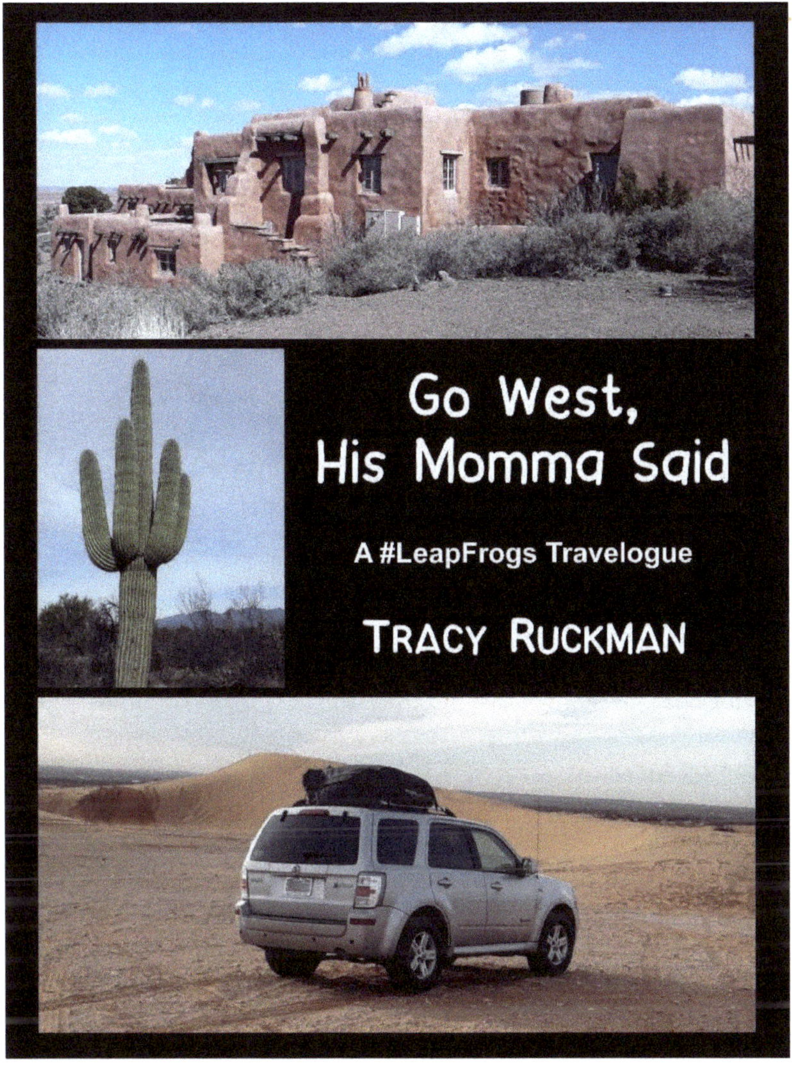

Go West,
His Momma Said
A #LeapFrogs Travelogue
TRACY RUCKMAN

Paperback ISBN-13: 978-1-948026-55-0
Hardcover ISBN-13: 978-1-948026-57-4
Digital ISBN-13: 978-1-948026-56-7

Published by TMPixArt, a division of TMP Books, 3 Central Plaza, Ste 307, Rome, GA 30161
www.TMPixArt.com
www.TMPbooks.com

Published in the United States of America.

Dedication

With immense love and immeasurable gratitude
to the
Mighty, Mighty
Prayer Warriors
who prayed—and continue to pray—for us
every step of this incredible journey.

We are eternally grateful.

Acknowledgements

We could not have done this trip without the support and
encouragement of so many friends and family members
(listed alphabetically):

Zach and Jessica Bolton

Jonathan Bolton

Margret & Matt Boyd

Janet & Rick Cadena

Peggy and Chuck Cunningham

Frieda Dixon

Annie & Dan Keys

Cynthia Kimbrough

Ann & Stan Knowles

Fay Lamb

Carrie Leeth

Laine McCall

Dorice Neir

Dr. Richard Nugara

Carolyn & Jay Priester

Melinda Pruitt

Andy & Kim Williams

Christi Williams

Thank you for your support, encouragement, prayers, gifts, phone calls, e-mails, and
patience.

Table of Contents

Preface 3

Chapter One 7

Chapter Two 11

Chapter Three 19

Chapter Four 25

Chapter Five 31

Chapter Six 39

Chapter Seven 47

Chapter Eight 53

Chapter Nine 61

Chapter Ten...65

Chapter Eleven..71

Chapter Twelve 79

Chapter Thirteen 85

Chapter Fourteen..91

Chapter Fifteen 97

Chapter Sixteen..103

Chapter Seventeen 107

Chapter Eighteen...111

Chapter Nineteen 117

Chapter Twenty...125

Chapter Twenty-One 133

Chapter Twenty-Two 137

Chapter Twenty-Three 145

Chapter Twenty-Four 151

Chapter Twenty-Five 159

Chapter Twenty-Six 171

Chapter Twenty-Seven 181

Chapter Twenty-Eight 183

Chapter Twenty-Nine 189

Chapter Thirty 199

Chapter Thirty-One 207

Chapter Thirty-Two 211

Chapter Thirty-Three 221

Chapter Thirty-Four 231

Chapter Thirty-Five 235

Chapter Thirty-Six 241

Chapter Thirty-Seven 243

Tracy's Travel Art List 245

Equipment 246

About the Author 259

Other Books by Author 260

PREFACE

The day after Christmas, my husband Tim and I received devastating news. After a few hours of shock, we decided to view the information from a different perspective, and once that took hold, we realized a life-changing opportunity presented itself. We had an immediate decision to make—continue life as things were or take a chance and do something different?

We leaped!

Have you ever heard the acronym for F.R.O.G.? **F**ully **R**elying **o**n **G**od. When we decided to take this route, a friend suggested adding the word L.E.A.P.—**L**eaving **E**verything **A**lways **P**raying **F**ully **R**eliant **o**n **G**od.

On January 8, 2019, we became the #LeapFrogs when we began the journey of a lifetime. That day, we set out on a cross-country road trip of an indefinite length, to see all we'd dreamed of seeing our entire lives.

Tim is retired, but I am not, so I planned to continue working, continue running my businesses online and on the road, publishing books for clients and for myself, consulting, creating art with my photography, and writing. I've even created a few products with our new #LeapFrogs logo!

We're not wealthy, and Publisher's Clearinghouse was taking too long to find us, so we set out equipped only with our SUV and a tent. A few other items, too, because our car was packed to overflowing.

In this book, I'll share how we prepped for the trip and I'll provide a few checklists to help others who are thinking about taking a similar journey. This was a dream come true, and we've been surprised to learn how many others share this dream, too.

Some of our interests include art, architecture, nature, western/cowboy stuff, and funky/fun/unusual. We're also foodies, but we are on a limited budget, so we'll be cooking a lot of our food as we camp, but on travel days, we're going to try to find local favorites.

At the end of a few chapters, I'm also including a section called **From the FROG Files**, snippets of emails we sent or received during our travels to provide deeper insight into our journey. The FROG Files are written in present tense and might seem a little choppy – I hope by doing so, I don't confuse or hinder your reading. I made the decision to use snippets from the emails, and not repeat any information I wrote in the body of the chapter.

Before we left, we learned that flexibility was crucial. But we also had to learn how to relax a bit, meander, savor every step of the journey, rather than pushing from destination to destination—a lesson we're still struggling to grasp.

📷 You'll find this camera icon placed below certain images within the book. These photographs, for the most part, have been digitally enhanced in different ways to create new art pieces, and are available as prints, on canvas, wood, or metal, or on a variety of merchandise. Many others not included in this book are also available for purchase.

All of my art can now be purchased at FineArt America and Pixels. More information is also available on my art website at www.TMPixArt.com

Chapter One

First Leg of our Leap Frog Journey

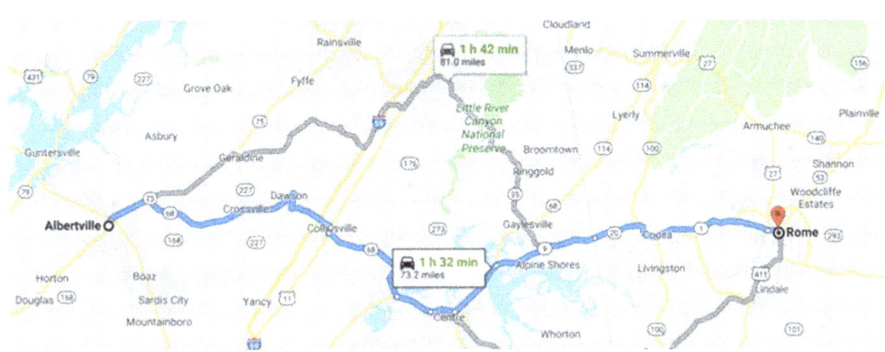

Rome, Georgia to Albertville, Alabama

We packed up the house, giving away or selling stuff for days, packing what was left into a one-size-too-small storage unit. But finally, it was done! A friend gifted us with one night in a hotel in town so we could recover from all that packing and moving, and we collapsed!

Before we left town, we took care of final things like refilling prescriptions and arranging for mail. Someone asked us about mail as we packed so I realized others may have the same questions.

For almost a decade, we've rented a mailbox. We receive packages often, so we needed a mailbox with a street address, and The UPS Store provides that and more, including mail forwarding services, as part of our box rental. Even though we're on the road, our mailing address remains the same. Whenever we want or need our physical mail, we call them and arrange for them to ship it wherever we happen to be. It's costly to do that often, but after canceling all the junk mail and switching everything else to paperless, we hoped we wouldn't need to use the service often.

We planned our first stop to be at my Mom's and sister's house for a short visit. This gave us time and space to reassess our car packing to determine how easy loading and unloading would be to get what we needed quickly. We purged a few items and picked up others we had forgotten before we left home.

For my entire life, we've traveled the same roads from Alabama to Georgia to visit grandparents, and then each other as we grew up and lived in one or the other state. This time, when we left Rome, Georgia, our Waze GPS app took us a different way, and I followed her lead, because I was honestly too exhausted to figure out where she was taking us. (Our Waze is named Jane, and Tim talks to her like he talks to me. I'm glad she doesn't talk back, or I'd never have any peace and quiet.)

This trip, Jane took us across a portion of Weiss Lake that I'd never seen before, through Cedar Bluff, Alabama. Totally surprised me to see how beautiful that side of the lake was compared to the other side. Then we discovered something else so fun, I quickly turned around and stopped to take pictures.

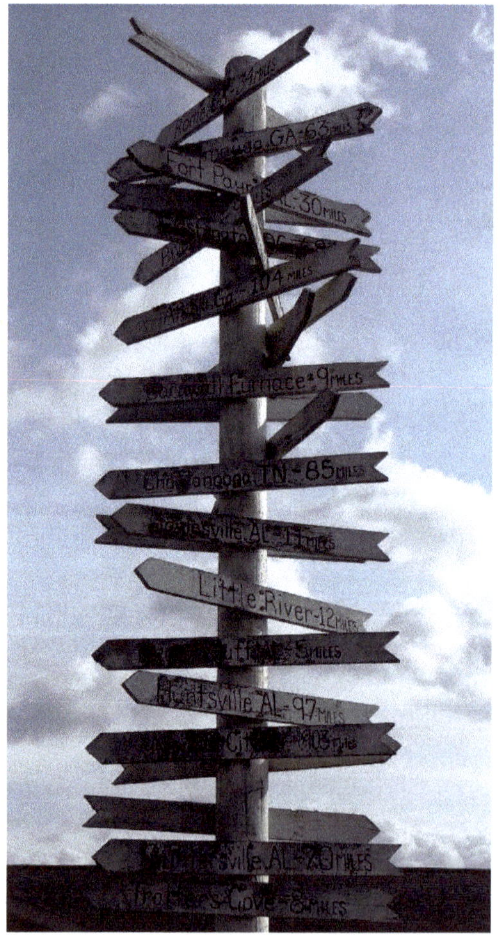

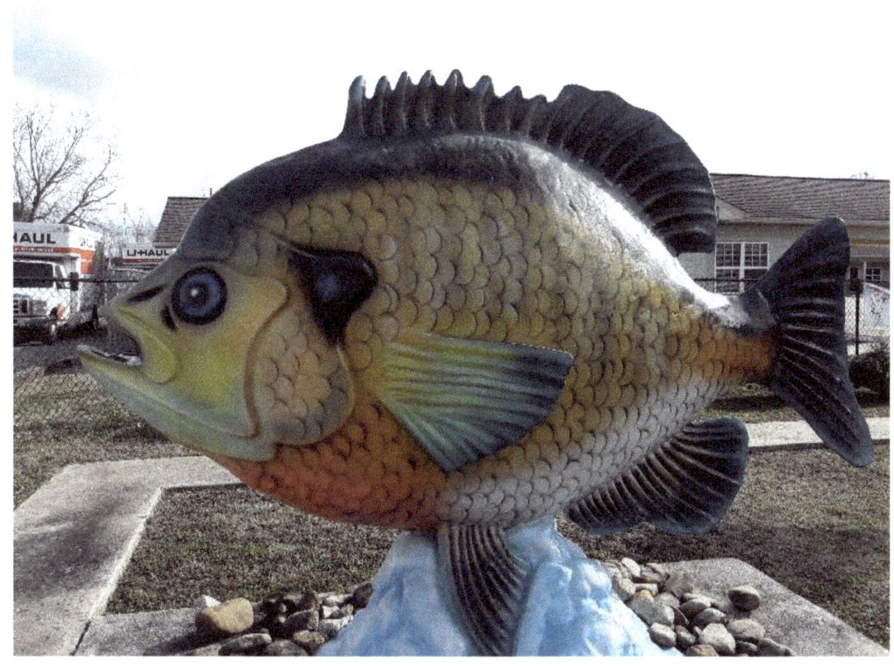

Above: Bluegill

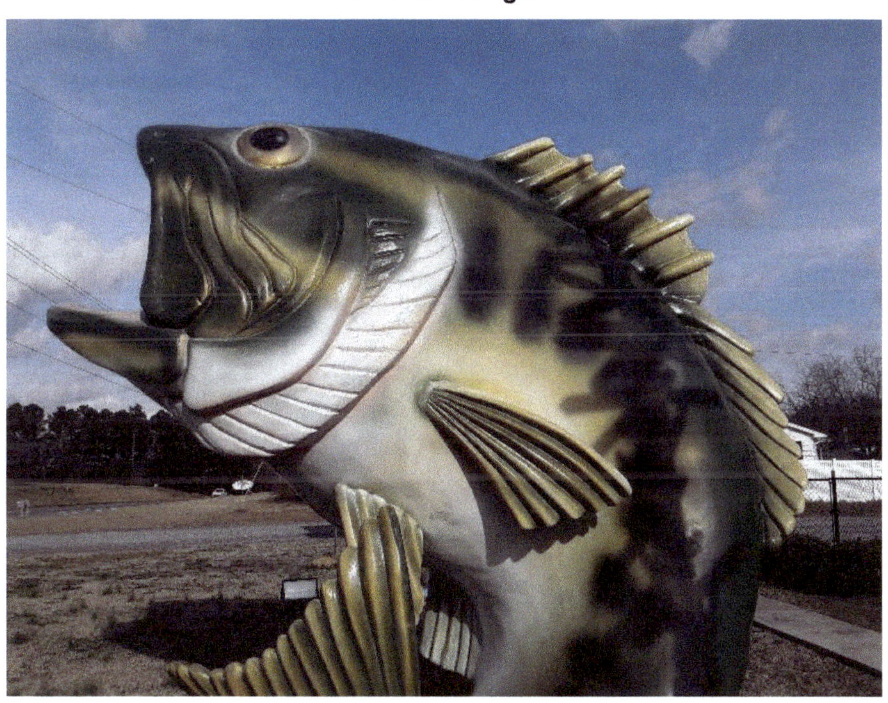

Above: Largemouth Bass

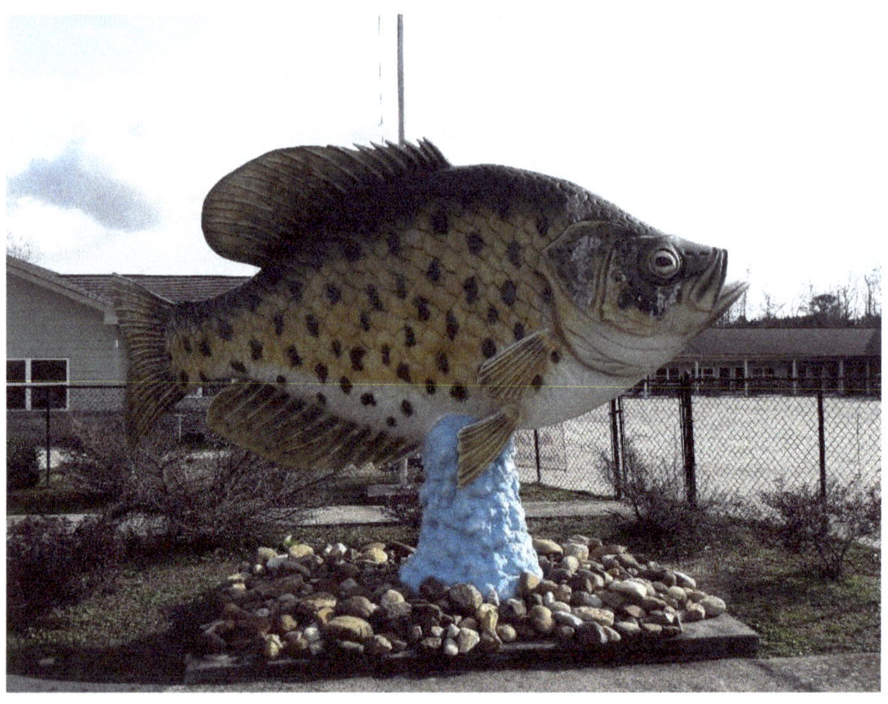

Above: Crappie

The Bluegill has always been my favorite fish to catch and to eat. Good thing my car was packed, or this beauty may have gone with me! Aren't the colors stunning?

My dad loved catching large-mouth bass more than anything! He would have loved this monster!

My grandad loved catching crappie. (Like some, he pronounced this fish like "crappy," but the rest of my family pronounce it like "croppy").

I was delighted by the fish and loved learning that they sit in front of Weiss Lake Lodge, so I'm sure I'll have to find an excuse to stay there one day!

The lesson learned on this leg of the journey—take the road less traveled. An unexpected delight could be waiting for you!

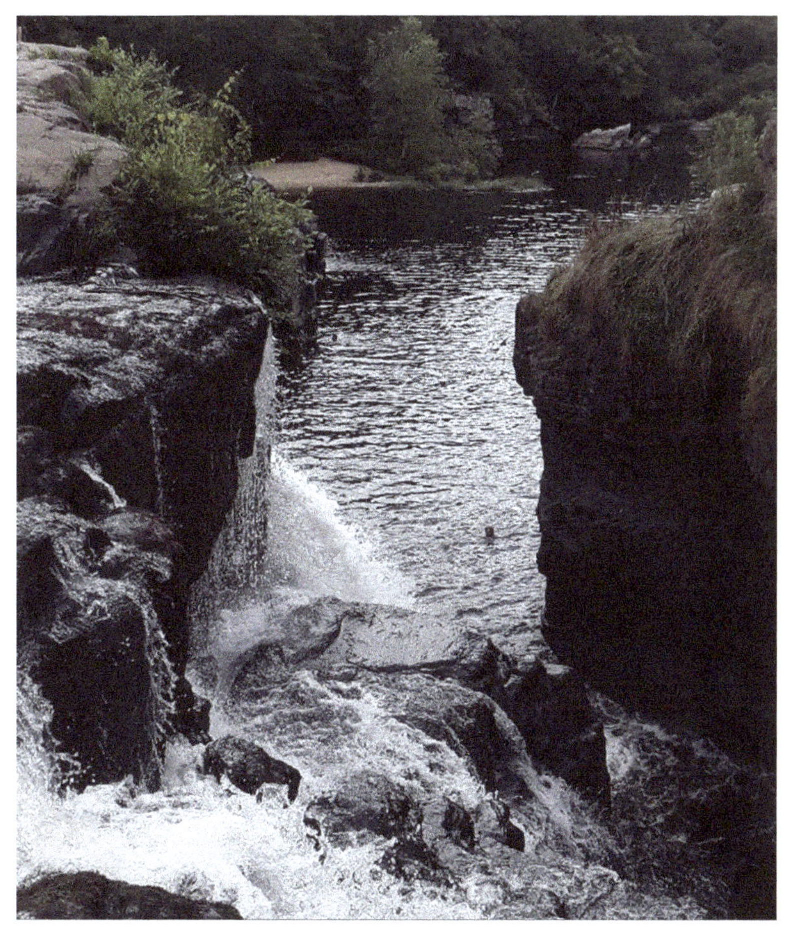

Above: High Falls Park; Below: Albertville

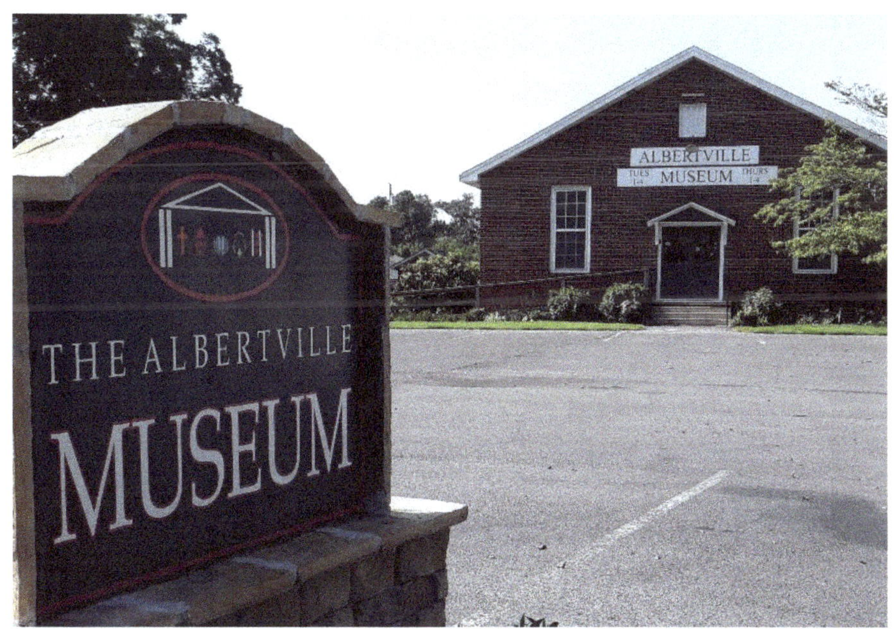

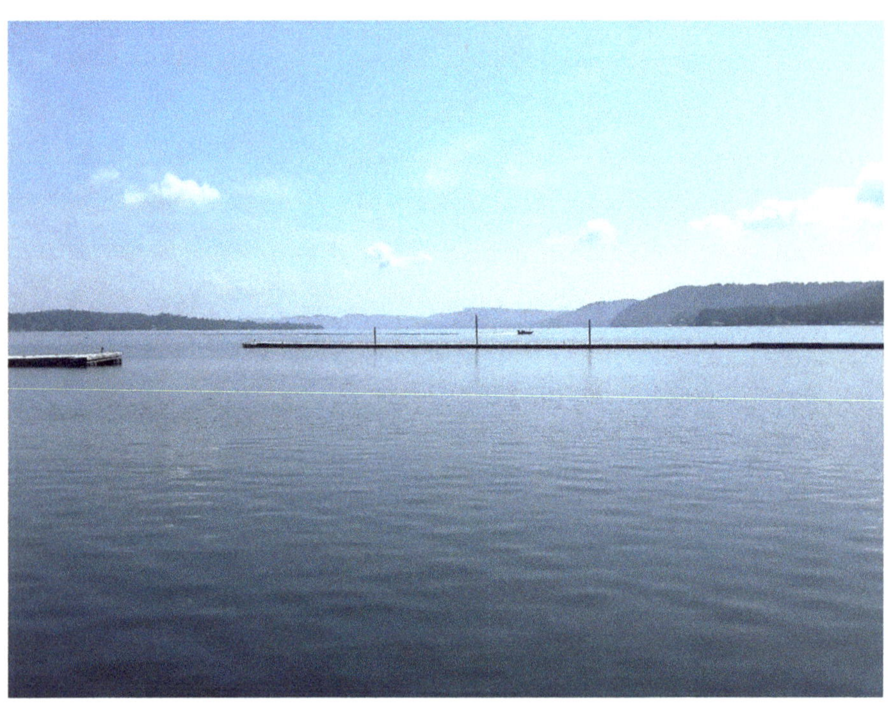

Above: Lake Guntersville; Below: Albertville

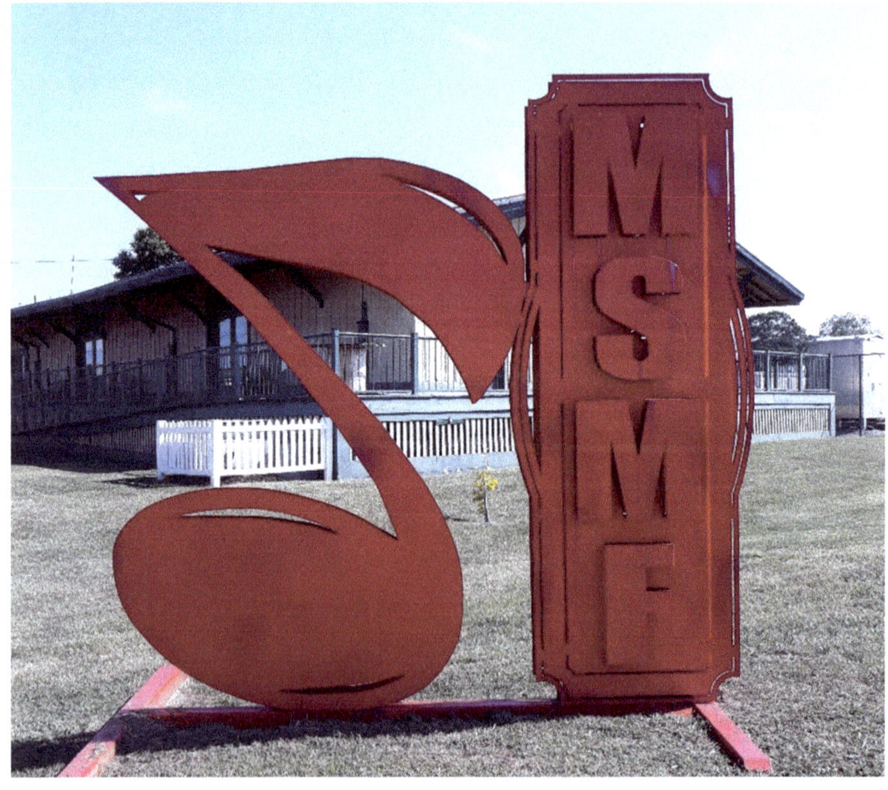

Chapter Two
Along the Natchez Trace

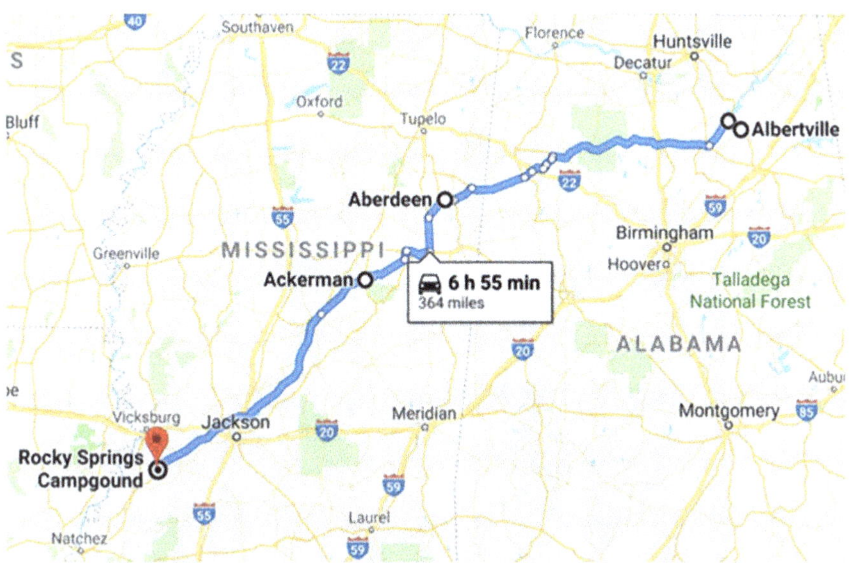

Albertville, Alabama to Hermanville, Mississippi

We left Albertville, driving through Guntersville, early in the morning, stopping briefly to snap a photo with our mini-mes, the plaster frogs who made our journey with us and popped in on blog posts from time to time as we traveled. (Photo at the end of the chapter.)

Our original destination was Ackerman, MS, where a free campsite was listed on www.freecampsites.net. We'd gotten an early start, so we stopped for lunch in Aberdeen to discuss staying put or moving on.

For years, we've used Trip Advisor to help us find local restaurants when traveling. This time, Tim found The Burger Shack. The quarter pound burgers were massive and tasty, and the home fries were salted well. under $11 for all of it, so my budget was as happy as our tummies.

The restroom had a fun surprise, too.

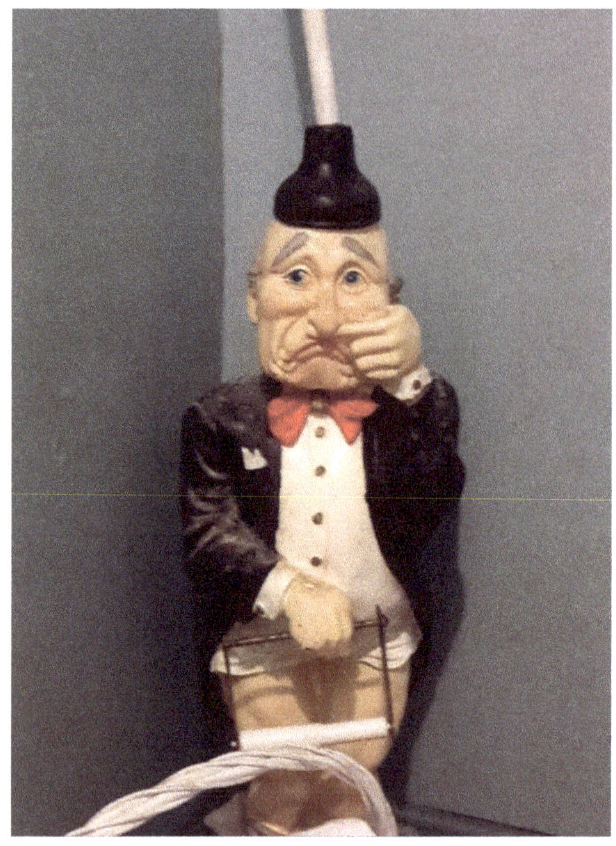

Something I'm fascinated by—our rooftop suitcase seems to attract attention in these small towns, and everyone wants to chat about our travels—even without us saying a word. I asked Tim if he'd put a "Road Trip Junkie" sign on my back or something.

When we share that we're camping our way cross-country, reactions have been positive but with a clarifier. Most say they could never do it, although they've always wanted to take off like we did.

Take the leap and hit the road. You won't be sorry.

During lunch, we decided to push on to the Rocky Springs Campground on the Natchez Trace.

One of the primary reasons was to get ahead of the weather, to get out of the cold and the rain. But instead, we landed smack in the middle of the wet stuff.

The Natchez Trace is beautiful, even in the dead of winter. The campground was great, but because it is part of the National Park system, it was affected by the government shutdown, which meant no services were available, including open restrooms.

Before we left, we'd purchased a used tent on OfferUp because 1) it fit our budget, and 2) it met our needs. Unfortunately, I trusted the seller to be honest in his dealings, and when I asked if all the parts were included, and he told me they were, I believed him. I didn't bother unpacking the tent before we left home, but we did purchase tent stakes, because you can never have too many of those.

As we set up in the Rocky Springs Campground on the Natchez Trace, we discovered the seller wasn't honest. Not only were tent stakes missing, but so was the rainfly for the tent—that keeps out all the rain—and the room divider that Tim had really wanted. The room divider we can live without, but the canopy, not so much. We had two smaller tarps that we used to cover part of the tent, but they weren't big enough to cover it all.

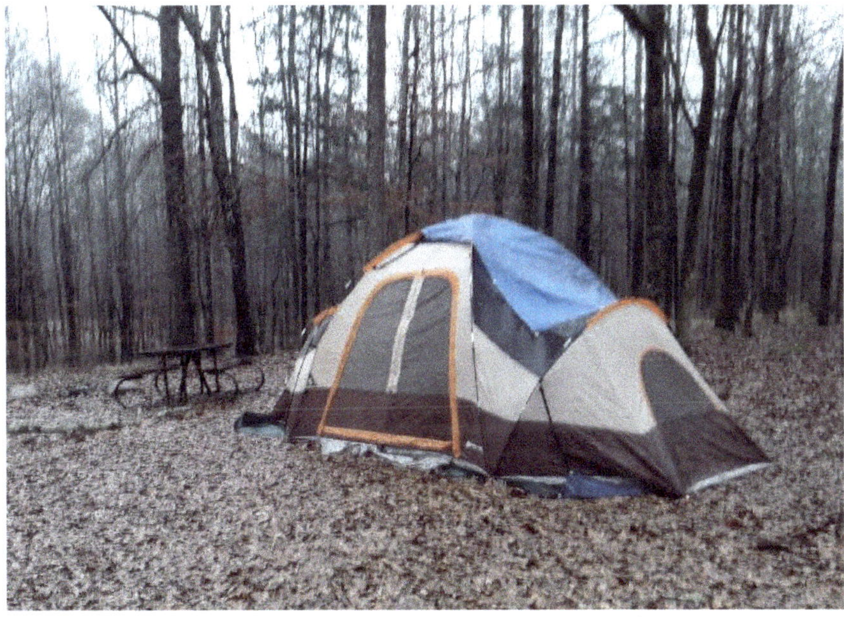

The forecast called for clear skies for the next few days, so I wasn't too worried about getting wet. But at three a.m., the rain hit.

At 5 a.m., I woke with a puddle of water at my feet, inside my sleeping bag.

We quickly packed up important stuff, and left blankets and Tim's chair inside the tent, and retreated to the car. At 5:30, we decided to head into town for coffee and figure out our next move. We stopped in at the McDonald's in Port Gibson. Again, people seemed to gravitate to us, asking about our travels. One elderly gentleman came over and shook our hand, told us he appreciated us visiting Port Gibson and hoped we had a great journey. We hadn't told anyone we were traveling at that point, and we were talking softly, so he couldn't have overheard us. Tim decided he must be the mayor of the town. Zach looked up the population and said the town was so small, everyone knew everyone else, so they knew we had to be strangers passing through.

Once we had internet service again, we learned the rain was settling in there for four days, so we went back to camp, packed up everything soaking wet, and hit the road again.

Before we went back to camp, I decided we'd venture out to a RoadsideAmerica recommendation in the area—one of the reasons we'd come that direction anyway! Unfortunately, The Frog Farm was not in operation. It appeared to have been abandoned. The ground was too soggy to park, so Tim dropped me off, and I made my way to a locked gate where I snapped these photos. You can see a couple of the large frogs in the distance. Disappointed that we couldn't explore more.

[NOTE: I checked online as I was finalizing this book, and The Frog Farm appears to be open again, with an admission fee. Discounts for children and seniors 55+. You can find them on Facebook.]

After we packed up camp, we drove to the Natchez Visitor's Center, hoping to get maps and general information. Overnight parking is allowed, with electric hookups for two nights, for RVs. At the Visitor's Center, we changed into dry, clean clothes and then went exploring.

We found a small, local restaurant, called Southern Style, where we feasted on the best catfish we've had in years, and the most affordable, too. The green beans, mac & cheese, and corn were all specially prepared and seasoned perfectly—nothing canned or boxed. The service was friendly, too. The ladies there all take pride in what they do. I was texting Zach while we waited for our food to arrive, and he informed me that Natchez was a dangerous place. When the ladies at the restaurant learned we were traveling through, they told us to be sure to carry weapons and not be afraid to use them around there if need be. Not once did we ever feel unsafe.

What I found so interesting was that different races and different generations were warning me of the same dangers.

To make our trip as affordable as possible, we're camping for free as often as we can. When I can find an internet connection, I'm scouring websites like freecampsites.net and Campendium.com, looking for random places to land. The first night was the Rocky Springs site, but after realizing the government shutdown would keep us from having bathroom facilities, we began looking outside the national park options.

We left Natchez en route for another free campsite across the Louisiana state line.

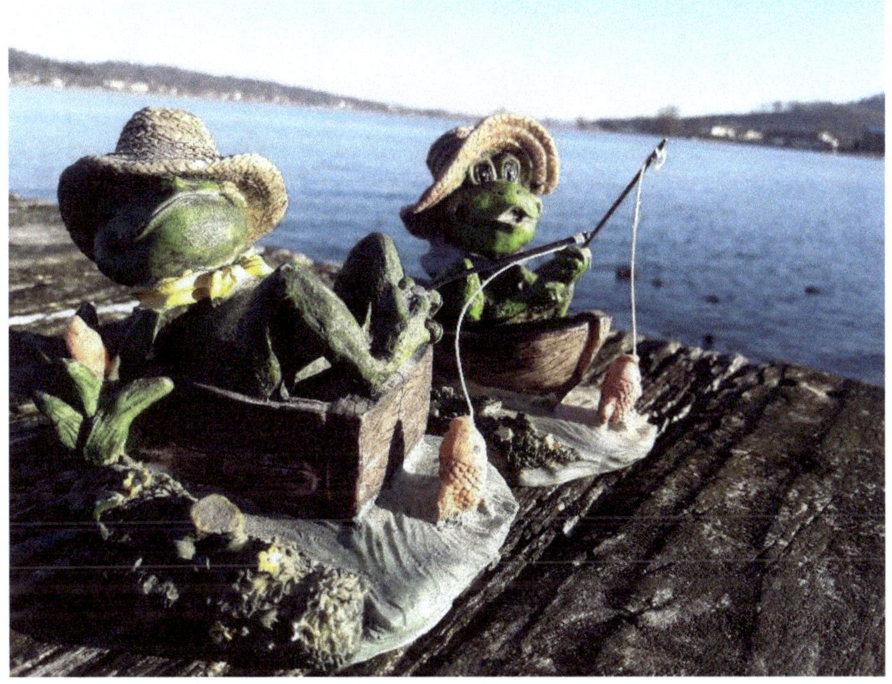

Our Mini-Mes

From the FROG Files:

The government shut down could affect our camping plans—some of the places may be closed or affected in some way, so we must be flexible and look at all options.

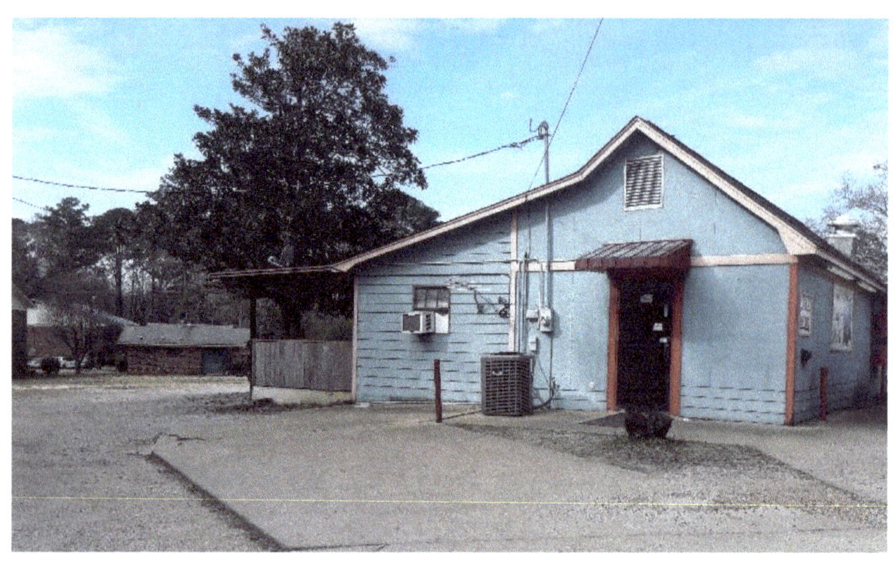

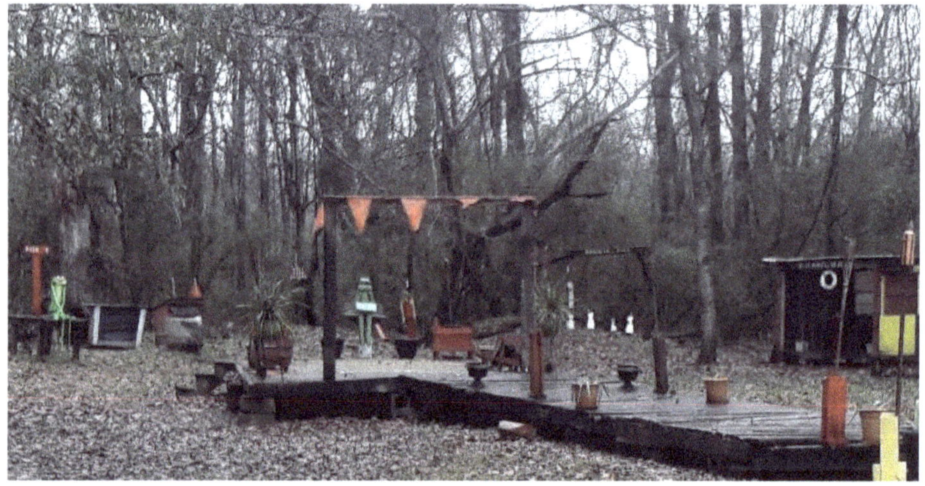

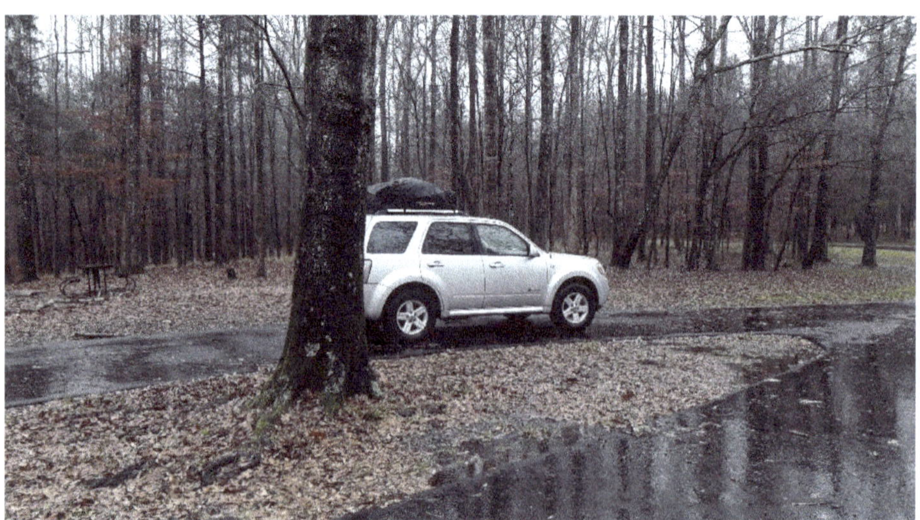

Above: The Burger Shack in Aberdeen

Below: The Frog Farm in Fayette, and the campground near Hermanville.

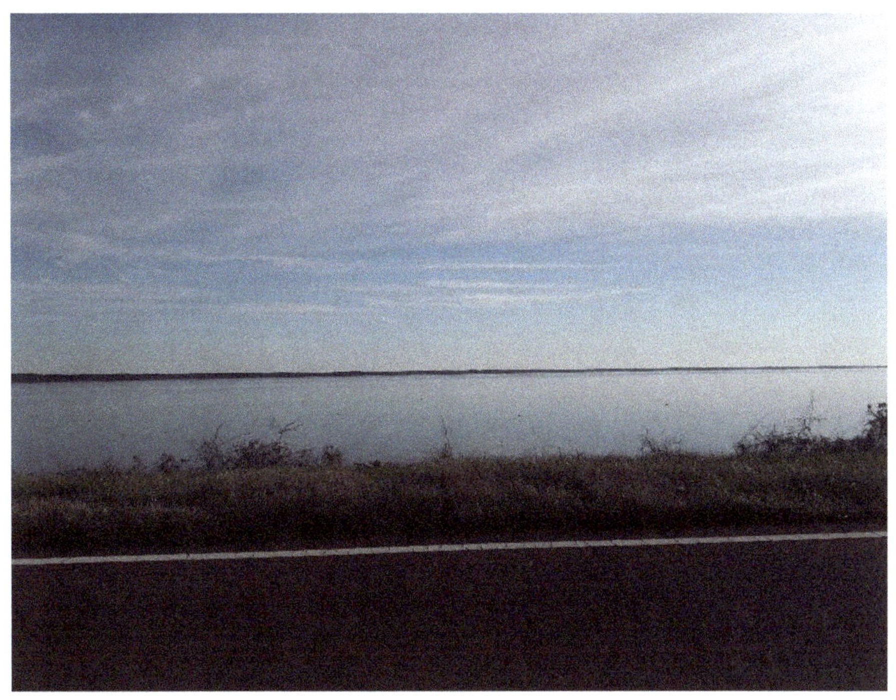

Above: Reservoir on the Natchez Trace

Below: The Natchez Trace Parkway 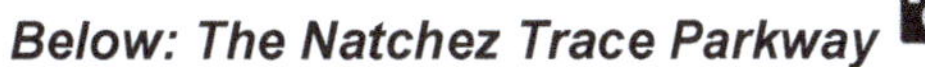

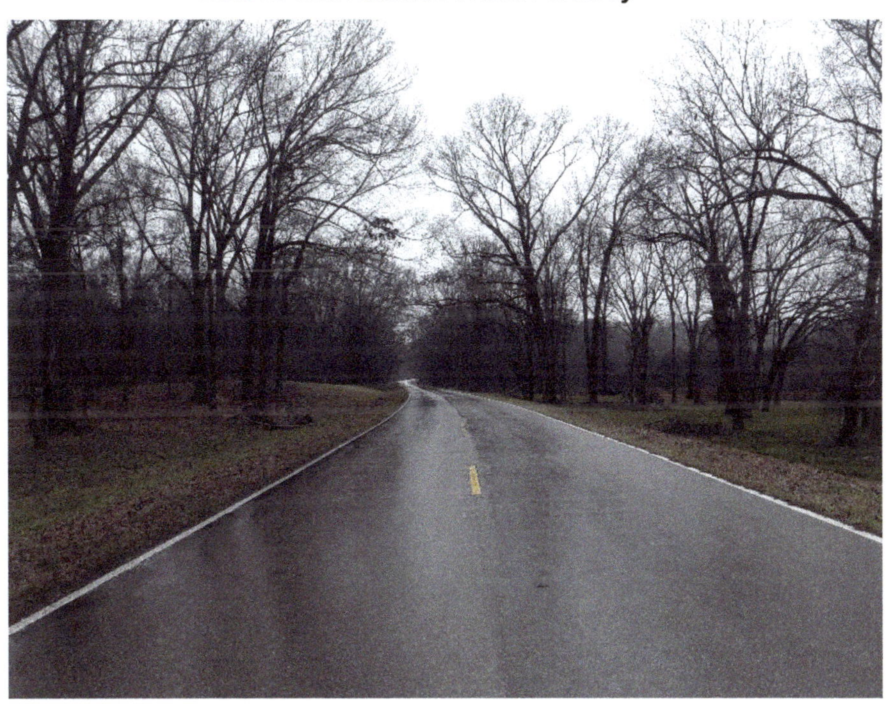

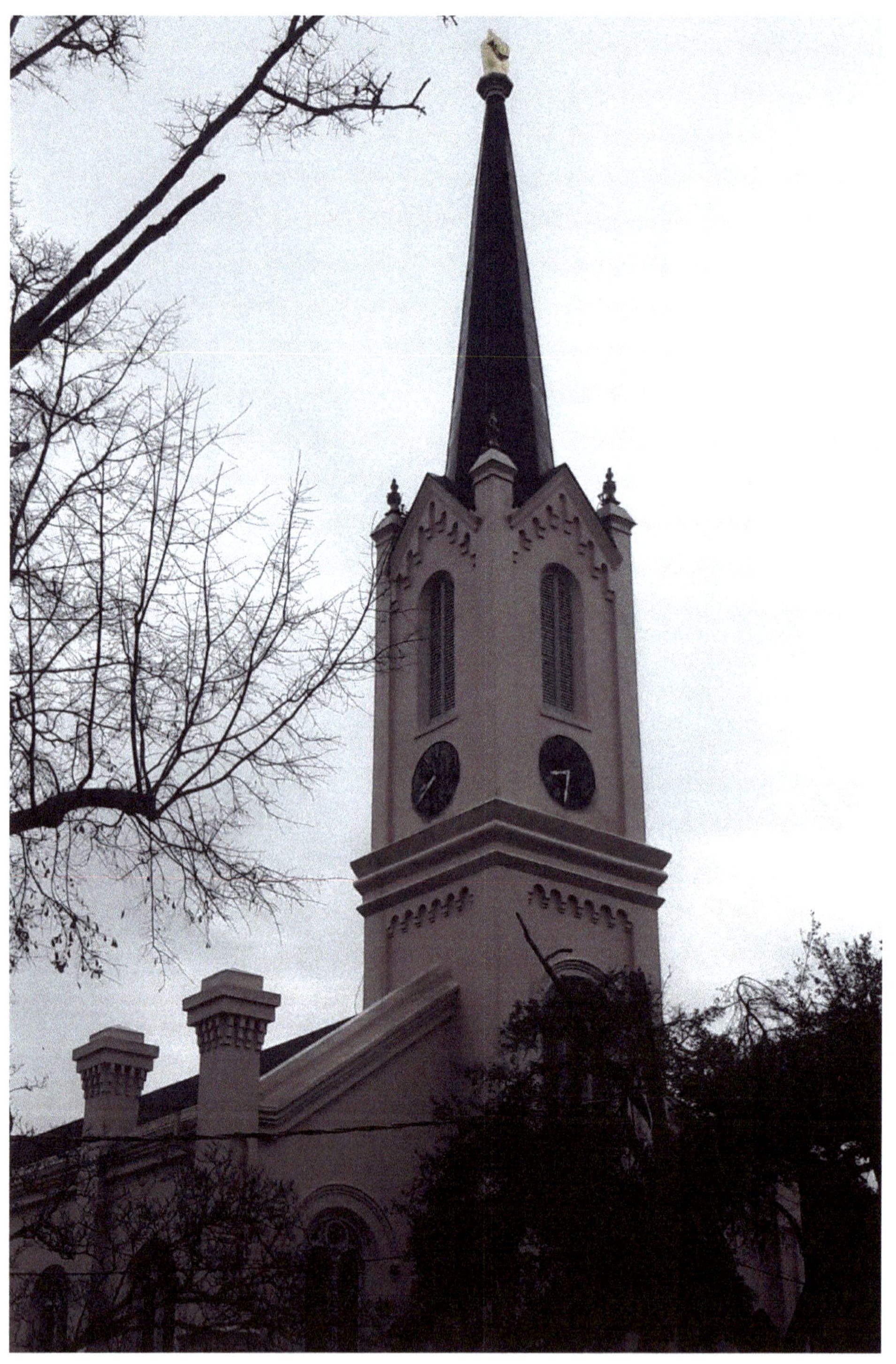

Church in Port Gibson

Chapter Three

Crossing Louisiana

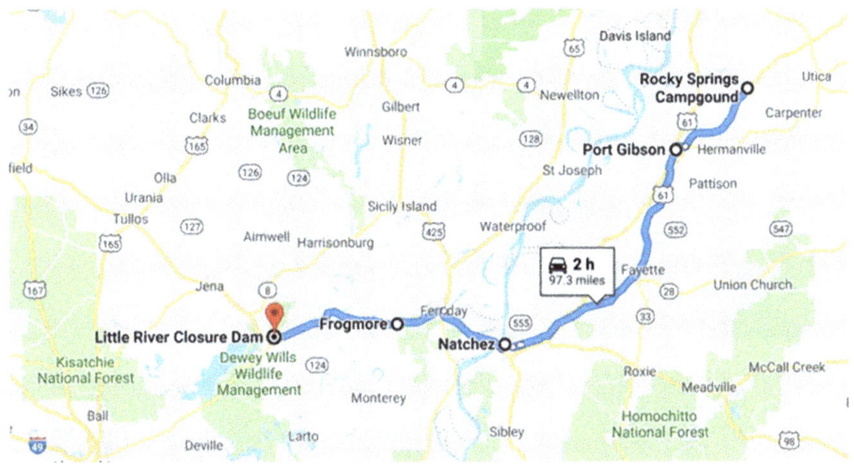

Hermanville, Mississippi to Jonesville, Louisiana

Still trying to get into warmer temps with less rain, we continued our journey southwest without too much lingering. We'd thought about staying overnight at the Natchez Visitor's Center, but it was still early enough in the day that we decided to push west a little more before stopping over the Mississippi Louisiana state line.

TIP: the drive through Frogmore, Louisiana (state road 84) is gorgeous at sunset.

We car camped for the first time near Jonesville, at the Little River Closure. The listing said there were "pit toilets" available and picnic tables, and that fit our basic needs, so we decided to check it out. The pit toilets were a thousand times cleaner and nicer than a gas station restroom I'd run from earlier in the day.

Campers define car camping several different ways, but for us, car camping means sleeping in the car, to differentiate from times when we set up our tent. Other campers still call it car camping if the car sits next to the tent, without having to hike into a site, but we never camp that way, so our definitions are more literal.

We'd already had dinner, so we took a stroll, then settled down and snuggled into our seats, not bothering to set up our tent. We knew it would be another cold night, with possible rain, so we chose to stay dry and warm. That worked well for us.

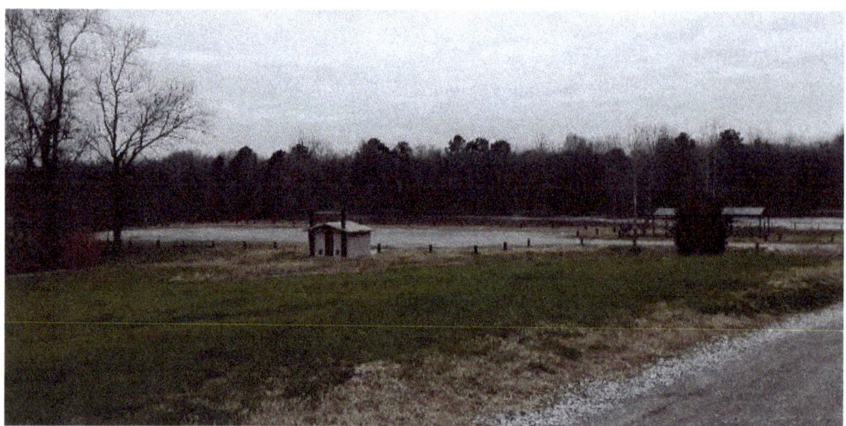

The place was dark, but we never felt unsafe. We could see cars as they came and went, but there weren't many. One guy had been night fishing, so he pulled his boat out of the water around midnight —the most action we saw all night, besides a beautiful shooting star.

The next morning, we made our way to Alexandria, Louisiana, where we found a laundromat that advertised WIFI—but they had none. We dried our blankets and coats, then picked up lunch at the local IGA store.

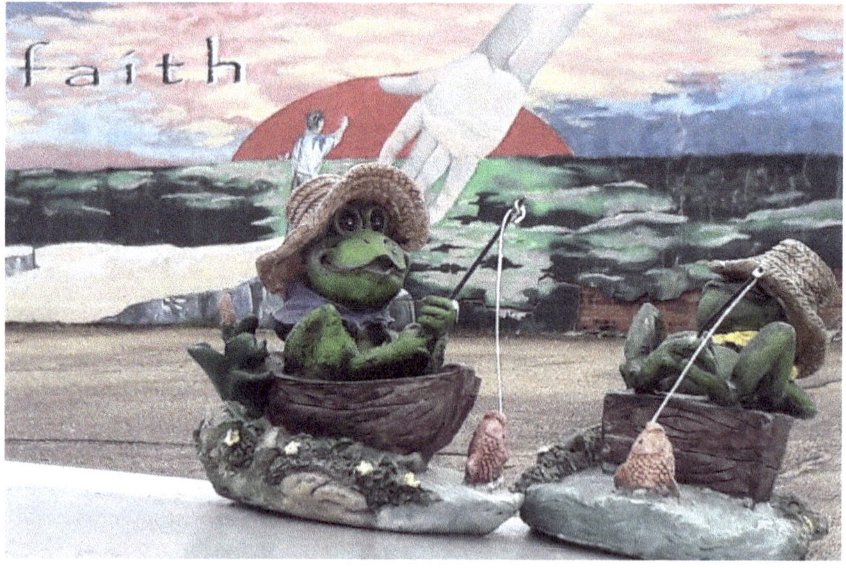

For our third night out, we'd planned to stay in a campground that offered $4 per night tent sites. When we arrived, the entrance looked beautiful, so we drove around to check things out. We saw the tent camping area, but something about the place didn't feel right. We knocked on the door and the host answered, telling us he was too sick to fool with us, so we left.

We made our way to another place on the Intracoastal Waterway in Sulphur, LA. The listing said they also had $4 tent sites available. We pulled in, saw they had gravel sites, with grassy spots on the back edge of the property. We stopped and talked to the host, explained we were tent camping. She said the ground was too soggy to pitch tents right now, but we were welcomed to car camp for the night if we wanted. She pointed to an area where we could pick a spot and said she wouldn't even charge us for the night.

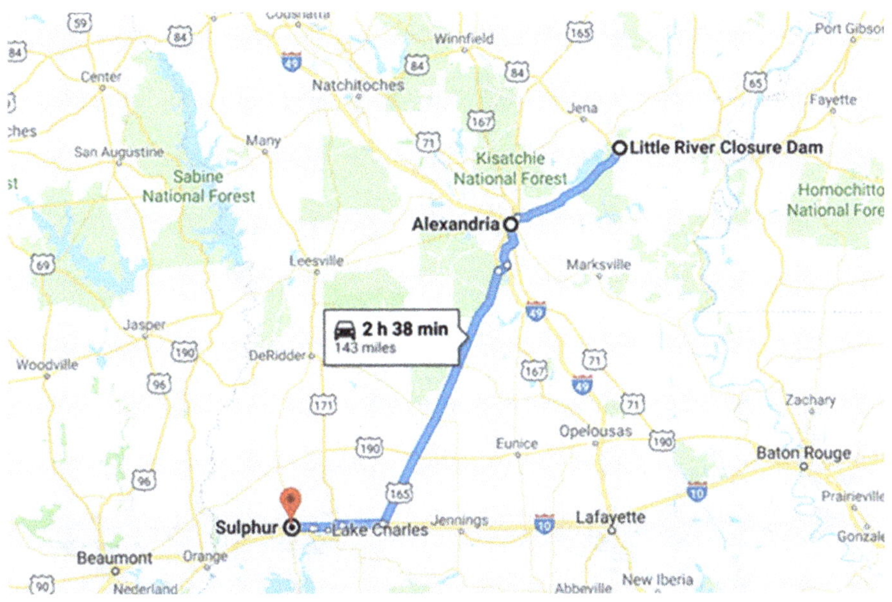

Jonesville to Sulphur

The parking lot held a bathhouse with showers and a picnic table where we could cook our own food. A huge bonus was being able to watch the tugboats and barges float up and down the river and waiting for the draw bridge to rise.

Our first night here was peaceful and delicious. Tim cooked pork chops that we'd brought from home that were finally starting to thaw a little. We also prepared potatoes and onions to pan fry. In the morning, he cooked bacon and eggs, then after breakfast, he sautéed chicken that was beginning to thaw, too.

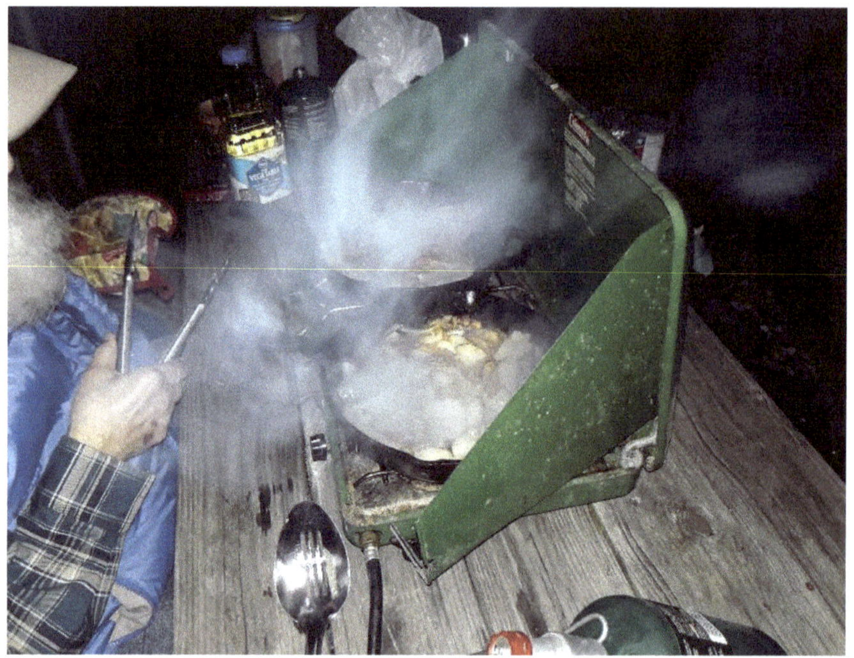

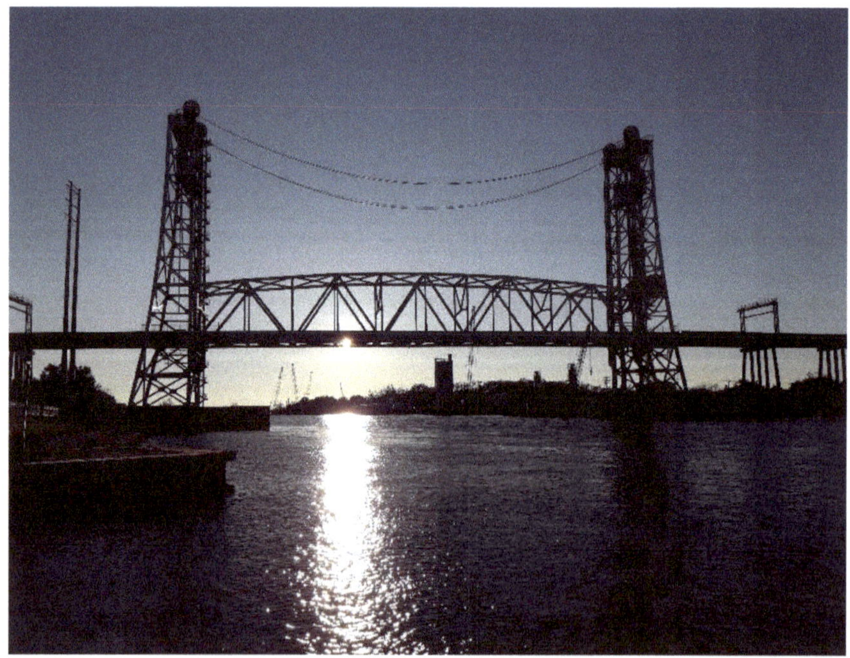

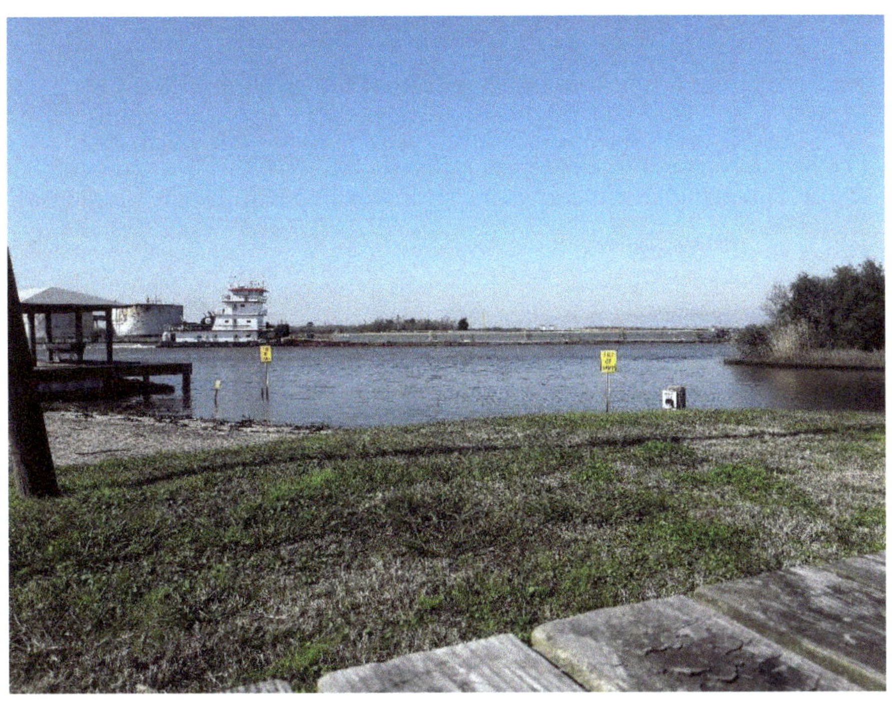

I was pleased to finally snap a photo of one of the barges and tugboats and had to smile when I saw its name: Blessed Trinity.

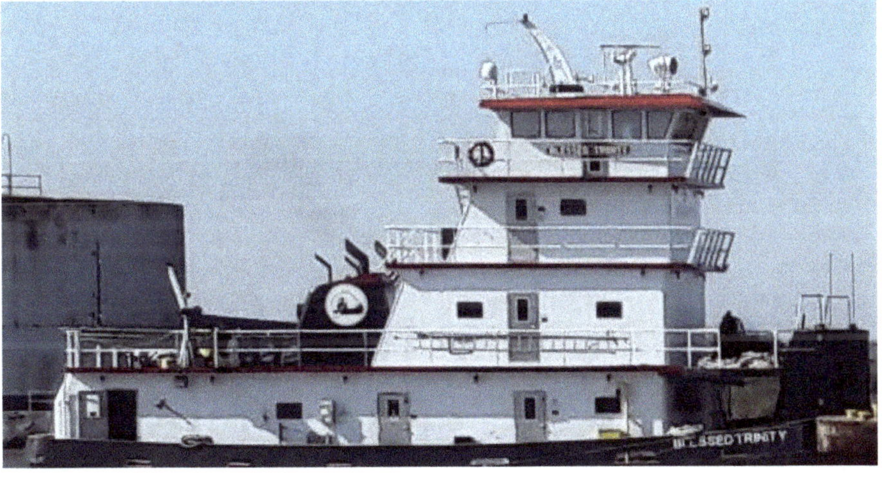

We stayed two nights (paying for the second night) and enjoyed the down time.

We spent a couple of hours in the laundromat today, drying blankets and jackets. We still don't have everything dried out, but we're functional, warm, and dry again.

I'm loving exploring all the various towns, but I'm realizing a couple of things about myself. I'm driven and I must fight the urge to keep moving forward, instead of lingering and soaking in what's around me. Today, we discovered a couple of cool murals in a town where I hadn't planned to stop. On another road, we spotted a red fox running through a field. Tonight, a raccoon is hanging out near our campsite.

I saw a falling star last night at the last car camp spot.

We're discovering we like car camping. (Tim keeps wishing for a small Class C RV. We saw two where we were camped—the long ones are entirely too big, so now he's wishing for a small one. LOL!)

Car camping is a lot less work than tent camping, so Tim's more in favor of it. He sleeps sitting up, so it's not much of an adjustment for him, but for me, it's been more challenging.

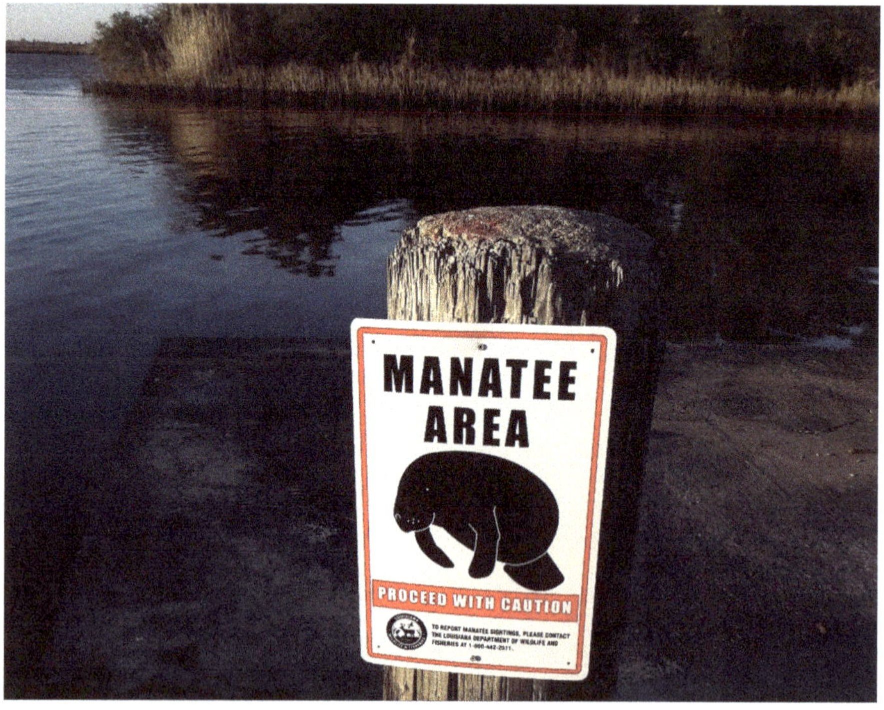

Chapter Four

Fort Anahuac, Texas

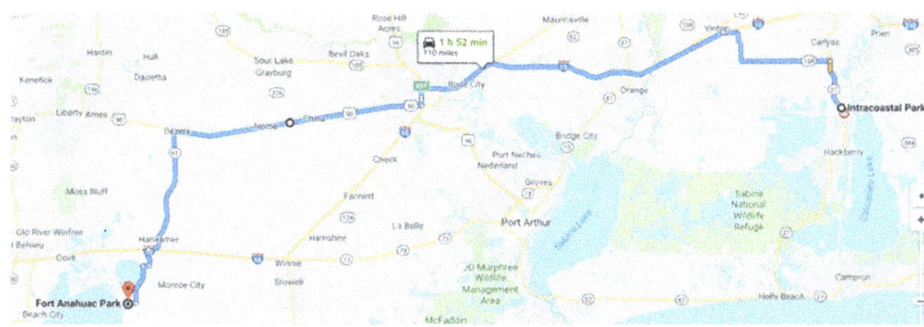

Sulphur, Louisiana to Fort Anahuac, Texas

Texas! Tim is a lifelong wannabe cowboy. He can quote almost every John Wayne movie from start to finish, and most other westerns, too. There aren't many westerns he hasn't viewed more than once—some of them dozens of times each. He wore cowboy boots every day until he retired, and his dream is to one day own a "two-pound Stetson with a six-inch brim" (from John Wayne's *McClintock*.)

But Tim had never been to Texas, and I couldn't wait to introduce him. I needed to catch up on work, so we spent the day in the Beaumont Public Library (and driving around town a bit), before continuing to our planned campsite at the community park in Anahuac, Texas.

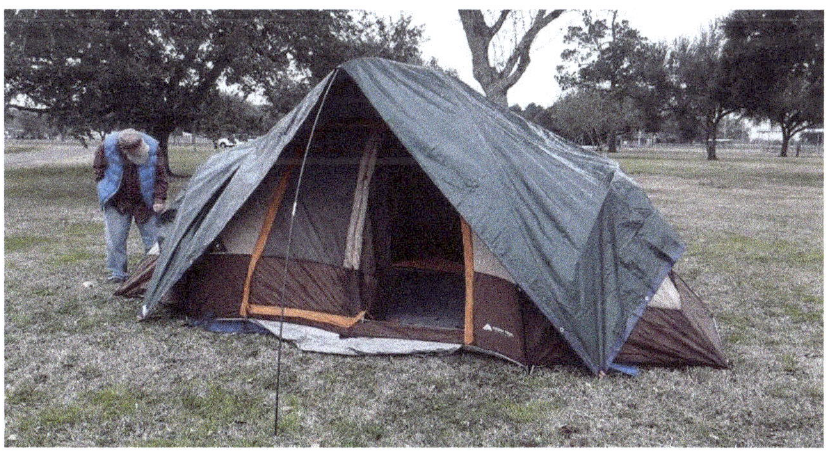

Our new tarp kept us dry and snug

Loved the overall park layout because we had almost the whole place to ourselves (although the bathrooms needed an overhaul!) A nature conservancy group had already picked out the best spot in the place, so we landed smack in the middle of the park, and because there were no boundaries on campsites, we spread out.

The restrooms were quite a hike though, so we picked the site closest that we could get without landing in water. We stayed dry our entire stay, which was a relief after all the rain we'd experienced since leaving Alabama.

Although the campsite was free, we had to get a three-day permit from the local commissioner's office, and could have renewed it for three more days, but the cold front was moving in, so we left to avoid overnight temps near freezing. The same commissioner's office oversees the Double Bayou Park a few miles away, with the same three-day permit required. We drove over to that park one day, to see what we were missing, and decided that Fort Anahuac was the best option. Double Bayou was totally secluded, and basically a large chunk of land. One bathhouse, next to the deputy's house on the property, but that was it. Roads weren't developed, basically paths.

TIP: If you go to Fort Anahuac, try to get the site at the back of the park, next to the monument. The site has a couple of picnic tables, under large trees, overlooking the marsh, with views of the water. Best place around.

But it felt good to settle in somewhere for a few days. Anahuac is relatively small, with a population of 2339. Driving around, we discovered a bank, Dairy Queen, Dollar General, a steak restaurant, and a Mexican restaurant. We also used their washeteria, which was only $2.00 per wash and took $1.50 to dry. (Cheapest laundromat so far.)

My favorite part of Fort Anahuac was walking out on the point and seeing Trinity Bay.

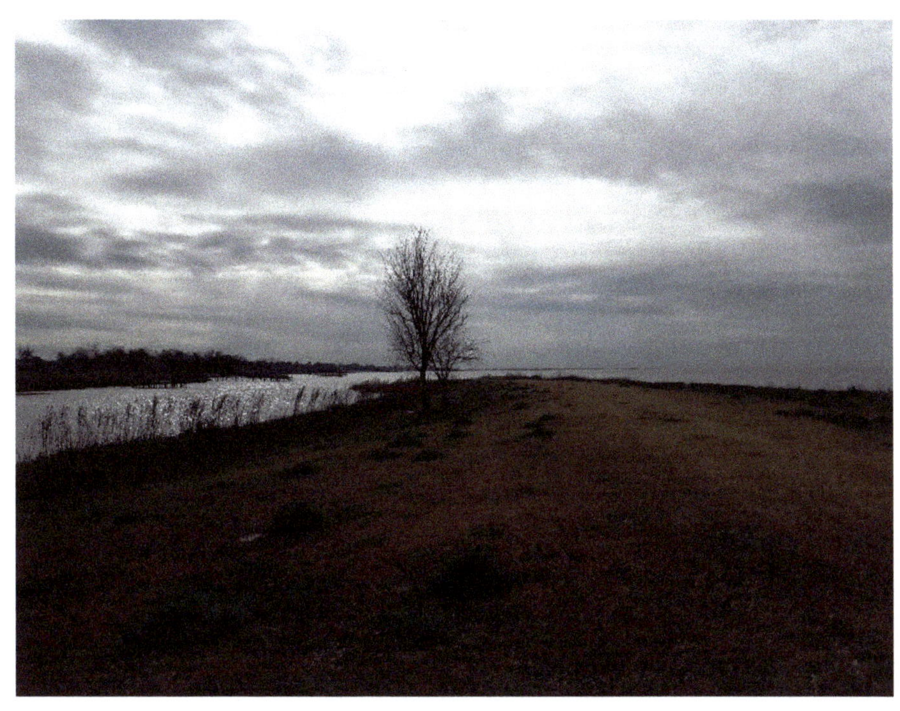

The Point at Anahuac 📷

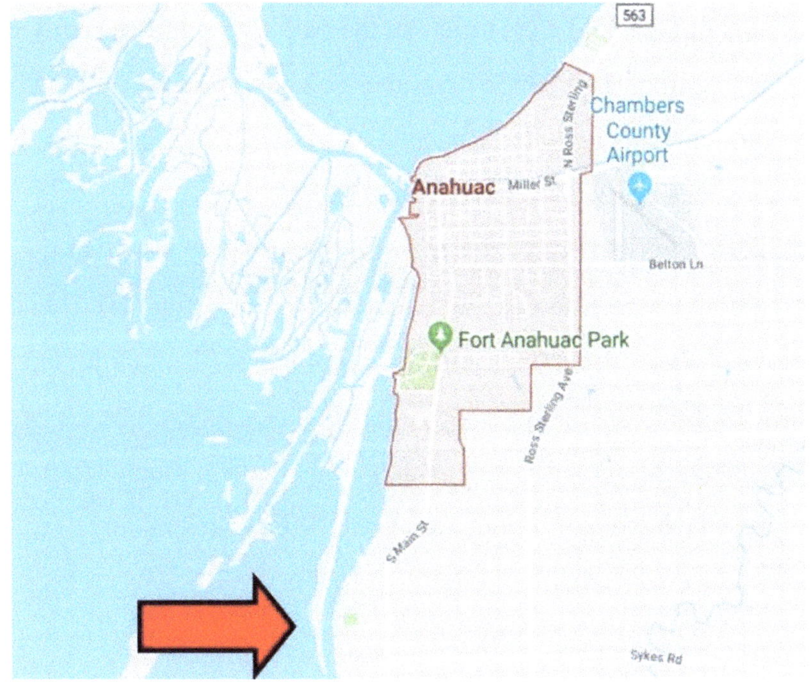

While we were in camp, we realized the need for groceries. The Dollar General there was basic, so we asked a customer where the nearest larger town was located. She laughed and said if we needed "real" groceries, there was a new H.E.B. store located in Mont Belvieu about ten minutes away. The grocery store was on my list of "must-visit" sites while in Texas, because of their kindness, compassion, and generosity to residents during and after Hurricane Harvey.

H.E.B. exceeded my expectations. Great prices, good service, delicious and cheap pastries for our breakfast, and this new location even offered free coffee. What's not to love about that?

From the FROG Files:

We're trying to decide now whether to stay another three days or move on. Severe thunderstorms are forecast for the weekend, then temps plummet. But our next areas of exploration have a similar outlook, so we can't avoid it.

Tim has come down with a cold, which is one reason we may stay put. He entered the tent, talking about the cold steel toilets in the bathhouse. It's currently 62 degrees, so what will they be like when it's 30? Another consideration for moving on.

We're in our tent, finally, with heat. Safe, dry, warm, and relaxed at the moment. I'm in my fuzzy socks again, so I'm a happy camper.

Surrounded by a parliament of chatty owls. Yes, I had to look that up.

Tim's breathing seems to be getting worse instead of better, like I'd hoped once we left the house. (We'd wondered if our rental home had black mold, but never had it checked.)

We re-organized the car yesterday, which made me feel much better. The car seems lighter, although we didn't purge anything. We packed better.

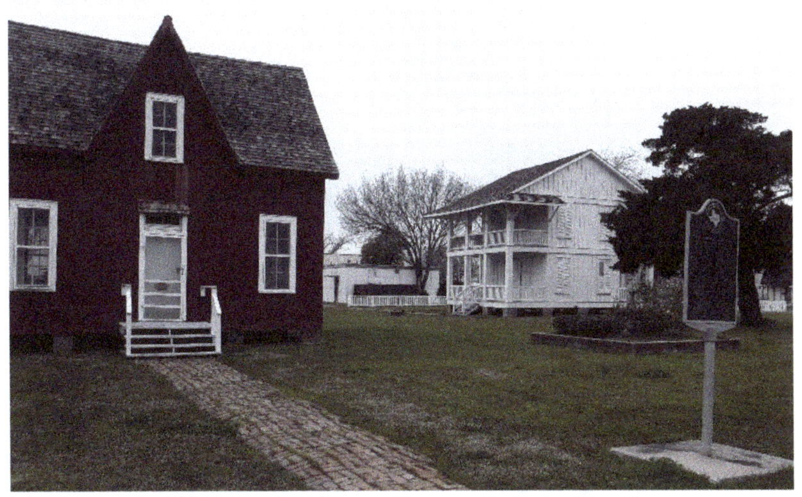

Above: Anahuac, Texas; Below: Heat!

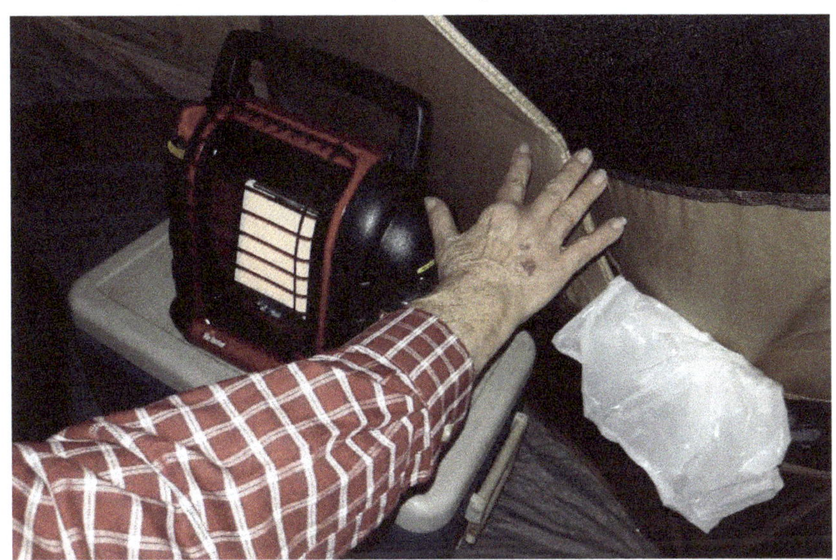

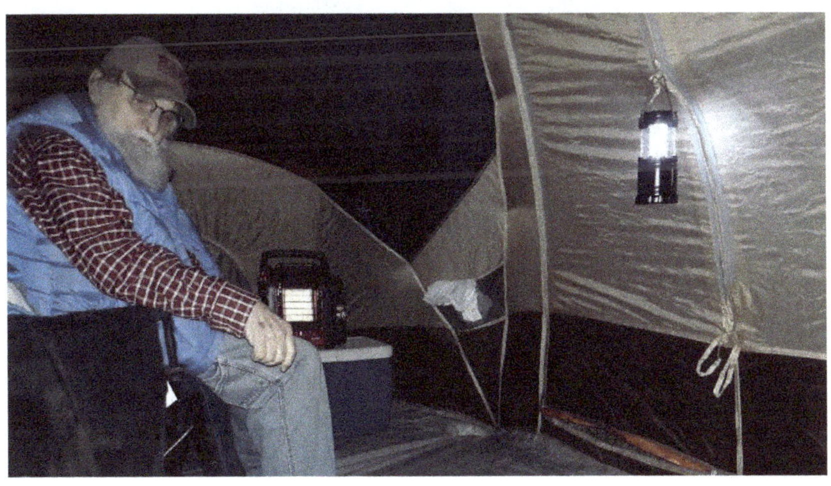

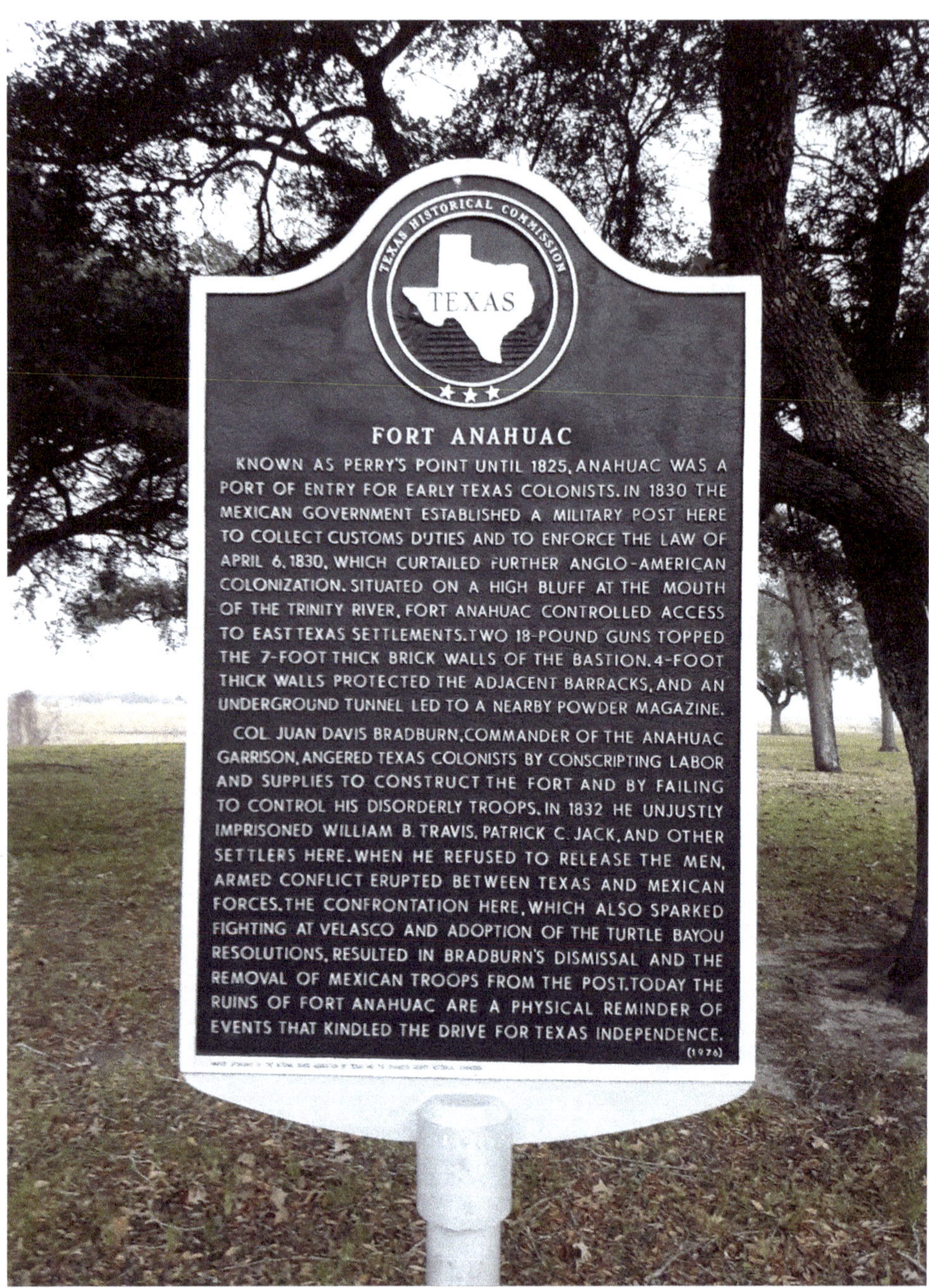

TEXAS HISTORICAL COMMISSION
TEXAS

FORT ANAHUAC

KNOWN AS PERRY'S POINT UNTIL 1825, ANAHUAC WAS A PORT OF ENTRY FOR EARLY TEXAS COLONISTS. IN 1830 THE MEXICAN GOVERNMENT ESTABLISHED A MILITARY POST HERE TO COLLECT CUSTOMS DUTIES AND TO ENFORCE THE LAW OF APRIL 6, 1830, WHICH CURTAILED FURTHER ANGLO-AMERICAN COLONIZATION. SITUATED ON A HIGH BLUFF AT THE MOUTH OF THE TRINITY RIVER, FORT ANAHUAC CONTROLLED ACCESS TO EAST TEXAS SETTLEMENTS. TWO 18-POUND GUNS TOPPED THE 7-FOOT THICK BRICK WALLS OF THE BASTION. 4-FOOT THICK WALLS PROTECTED THE ADJACENT BARRACKS, AND AN UNDERGROUND TUNNEL LED TO A NEARBY POWDER MAGAZINE.

COL. JUAN DAVIS BRADBURN, COMMANDER OF THE ANAHUAC GARRISON, ANGERED TEXAS COLONISTS BY CONSCRIPTING LABOR AND SUPPLIES TO CONSTRUCT THE FORT AND BY FAILING TO CONTROL HIS DISORDERLY TROOPS. IN 1832 HE UNJUSTLY IMPRISONED WILLIAM B. TRAVIS, PATRICK C. JACK, AND OTHER SETTLERS HERE. WHEN HE REFUSED TO RELEASE THE MEN, ARMED CONFLICT ERUPTED BETWEEN TEXAS AND MEXICAN FORCES. THE CONFRONTATION HERE, WHICH ALSO SPARKED FIGHTING AT VELASCO AND ADOPTION OF THE TURTLE BAYOU RESOLUTIONS, RESULTED IN BRADBURN'S DISMISSAL AND THE REMOVAL OF MEXICAN TROOPS FROM THE POST. TODAY THE RUINS OF FORT ANAHUAC ARE A PHYSICAL REMINDER OF EVENTS THAT KINDLED THE DRIVE FOR TEXAS INDEPENDENCE.
(1976)

Chapter Five

Kemah, Houston, Wharton

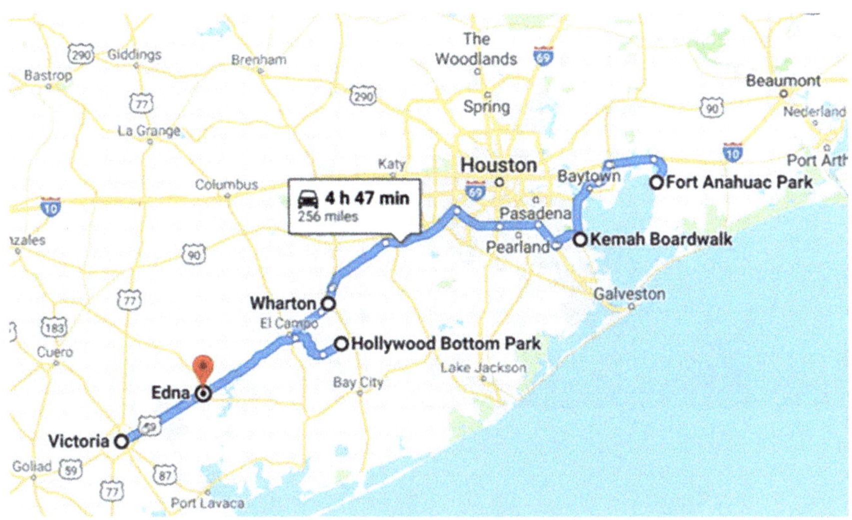

Fort Anahuac to Wharton to Victoria to Edna

After Fort Anahuac, I picked Kemah, Texas for our next stop because I began writing a script a few years ago and my character landed on the Boardwalk there. I'd never heard of it before writing and researching for the script, but I ended up falling in love with the place. I wanted to see if my imagination—and Google Earth—had given me a good representation of the area.

Kemah is located diagonally opposite of Anahuac on Trinity Bay. We arrived early morning, before the Boardwalk opened at noon, so we were able to see the buildings and layout instead of throngs of people. A light misty rain fell as we parked the car.

The businesses and residences in the surrounding blocks all had that beachy, tropical look—something that made me want to stay for a while.

The one thing that surprised me about the boardwalk was the ginormous rollercoaster. I'm not sure if it was new since Google last visited, or if I missed it in all my research. I love the Dahlonega Mine Train at Six Flags and the Alpha and Omega and Disney, but that's the extent of my roller coaster bravery, so I may not have paid it much attention. But in person, you sure can't miss it!

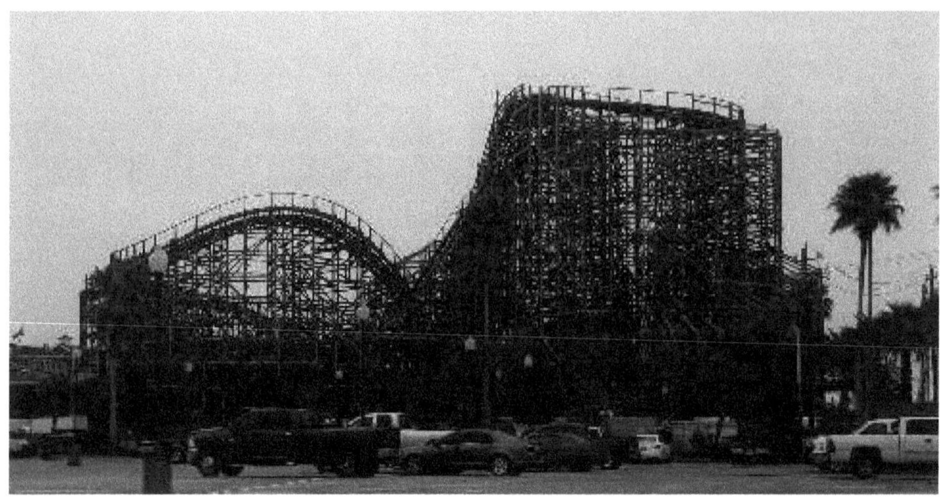

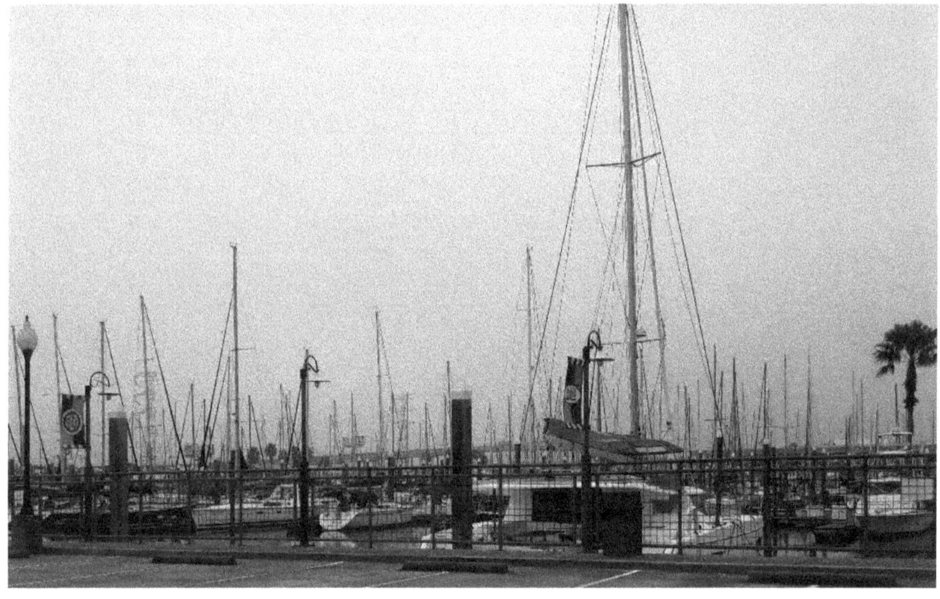

We were still trying to outrun the cold and rain (and you can tell from the photos we're not there yet!), so we didn't stay at Kemah long before we hit the road again. (The next morning, I saw Kemah's temperature was 31 degrees. It had been 55 when we were there.)

We had originally planned to go into Houston to visit a family member, but plans changed so we hit the outskirts. When Texans tell you how big that city is, believe them. We got on Hwy 80 on the east side and seemed to drive all day long. Eventually we saw a "leaving Houston City Limits" sign. An hour later, we saw another one.

We drove toward a free camping spot near Wharton, Texas. The whole drive, the name of the town bugged me, because I felt I wasn't pronouncing it properly. When I tried to say it one way, it came out "Horton," but I knew that wasn't right. When I really tried to sound it with the "Whar" sound, it garbled.

Before going to the camp site, we stopped in town so I could introduce Tim to Texas barbecue. In a quick internet search, I found that Hinze's BBQ had been in business since the 1970s and knew their stuff. The beef brisket began calling my name.

On the way, we spotted the coolest place—if my budget would have allowed, we'd have stayed at the TeePee Motel that night. What a fun place. They even offered free WIFI.

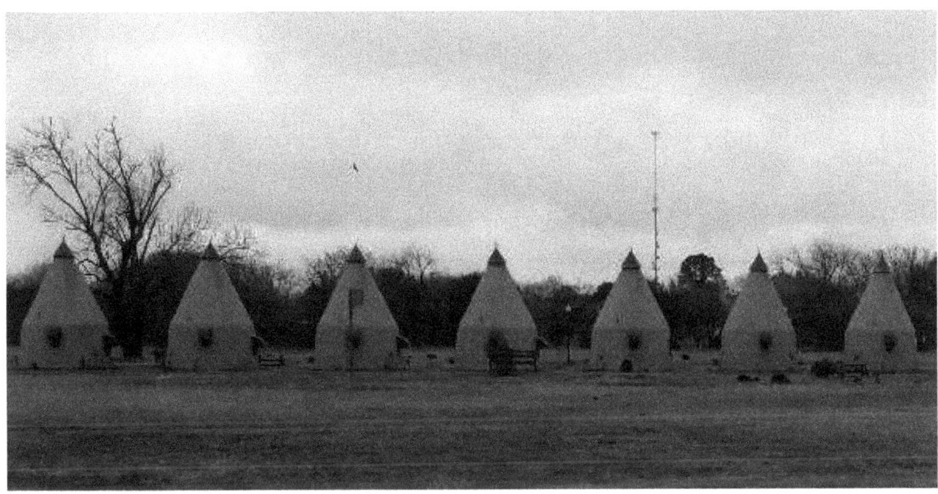

But we kept driving toward the food and Hinze's BBQ did not disappoint. Tim was instantly at home: two framed images with John Wayne greeted him as we walked to the register. We knew we had truly entered a local joint, all talk ceased as heads turned toward the strangers. The crowd was all ages, all races, but mostly local, so our arrival seemed to surprise them all.

My order of beef brisket was the best I've ever eaten, two delicious pork ribs, two sides, a slice of onion, a pile of dill pickles, and a slice of soft, white bread. Tim got chopped beef (he said he'd listen to me and next time get the brisket) and smoked sausage. We ended up trading out sides, but they were all delicious. Blackeye pea salad (except they looked more like crowder peas or lady peas than blackeyes) that was sweet, vinegary, with a slight hint of jalapeno, cucumber salad in a light creamy dill dressing, mashed/chopped potatoes mixed with bacon and onion—I was told similar to German potato salad, but I felt it missed that mark—but Tim loved them, so I got his pea salad. And mustard greens—Tim got those, but I could have eaten a pot of them, too. The best part, after the brisket, was the price—only $10.50 per plate. I love finding such great food at bargain prices. Tim was already chowing down on his before I could get a picture of both plates.

After our tummies were full, we stopped in at a local store down the street, only because of its name: TNT Western Wear. (TNT—Tim N Tracy?) The employees were friendly and beautiful, and fitted Tim for a cowboy hat. A couple of guys at a rodeo fitted and sold him one several years ago, but he said it never fit right. These ladies sized him up and proved that the rodeo guys had been wrong. Tim was content to know his correct size and I was relieved he didn't want to break the budget!

While we were in the store, I asked them about the pronunciation of the town's name and found out they all pronounce it Warton (or more like Wertn). I feel better.

Too late in the afternoon, we finally turned toward the free camping site out in the country. Way out in the country.

We drove ten miles without seeing a car or even a business. On the final turn to the park, we landed on a dirt road that was all washboard. It seemed treacherous, and with the coming storm, we were afraid the road would wash out and leave us stranded out in the boonies. We weren't sure how long our cell signal would last, so we decided to get out of there and head toward Victoria, but our camping destination still unknown at that point.

The countryside was gorgeous, and I have a tremendous amount of respect for the farmers who have worked that land for generations. The soil was rich, and the vastness of it all went on as far as the eye could see in every direction.

I took a couple of panorama shots on either side of the car from the same location, trying to capture the vastness of it all. Photos still reflect the dreariness we're facing with the weather.

Just before we got to Victoria, our tire sensor light flashed on and off a few times, so we decided to go into the town and have our tires check. Walmart Auto Center was almost ready to close, but they pulled us in and aired up our tires, told us which one was low, and sent us on our way.

By this time, it was dark. We'd passed a rest stop a few miles back, so we checked online, learned that overnights were okay, so we went back, and car camped for the night.

But the next morning, we had decisions to make.

From the FROG Files

We drove way out in the country—and I mean the deep Texas country—toward our next campsite. We drove for ten miles without seeing a business or even another car. Houses were miles apart. I never get scared out in the country, but the vastness of nothingness sort of freaked me out a bit. I kept thinking of all the what ifs (what if we lost cell signal, had a flat, etc.), while at the same time marveling at the beautifully rich, dark soil and wide, open skies.

We escaped the colder temps, finally, and spent most of the afternoon at 65 degrees or above (at one point, it was 71 degrees). Right now, I'm sitting at a picnic table in the rest stop and it's 68 degrees at eight p.m. Yay!

Tonight, we're both tired. We drove entirely too many miles and had too many excursions to set up camp. Texas is huge and we need to learn to pace ourselves. We're also finding that this must be peak season because a lot of the free campgrounds we found before leaving home are no longer free.

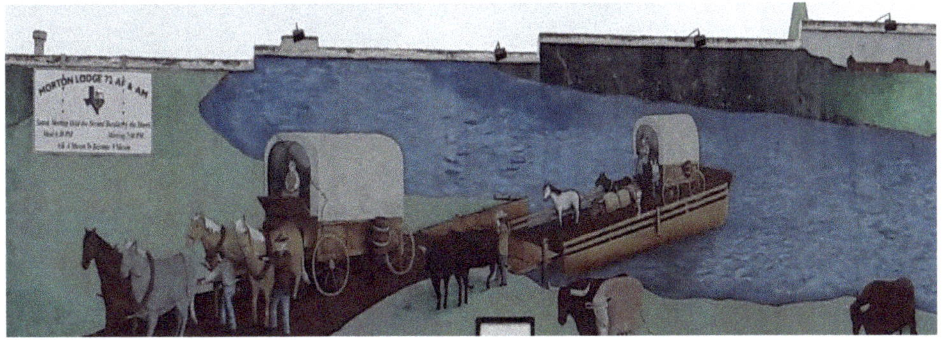

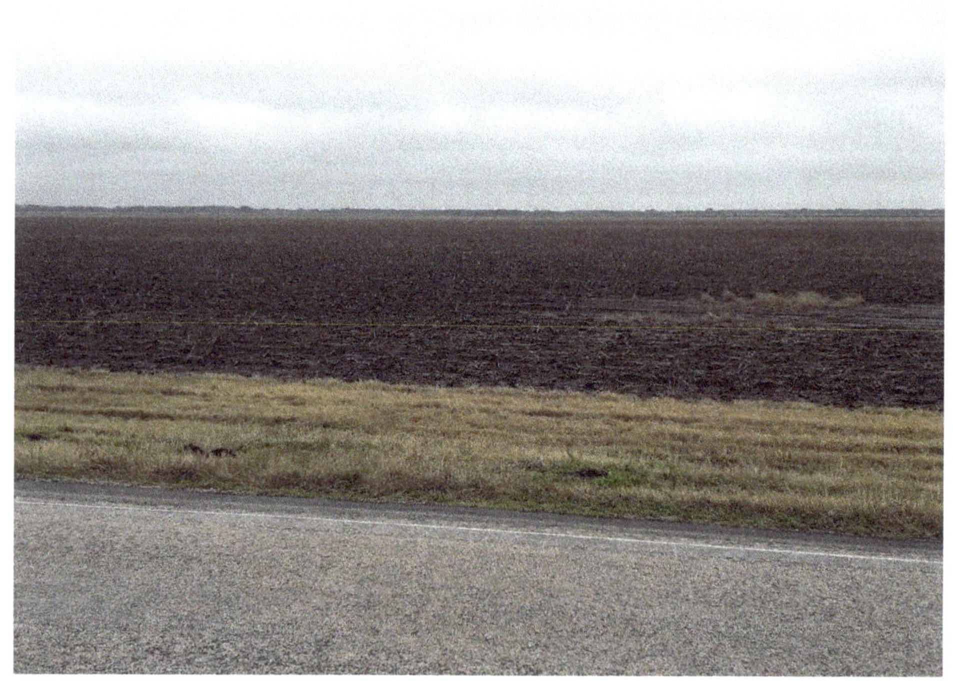

As far as the eye can see of Texas countryside.

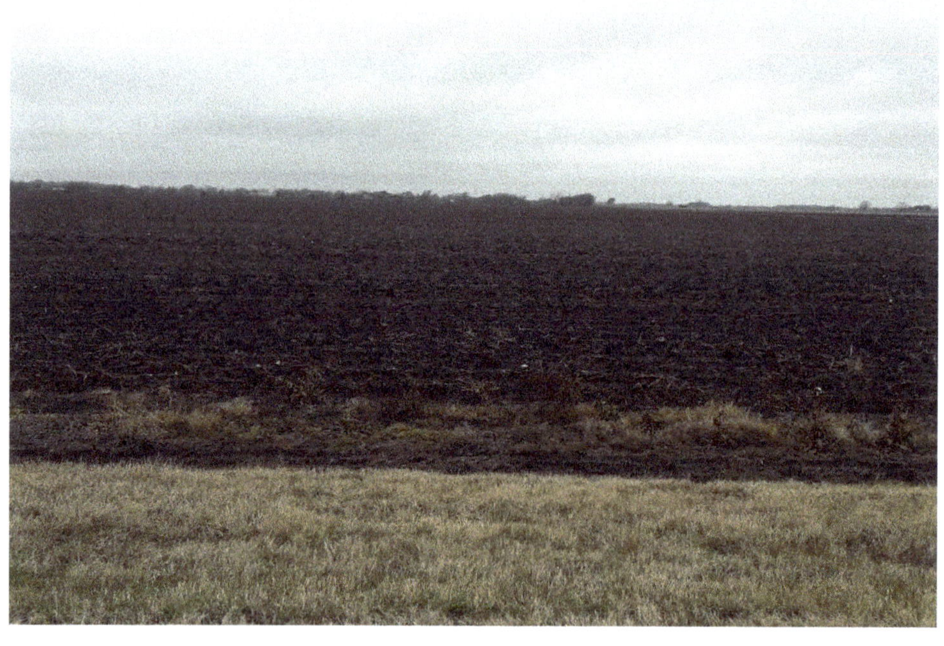

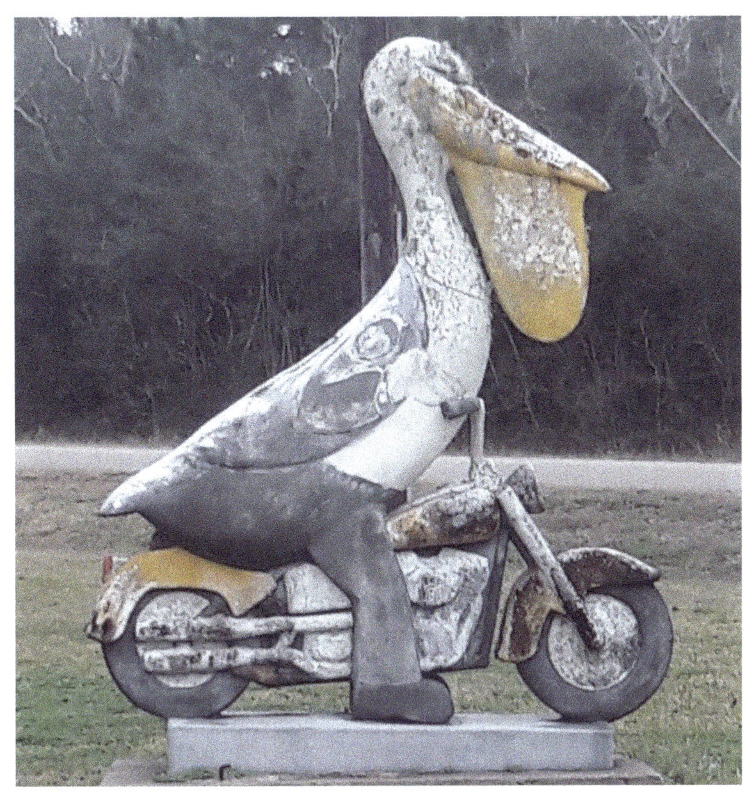

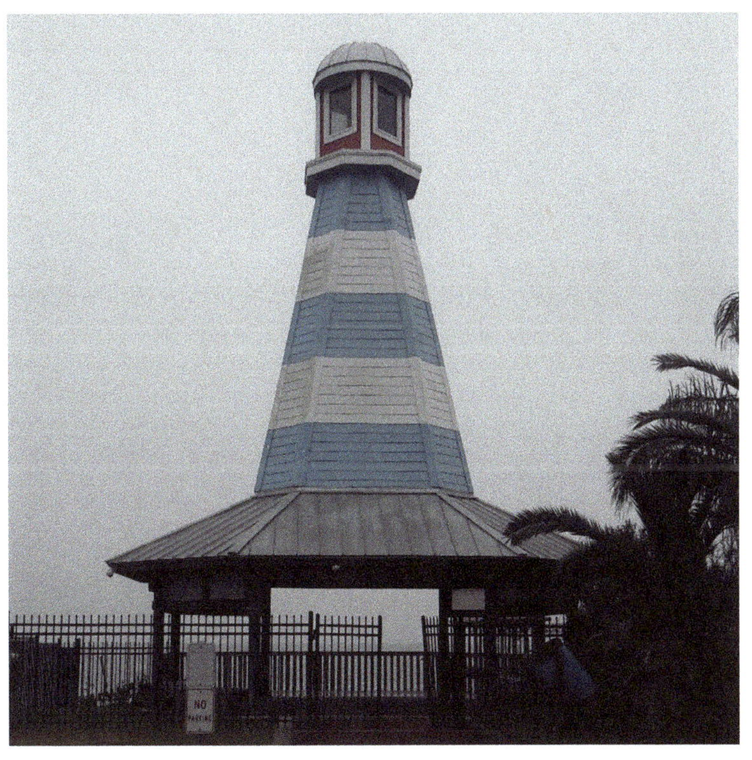

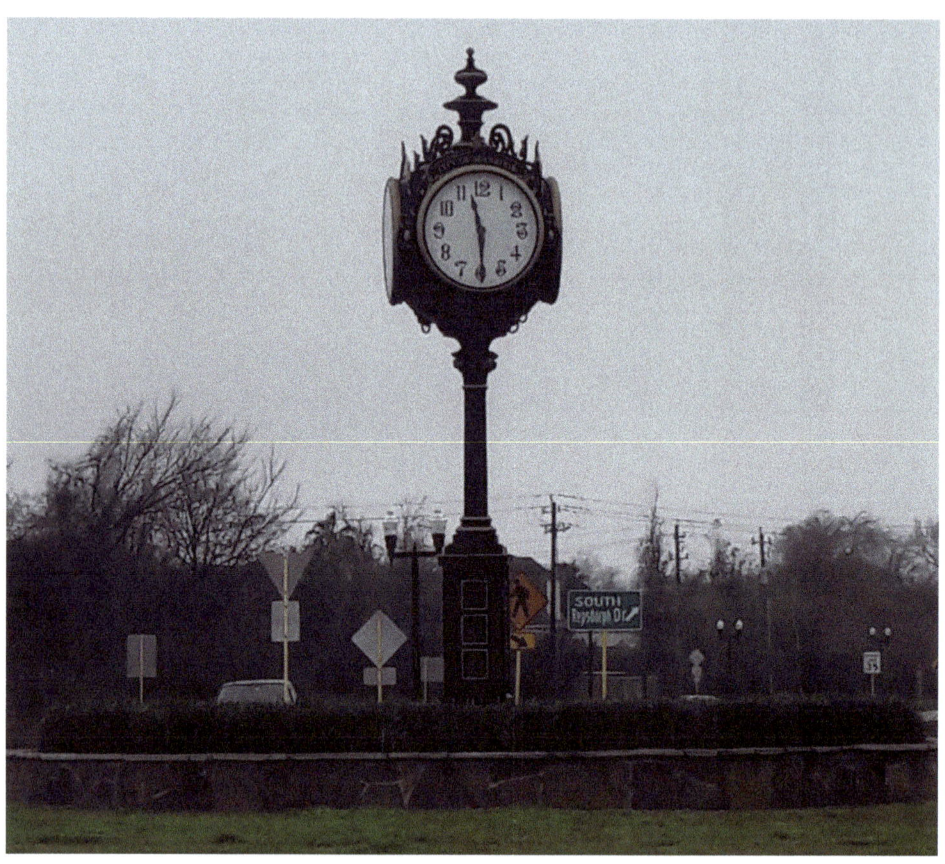

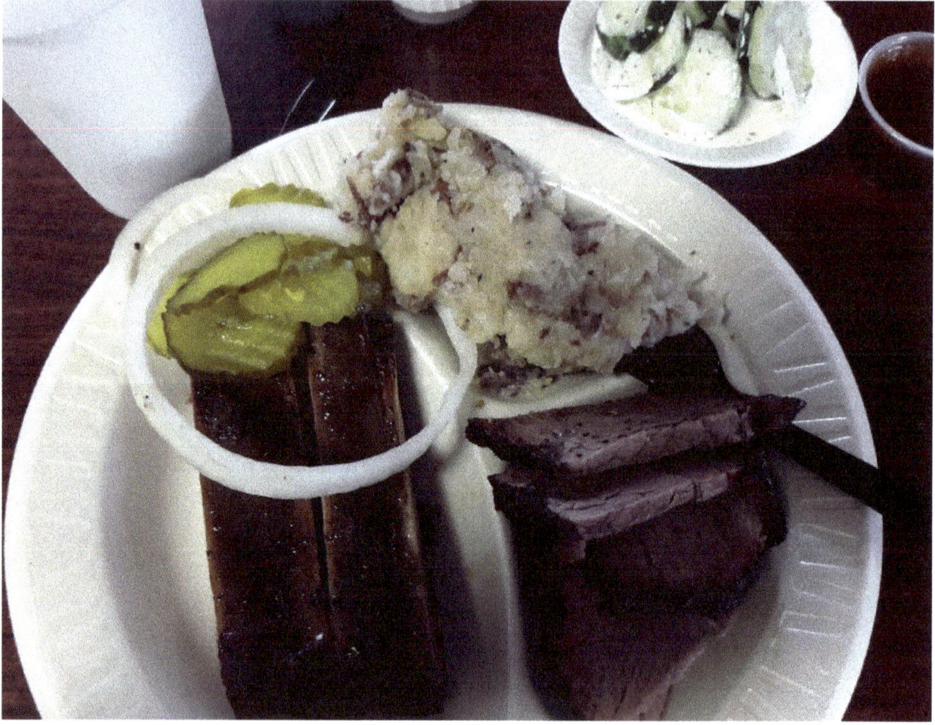

Chapter Six

Rockport and Mathis

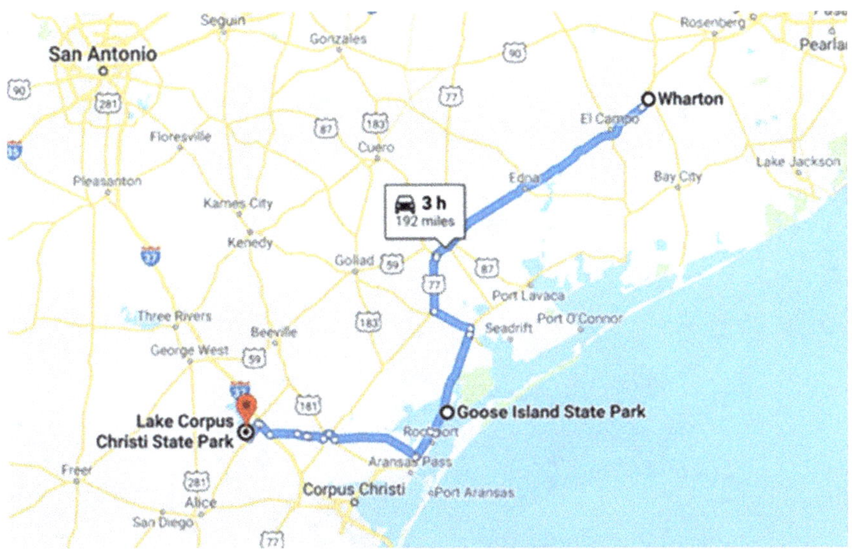

Wharton to Goose Island State Park to Mathis

After our overnight at the Victoria rest stop, we made the decision to head south to Goose Island State Park. The website said the rate would be $10 per night, so I thought three nights at the coast would be good. There were free sites in the area, but most of them are on the beach, and I wasn't yet confident enough about setting up a tent with all that blowing wind. We thought the state park might offer more of a wind break and we wouldn't have to drive on the sand.

But when we arrived, the gatekeeper told us the fees would be $10 a day for camping, plus $5 per person per day entry fee.
No discounts, no passes. My budget didn't allow that, so I told her we'd have to go elsewhere. She suggested we check out the Big Oak at the end of the road and gave us directions.

TIP: If you're going to spend time at any of the Texas State Parks, I highly recommend buying a State Park Pass for $70. The pass is good for a carload of up to

We followed the road around and around to the Big Tree.

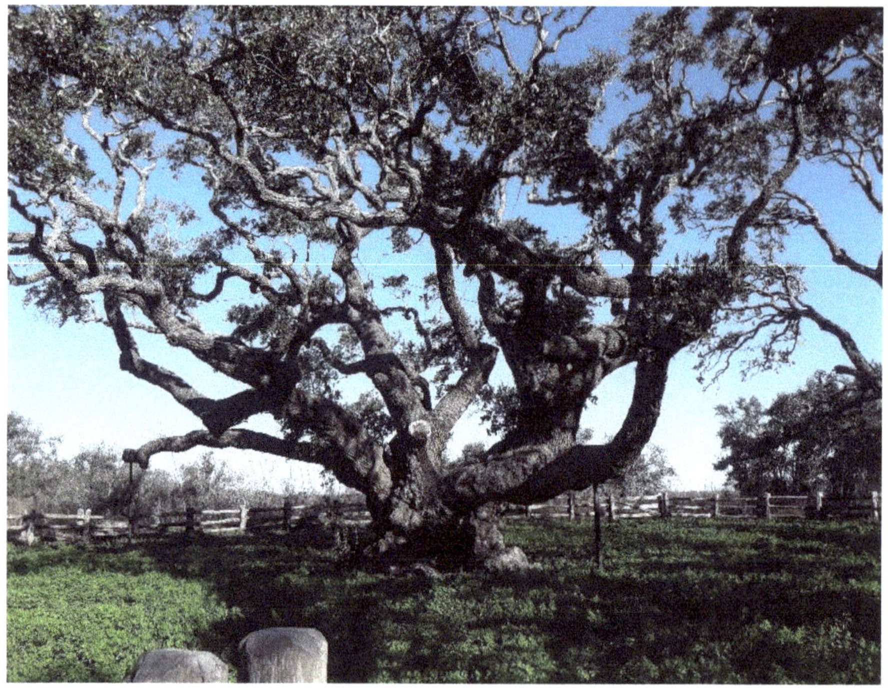

The Big Tree, Goose Island State Park 📷

A 1,000-year old Big Coastal Oak tree that has withstood all those massive
hurricanes through the years. It was gnarled and twisted and had been given support in
areas—and every inch of it was beautiful. I walked around it, snapping photos,
enjoying the way the sunlight poured through the branches leaving shadows. On one
side, as I neared the full circle, I was greeted by a frisky orange and black butterfly
that landed in front of me on a railing, then flitted to the grass, before landing on me
for a few moments. I tried to snap a photo, but it was never quite still enough for me
to get a good one.

Due to the high winds we were experiencing at the coast, we made the decision to
head more inland. Tim was ready for "cowboy country" and that didn't include coastal
destinations.

We picked a road and started driving. Windmills as far as the eye could see on one stretch of road. And they were massive!

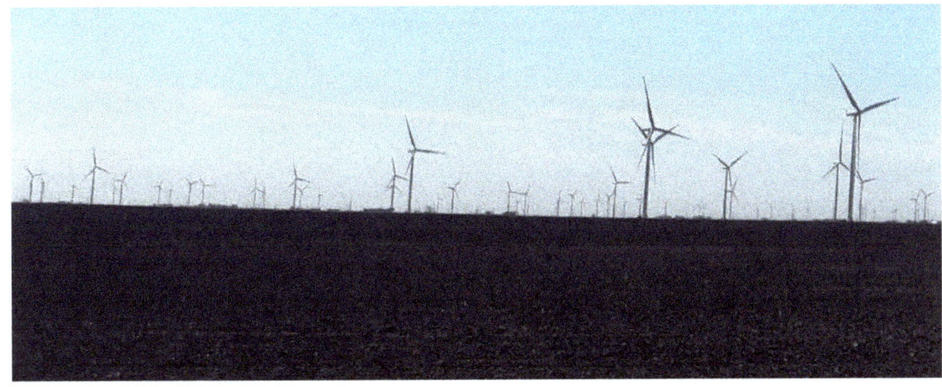

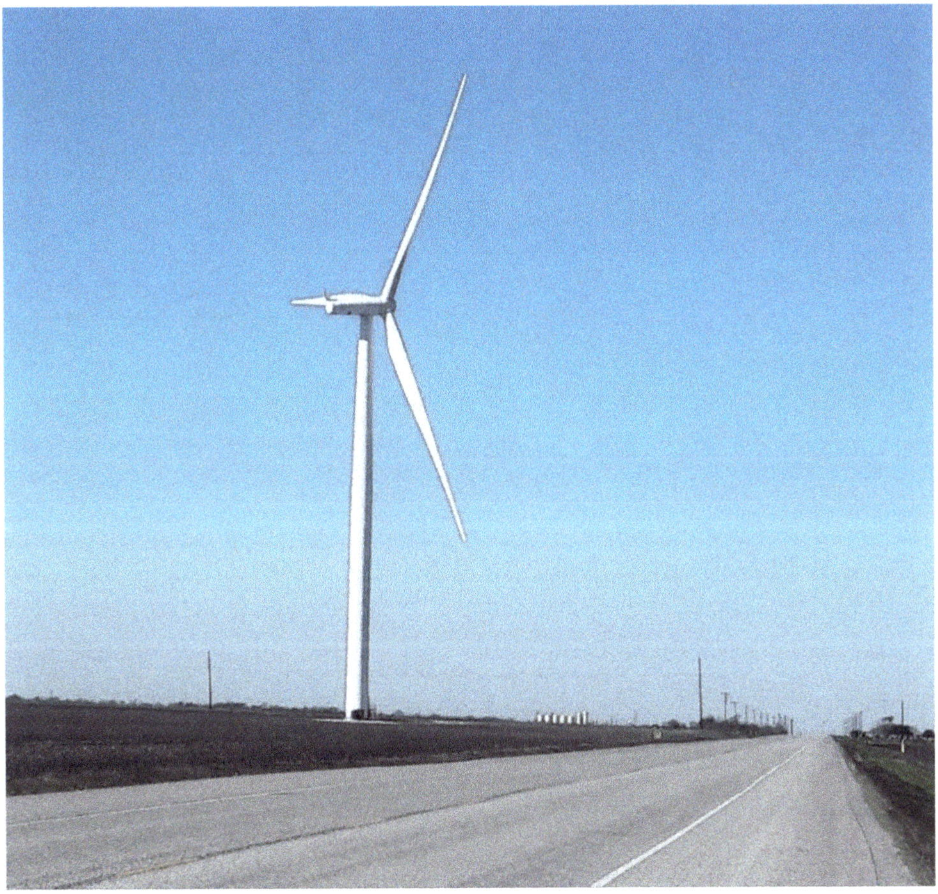

While we were driving, Zach called and said we had a reservation for two nights at Lake Corpus Christi State Park. Their reservation system wouldn't allow for a same day reservation, but they had room for us that night if we wanted.

The park was deserted but beautiful. Tiny yellow flowers cover most the land, and the moment we got out of the car, we could smell them.

But the wind. Oh my goodness, the wind.

Have you ever set up camp in the Texas wind?

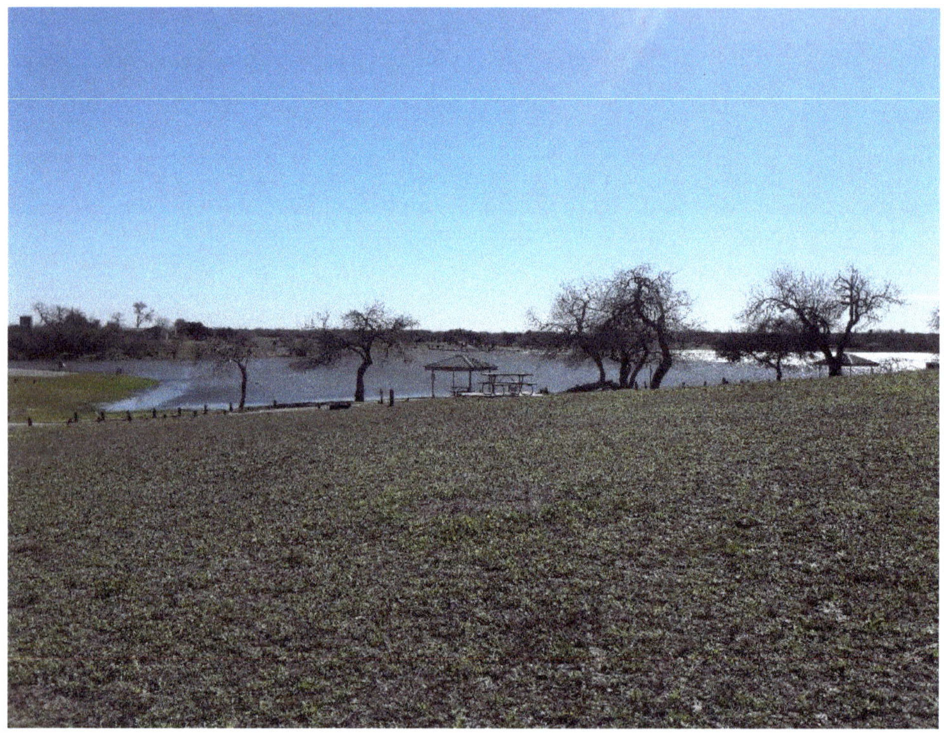

Tim finally checked the weather and learned that the wind, 25-30 mph with gusts up to 40 mph, was something that would last only until midnight, and thankfully, it died down a few hours early. But it was fierce. Our campsite had a covered picnic table, so we were able to wrap two sides of it with a tarp to block that wind. (The wind the next two days change directions, so while the tarp helped immensely the first day, it didn't help as much the rest of the time.)

[Confession: tarp aeronautics is beyond my comprehension, and above my head, both literally and figuratively. I never could figure out how to position the tarp, even with the numerous videos Zach sent me.]

How strong are 25-30 mph winds with gusts up to 40? Strong enough to break every string we tried to use. The wind broke tent poles and even one strip of duct tape—but not after I doubled it.

And yes, we pulled out the zip ties, but even our longest weren't long enough and before Tim could join them together, I'd pulled out the duct tape.

The Mesquite section where we pitched the tent had approximately 25 campsites that were spread out, but only two other campers were in the area. The lake was gorgeous and overall the park was clean, and grounds maintained. The bathrooms could have been a bit cleaner, but after discovering someone used the restroom to dye her hair and smeared hair dye all over the walls because—well, the bathrooms were in pretty good shape if that's what they're dealt regularly. Water was hot and pressure was great; two sinks with a vanity top in the bathroom and a real mirror—all things I don't take for granted these days. The showers are large and have a small bench to set your belongings to keep them within sight but out of water's reach. Something else I don't take for granted.

My only complaint about the bathhouse in our particular area was that the stall door locks weren't operational. They're in place, but don't fit properly on any of the stalls.

The campground winds around the shores of Lake Corpus Christi and is divided into several sections: two water-only sections (where we camped), a full hook-ups section with pull-through sites for RVs, and water & election sections that are back-in. While our section was almost empty, the RV sections were full.

After a beautiful day of exploring, the winds hit again.

Before it was over, the winds had destroyed our tent, breaking two tent poles and ripping one wall. The winds also pulled up and sent flying four of our eight-inch heavy-duty tent stakes. I'm so grateful no one was hurt as they flailed through the air. I was able to catch some midair, others fell out of the whipping grommets and hit the ground without further damage.

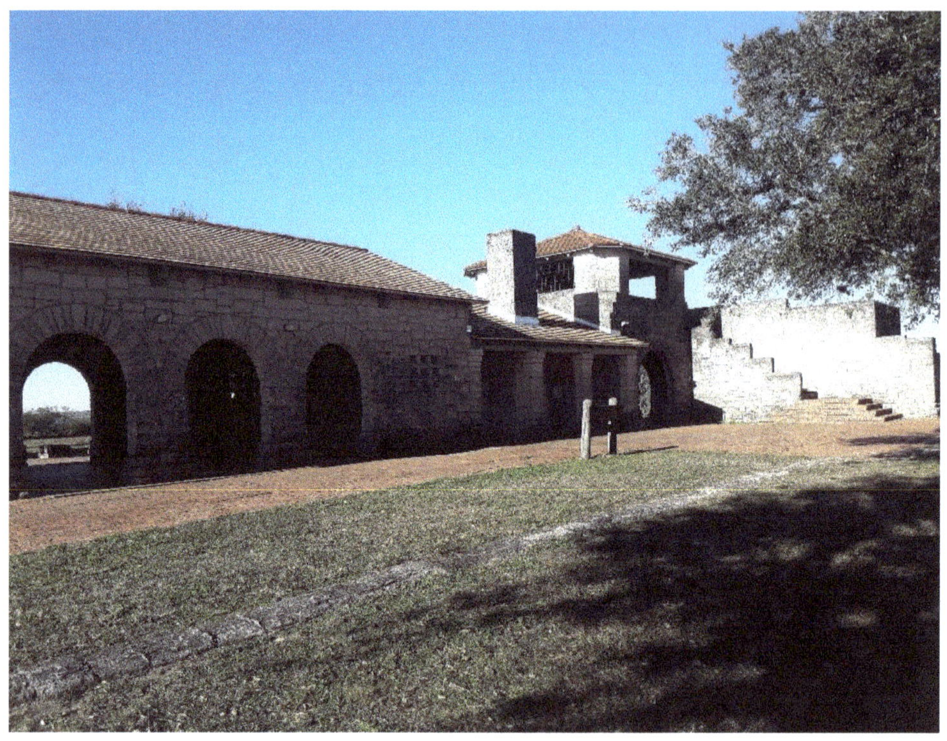

Old Pavilion built by the Civilian Conservation Corps in 1933-34

With the tent caved in, we began packing the car as quickly as possible. Originally, I thought setting up camp in the wind was bad, but breaking camp during these awful winds was much worse.

We couldn't fold our tarps or sleeping bags properly, so our packing was a disaster. We managed to literally squeeze everything into the car—minus the tent— and we slept in the car overnight. We planned to car camp for the next few days until we found a replacement tent or camper.

At this point, we began considering a low-profile pop-up camper, but budget kept us from doing anything immediately. We decided a new tent was in our future, because we sure weren't going the used route again.

From the FROG Files:

While I stood in awe in front of that 1000-year-old oak tree, amazed at its fortitude and the beauty of its limbs, Tim wasn't impressed at all. I found that odd and puzzling, perhaps even a little alarming.

I had a very rough night - lots of nightmares and disturbing dreams, and I kept scooting myself to one end of the tent, so I wasn't in Tim's way as he climbed in and out. At the very end is where the tarp kept flapping, so the cold winds kept blowing on me. I finally got up at five a.m. with a sore throat and cough.

The winds seem to have died down now, but the temp is currently 35 degrees. Tim chose not to light the heater all night, so I'm currently sitting in the car charging electronics and taking advantage of the seat warmers. He's lit the heater and I'll return there after I do some writing.

Tim's cold seems to be gone, so I'm very grateful for that.

Unfortunately, the tent went in the dumpster. We asked the campground if someone might be able to put it to use and was told that these kinds of tents did not have replaceable parts, so when they found them, they threw them in the dumpster. They asked us to toss ours so they wouldn't have to do it, so we did.

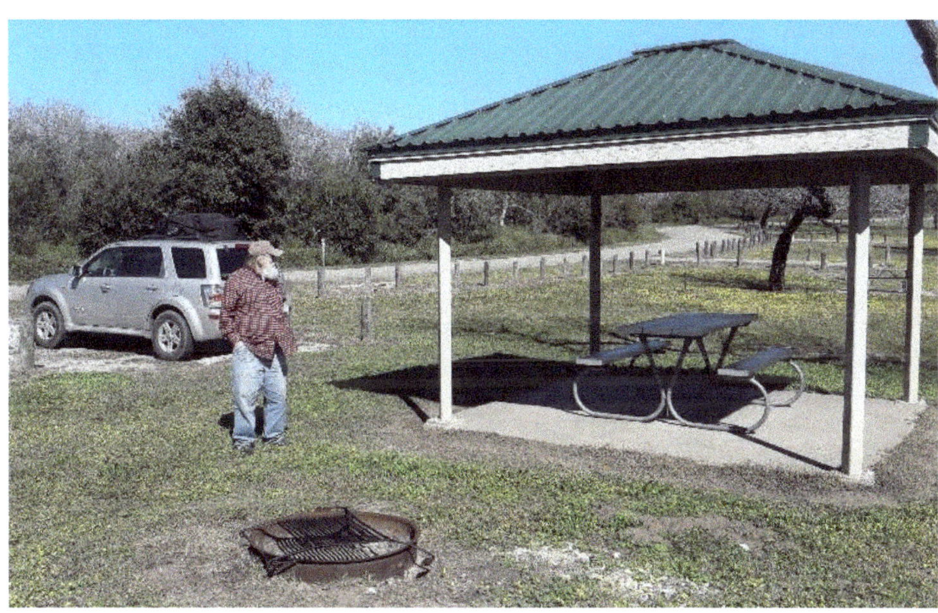

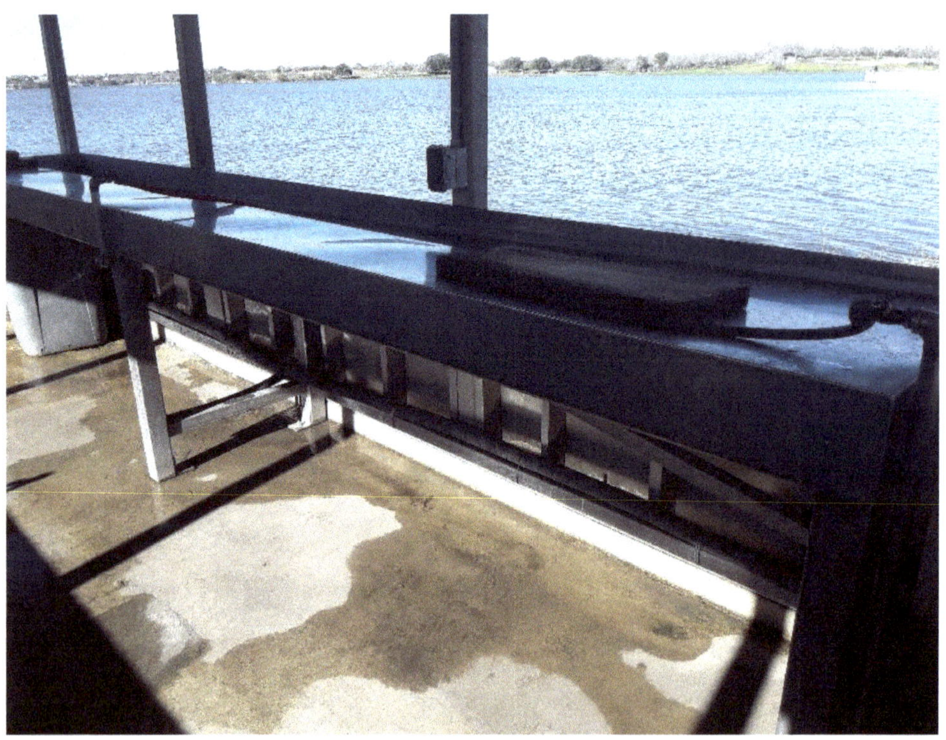

Above: Fish Cleaning Station in State Park

Below: Old Pavilion Archway 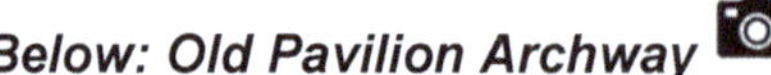

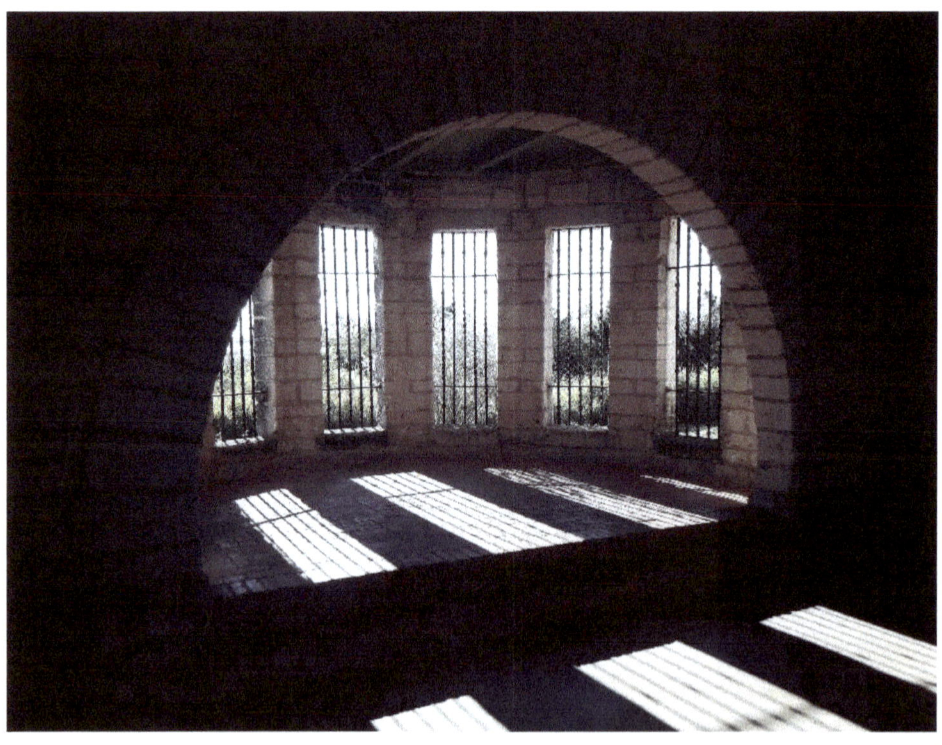

Chapter Seven

On the Way to San Antonio

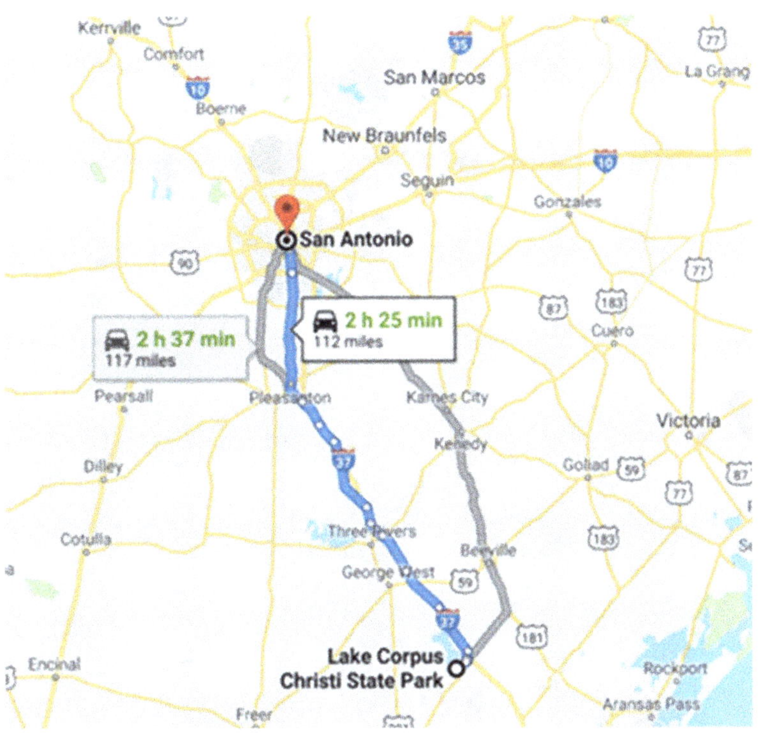

Mathis to San Antonio

Amazingly, we managed to get dinner (and our breakfast for the next day) cooked before the tent collapsed and we started packing the car.

For dinner, we cooked "flappin' jacks in the wind" with bacon, and then, the next morning, we ate the rest of the bacon with hard-boiled eggs. Yes, Tim travels with bacon and hot sauce. (It's Tabasco, the Garlic variety—wonder if they'd sponsor the #LeapFrogs? He told me to try for a bacon sponsorship, too! Ha!)

After leaving the lake, we took the backroads into San Antonio, taking our time and soaking in the countryside.

We drove into the Choke Canyon Reservoir area to see if it might be a good camping area for any future trips to the area. As we drove around, we spotted a wild hog. Photo is not great, because it was taken with my phone from so far away, but I was glad not to be any closer!

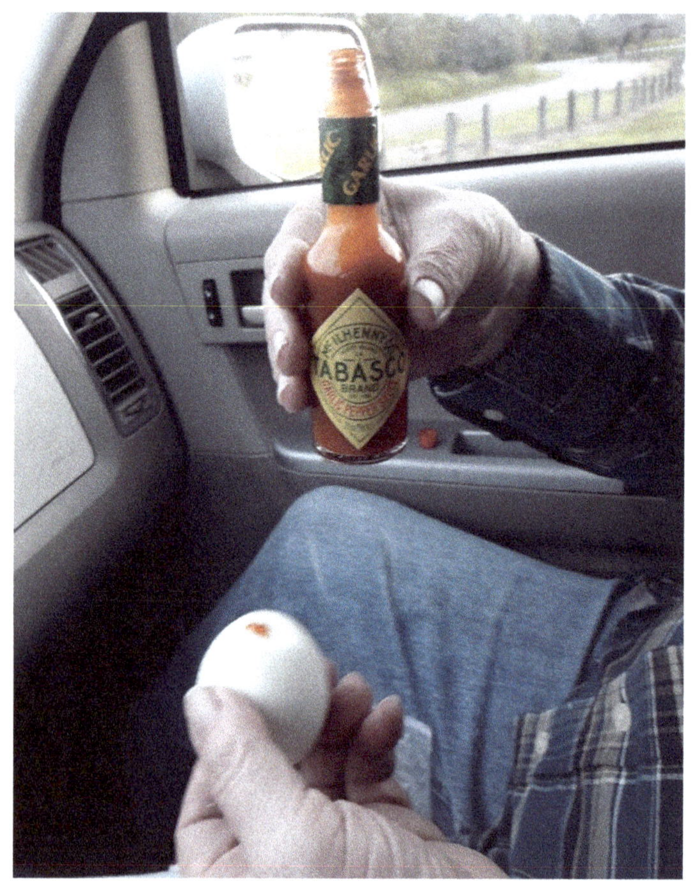

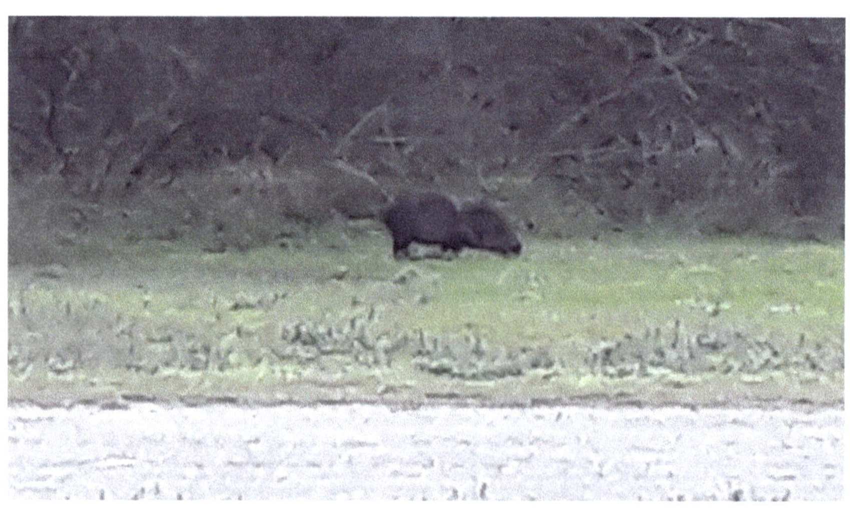

Small towns always intrigue me, so we usually stop and take a few photos of their main street areas.

The town of George West had a cute little square with red streetlamps, and a BBQ place across the street that smelled heavenly—but we'd just finished breakfast!

The Atascosa County Courthouse in Jourdanton is on the National Historic Register.

The town of Calliham had a post office almost smaller than the sign pointing to it.

We eventually got to San Antonio, but the small towns along the way help me remember that life isn't about the destination but about the journey—the places we see and the people (and critters) we meet along the way.

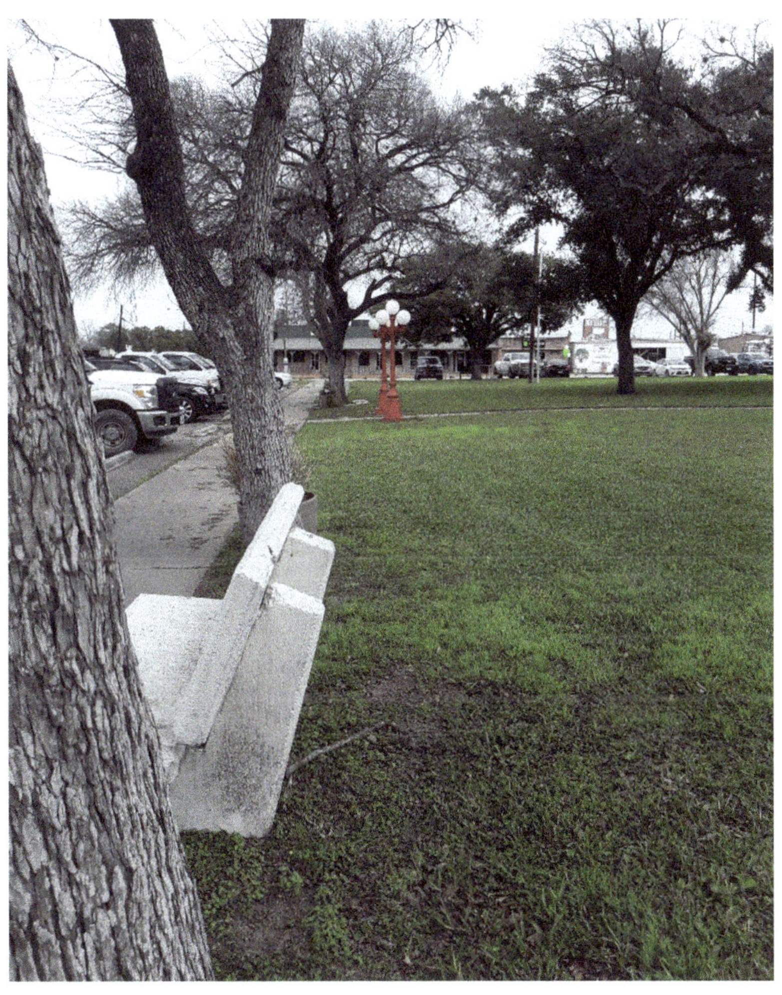

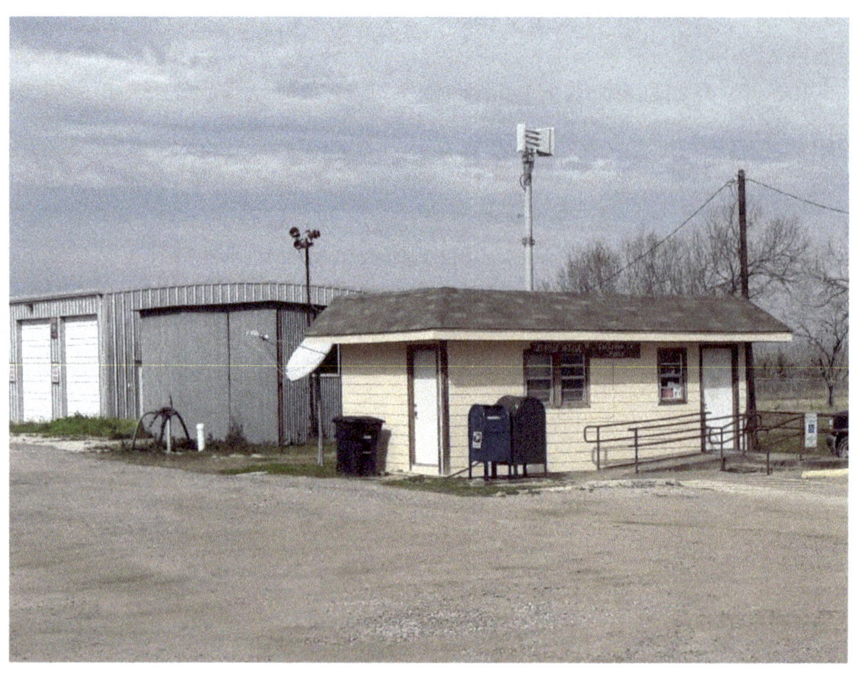

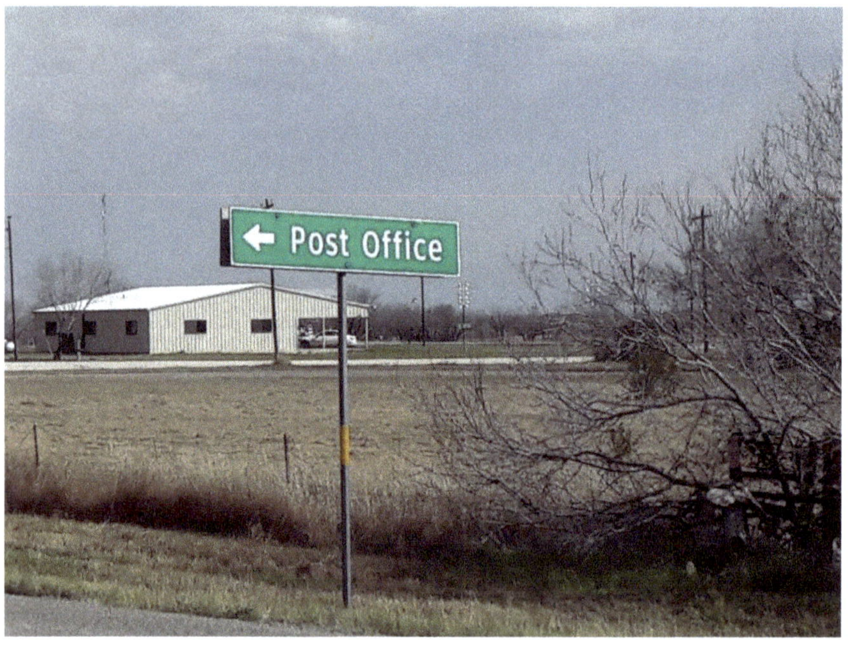
Post Office

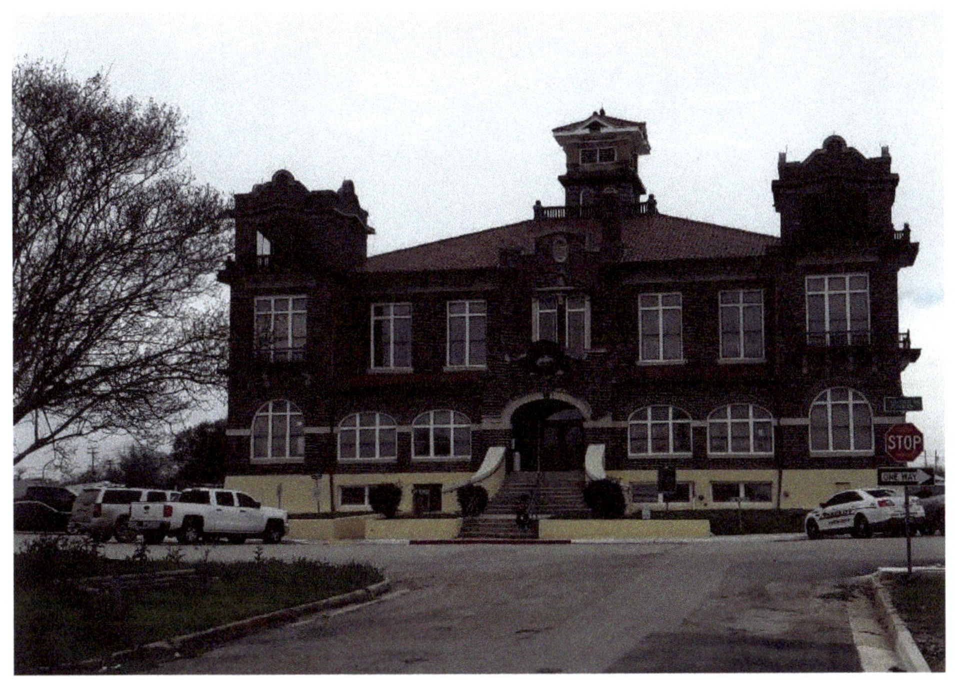

Above: Atascosa County Courthouse in Jourdanton

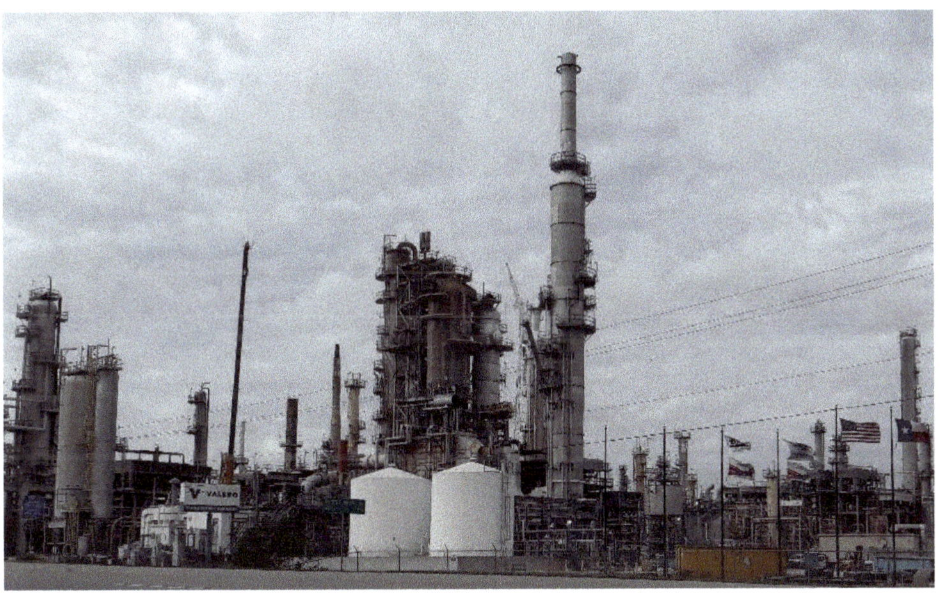

Sample Artwork:

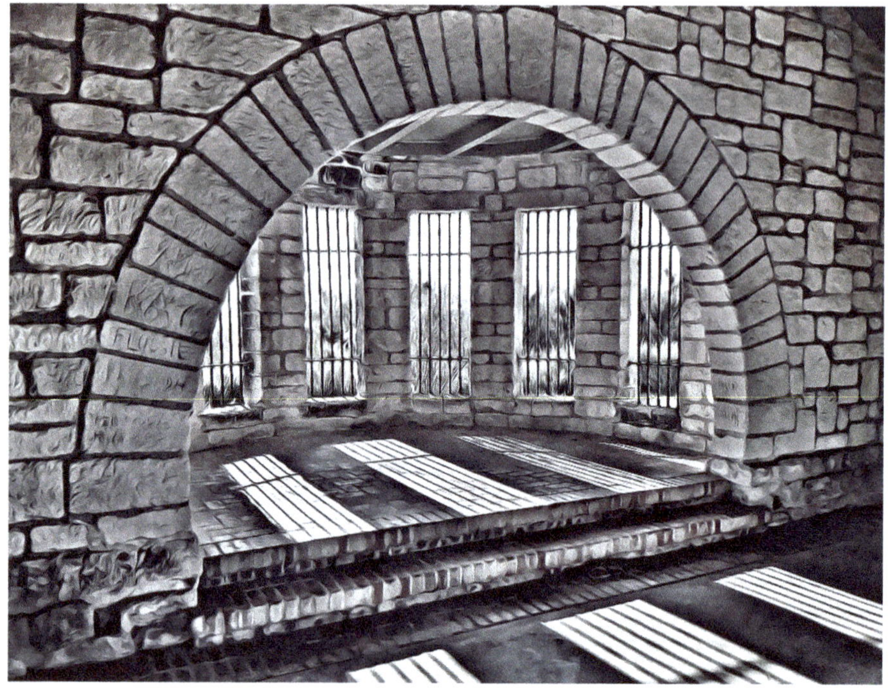

Old Pavilion Archway 

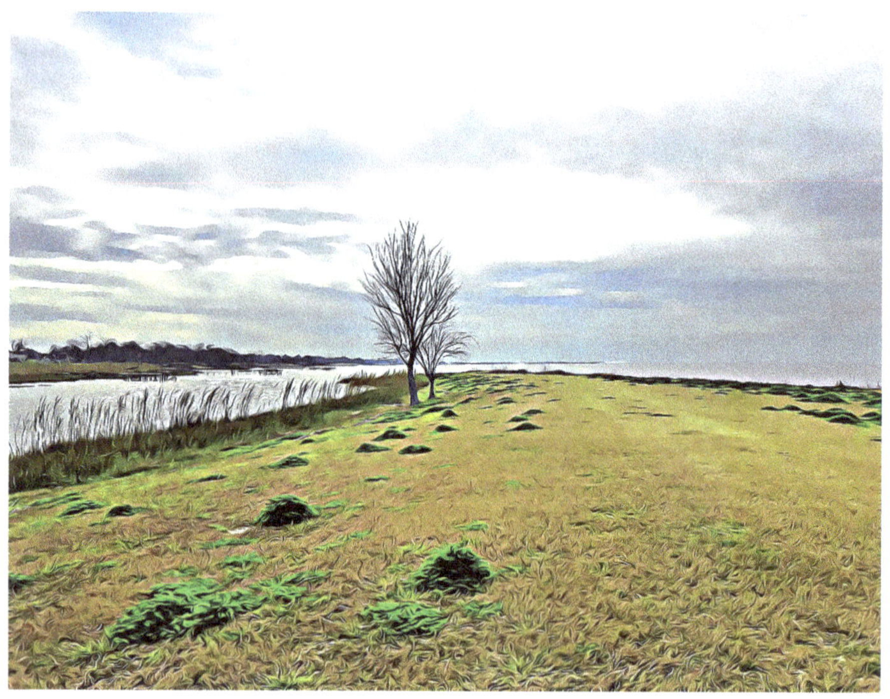

Late Winter on the Point of Fort Anahuac

Chapter Eight

San Antonio!

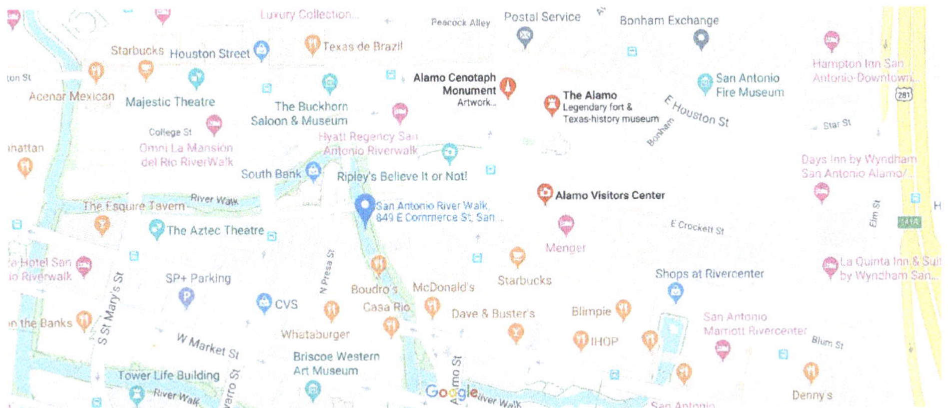

After all the wind at Lake Corpus Christi, we were relieved but weary upon our arrival in San Antonio. Without a tent, and without a backup plan, we knew we were in for several days of car camping.

I also had work to do, so our first stopping point in San Antonio was the public library, where I hoped to recharge all our electronics and get a few hours of work done.

The main branch of the San Antonio library is ginormous and busy. The first parking space we found was on the roof of the parking deck—several stories high. The library itself had escalators (out of service while we were there), elevators, hallways, and people giving directions—and they weren't always correct. The place was busier than most malls I've been to in recent years. So busy, I couldn't work, so we cut our stay there

short and went in search of food.

In case you haven't figured out by now, we're foodies and we search (usually on TripAdvisor) for the best local places we can find that fit a small budget. For Texas, I also created a list of foods we must eat while here: barbecue, enchiladas, tacos, and tamales, and other Tex-Mex as we encountered it. San Antonio did not disappoint!

The first place we went, I still can't pronounce the name, and I cheat by copying and pasting the name when I see it in print. I know *Pollos* means chickens, but that's as far as my own translation goes. Google Translate gives me the word Roasted, but that's not an accurate description of the food we got.

Pollos Asados Los Nortenos offers charbroiled chicken, served with rice, a grilled onion, lime wedge, and tortillas. You can order half a chicken or a whole one and add beans to your order for an additional charge if you wish.

We both ordered a half chicken meal, not really thinking it through, so we each ended up with one breast, one wing, one leg, one thigh. We had a full meal leftover for our dinner, so that worked out great! Flavors were incredible, and the prices affordable.

I was working while we were in San Antonio, but after the busy-ness of the main library, I sought another and found a delight in the San Pedro branch, located in the San Pedro Springs Park, the second oldest park in the whole country.

The park wasn't large, but seemed slightly inaccessible, at least from a visitor's point of view. Roads through the park had been blocked off, and there was limited street parking around it. The library parking lot had meters—we had to pay to park there. Library staff told us they were the park's meters, so we could stay there to utilize the park if we wanted—but we had to pay.

When we went back later, we found other parking in the lot of the Playhouse, which is part of the park property, too.

We ran into another problem while we were car camping in San Antonio.

We woke up one morning and discovered Tim's legs were swollen. We knew he had to get flat, so I found a cheap, cheap hotel on Hotwire and booked it that morning. We drove straight to the hotel, the Super 8 on N. St. Mary's, and they let us check in at seven a.m. Tim took a shower, crawled into bed, and slept until noon, while I worked and washed clothes. The hotel provides a washer and dryer for guests, so I didn't have to leave the property. They'd recently undergone a few renovations, and apparently, folks decided to try to destroy the good work, so now the hotel requires a refundable $50 deposit upon check-in. It was refunded to my bank IMMEDIATELY upon checkout, so I got over my frustration about that. (I thought they might delay the deposit several days, like places tend to do, but they did not.)

The hotel also served another great purpose, so although it was an expense we weren't counting on, it ended up paying for itself in several ways. 1) The laundry was cheaper than elsewhere so we saved money that way; 2) free breakfast and coffee; 3) they let us check in early in the day, so we got maximum use of our time there; 4) they graciously let us leave our car parked in their lot while we took the city bus to see the Alamo and Riverwalk after we checked out the next morning, which saved us tons on parking.

My budget really appreciated San Antonio. An all-day City Bus pass, purchased at the VIA bus office (or can be purchased at most HEB stores and other locations) was only $2.75 for me, $1.30 for Tim and good on any city bus or trolley all over the city. (Not good on the specialty Hop On-Hop Off buses, but still a great option.) Routes were a little confusing, but we eventually figured it out, and the more lost we got, the more we saw of the city, so no complaints at all.

The Alamo, as expected, was swarming with tourists. Signs posted everywhere warned us not to touch the walls, but that's what I wanted to do most—touching the history somehow makes me feel part of it. And I wanted to touch the walls before I ever saw the first sign—but they made the urge even greater. (I resisted.)

Sunshine peeked through the clouds a few times during the day, but it was still dreary and cool.

Getting to the Riverwalk proved quite challenging. I haven't figured out if they like to give tourist the runaround, or if they're trying to keep it hidden, but there seemed to be no easy way to get there. For most folks, this may not be an issue, but for Tim, walking had become quite a chore, so we adapted best we could.

Another budget friendly aspect of San Antonio was the Riverwalk boat cruise. The tourist office (across from the Alamo) was keen to sell us the short cruise, which we purchased. Tim got a senior discount, so both passes were only $21 total. If we ever visit again—in warmer weather and with more time—I think we'd opt to buy the shuttle pass instead of the tour. The tour guide was fun, but I would have enjoyed seeing more of the actual Riverwalk than the short loop this tour cruise provided.

San Antonio was a great place to visit, and we will one day return.

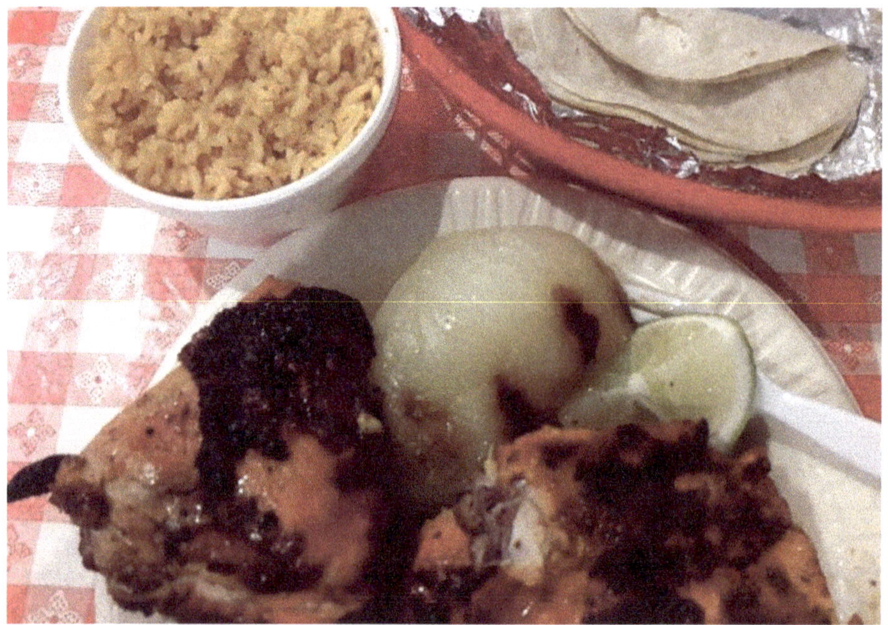

Pollos Asados Los Nortenos

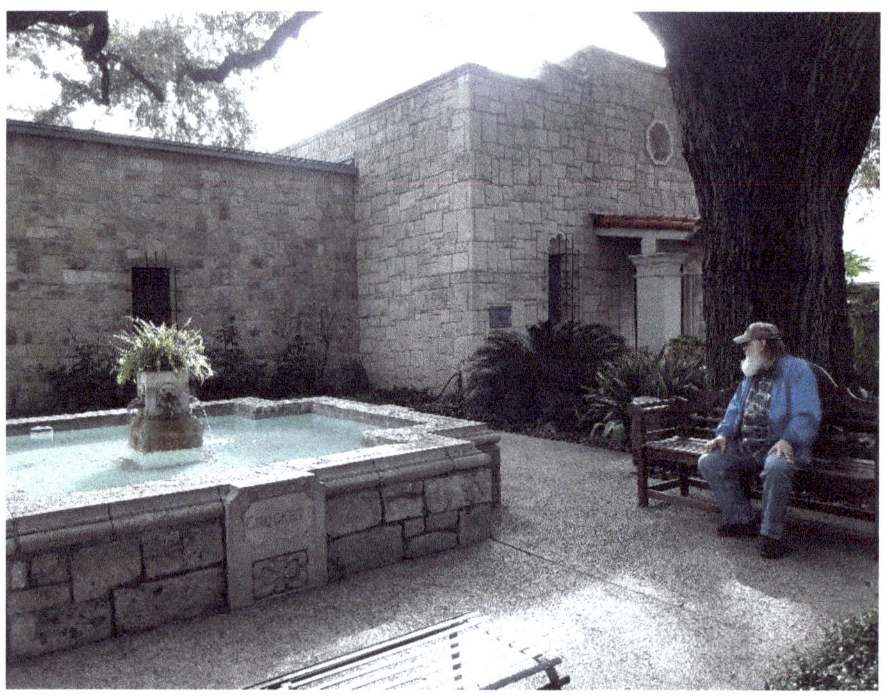

Courtyard at The Alamo

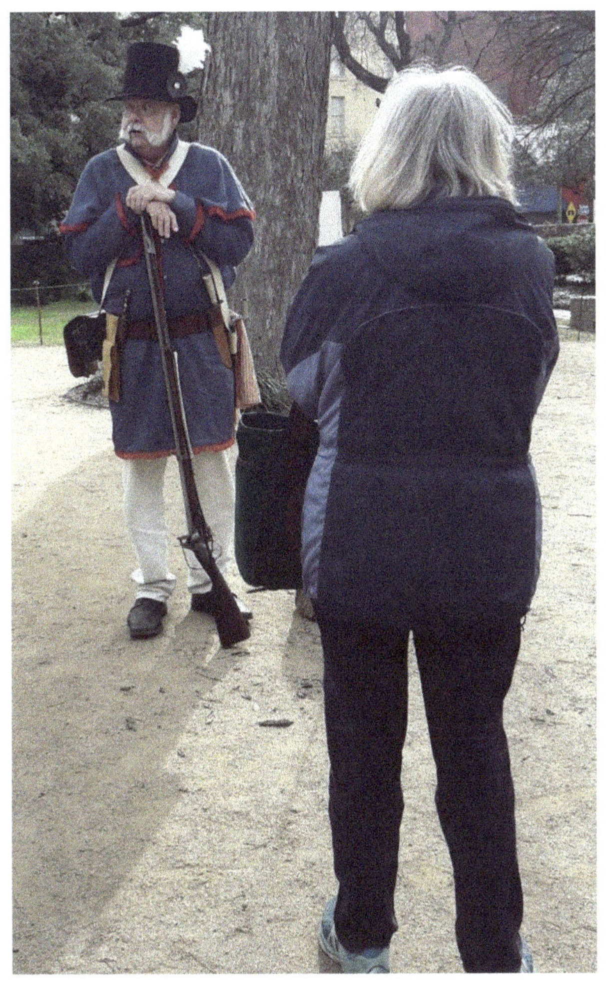

An Alamo docent answering questions

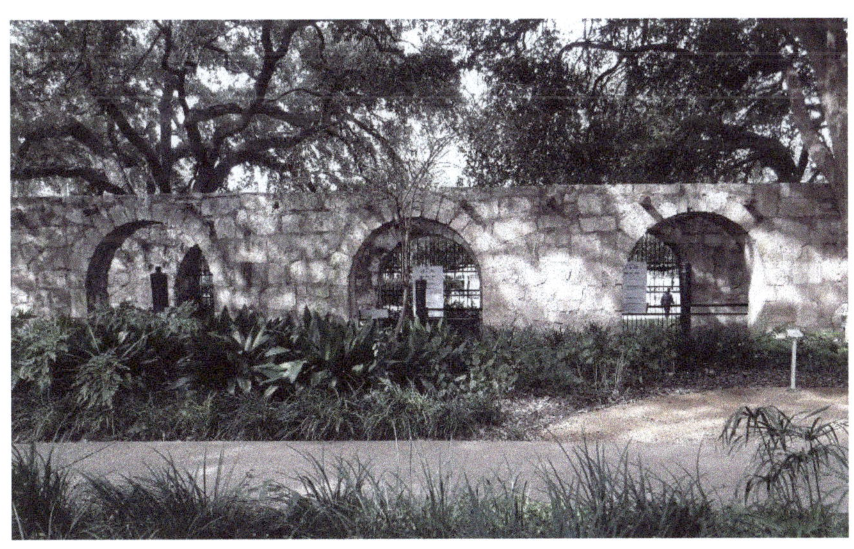

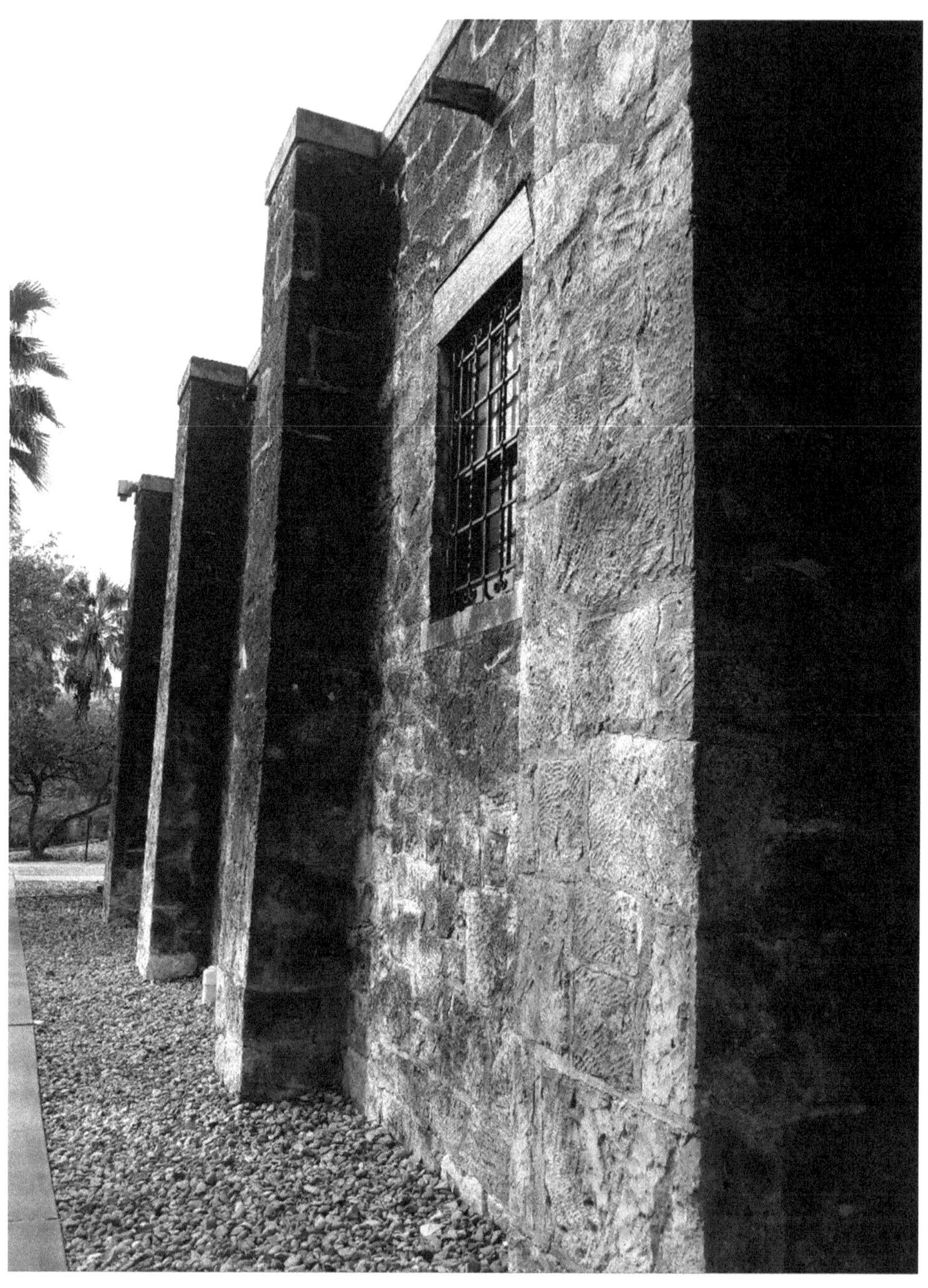

The Alamo exterior wall
(Don't you want to touch it?)

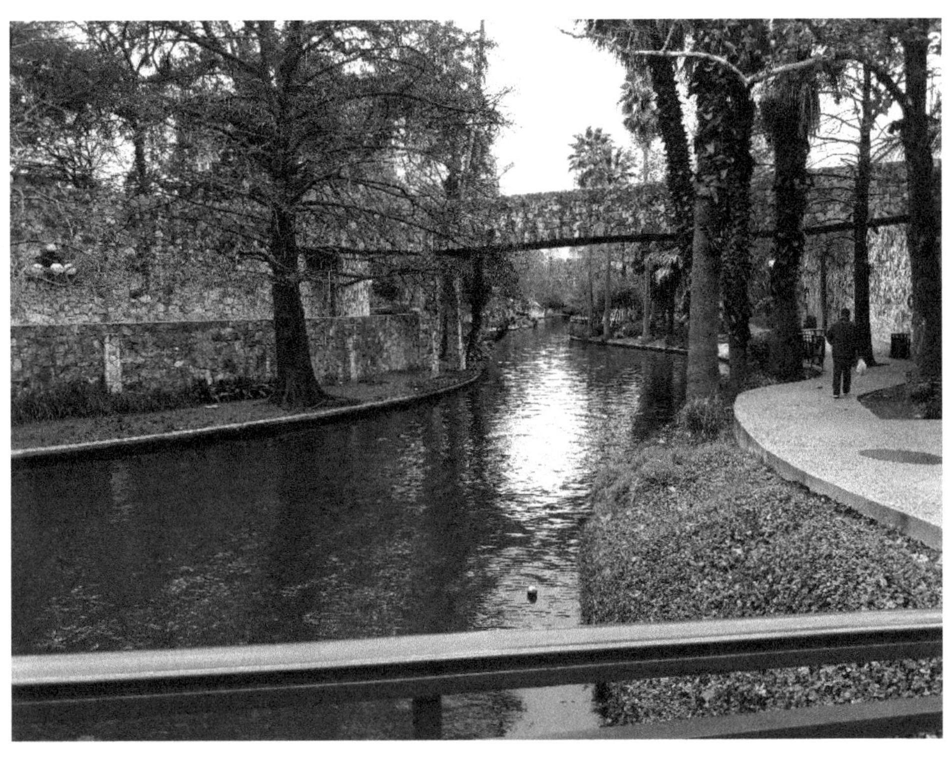

The Riverwalk

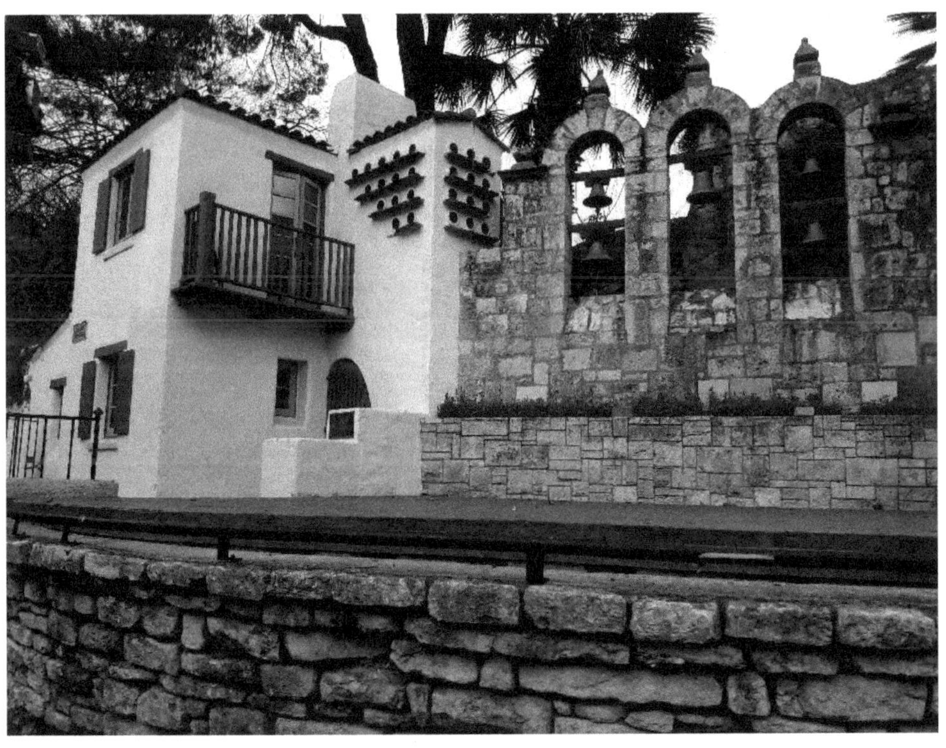

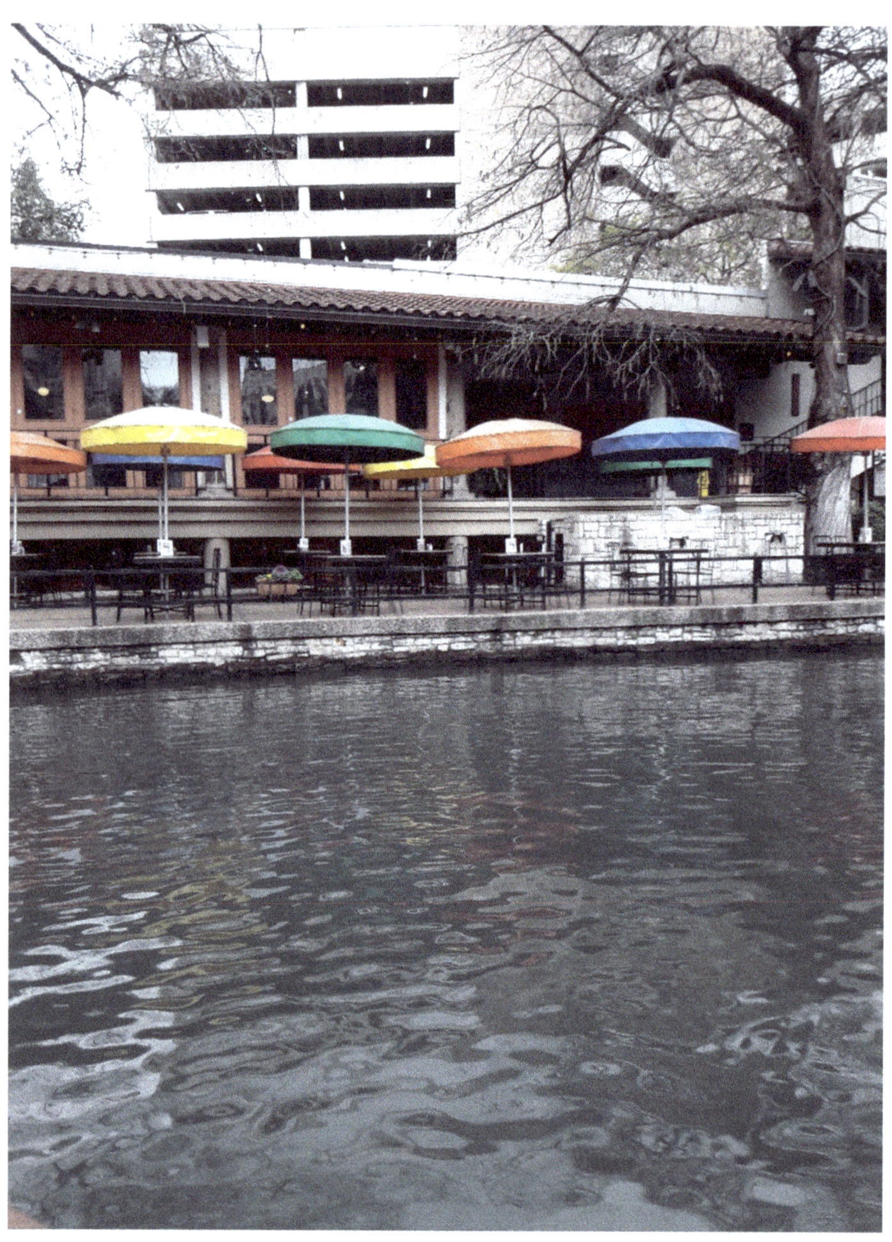

The Riverwalk's Famous Umbrellas 📷

Chapter Nine

A Day Trip from the Road Trip

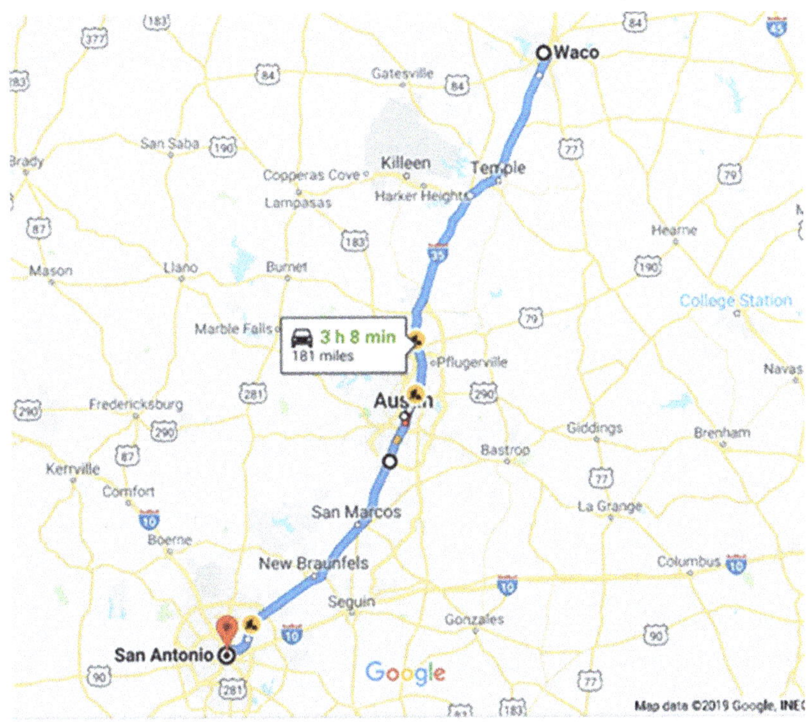

San Antonio to Waco

After our timeout in San Antonio, we hit the road again, knowing the towns we wanted to visit next, but not really having much of a plan. (Yes, I'm learning that even wanderers need a plan to get the most out of the journey.)

Our original plan included San Marcos and then Austin, but because of weather, we'd decided not to go to Waco.

We arrived in San Marcos on Saturday and quickly discovered that our primary reason for going there would not be open again until Monday. That threw a kink into our plans, and upset Tim more than it should have, so I made a hasty decision to take a day trip from our road trip and go to Waco, for the day.

Honestly, it was poor planning on my part. But it seemed like a good distraction at the time, and we knew the coldest weather would avoid Waco for only 24 more hours, so we went.

Going to Waco from San Marcos, we bypassed Austin, and planned to stop there on the way back to San Marcos, so we drove straight to Magnolia Market.

Since this was a side trip, we stayed on the interstate the entire way, and from town to town, interstate drives look pretty much like interstate drives everywhere else—all the regular chains and stops.

This drive offered a fun stop, though—a Bass Pro Shop that seemed out in the middle of nowhere. Fact about me: I could move into a Bass Pro Shop and be right at home. Apparently, so could Tim. He wondered if they might offer him a job as mannequin.

Another reason going to Waco on the spur of the moment wasn't such a good idea—it was Saturday, and Magnolia Market was a madhouse! People everywhere. Lined up around the block to get into the bakery—we didn't even try to go there.

Thankfully, the Lord blessed us with a parking spot right at the back entrance— we pulled up as someone was leaving, and didn't even have to circle around once, so that made it much easier on Tim.

We walked through the store, Tim got to hold Chip's hammer (I still don't know what that was about—not sure if it was one for sale or a display—but he held it!) I was busy looking at wall art.

We went back outside to the picnic table area so Tim could rest a bit. As I looked around at the families and all the happiness there, I realized how much God had redeemed the atrocities of the 90s in the town, and had created such a beautiful witness to the whole world through Joanna and Chip Gaines, their family, their work, their business. May God continue to use them in such powerful ways, and may He protect them from the evils of this world.

I didn't research Waco before we went, so we missed the Texas Rangers Hall of Fame and Museum—but it's at the top of the list for our next visit.

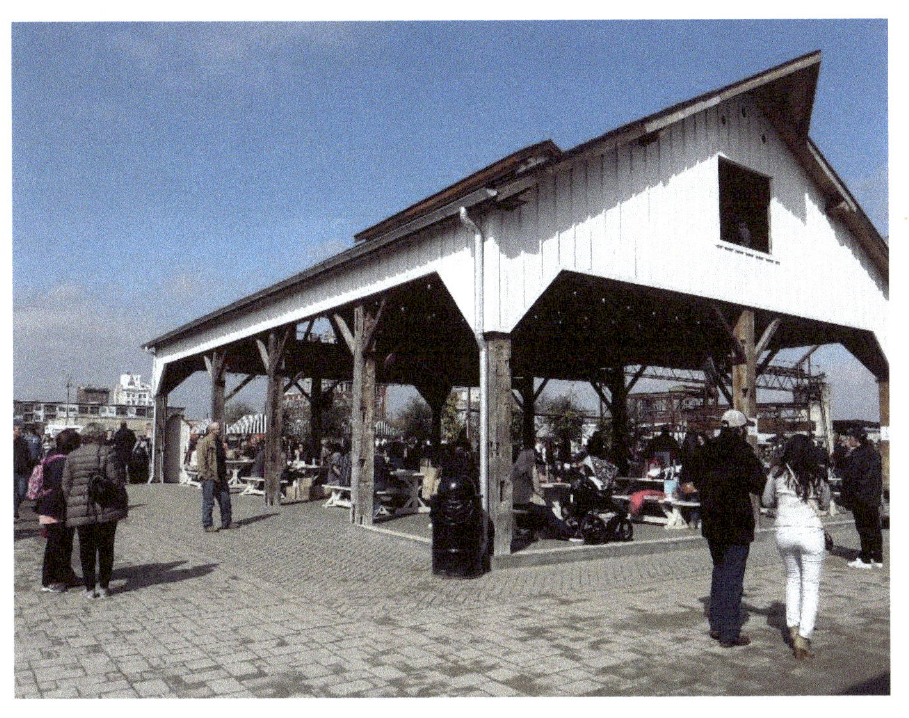

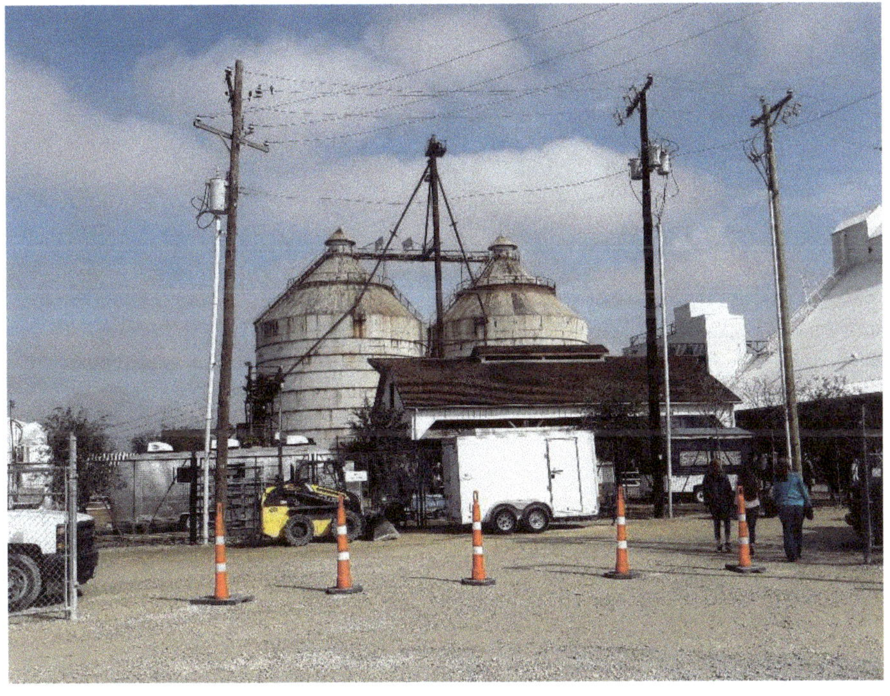

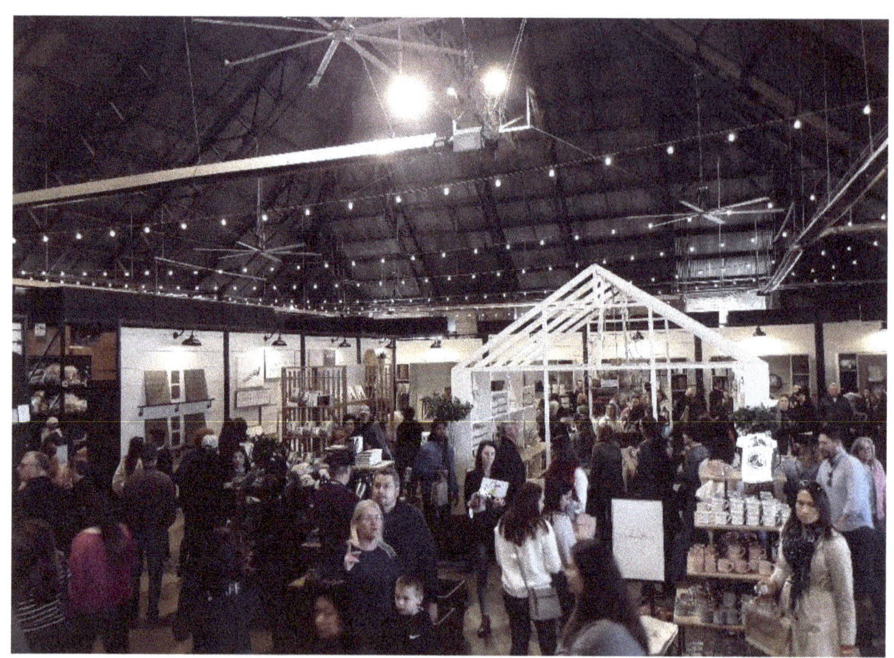

Inside Magnolia Market, above; Tim-Mannequin, below

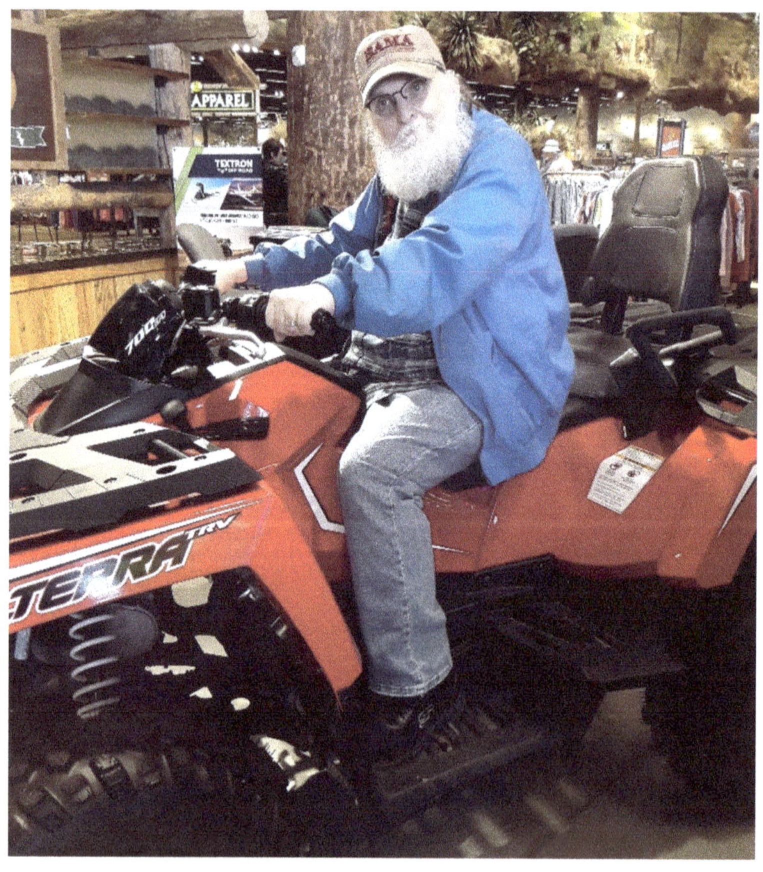

Chapter Ten

Austin

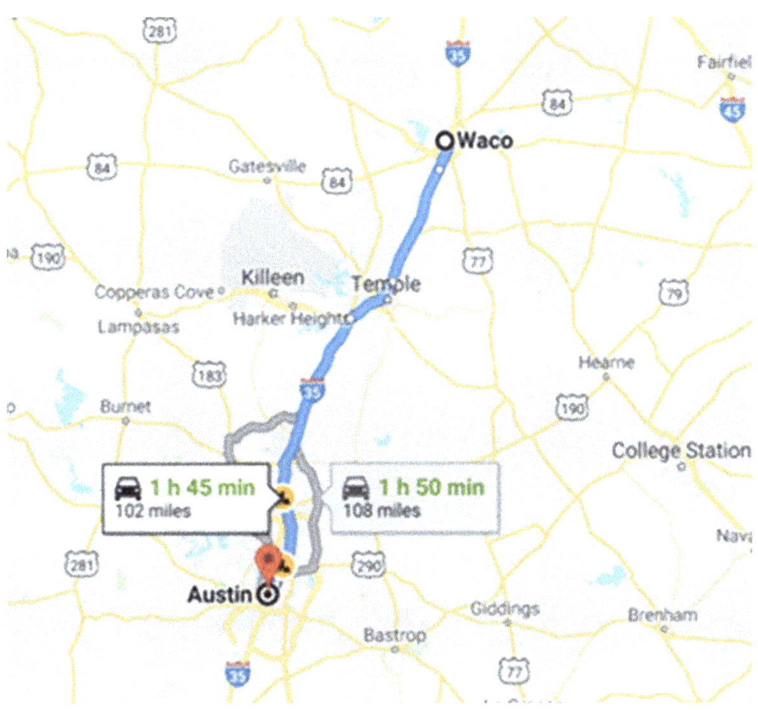

Waco to Austin

We left Waco late afternoon and car camped at the awesome rest area on I-35 between Waco and Austin. The rest areas welcome travelers and provide a safe haven with restrooms 24/7.

We had a special reason for wanting to visit Austin—Tim has family there! One of his first cousins lives there, and one of her sons and daughter-in-love own a really cool business that I've wanted to visit since they opened—Stouthaus Coffee Pub. We stopped in for a coffee (and an addictive mocha!) Sunday morning, but knew we wouldn't see the family until the next day, so we played tourist and visited the Texas State Capitol. (The best time to visit any big city downtown area is on Sunday— mostly deserted, except for a few tourists, so there's minimal traffic.)

The state capitol building was beautiful. Downtown parking is free on Sundays, and the sun was shining bright and warm during our visit.

Then we drove to Mount Bonnell, the highest point in Austin. We asked folks leaving the hiking area how difficult the trail was to manage, because Tim wasn't sure he could do it, but they assured us it was relatively easy, and they were right. A gravel path led to the right down to a picnic table, and to the left, with a gradual climb upward, overlooking the Colorado River.

We car camped at Walmart. The next morning, I had a conference call with a client, and then we went back to Stouthaus, where we got to see Tim's cousin Sandy.

We had a great visit and loved seeing her. We missed seeing Cecelia, but she was busy helping her daughter's family as they welcomed a new little one to the family!

While we were in town, we had to try Austin BBQ, and to fit our budget, we landed at Slab BBQ (we later learned they're friends of Stouthaus!)

Their specialty sandwich is called The Donk, a full pound of smokey goodness, so we decided to split it. When we ordered, we told them we planned to share, so they asked if we wanted it deconstructed, and we did! They brought it to us like this:

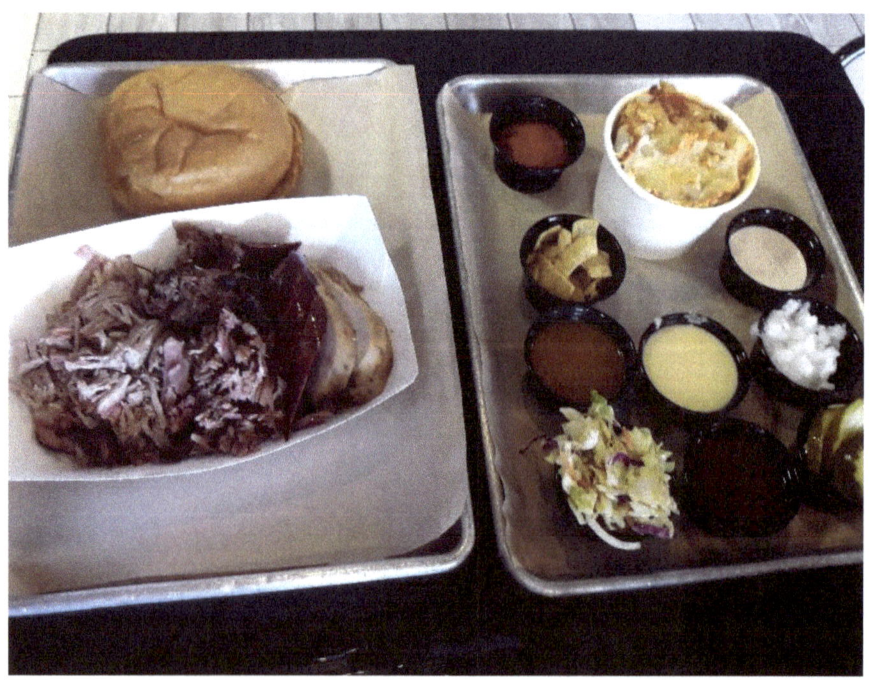

The Donk, deconstructed

Such fun. The pound of meat included chopped pork (our least favorite), rib meat that had been pulled from the bone and shredded (Tim's favorite), chopped beef (my favorite), a few slices of smoked sausage, and three thick slices of chicken breast. The sandwich came with one side—we chose the twice baked potato casserole—and a bunch of condiments, which included mustard slaw (had never had this before— yum!), pickles, onions, queso, Fritos, and several different sauces. I loved playing with the food and mixing and matching different flavors. Tim ate the bun, but I never missed it.

We drove around the town quite a bit and discovered why people come to visit and never leave. It's a town I could move to quite easily.

Another town I'll look forward to visiting again in the future.

From the FROG Files:

This morning, I'm the one with one swollen foot. But we're back at the library, this time in a quiet room without an intercom like yesterday, and I have my foot propped up. So we're good. All the swelling in Tim's legs seem to be gone, but he did develop a blister that popped on the top of one toe yesterday, because he tried to put orthotics into a pair of shoes they weren't made for. Once he took those out, the pain went away and the rubbing stopped.

New shoes would help us both. LOL!

I think we're going to stay here one more night - then the worst of the cold will be gone. The areas we're wanting to go next had colder temperatures than here, so that's why we decided to stay.

I spent time this morning planning our route for the next week or so. I found some great things to explore and we're looking forward to going into west Texas. The southeast was so similar to back home, we hardly realized we were in TX. The middle corridor that we've spent the last several days is all "citified" so, again, still seems little Texan. I expect that's about to change as we make our way west.

As odd as this sounds, I'm still grappling with the fact that we're actually traveling and that I can breathe and enjoy the trip. I must remember that part of my actual job right now, is discovering and exploring and recording, so that I can turn these things into books and art. (It seems so luxurious to think that way!) I spend so much time planning, and trying to just keep us functional, that sometimes, I forget to soak it all in. I realized the importance of that after our hurried trip to Waco, where we missed something I didn't know about until after we'd left.

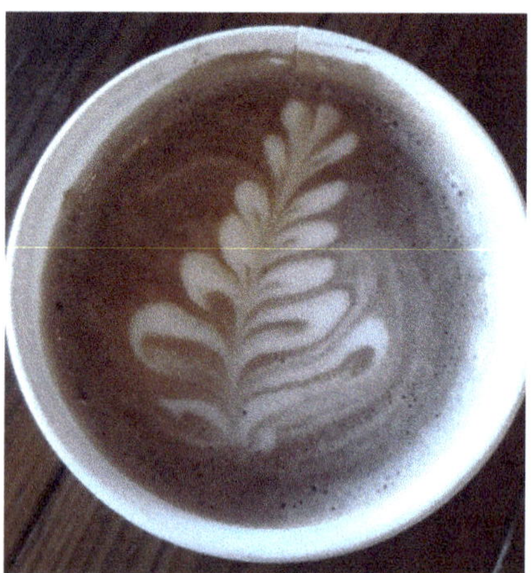

Stouthaus Mocha! Craving one now!

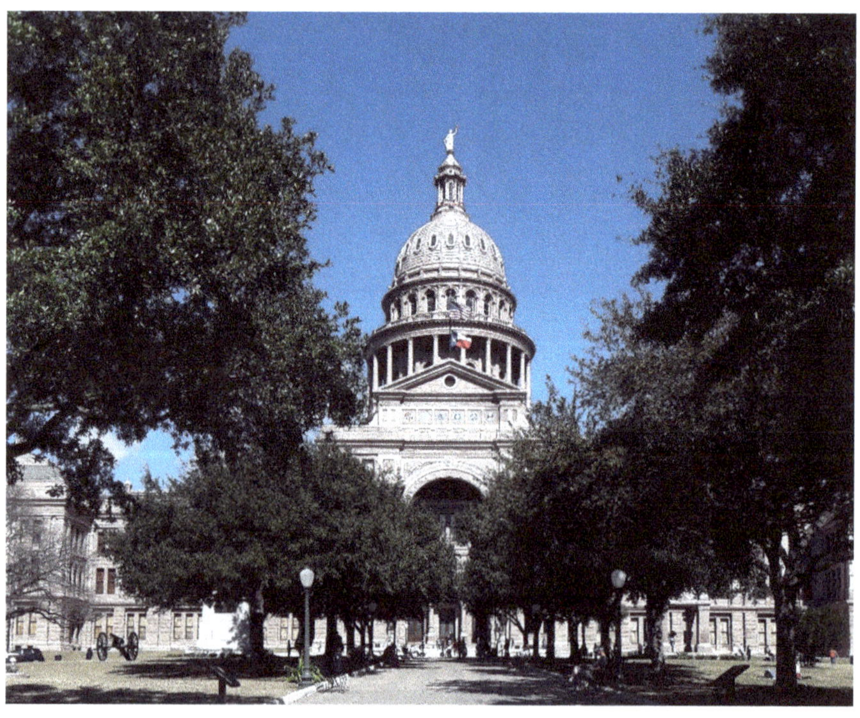

Texas State Capitol, Austin 

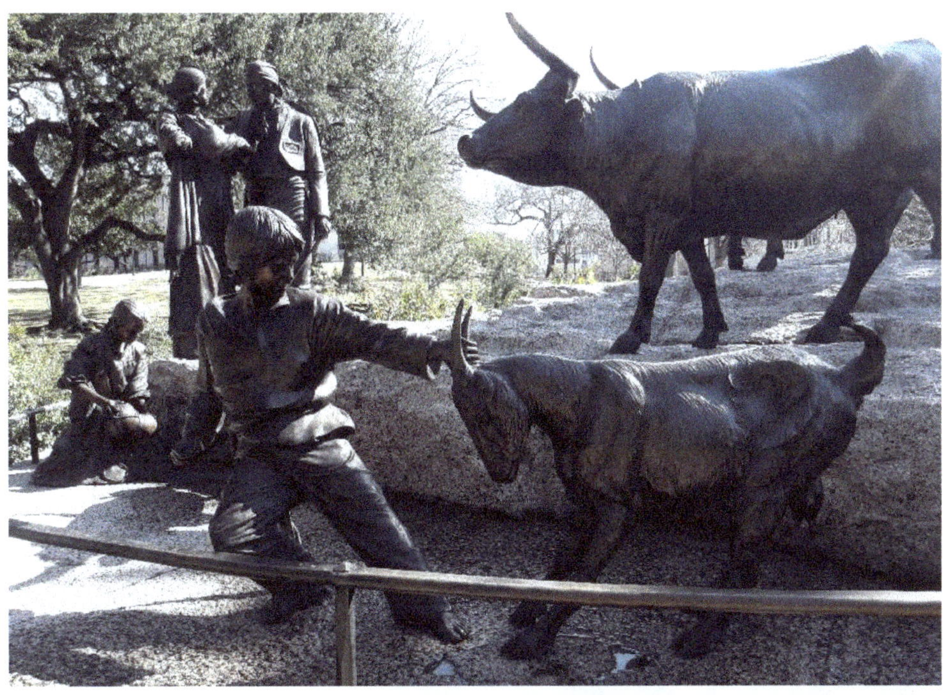

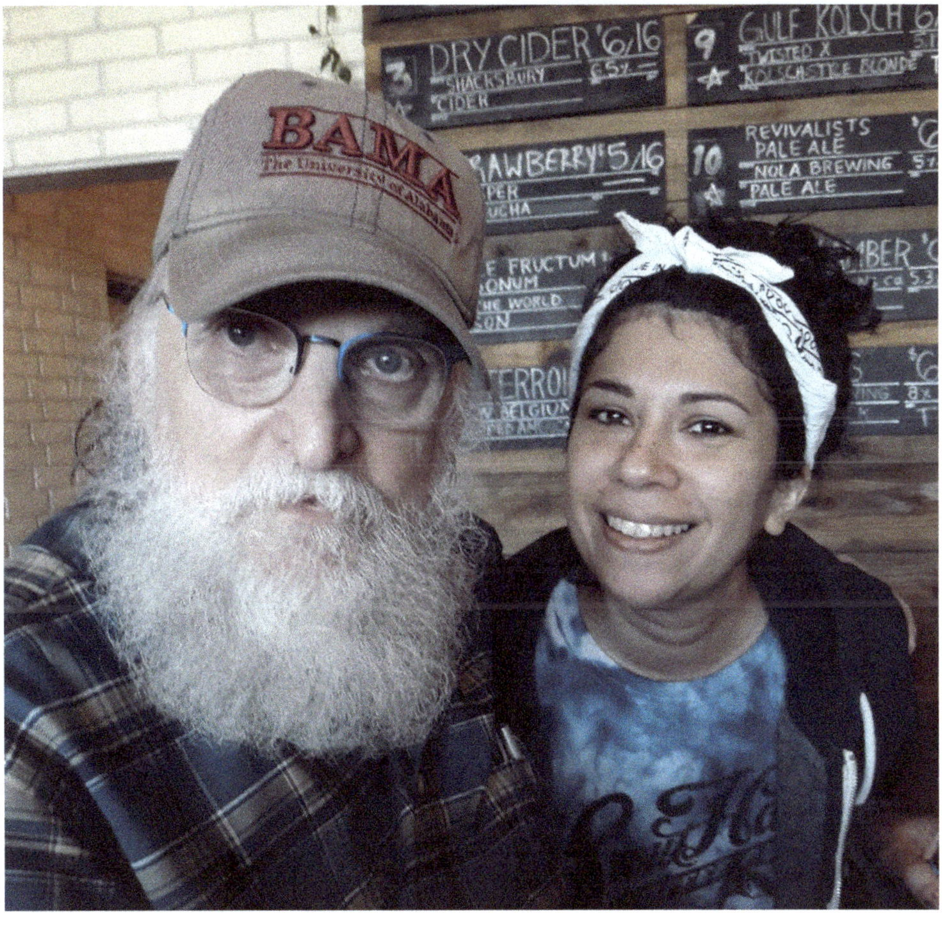

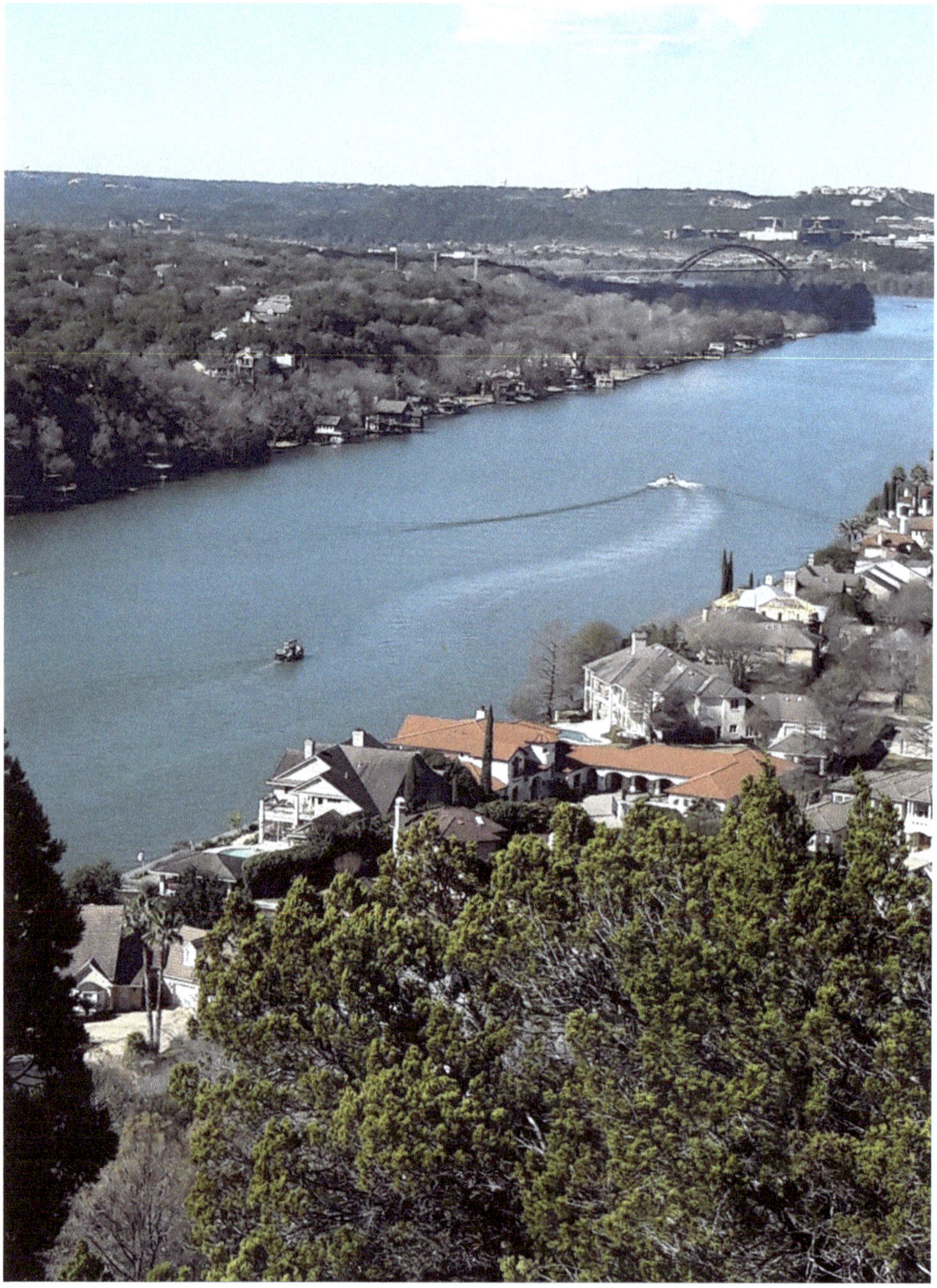

Atop Mount Bonnell, overlooking the Colorado River

Chapter Eleven

San Marcos and Lonesome Dove

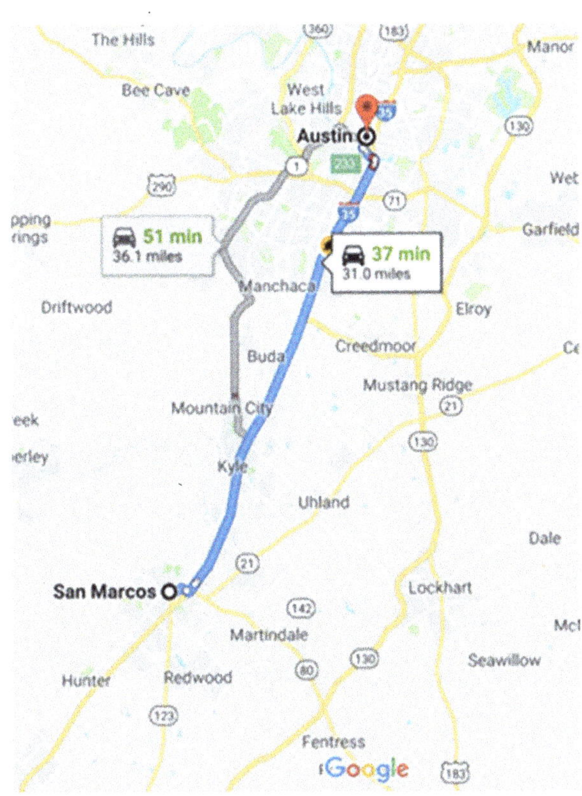

Austin, Texas to San Marcos

We continued south from Austin and returned to San Marcos. I haven't figured out why we were so drawn to this town – I'd never heard of it before this trip. While we were there, *Forbes Magazine* named San Marcos the best city in Texas for retirement, so I guess others are drawn here, too.

One thing we noticed—everywhere we wanted to go in town was only a mile or two away, regardless of where we were at the time. We found that pretty funny because it's not exactly a small town with a population of 45,000.

One of Tim's favorite westerns is *Lonesome Dove*. He's watched the mini-series several times (including with me, for my first time viewing it). I bought the book for him on Kindle, and he's let Kindle read the book to him twice already. (Tim has a learning disability and didn't learn to read until he was 22—and he's still a reluctant reader. Kindle reading to him has opened up the world of books to him!)

When we began talks of this trip, he said he wanted to follow the Lonesome Dove trail, so I sought information to see if that was possible, and that's when I learned about San Marcos.

The screenwriter of the *Lonesome Dove* series, Bill Witliff, had assembled, acquired, and donated a collection of *Lonesome Dove* artifacts and memorabilia to Texas State University in San Marcos, so that went to the top of our "must see" list in Texas.

The exhibit is only available Monday–Friday, and only by request. They unlocked a special room and let us browse at our leisure. The first draft of the first script was on display, as was the cover page for the final script of the series—signed by the cast and crew. Witliff supplied illustrations of set designs, maps, and costumes, and actual costumes and props were on display, too.

The characters became more alive to us once we got to Texas, and Tim made regular comments about Augustus McCrae or Woodrow F. Call—about trails they took or towns they visited. He was determined to see where Gus was buried, even after I tried to explain that Gus was fictional so there would be no burial place. Thankfully, Gus's "remains" were on display in the museum, so we could finally stop grave hunting.

The Witliff Collections include other areas of interest, too, focusing primarily on southwestern writers. Well worth the visit. Employees told us that Witliff had acquired more artifacts, so the *Lonesome Dove* collection would more than double later in the year.

San Marcos was cute, quirky, and fun. The town held a mermaid contest, so there are brightly colored mermaid sculptures on display all over town.

One day, as we drove down a neighborhood street, we discovered other fun art. The first time we drove past, this conversation took place:

"Hey, what was that?"

"Looks like junk to me."

"Tim, that was art."

"Hey, don't get mad at me. I don't know what art is."

I kept driving, but we ended up on that street again, so I turned the corner and jumped out to snap photos. I laughed when I saw that we were both right—junk and art!

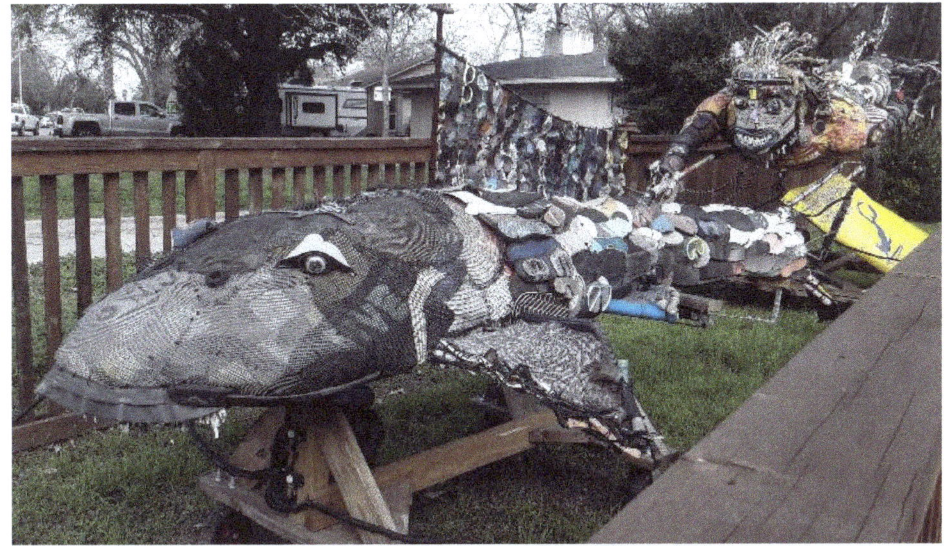

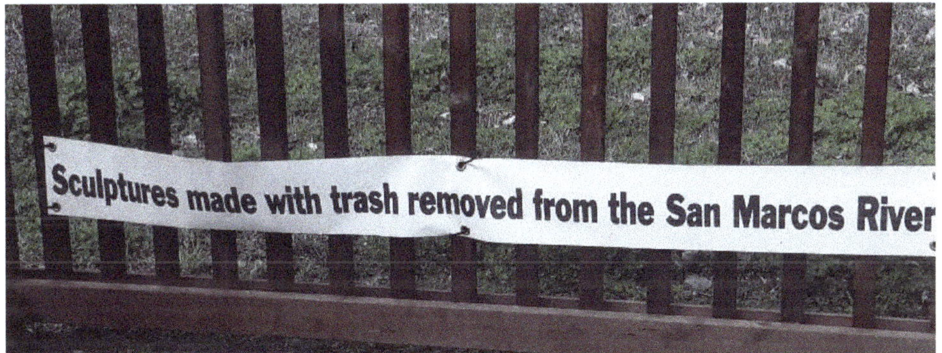

San Marcos has a convenient library, but it was rather noisy until we discovered the quiet room.

They also have an active activity center that welcomes day use visitors, and we took advantage of that for showers.

Spending time at the library, I realized that we needed to slow down. We'd been speeding along on this journey, trying to take in as much as possible as fast as possible, and we missed things we would have enjoyed. Taking the time to research each area before we get there has already proven useful and sent us to our next two fun surprises. And yes, I was able to keep them as a surprise for Tim until we got there!

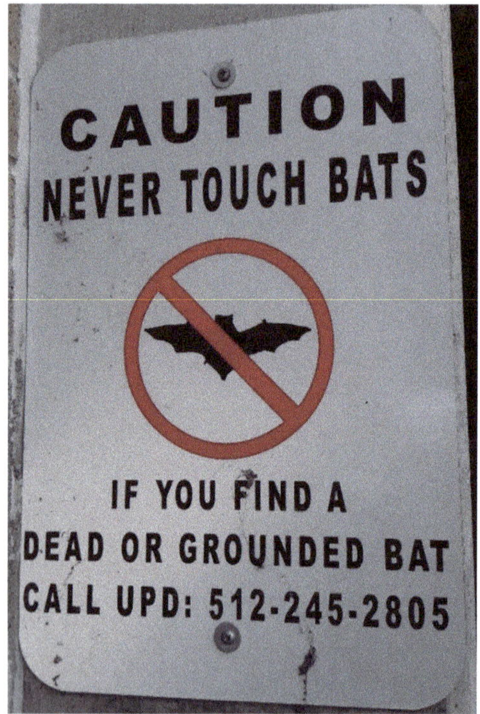

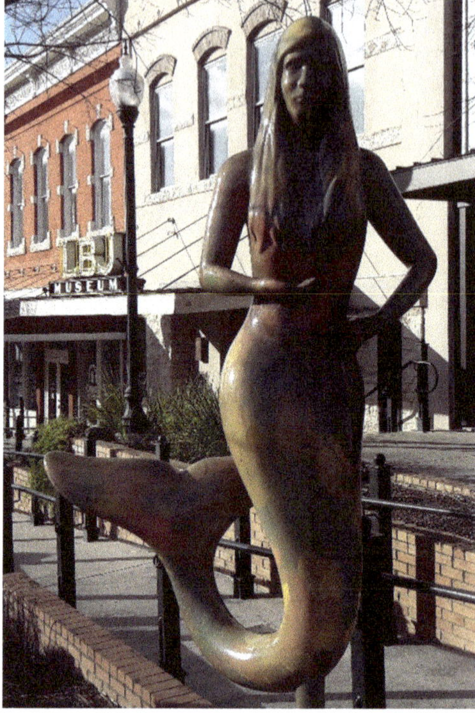

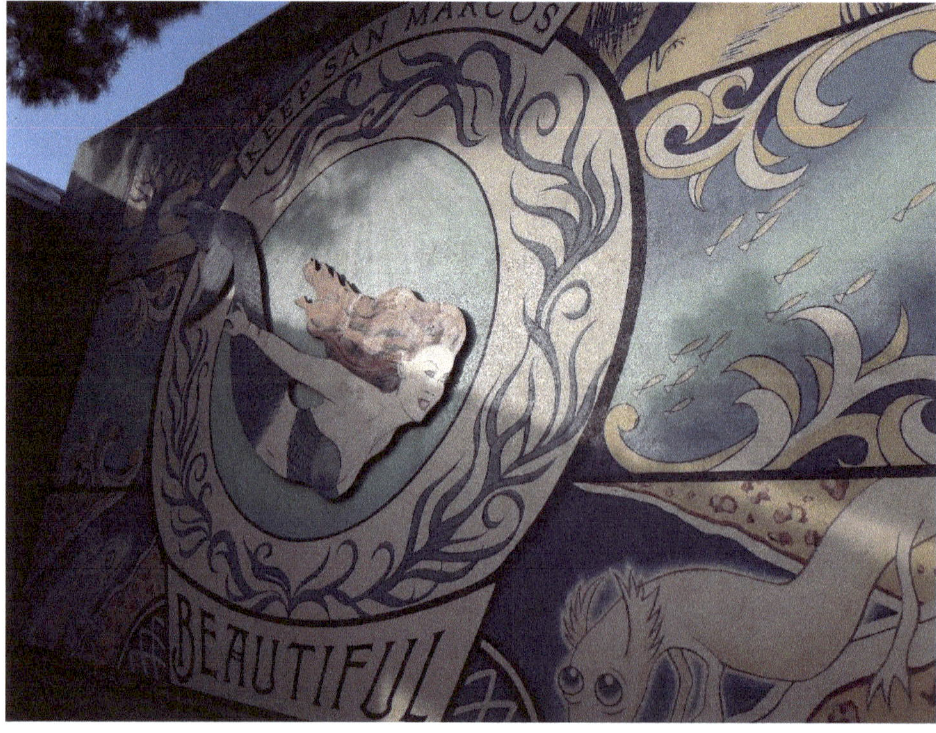

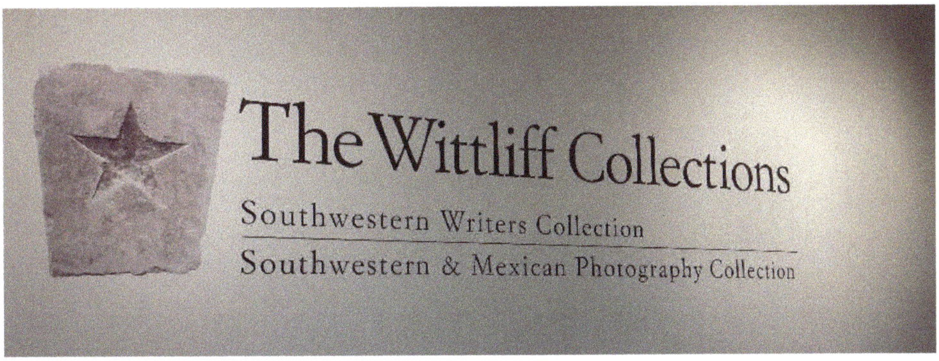

Artifacts of *The Lonesome Dove* series in The Witliff Collection

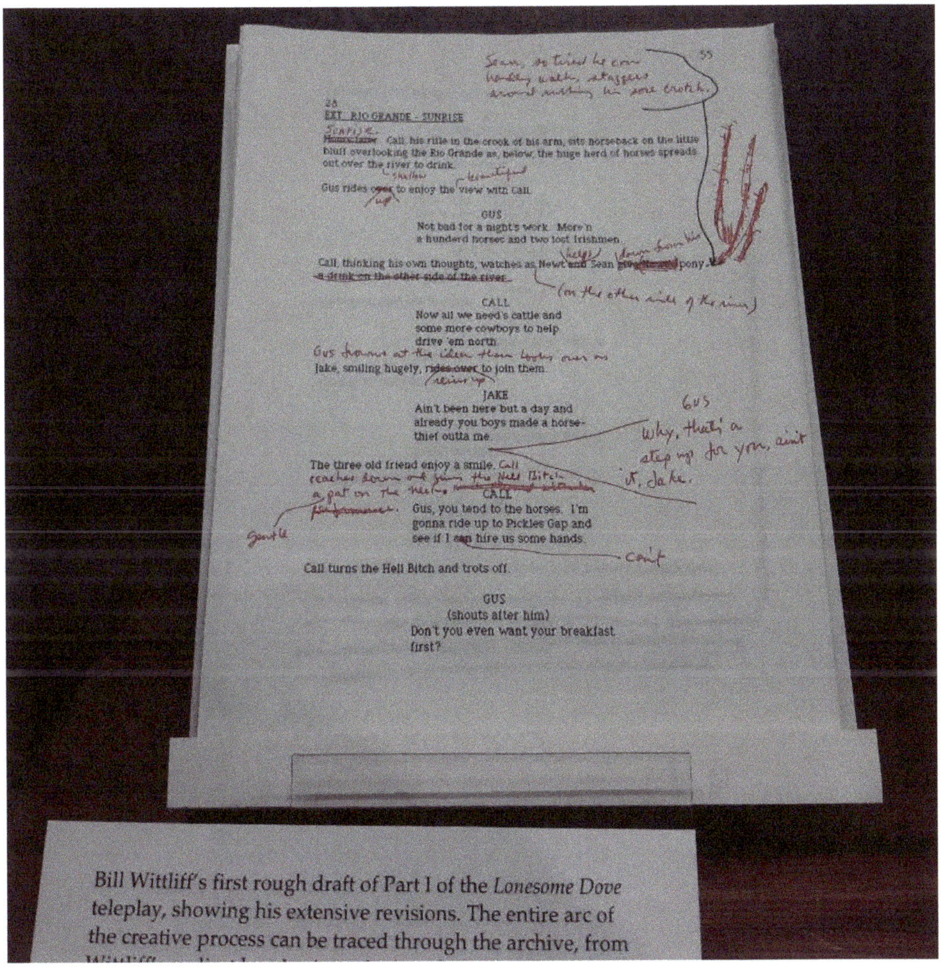

Bill Wittliff's first rough draft of Part I of the *Lonesome Dove* teleplay, showing his extensive revisions. The entire arc of the creative process can be traced through the archive, from

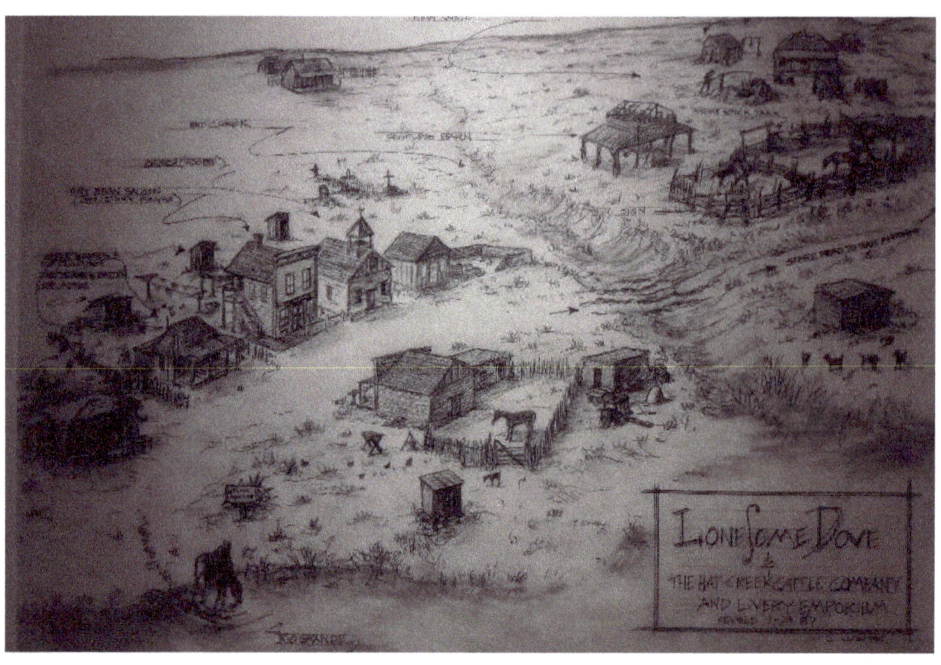

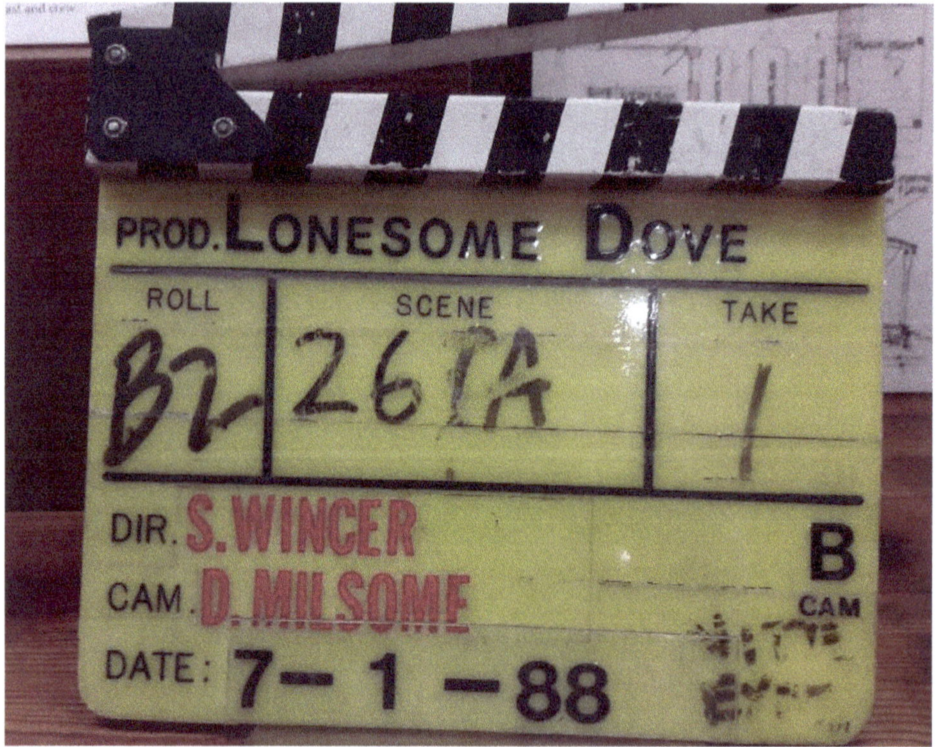

PROD. LONESOME DOVE
ROLL
SCENE
TAKE
B2
261A
1
DIR. S. WINCER
CAM. D. MILSOME
B
CAM
DATE: 7-1-88

While the action in *Lonesome Dove* ranges from the Texas-Mexico border to the mountains of Montana, the film was shot on locations in Texas and northern New Mexico. Because Australian Director Simon Wincer was not familiar with the geography of the American West, Production Designer Cary White created this annotated map to detail the action in *Lonesome Dove*. The map allowed the director to match the terrain in the shooting locations to the places depicted on the map.

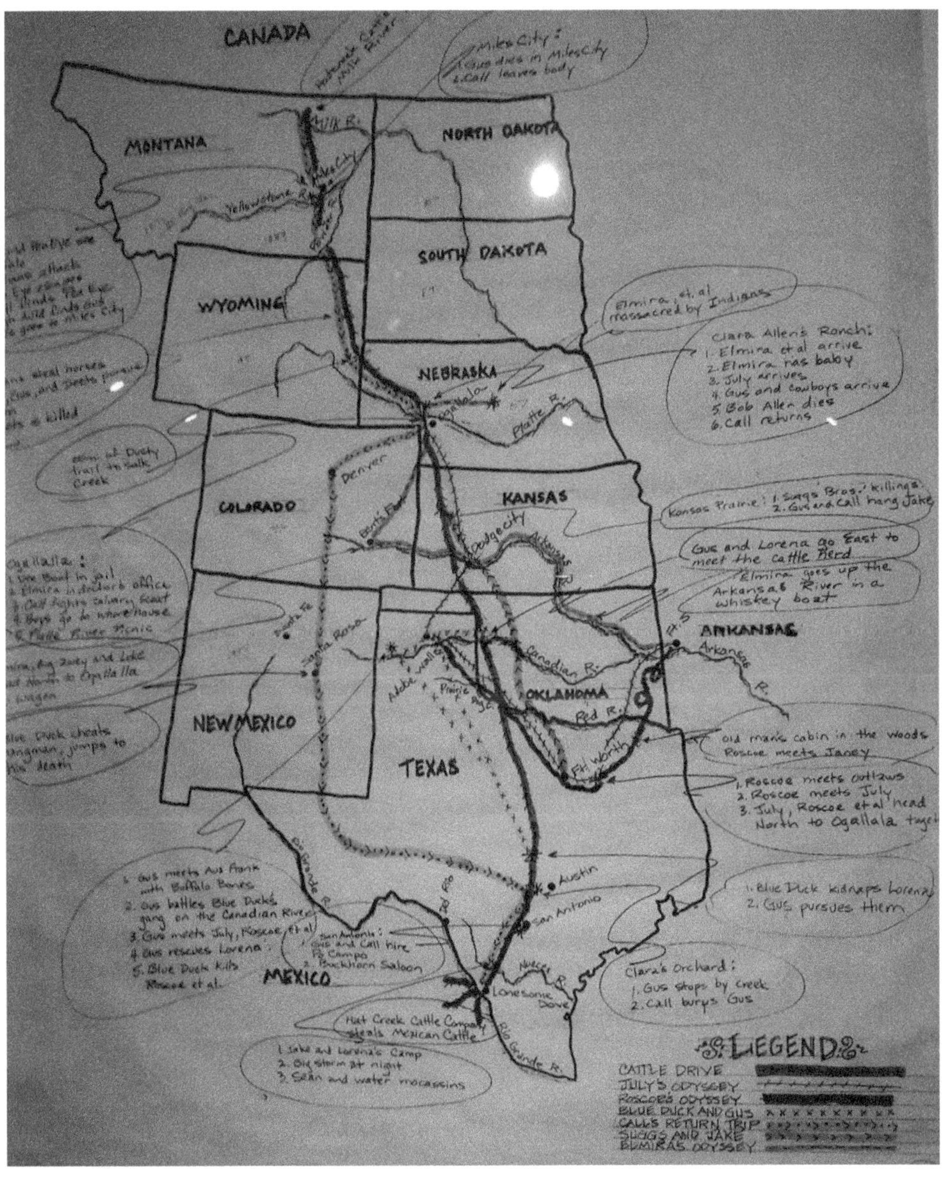

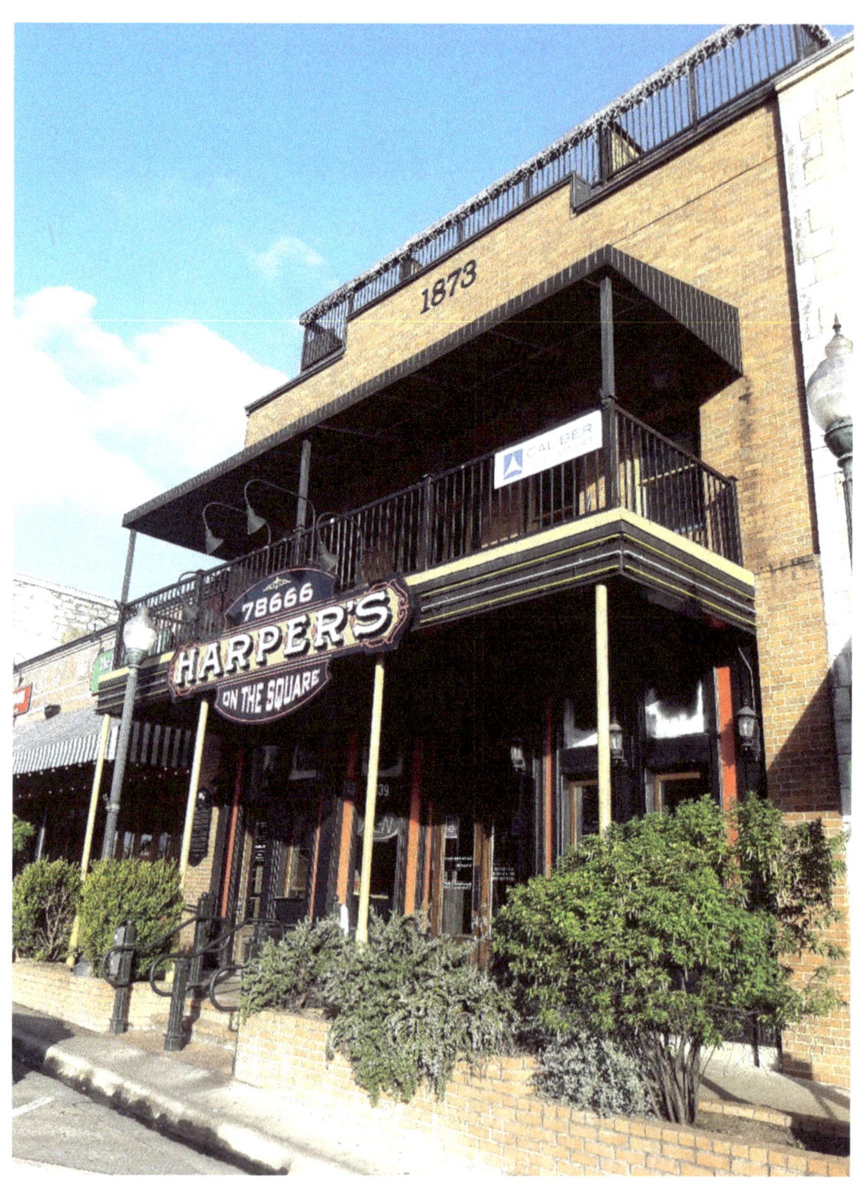

1873
78666
HARPER'S
ON THE SQUARE

Chapter Twelve

A Glimpse of the Old West

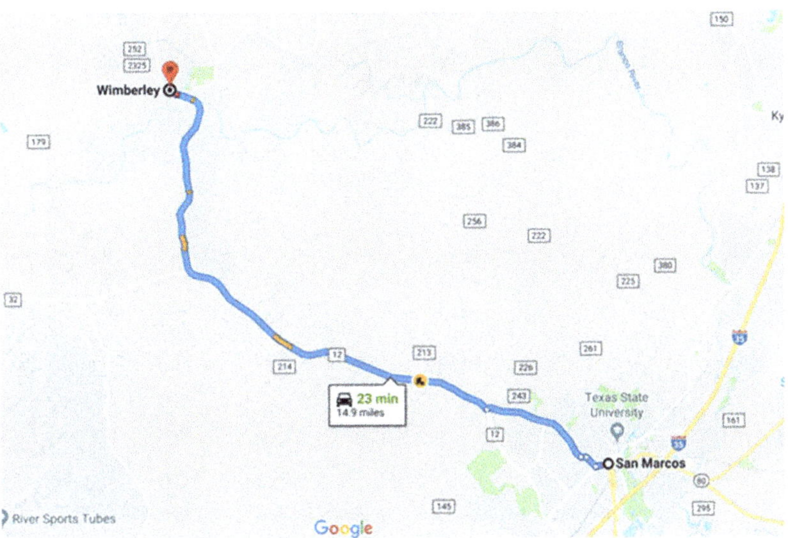

San Marcos to Wimberley

Even though we'd been heading west since January, we ended up going north and south in Texas for some time. From San Marcos, we headed west, excited about what we'd see next.

While hanging out at the San Marcos library, I searched Roadside America, TripAdvisor, and other sites, and discovered a couple of nearby fun spots to surprise Tim with as we got back on the road, heading toward Johnson City, Texas.

In our first stop in Wimberley, we found Pioneer Town. Based on what I'd read, I thought it was a small replica of a pioneer town but was pleasantly surprised to discover it was so much more!

Pioneer Town isn't "just" a replica. It's also a laid-back resort, offering cabins for rent, with 10-bedroom lodges for big groups. They have a resort-style swimming pool, and in warm weather, the Blanco River is available for play, too. The Boarding House in the middle of Pioneer Town also provides hotel-style rooms for rent. I've already told my family we should have a gathering at the 7A Resort—such fun!

Tim was sold when he heard the ice cream parlor is operational during summer months so that made the place even sweeter.

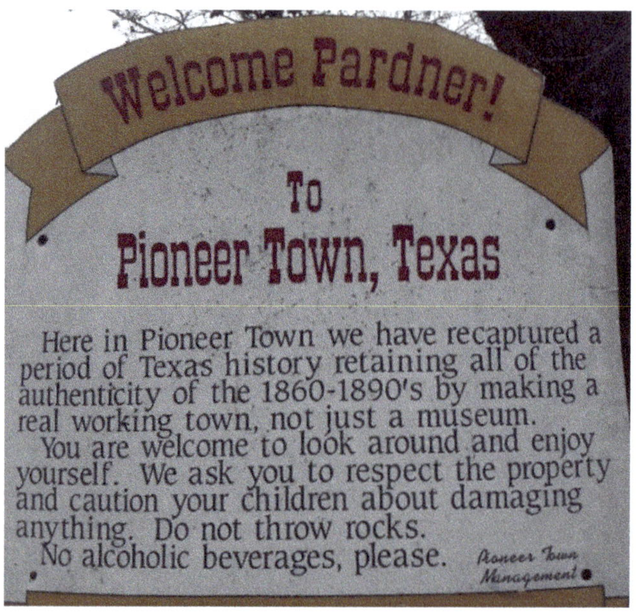

I hear there's a rough one on the loose though, so beware!

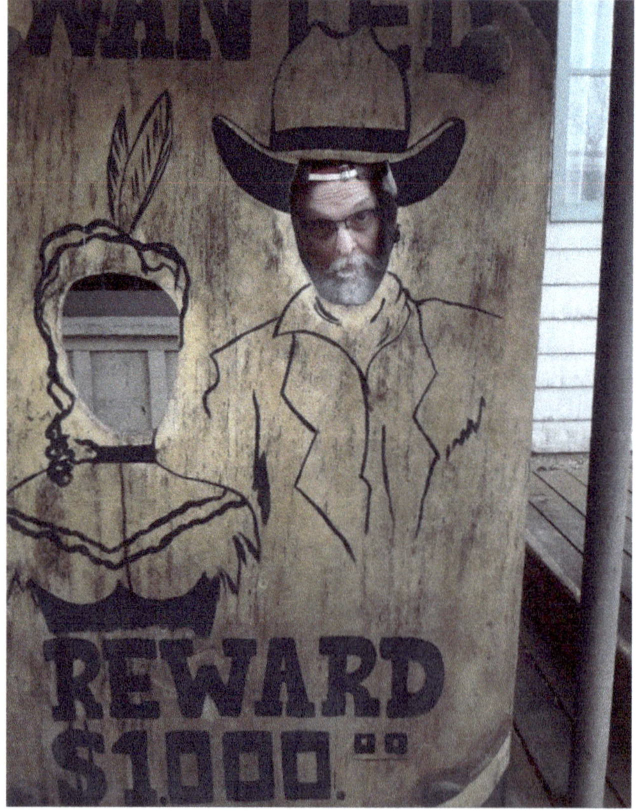

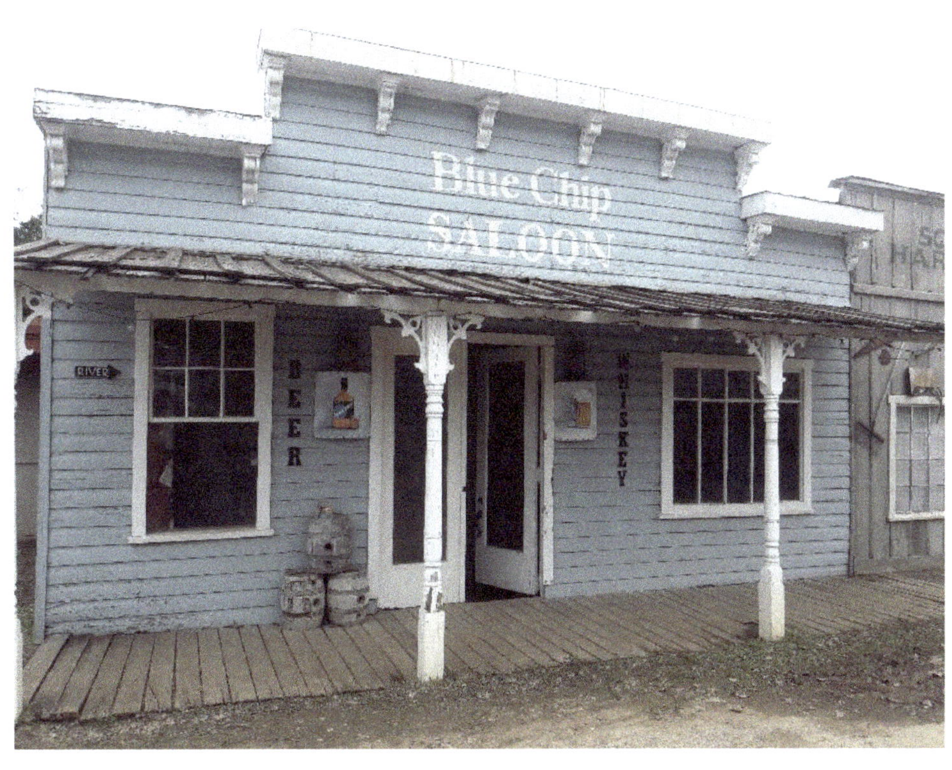
Blue Chip
SALOON
RIVER
BEER
WHISKEY

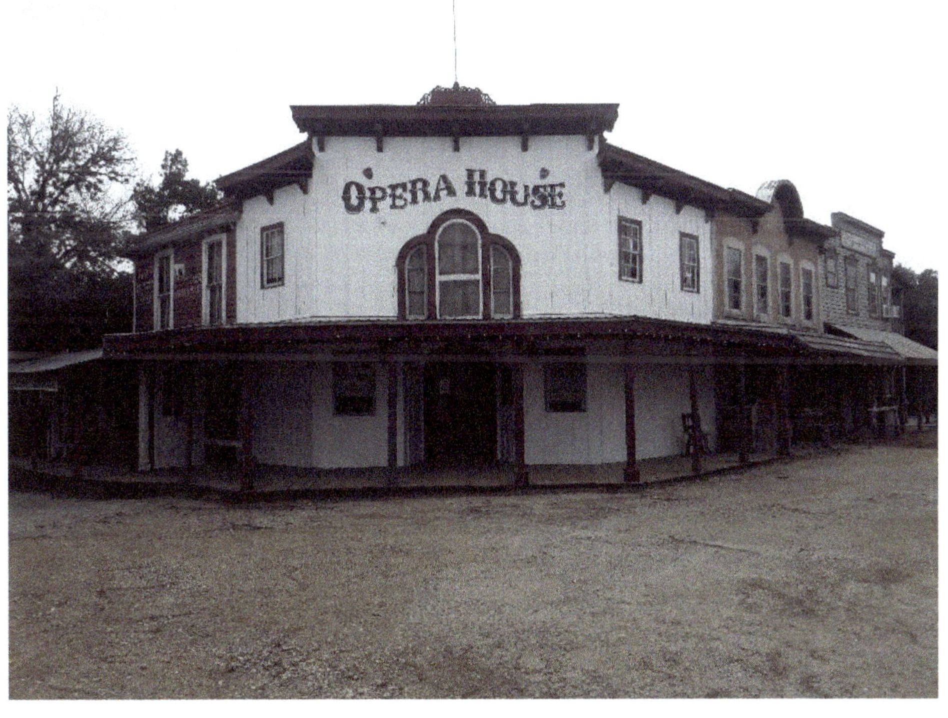
OPERA HOUSE

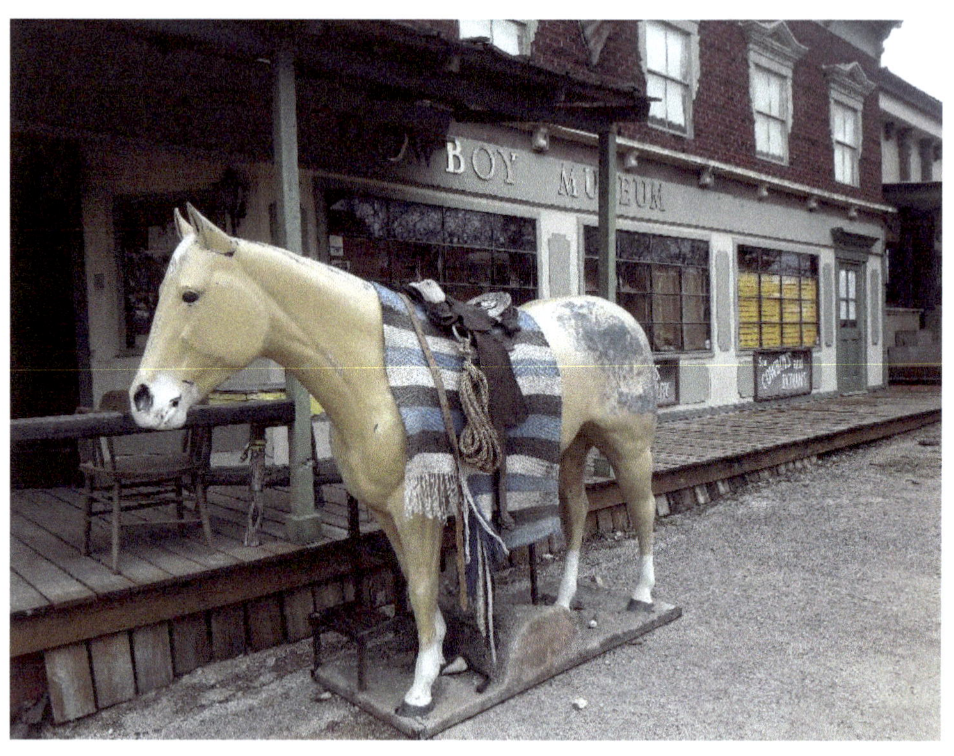

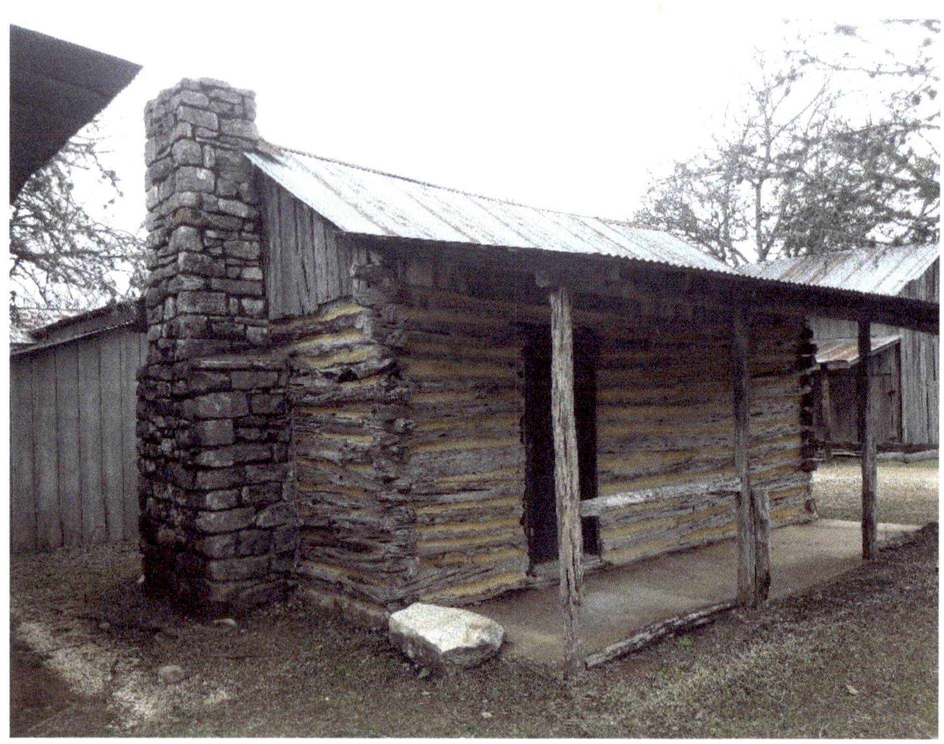

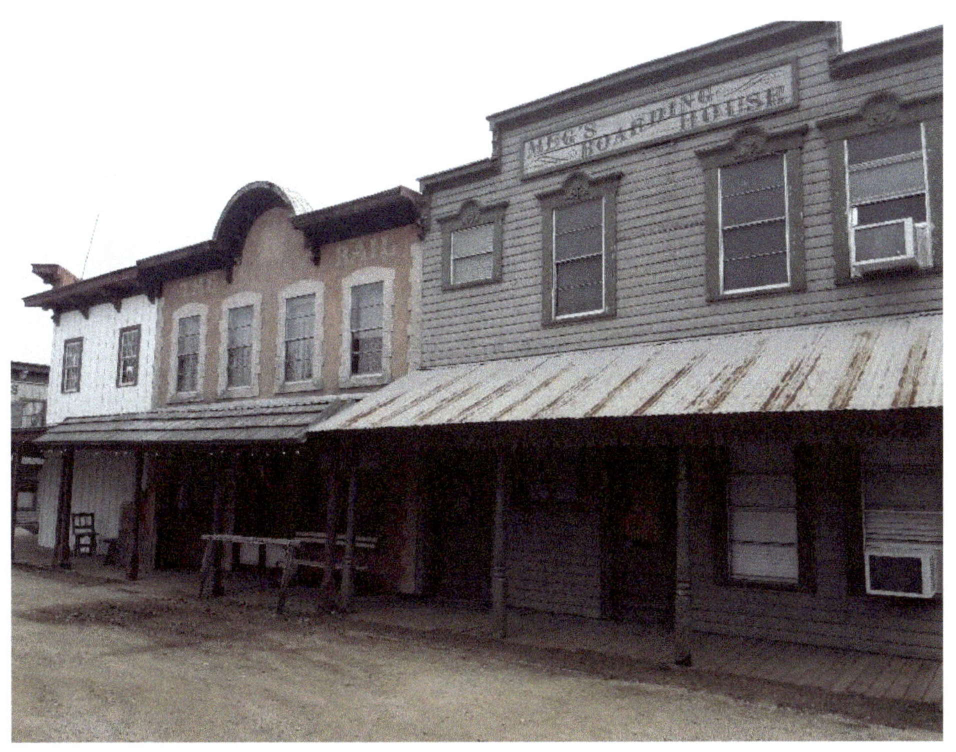

Boarding House modernized, slightly, for guests.

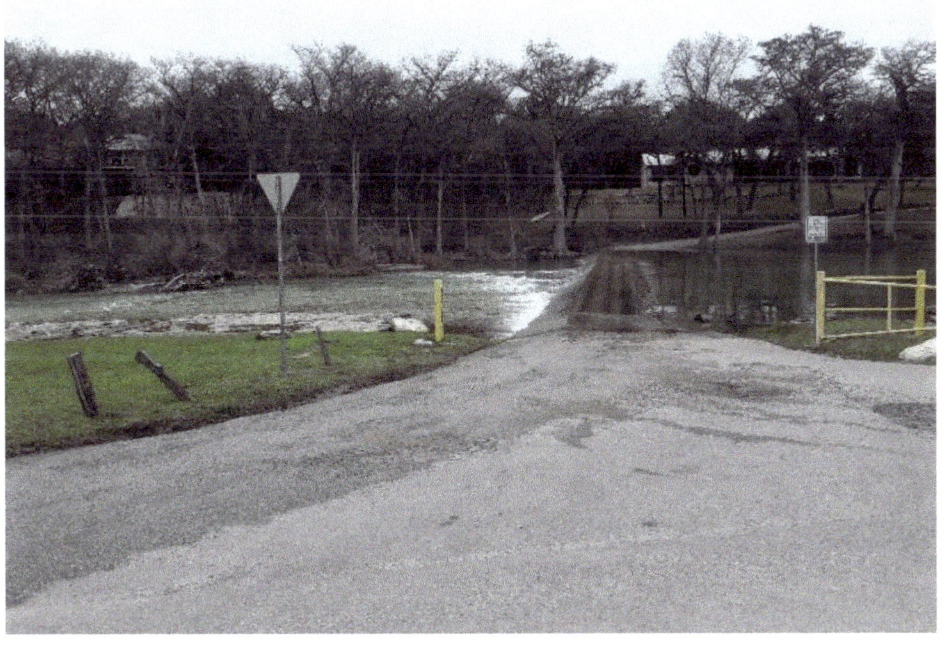

Yes, we drove over the aqueduct!

Sample Artwork:

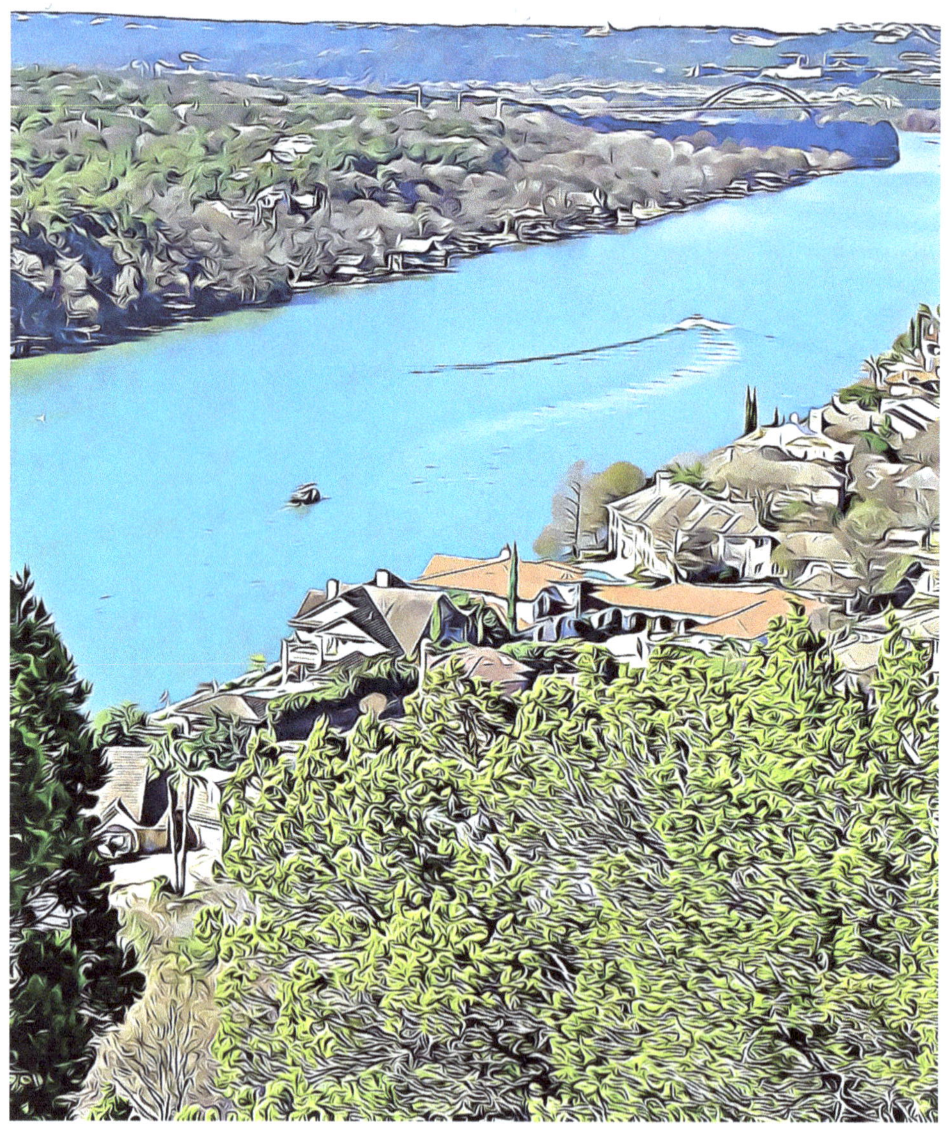

Austin View of Colorado River 📷

Chapter Thirteen

From One Pioneer Town to the Next

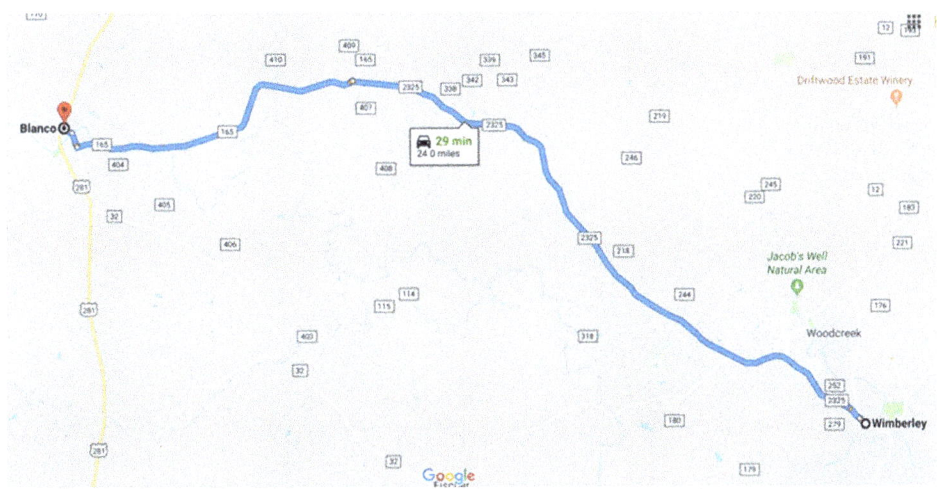

Wimberley to Blanco

From Pioneer Town in Wimberley, Texas, we drove to The Buggy Barn Museum in Blanco. I'd read online that they had wagons used in John Wayne movies, so I knew Tim would love it. But, like so many things on the internet, that wasn't quite true. They did have several wagons and buggies that were used in the new version of True Grit (2010, with Jeff Bridges), but only one of them was marked.

The "barn keeper" was friendly and turned us loose to explore the buildings on our own but kept popping up here and there to give us different facts about the artifacts. After we'd been all over the barn looking at the wagons, buggies, stagecoaches, and more, he told us to keep walking toward the back, where they had their own pioneer town set up.

From Pioneer Town and The Buggy Barn Museum of the 1800s, we leaped forward to the 1960s with our next stop.

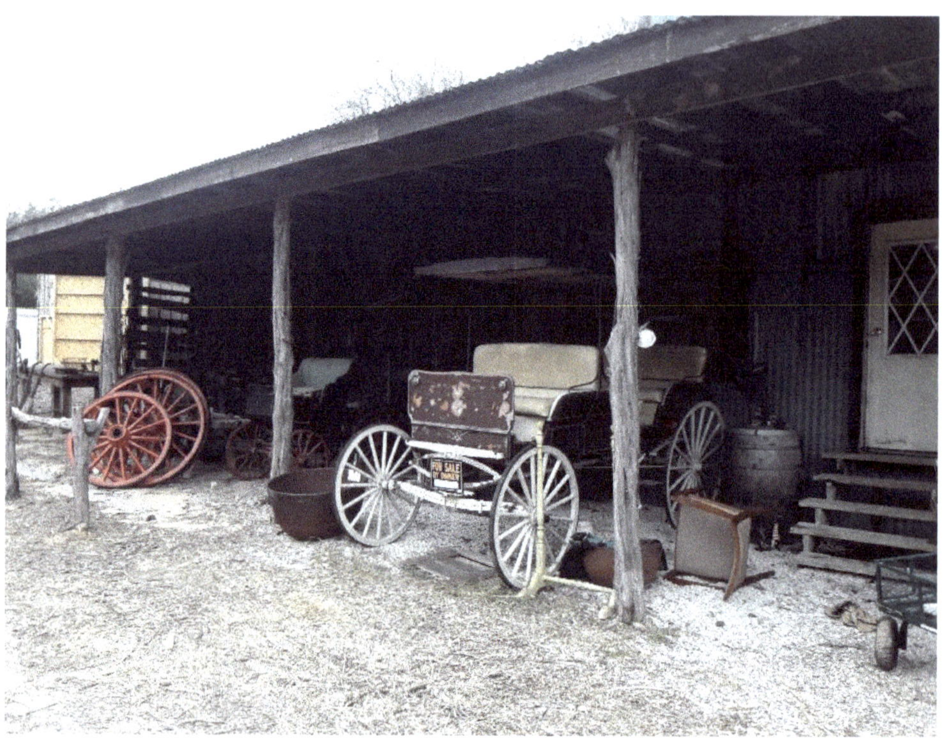

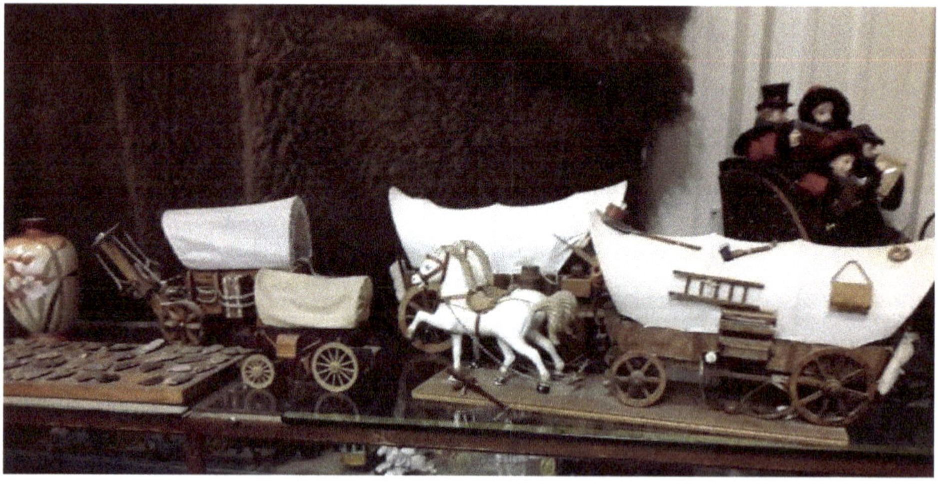

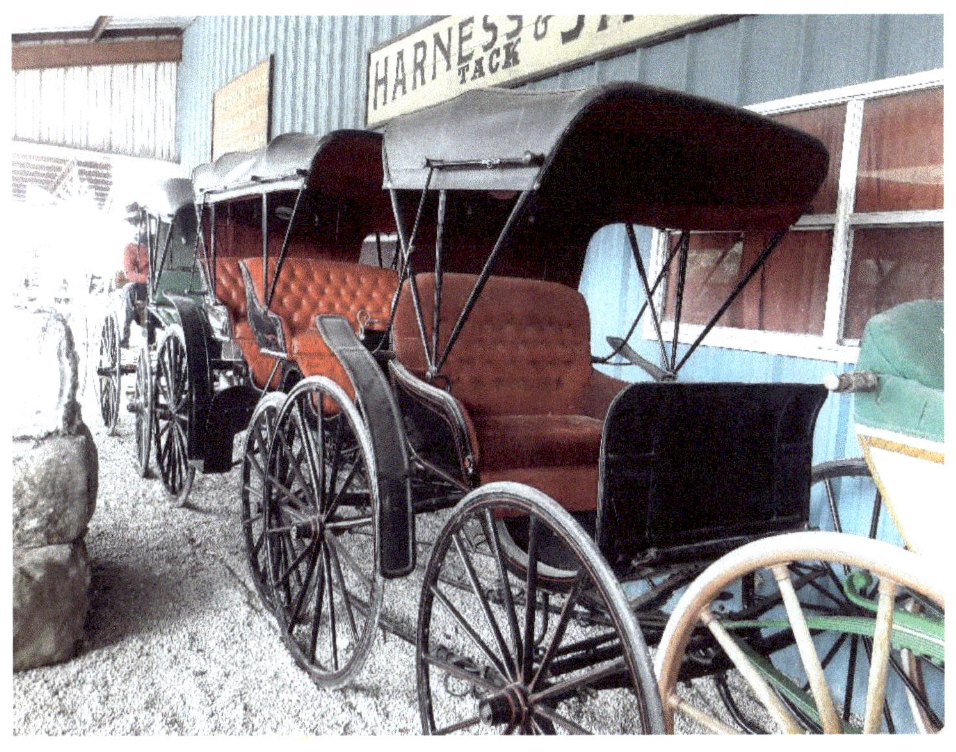
HARNESS &
TACK

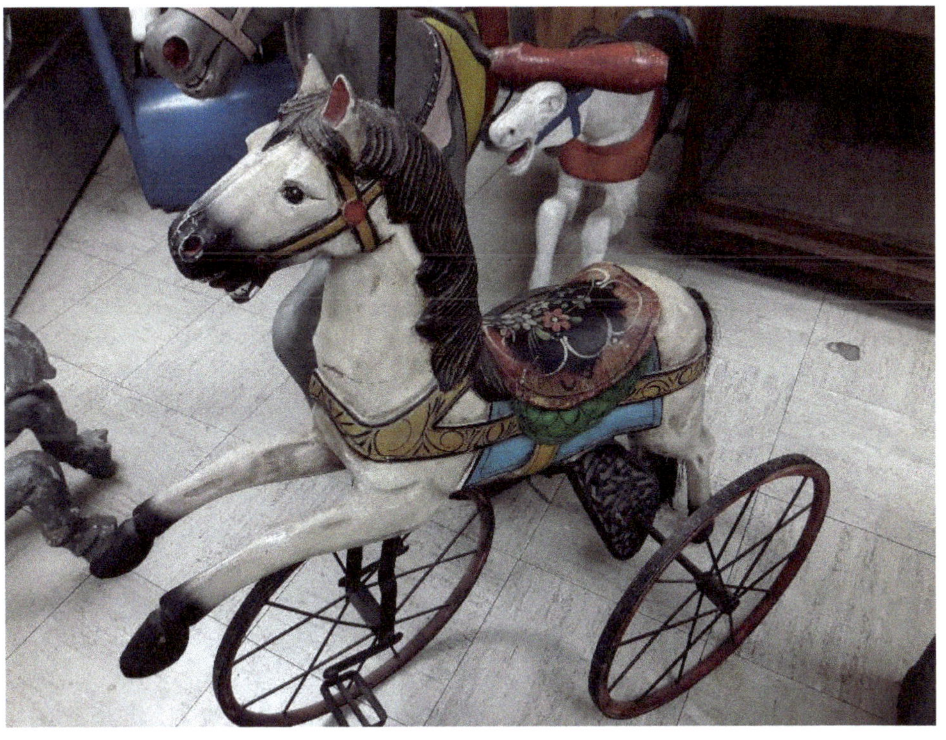

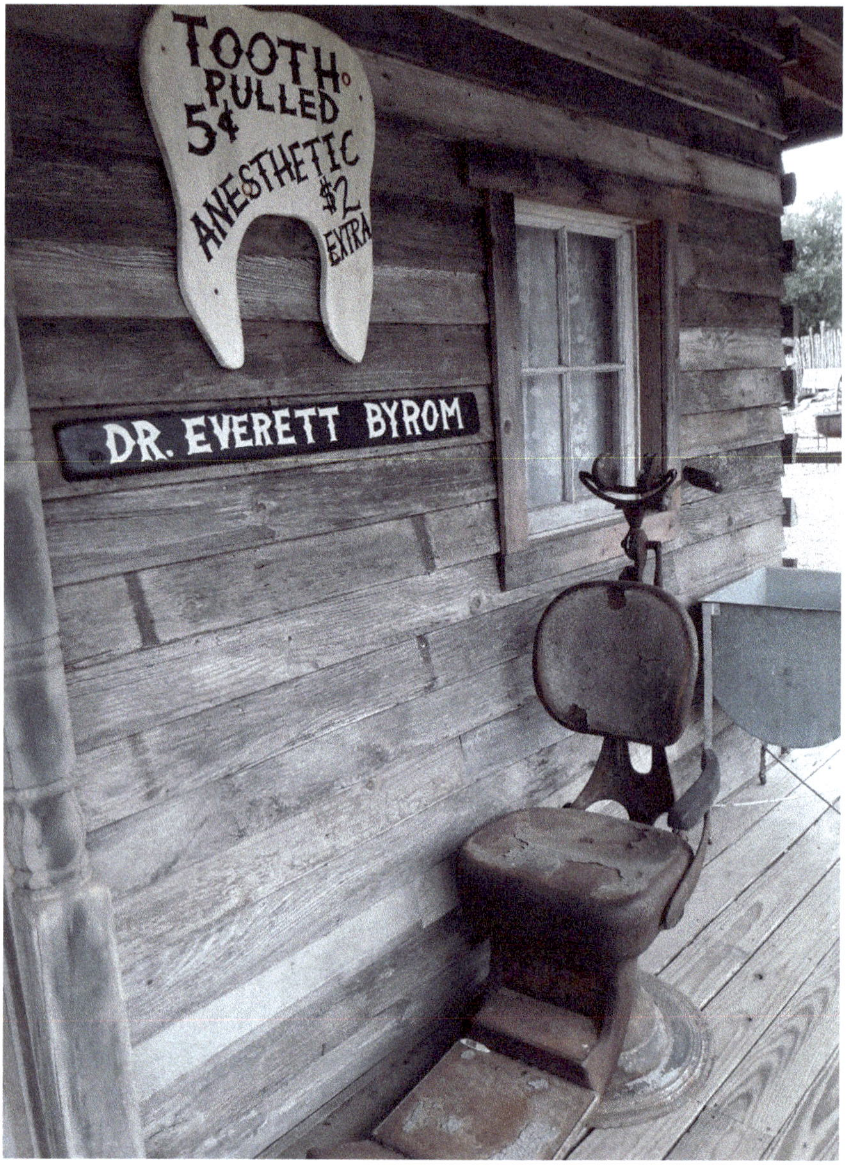

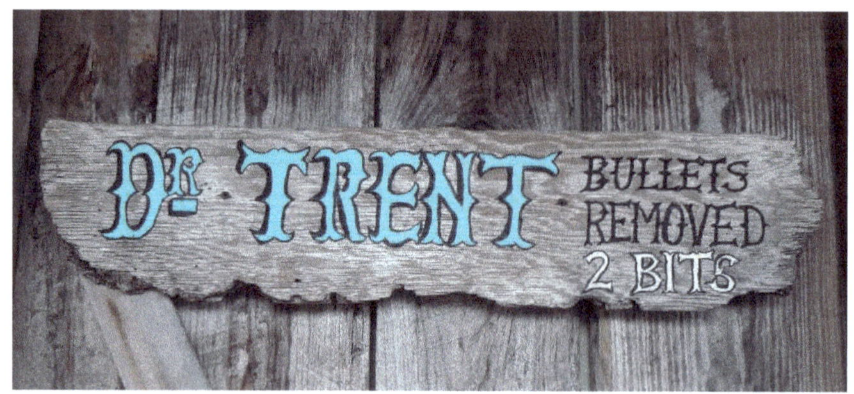
DR. TRENT BULLETS REMOVED 2 BITS

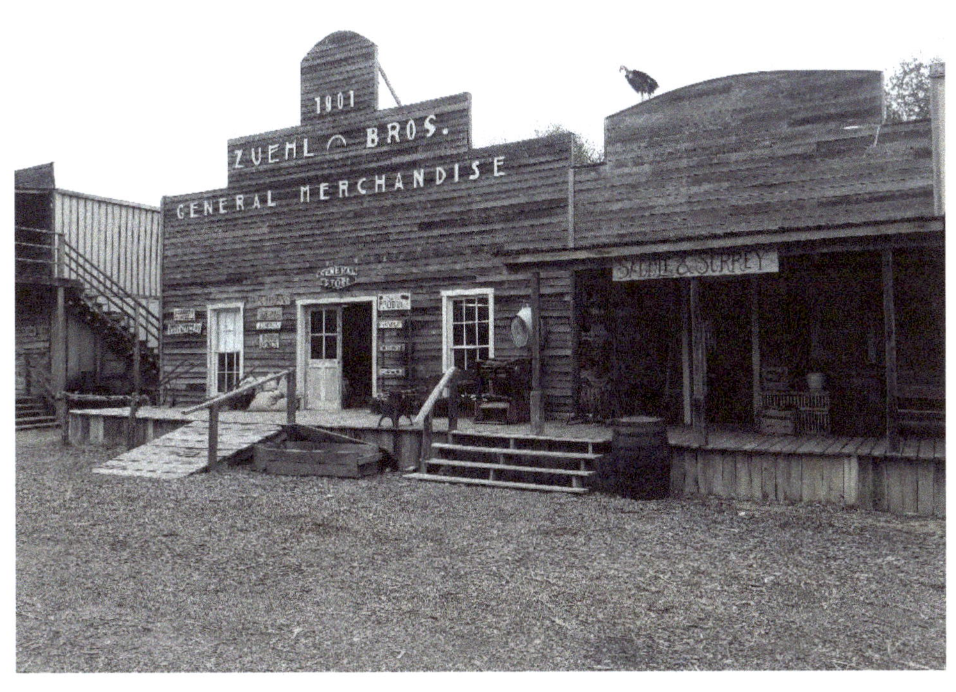

1901
ZUEHL BROS.
GENERAL MERCHANDISE
GENERAL STORE
SADDLE & SURREY

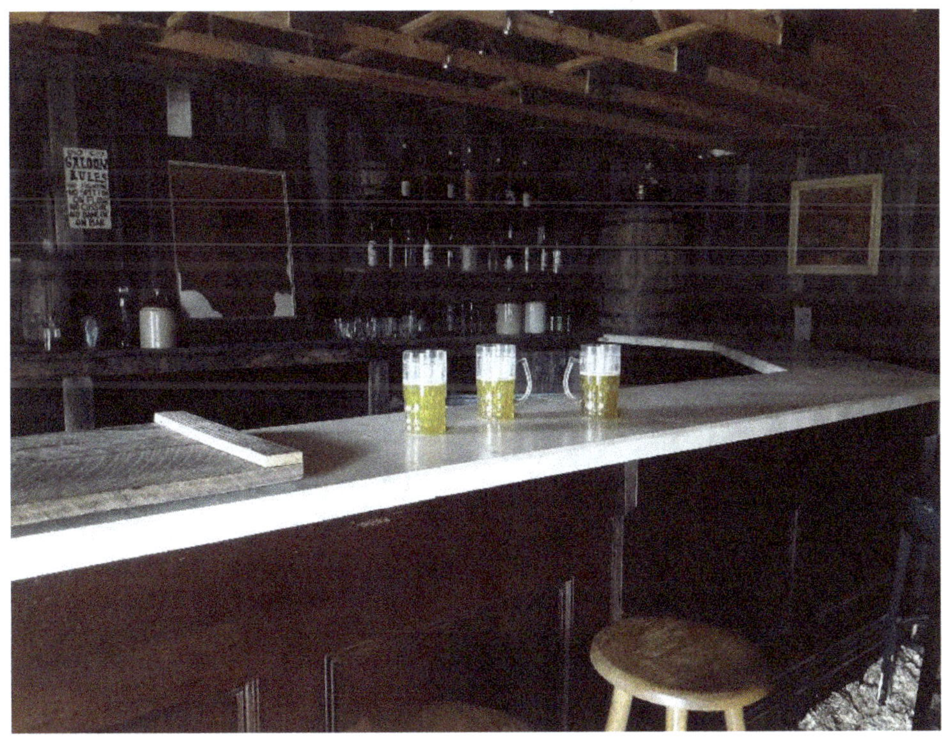

SALOON
RULES

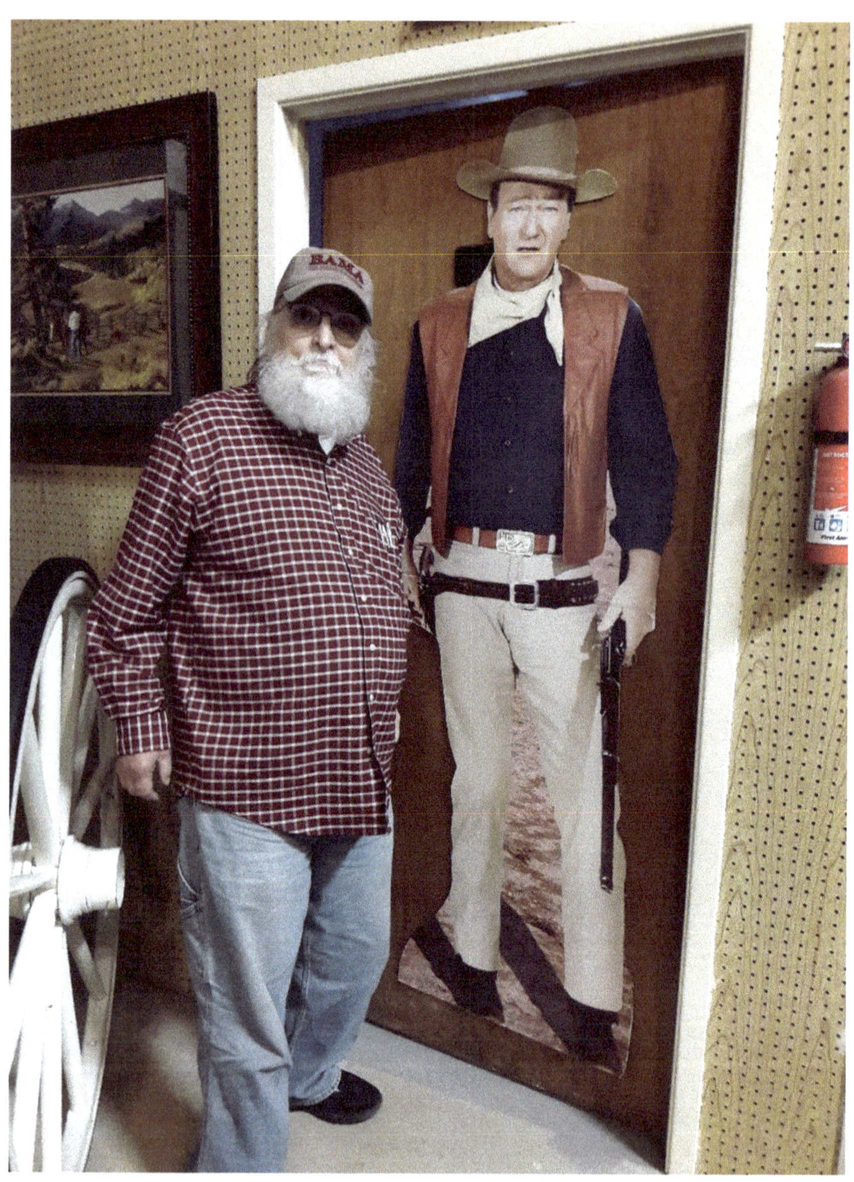

Chapter Fourteen

Johnson City and the LBJ Ranch

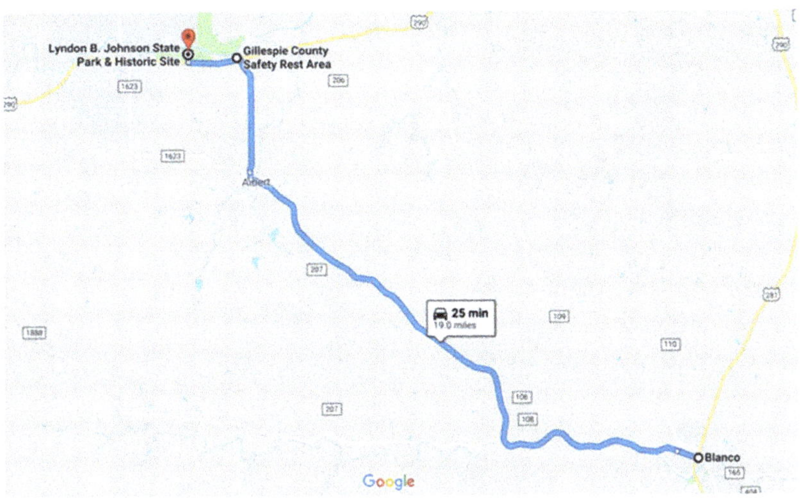

Blanco to Stonewall

I was never much of a history student in my early school years, but then I began homeschooling my kids, and I determined to make history come alive for them. Later, when I took history as I sought my bachelor's degree, my professor made history come alive for us too. But through it all, we never studied Lyndon Baines Johnson or Lady Bird Johnson, except in passing. When I saw we were going to be near their ranch, I knew I wanted to visit and get acquainted with their legacy.

We arrived in Johnson City late in the day, after our visits at Pioneer Town and The Buggy Barn Museum, so we sought out our overnight stop first. The Gillespie County Rest Stop, located in front of the LBJ ranch, was beautiful and reminded me of travel during my childhood.

As you can see from all the photos, our dreary weather continued.

Behind welcome center sits a beautiful church that can be seen across the river from the Johnson family cemetery.

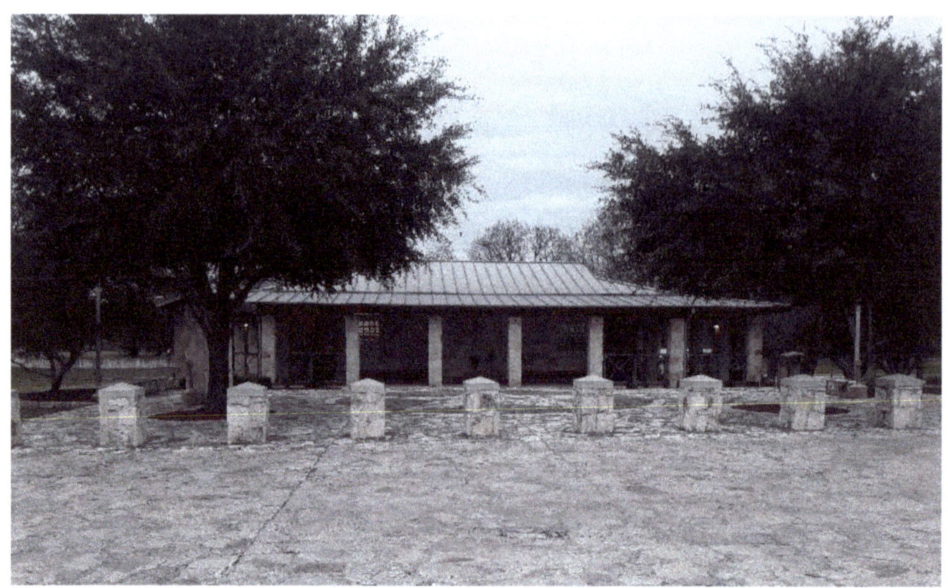

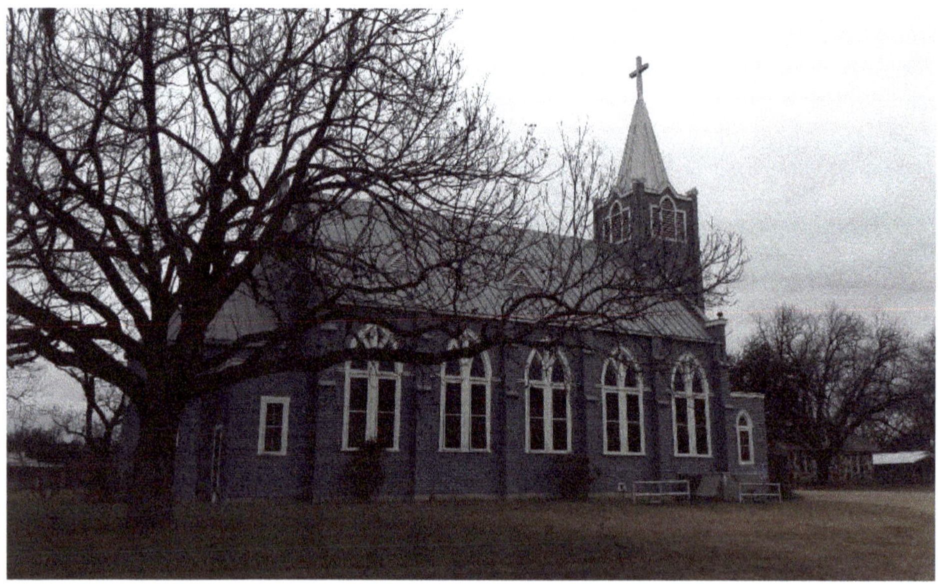

The next morning, we went to the historic site, a mile down the road. Visitors are sent first to the state park site, where we picked up a free permit to drive the self-guided seven-mile route through the ranch. Before we left the building, we were invited to view a short film (25 minutes) about LBJ. It was a TV special by NBC that aired while Johnson was President—he gave a tour of the ranch. He came across so laid-back and more like a farm hand than leader of the free world. (And nothing like politicians of today, although I learned from a local a few days later that the TV persona did not reflect who he was to the locals.)

Unfortunately, the Texas White House (the Johnson's home on their ranch) is closed to the public indefinitely, so we were unable to see it. Buildings surround it though, including the hangar that is now the National Park Visitor's Center and gift shop, and the communication buildings, so we had plenty to see.

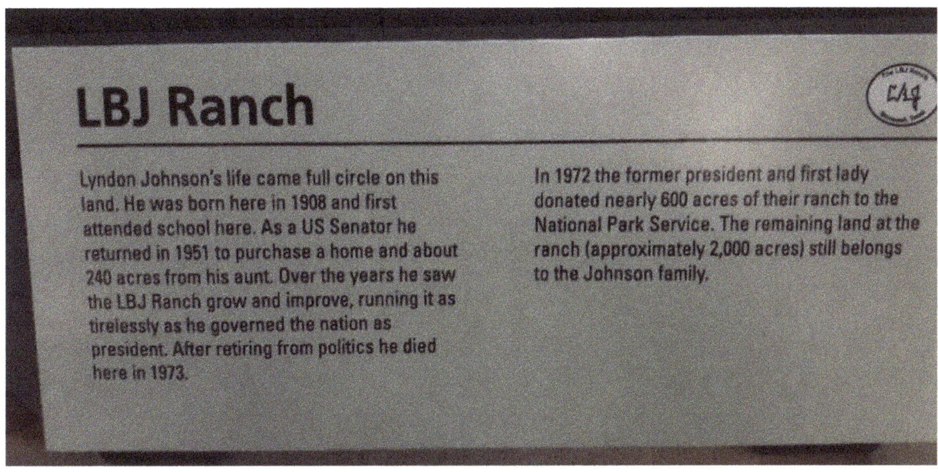

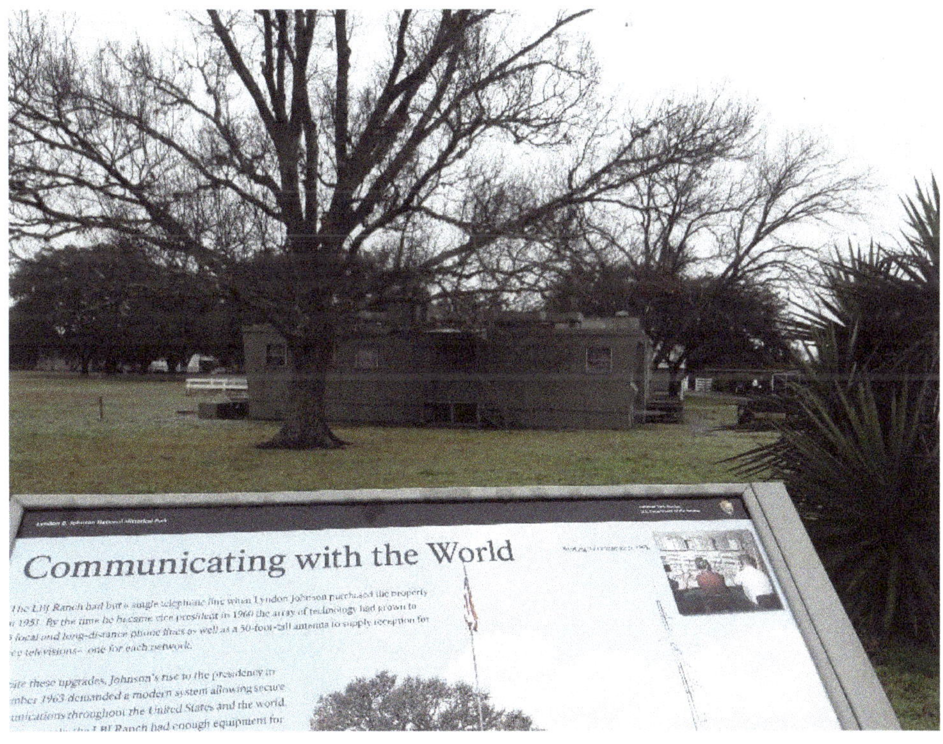

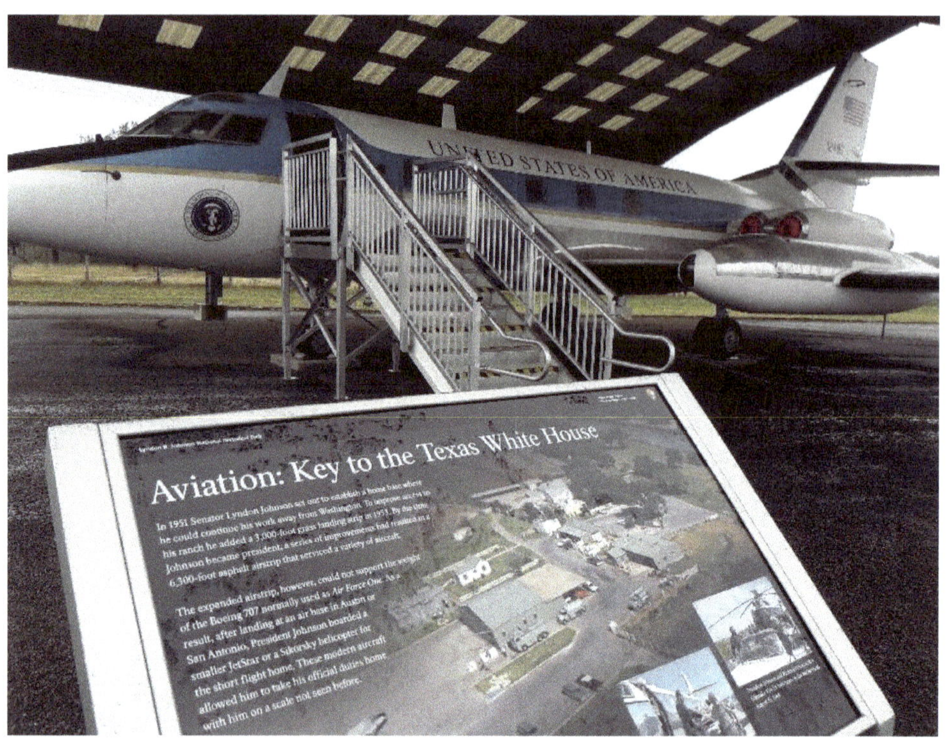
Lyndon B. Johnson National Historical Park
Aviation: Key to the Texas White House
In 1951 Senator Lyndon Johnson set out to establish a home base where he could continue his work away from Washington. To improve access to his ranch he added a 3,000-foot grass landing strip in 1951. By the time Johnson became president, a series of improvements had resulted in a 6,300-foot asphalt airstrip that serviced a variety of aircraft.
The expanded airstrip, however, could not support the weight of the Boeing 707 normally used as Air Force One. As a result, after landing at an air base in Austin or San Antonio, President Johnson boarded a smaller JetStar or a Sikorsky helicopter for the short flight home. These modern aircraft allowed him to take his official duties home with him on a scale not seen before.

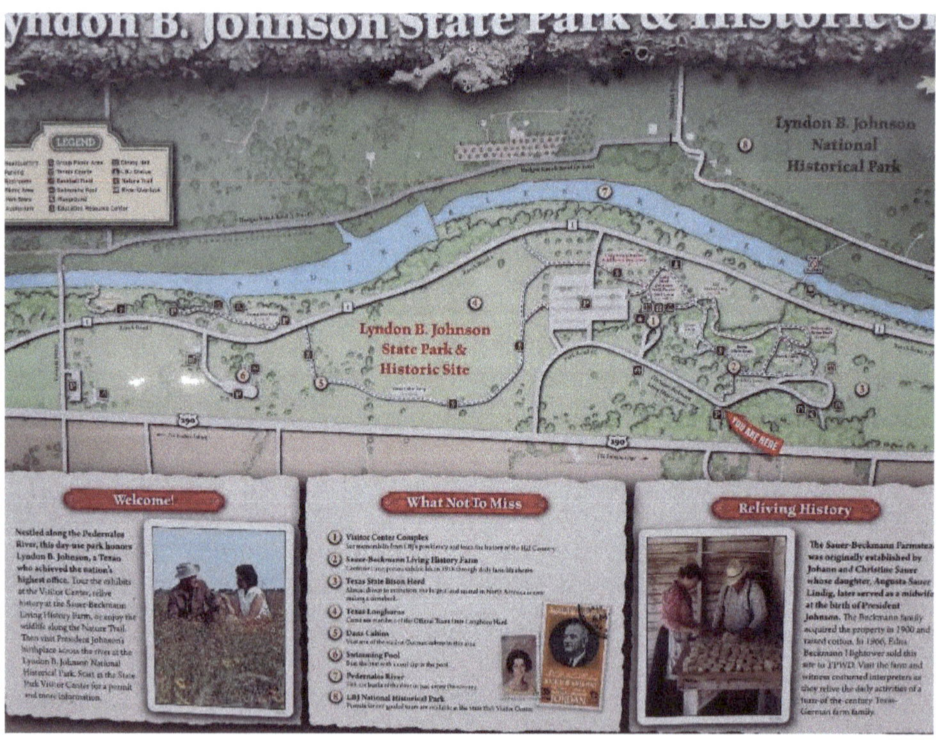
Lyndon B. Johnson State Park & Historic Site
Lyndon B. Johnson National Historical Park
LEGEND
Lyndon B. Johnson State Park & Historic Site
YOU ARE HERE
190

Welcome!
Nestled along the Pedernales River, this day-use park honors Lyndon B. Johnson, a Texan who achieved the nation's highest office. Tour the exhibits at the Visitor Center, relive history at the Sauer-Beckmann Living History Farm, or enjoy the wildlife along the Nature Trail. Then visit President Johnson's birthplace across the river at the Lyndon B. Johnson National Historical Park. Start at the State Park Visitor Center for a permit and more information.

What Not To Miss
1 Visitor Center Complex
See memorabilia from LBJ's presidency and learn the history of the Hill Country.
2 Sauer-Beckmann Living History Farm
Costumed interpreters exhibit life in 1918 through daily farm life chores.
3 Texas State Bison Herd
Almost driven to extinction, the largest land mammal in North America is now making a comeback.
4 Texas Longhorns
Come see members of the Official Texas State Longhorn Herd.
5 Dans Cabins
Visit one of the oldest German cabins in this area.
6 Swimming Pool
Beat the heat with a cool dip in the pool.
7 Pedernales River
8 LBJ National Historical Park

Reliving History
The Sauer-Beckmann Farmstead was originally established by Johann and Christine Sauer whose daughter, Augusta Sauer Lindig, later served as a midwife at the birth of President Johnson. The Beckmann family acquired the property in 1900 and raised cotton. In 1966, Edna Beckmann Hightower sold this site to TPWD. Visit the farm and witness costumed interpreters as they relive the daily activities of a turn-of-the-century Texas-German farm family.

94

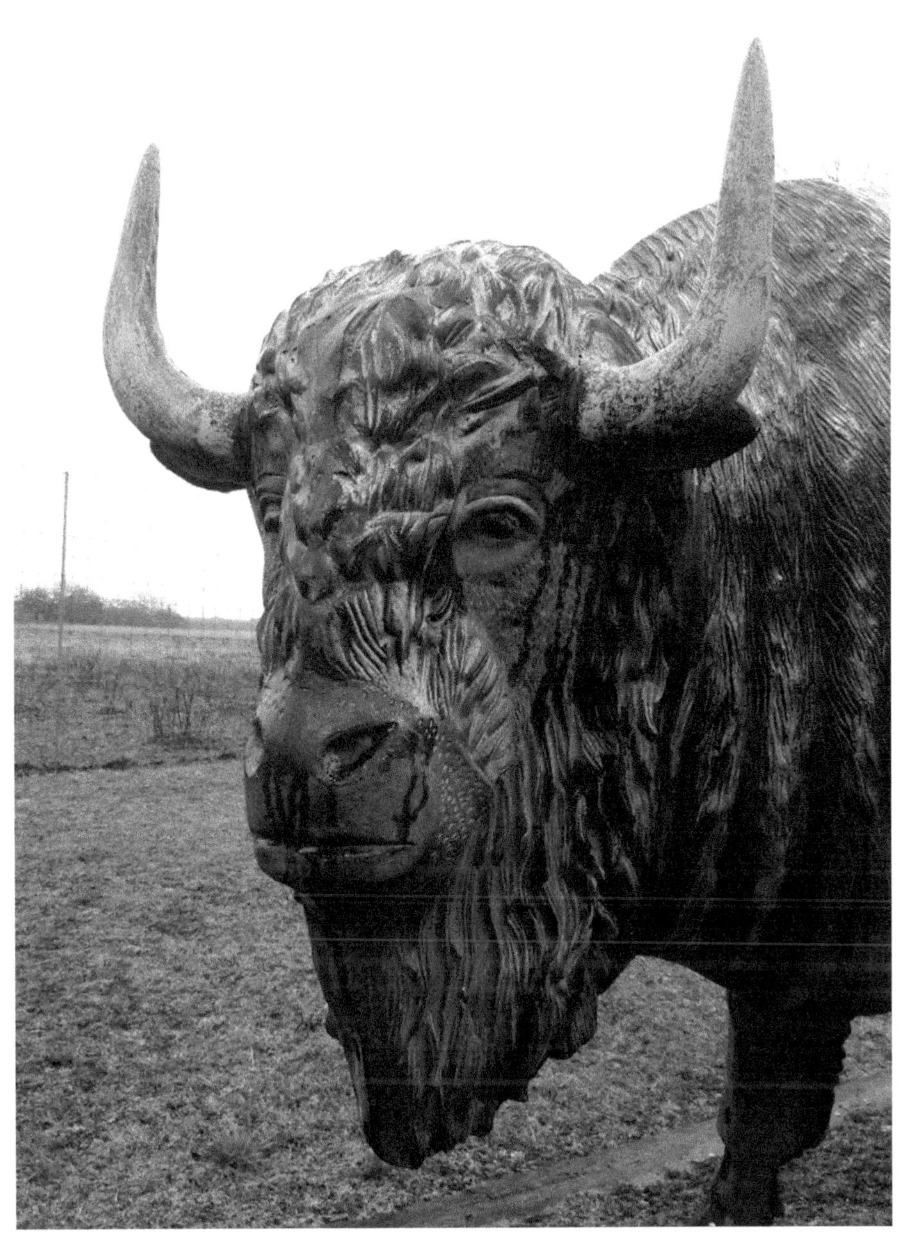

Sample Artwork:

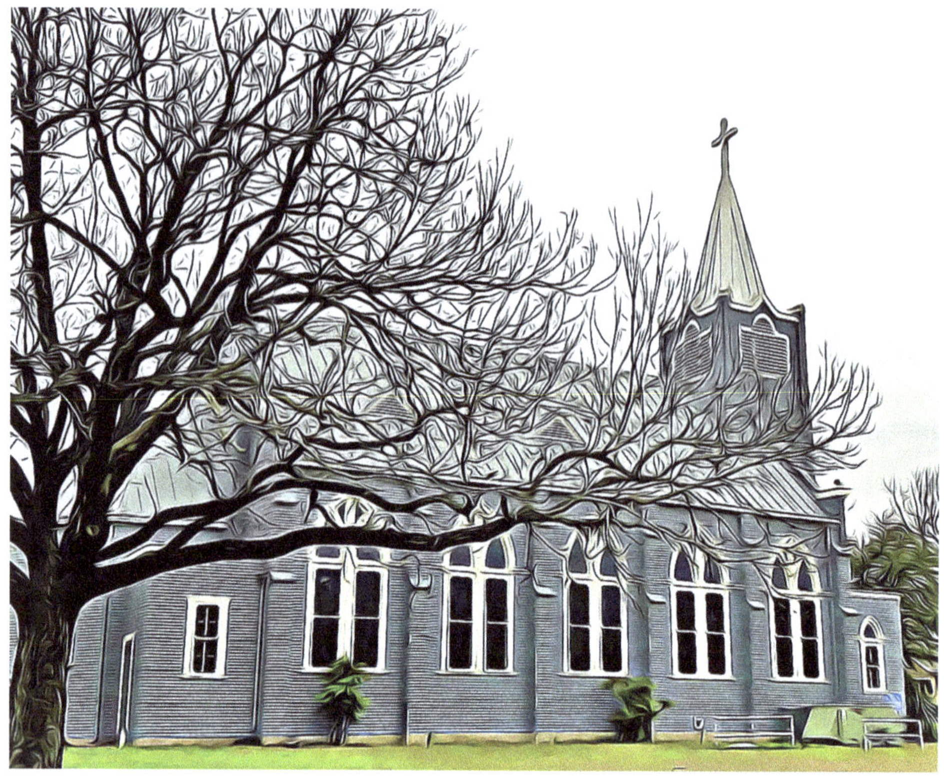

Trinity Lutheran Church Stonewall Texas 📷

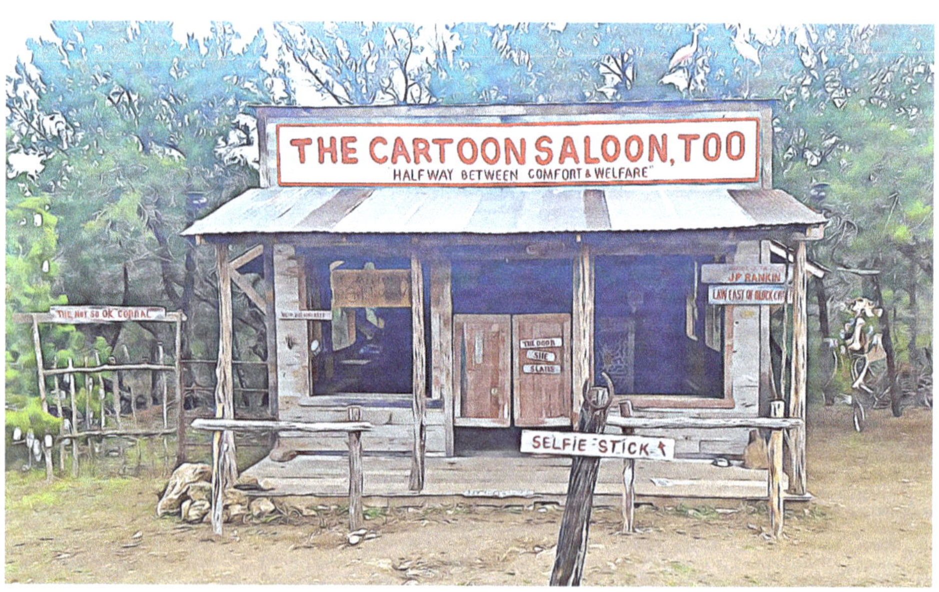

Cartoon Saloon Too 📷

Chapter Fifteen
The Living History Farm

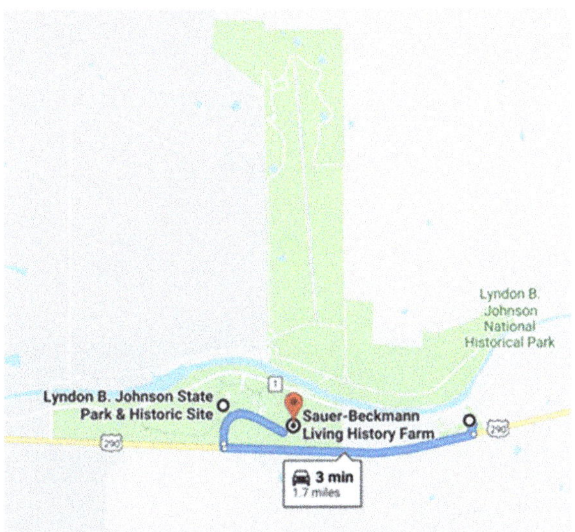

The first stop after we left the LBJ State Park facility was at the Sauer-Beckmann Living History Farm, and what a delight!

From the minute we walked through the gate, we knew we were on special property. Volunteers and employees were dressed in period costumes, and the farm was in full operation—an operation set in 1915, said one of the docents.

Animals roamed freely around the property—some were in pens, others not. This day, the sheep were roaming, and the ram caught my eye—and apparently, I caught his, too, and made a new friend before we departed.

As we walked around, we smelled food cooking, and soon found a costumed docent cooking a pile of onions in an iron skillet on a woodburning stove. She told us about the three houses sitting side by side on the property—one the original, then an add-on (the one we were in), and then the new one, built in 1915 from materials bought through the Sears catalog. It was fun to compare the differences.

We asked about the milk sitting around in bowls, and she explained the cheese making process—all of it quite fascinating.

Ranch hands popped in and out for coffee and invited us to come watch the butchering of a steer that would take place shortly.

The garden was beautiful too—the cabbages were near perfection, along with broccoli, carrots, turnips, and more.

This was a great stop, and one I was reluctant to leave. As sappy as this sounds, all felt right in the world as we stepped back in time.

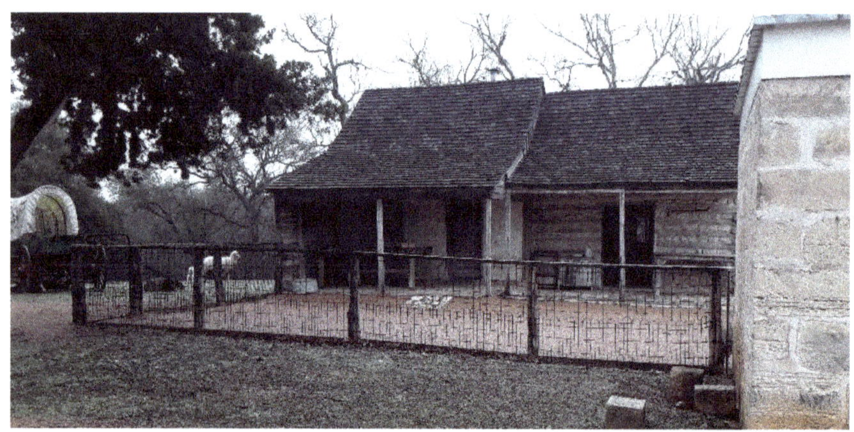

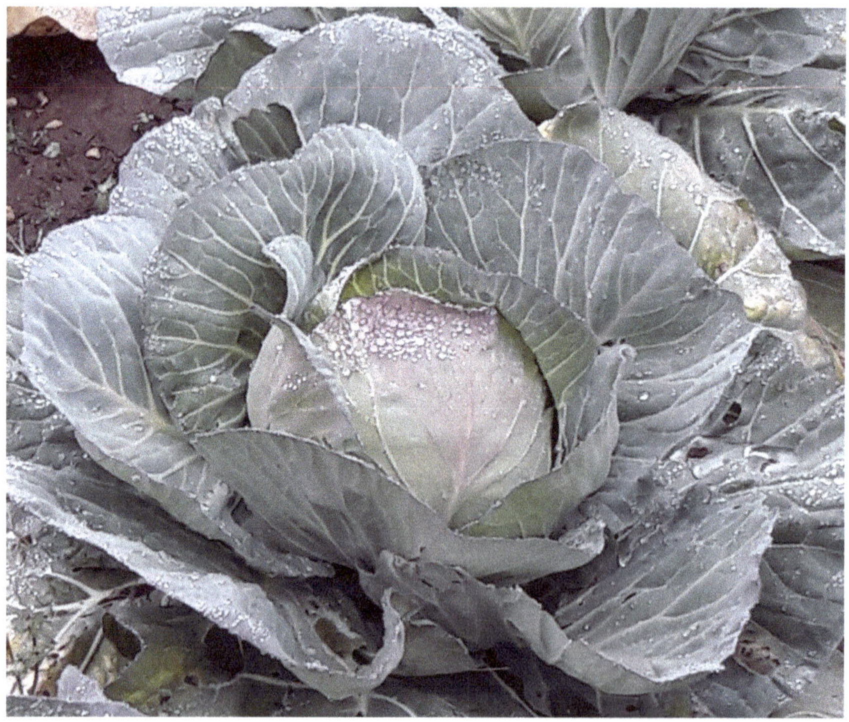

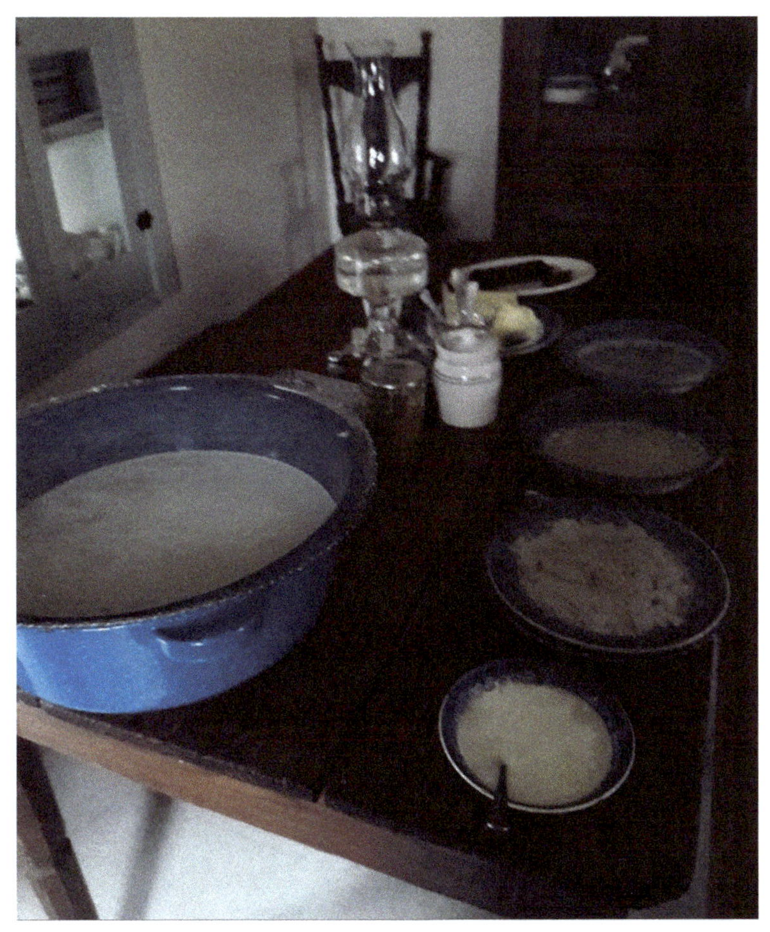

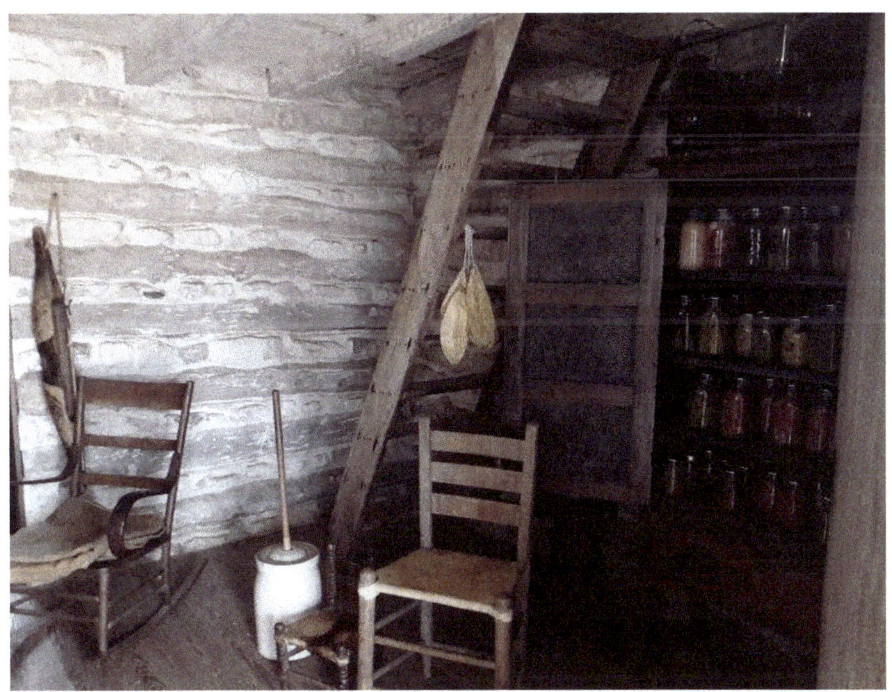

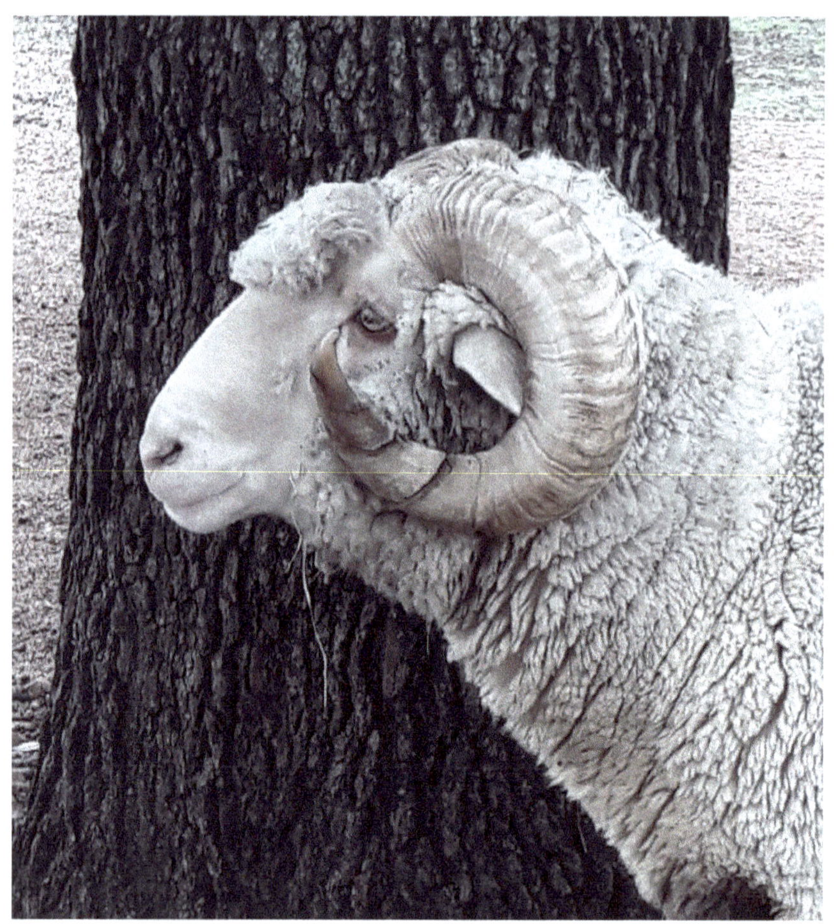

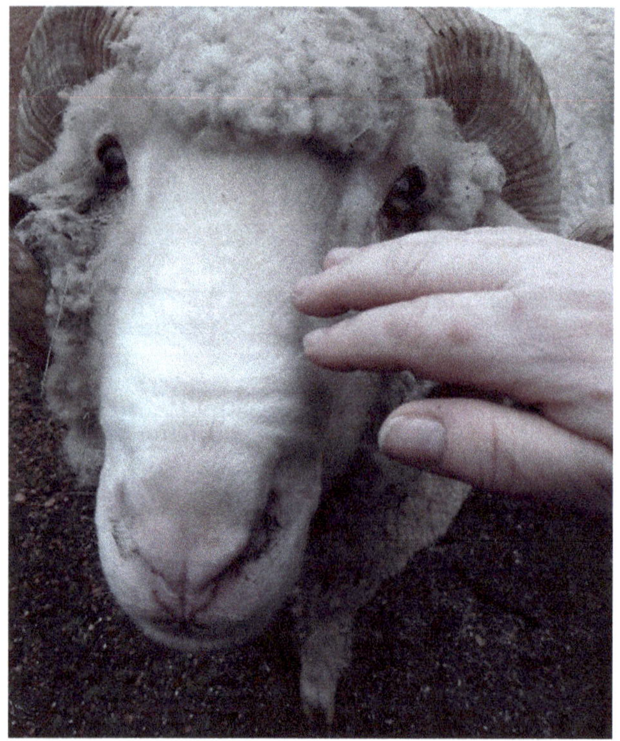

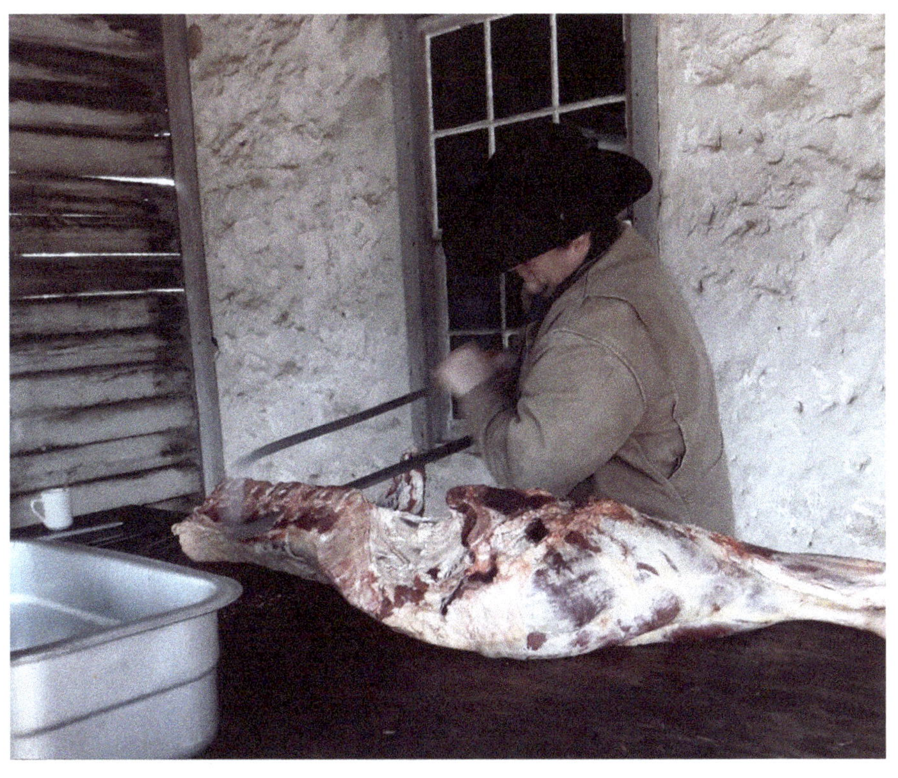

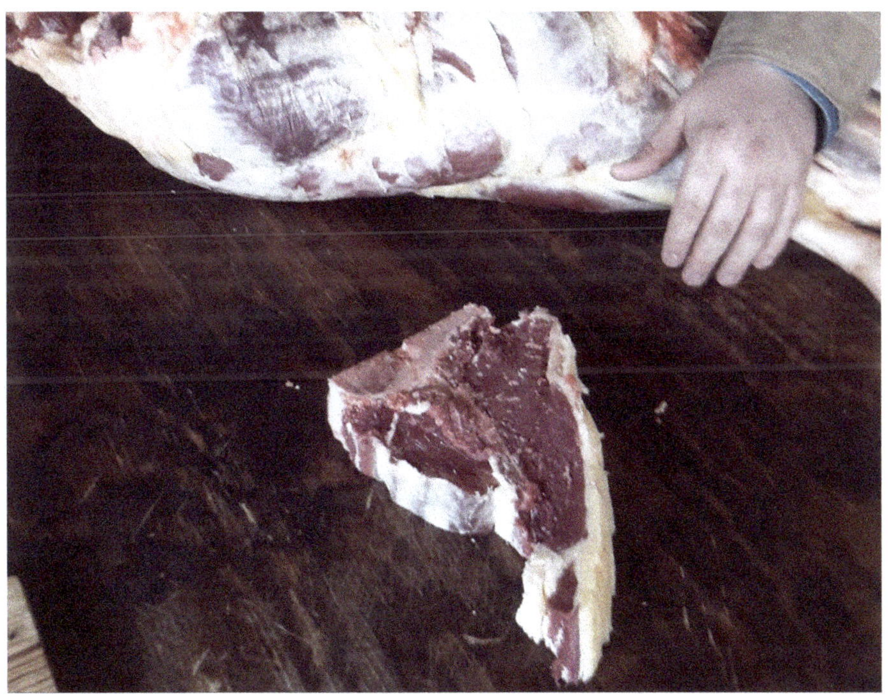

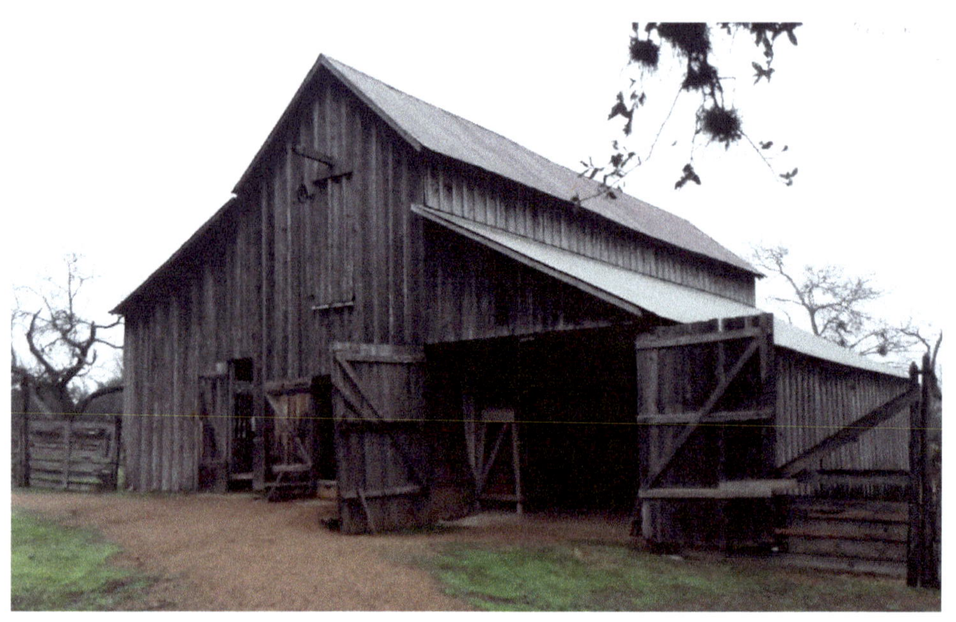

Sample Artwork:

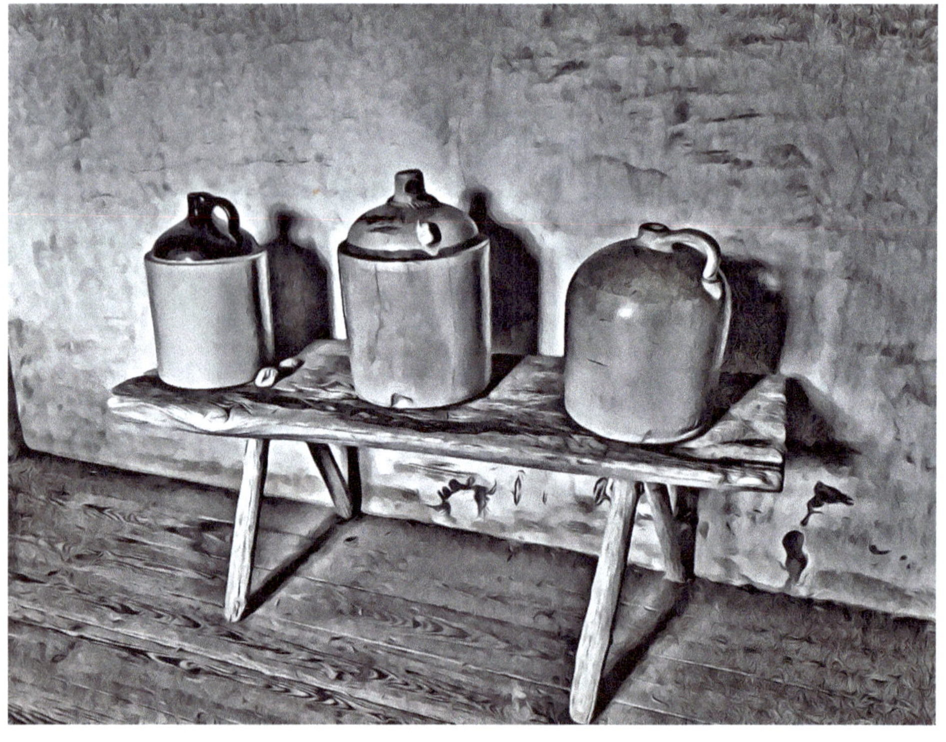

Old Fashion Farmhouse Jugs

Chapter Sixteen

From the Old West to German Influence

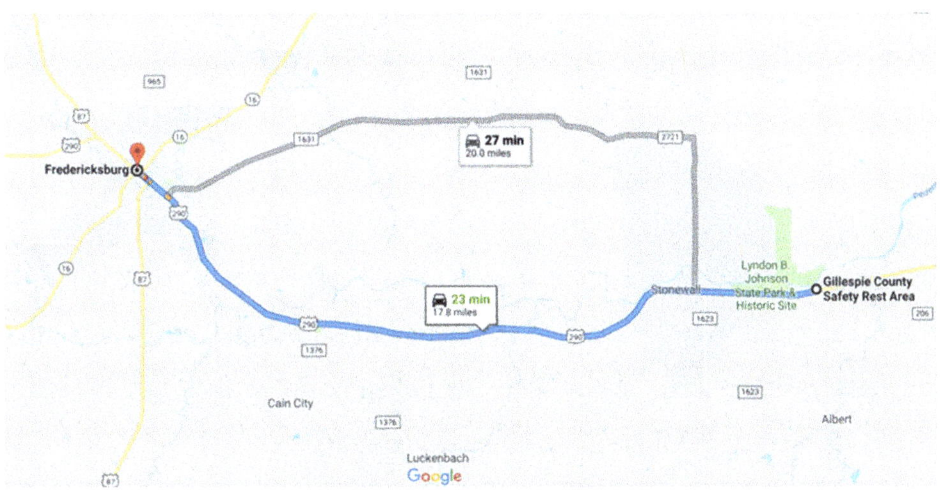

Stonewall to Fredericksburg

I had work waiting for me after all our play time in Stonewall, Blanco, and Wimberley, so when we got to Fredericksburg, our first stop was the public library.

The minute I walked in the door, I wanted to move in there! When we asked the librarian the best place for us to work for a few hours, she told us to head upstairs where it was quiet. Upstairs, we found large worktables with charging stations and a quiet nook with two armchairs, two ottomans, and electrical outlets—just what we needed. I set up shop in one of the chairs while Tim napped in the other. He said at one point all we needed was a fireplace, and while I agreed that would be awesome, I was perfectly content.

Fredericksburg turned out to be a touristy town, but it took us a couple of days to discover that fact. The town held a lot of contrasts—young and old (people and culture), new and old (architecture and attractions), Old West and German, past and present.

We are still car camping, so one night, we decided to go hang out at the local Whataburger and discovered that this location served as the town's diner. Locals of many generations hung out there, and apparently, our presence created quite a stir.

First, the woman who brought us coffee asked where we were from. (Tim's Bama hat was still giving us away.) When she learned we were from Georgia and Alabama, she told us about her relatives who lived back east. She went back to work, but soon, we heard her tell someone else that we were from Alabama. Another employee came over and said her brother was from Huntsville. She talked for a while, then brought us a great map of Fredericksburg that we hadn't found elsewhere. We sat studying the map after she went back to work, but soon, a couple came up and asked where we were from. They said they'd noticed we were looking at the map and wanted to give us a few pointers about town. We invited them to sit down with us, and the wife perched beside me, but the husband remained standing.

We learned all about the National Museum of the Pacific War and about LBJ's power and influence in the area (and how he got it). The conversation was lively, although a bit one-sided, but we learned a lot. His wife was precious (although she never uttered a word.)

The downtown area is lively on Saturdays, with shops and many restaurants. Our Whataburger friend told us to try the ice cream shop downtown, so that's how we ended up there the next night.

My favorite part of Fredericksburg was the Lady Bird Johnson city park. We spent a few hours there (over a couple of days) because it was peaceful and spacious—and greeted us with a fun surprise on our first visit.

Fredericksburg was a nice town that proved much more interesting than I expected.

From the FROG Files:

Today, we're snuggled into the Fredericksburg, TX Pioneer Memorial Library. And I do mean snuggled in. As I write this, I'm the most comfortable I've been in weeks. The librarian told us we'd have more peace and quiet upstairs to work, so we came up here to discover large work tables, shelves of Texas books, and two very comfortable arm chairs with footstools, right next to an electrical outlet so I can recharge, work, and elevate our legs as I do.

Overall, we're doing okay. Legs still swelling, but we're managing. Grateful to be in some warm temps again. Last night's low was 55 - Tim didn't even use a blanket, and I didn't pull out the Mylar. Should be 55 or warmer for at least the next week, and I'm hoping longer. At least one day of full sunshine in the forecast, too, with clouds the rest of the time.

We still have a lot of west Texas to explore. At some point yesterday, Tim said, "Ah, now THIS is Texas." I guess the Hill Country must be on most westerns.

He's currently snoring away in the armchair next to me.

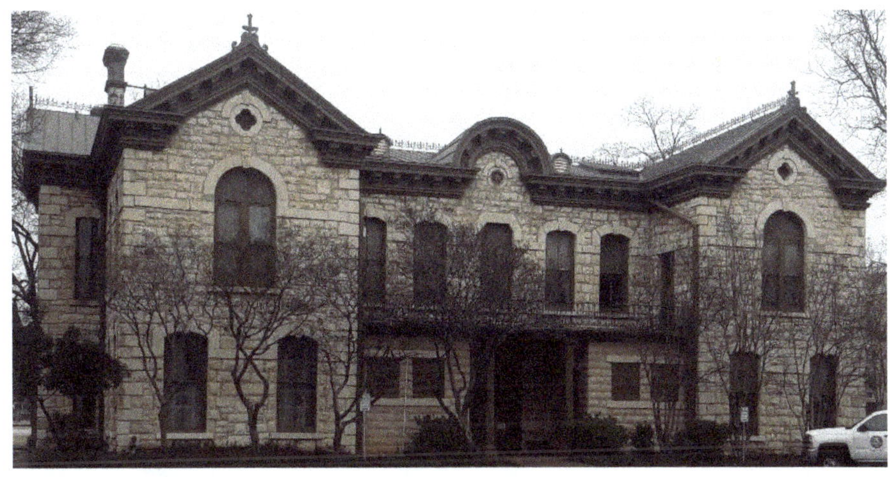

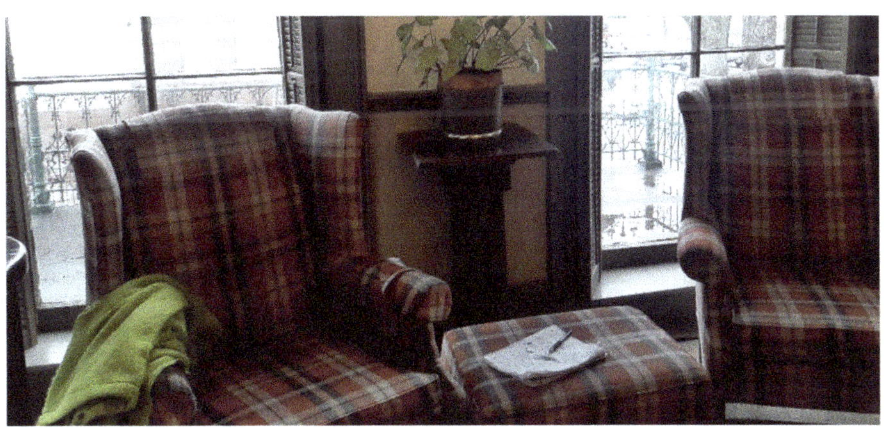

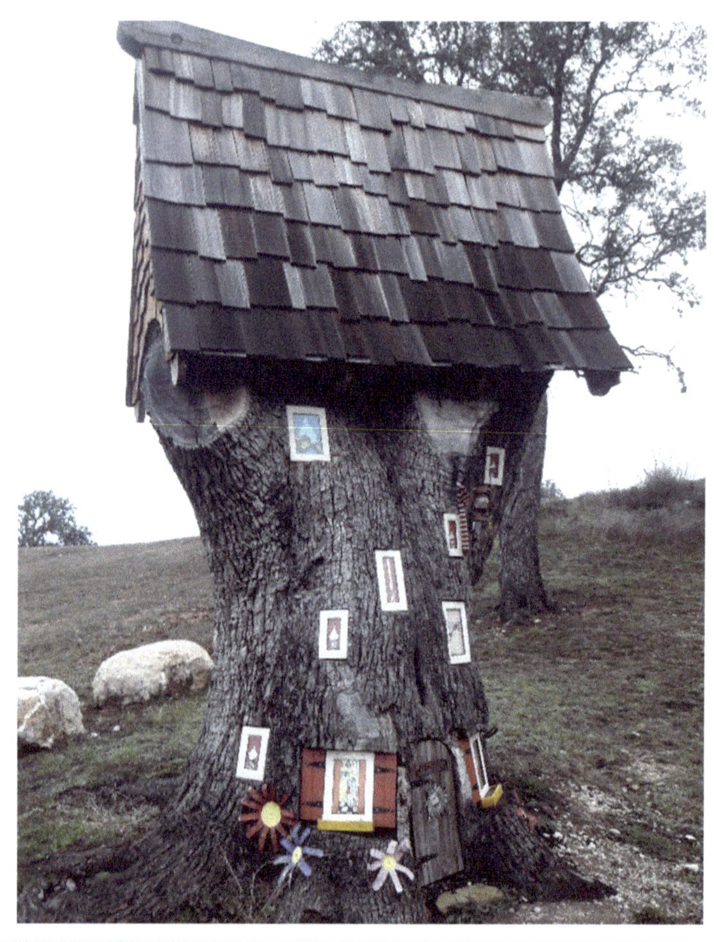

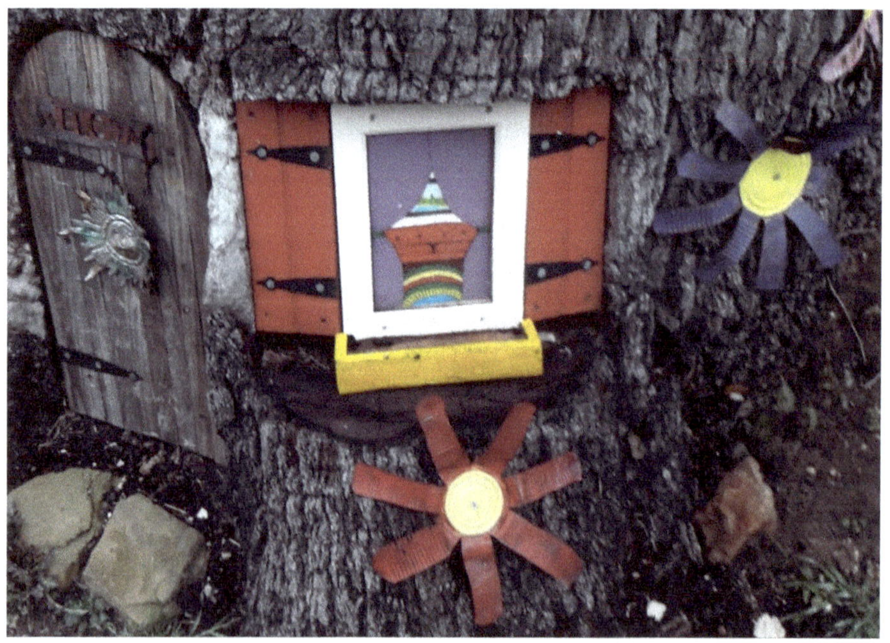

Chapter Seventeen

Holy Ground in Kerrville, Texas

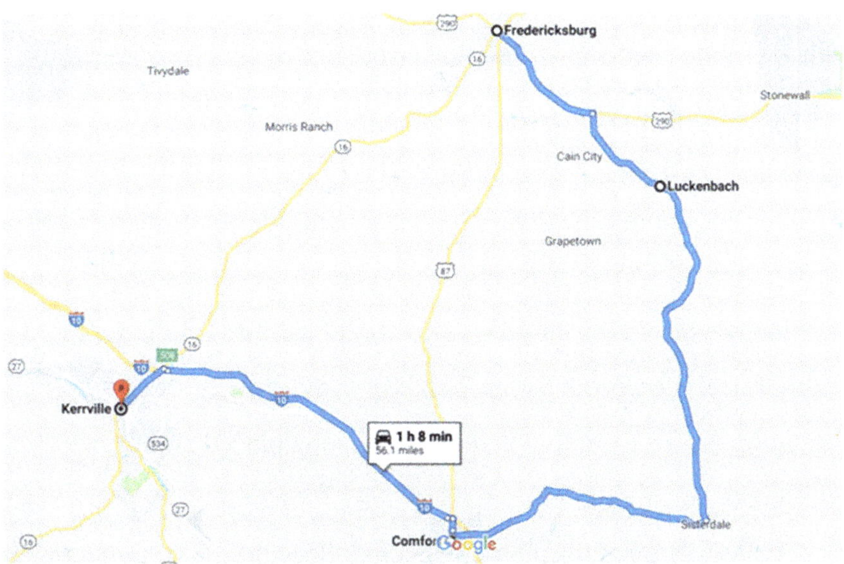

Fredericksburg to Kerrville

Sometimes we go roundabout to get where we're going, and once we'd seen the sign for Luckenbach as we entered Fredericksburg, we knew we'd have to check it out. After all, with a population of three, and the possibility of finding Willie, Waylon, or the boys hanging around, who could resist?

So many towns surprised us with their offerings—towns we'd never heard of or even seen on a map before this trip. Our next stop offered a time of worship and rest that we never saw coming.

Kerrville, Texas is home to the Empty Cross, as it is commonly known, or officially "The Coming King Sculpture Prayer Garden." I'd heard about the cross only a few days prior and made it our first stop when we arrived into town. Attractions like this end up being cheesy or have other intentions, so I had no expectations when we got there. The drive up the mountain almost caused us to turn away (Have I mentioned I tend to fear mountain roads and high bridges—but usually force myself through?)

but my desire to see the cross was greater than my fear so I kept driving upward.

The moment I stepped into the garden, I knew I was indeed standing on Holy Ground, and I removed my sandals. (Grateful for the sunshine and warmth that day, too!)

A concrete path leads visitors to the cross. Inserted in the concrete are engraved plaques with Scripture on them, offered in Spanish, English, and German.

The walkway leads to a statue, and then to the Empty Cross.

Lining the walkways are rock gardens—flat stones with prayers written on them. In various places throughout the area, they've placed piles of empty rocks for anyone to take and write prayers on to place along the way. I spent time praying over the requests—so many prayers for families as a whole, and for individual family members, too. Prayers for homes, jobs, healing. Wayward children, aging parents. Prayers for addictions. Prayers for finances. Someone placed a marriage proposal in the midst of the prayers.

Our time there was precious and unexpected. Peaceful. We were indeed standing on Holy Ground.

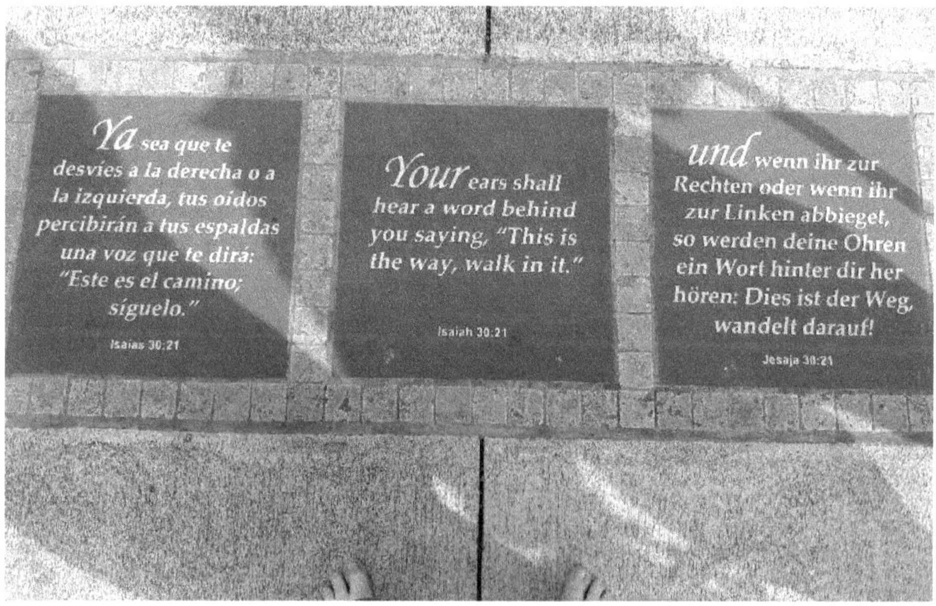

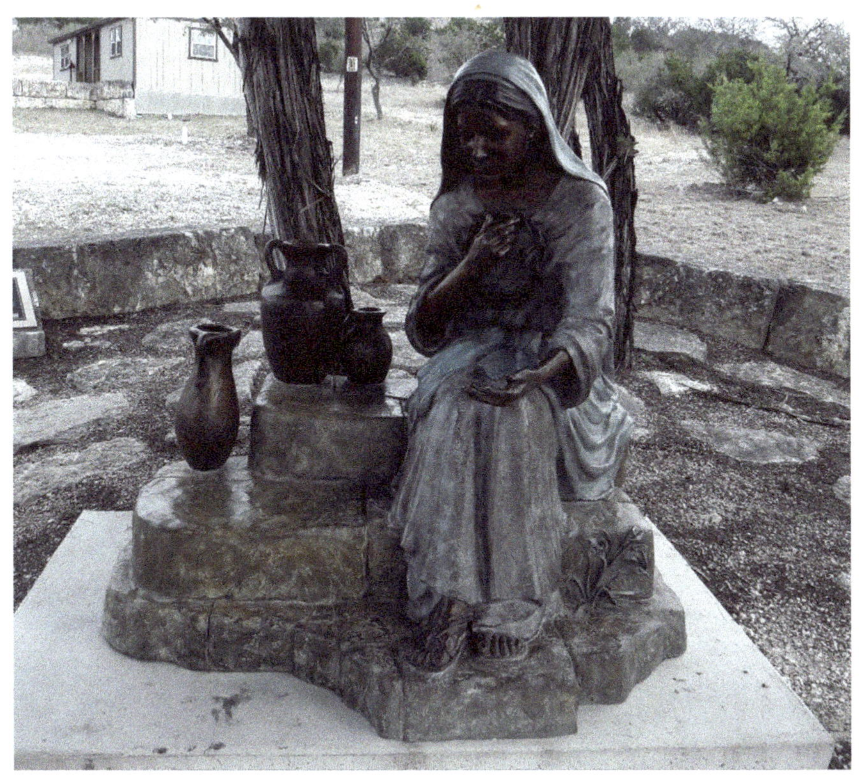

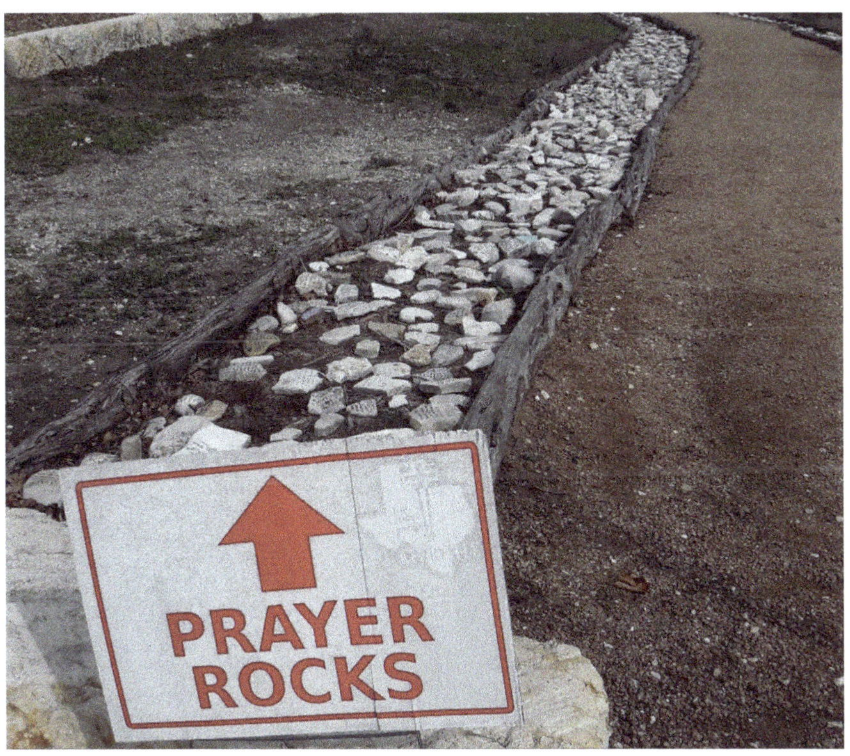
PRAYER
ROCKS

Sample Artwork:

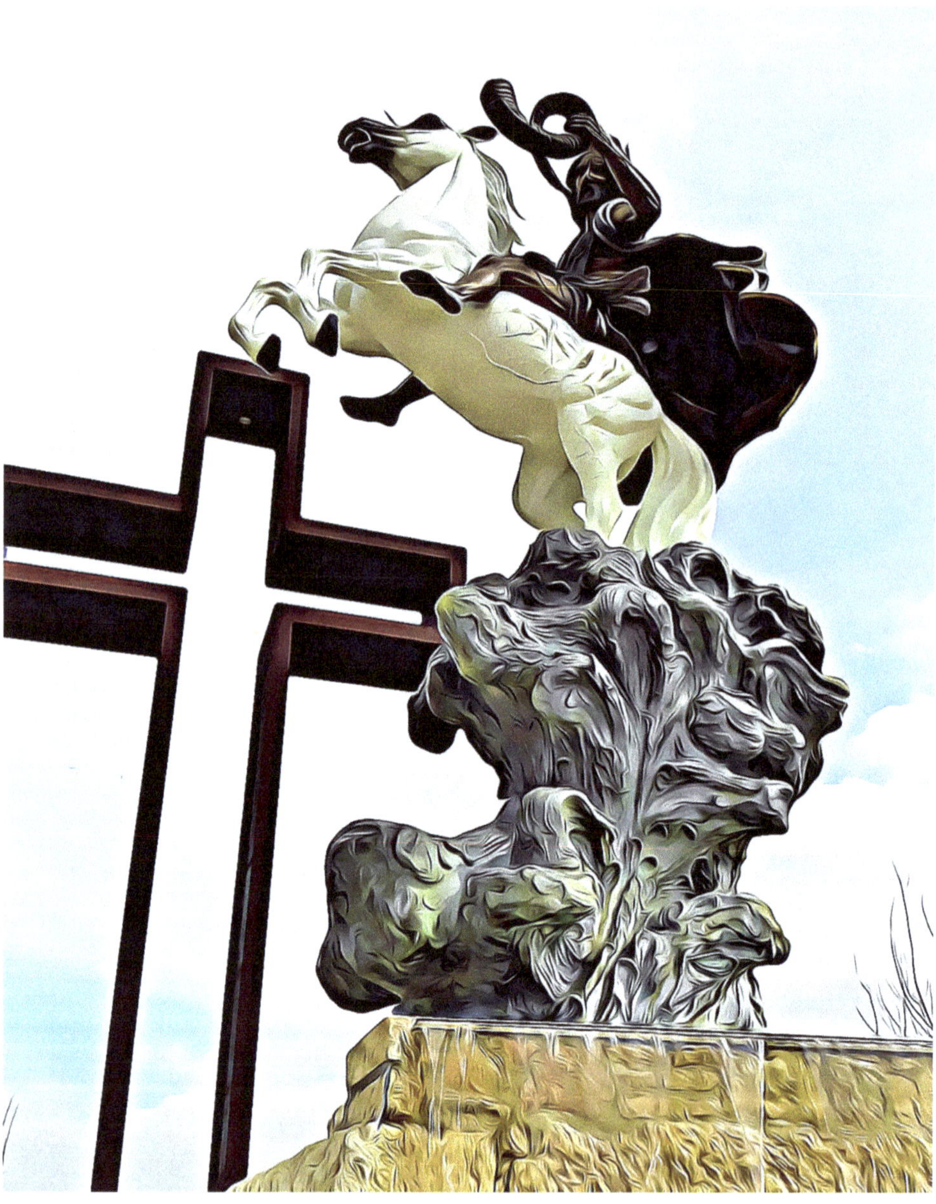

<u>The Empty Cross and The Coming King</u>

The Coming King sculpture by Max G. Greiner, Jr. of Kerrville, Texas

in front of The Empty Cross

Chapter Eighteen

Covering a Lot of Miles

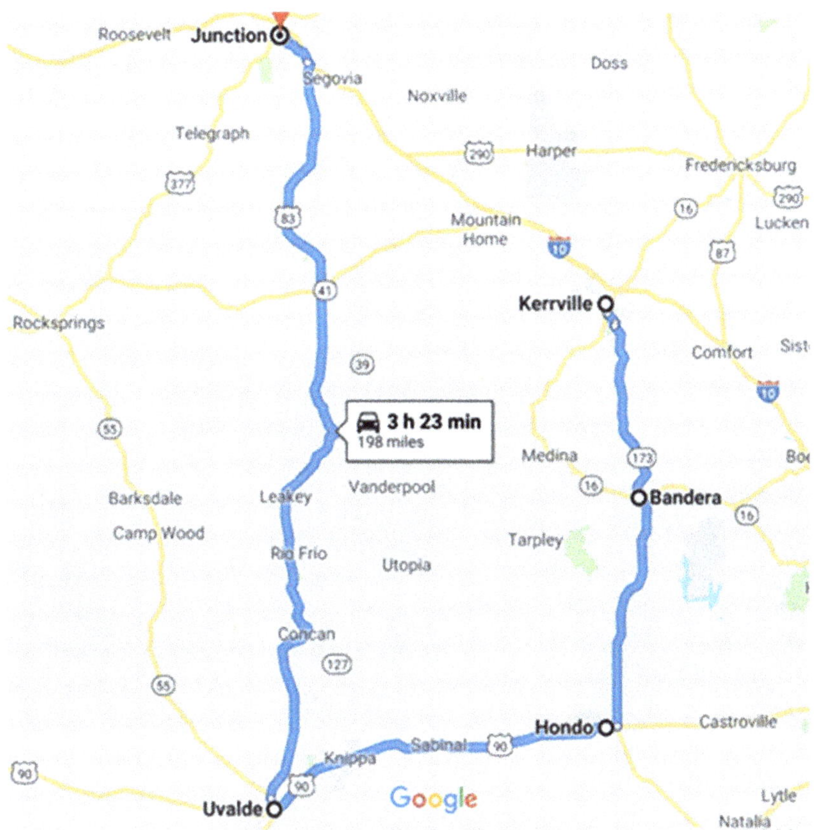

Kerrville to Uvalde to Junction

At this point in our trip, I expected us to be settling in a little more, but instead, we found ourselves speeding along and covering a lot of miles.

As we traveled, I checked several different websites regularly so we could visit the "must-sees" along the way. I checked RoadsideAmerica.com—sometimes for really wacky things, and other times, I'm surprised with something special, like our visit to the Empty Cross in Kerrville. I also checked TripAdvisor and do a general search for towns we're visiting.

Somewhere, I learned that Bandera, TX was supposedly home to one of the best ranches in the world, and although our budget didn't allow for a visit to a dude ranch, we decided to drive that direction to see the land. Then we saw Hondo on the map, and Tim said we had to go to Hondo, because of the movie. But I discovered on RoadsideAmerica that there were church ruins in Hondo, so we aimed for that direction.

The gorgeous courthouse in Bandera seemed larger than the town itself. 

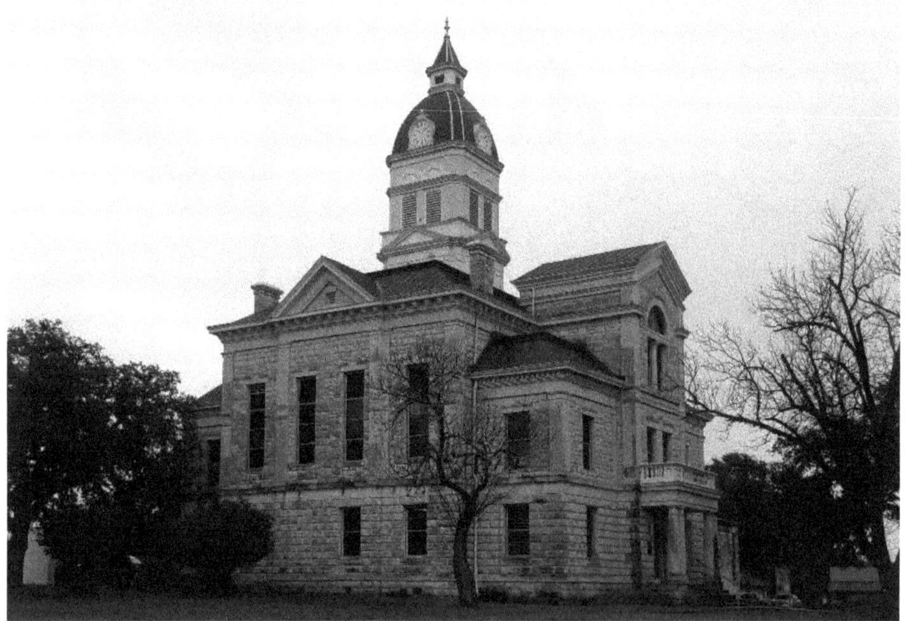

Then we found the ruins of St. Dominic's Church near Hondo.

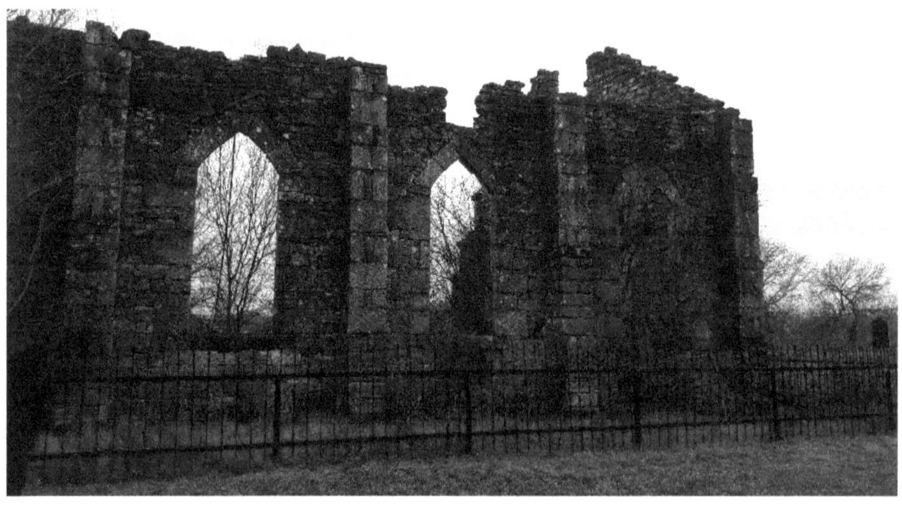

When I took this second photo of the church ruins in Hondo, I noticed something odd: cactus growing on top of the wall.

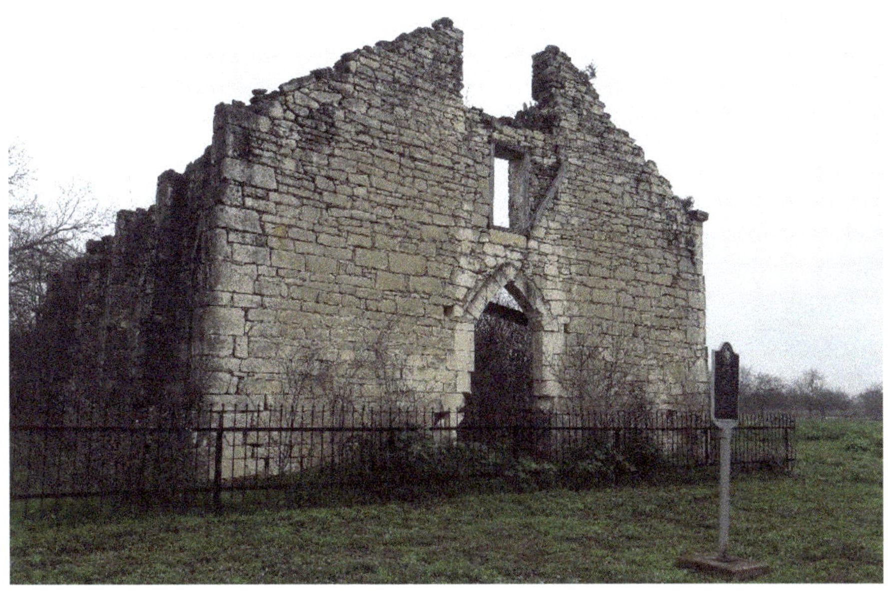

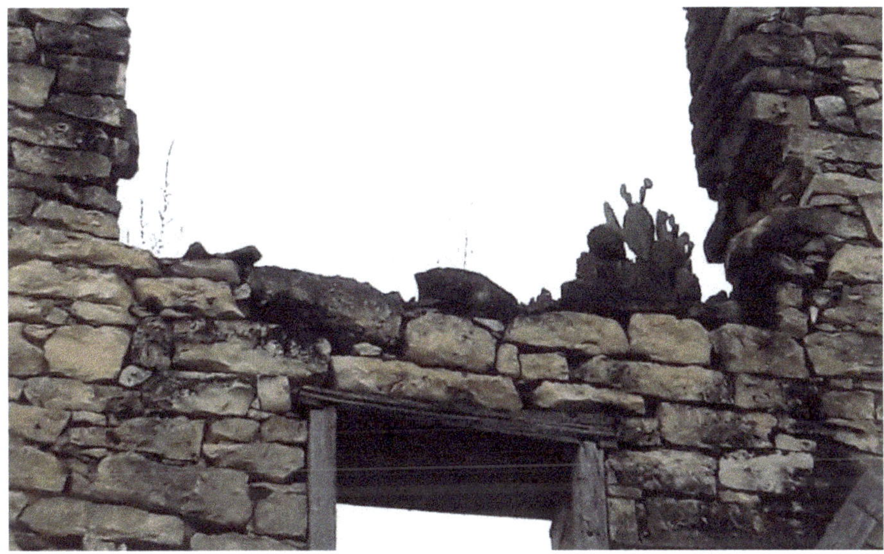

We continued westward and landed at a library in Uvalde so I could work. We found a magnificent tree in the middle of the road before turning into the parking lot.

Beautiful library, and the day was comfortably warm, but apparently, whoever controlled the thermostat was hot, so they cranked the a/c down so much we froze while I worked.

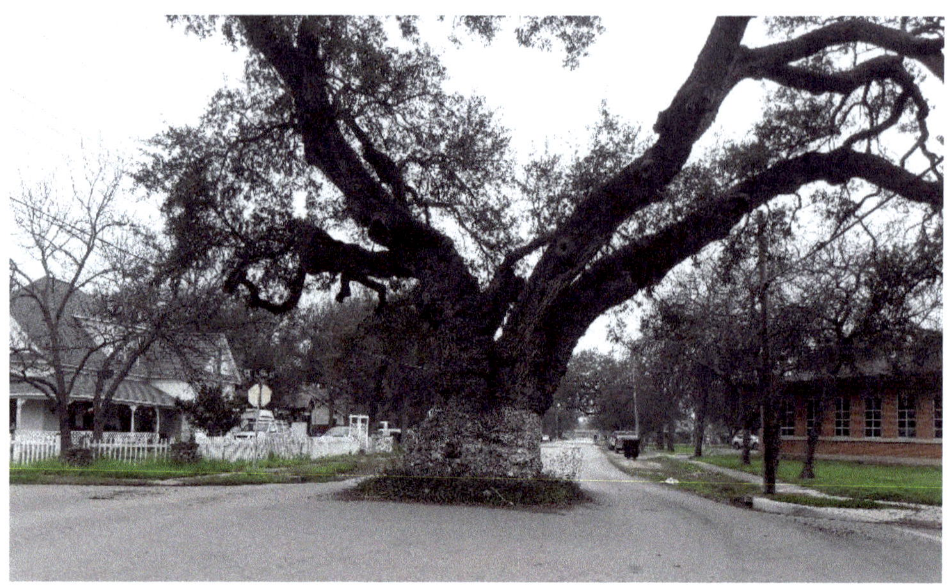

By mid-afternoon, we were famished and went hunting for local food. On TripAdvisor, we found a local joint that specialized in tortilla soup and homemade gorditas. After freezing in the library, soup sounded great.

When we arrived at Live Oak Drive-Thru, I never saw a drive-thru, so I parked. The building was a shed for cooking and a screened porch for ordering and dining in. I went to the window and ordered two soups and two gorditas. The gentleman told me, in broken English, "No Soup, it's Summer." I nodded. I understood his words. He was so convincing, it took me a minute to remember that it was FEBRUARY, and while it was a fairly warm day (60s, maybe), the cold was coming back the next day, so summer hadn't quite arrived. But no soup.

The gorditas, however, were divine! I should have taken a photo of the insides, but we dug in before I thought about it. Tim had the brisket and I had the chicken fajita—both "with the works." They were loaded with lettuce, tomato, onion, and avocado. While I was waiting on the food, a diner told me he loved the gorditas here because they're loaded but don't fall apart. He was right—they held together, and it was the homemade outer "bun" that made all the difference. I could eat those by themselves they were so good and quite different from the version of gorditas we normally eat.

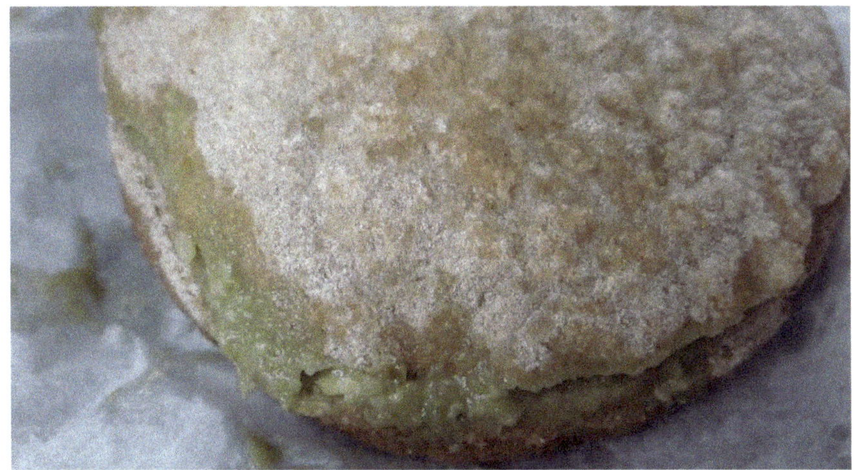

The diner alerted me to action taking place not far from town that was leading to heavy tension in the area, due to the caravan and the border-crossing issues. He said things were probably going to get worse before they got better.

Tim and I talked about all he told us and decided it might be wise for us to go ahead and begin our trek north. It was early afternoon and we had no idea where we would stop for the night, but we decided to drive and see where we'd land.

Two roads lead north out of Uvalde, but I was the driver, not the navigator, so we ended up on Highway 83, which took us due north into Junction, instead of northwest into Sonora.

By the time we got to Junction, I was beat and feeling quite discouraged. Physical problems became an issue, too—our legs were beginning to swell from all the driving and car camping. (For those younger than we are, we didn't expect this to be an issue either!) But until we could get a new tent, our options are limited. We pulled into a truck stop, found a place to park overnight, and settled in.

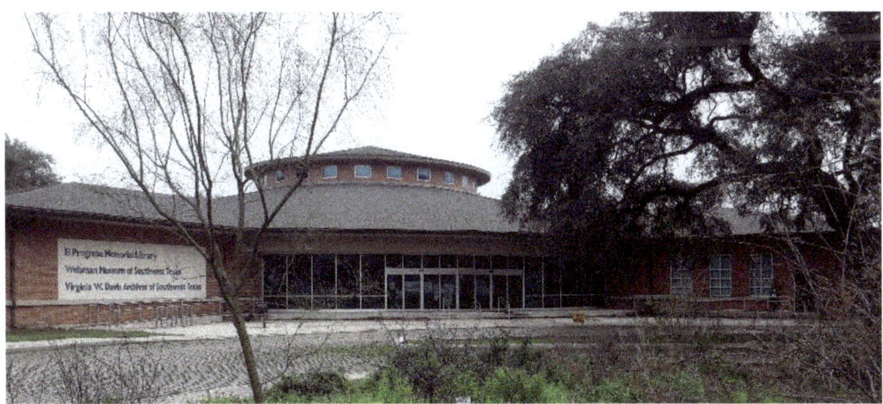

Someone warned me in Uvalde that things could get dicey there the next few days because of the wall and the caravan. Troops had already been sent to a location south of the town, and residents were preparing for the worst. Everywhere we tried to land, something happened that we either didn't feel safe or that something just wasn't right - weird internet connections, odd encounters. Tim got adamant that we leave the area, so we did.

Somewhere on one of the empty roads between Leakey and Junction, someone had dropped two big cardboard boxes - each about the size of a dishwasher - in the middle of the road. It was late dusk - just before it got really dark, but way past any daylight. God's Hand is the ONLY reason I saw those boxes and missed them. I have no idea if they were empty or full - but they didn't budge as I blew past them, so I'm thinking they were full and could have done some major damage to our car, and perhaps to us. But for God.

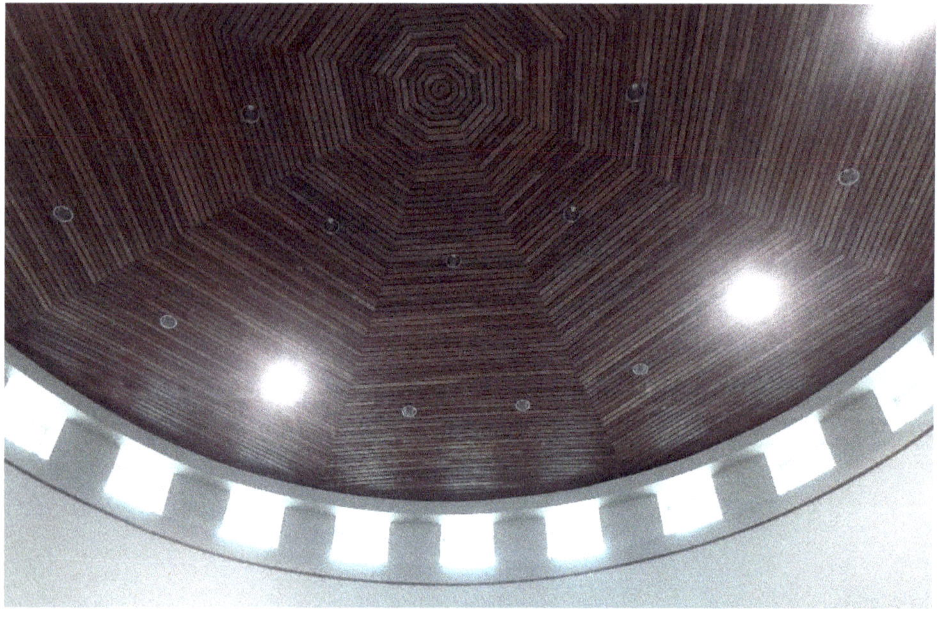

Ceiling in the El Progreso Memorial Library

Chapter Nineteen

San Angelo

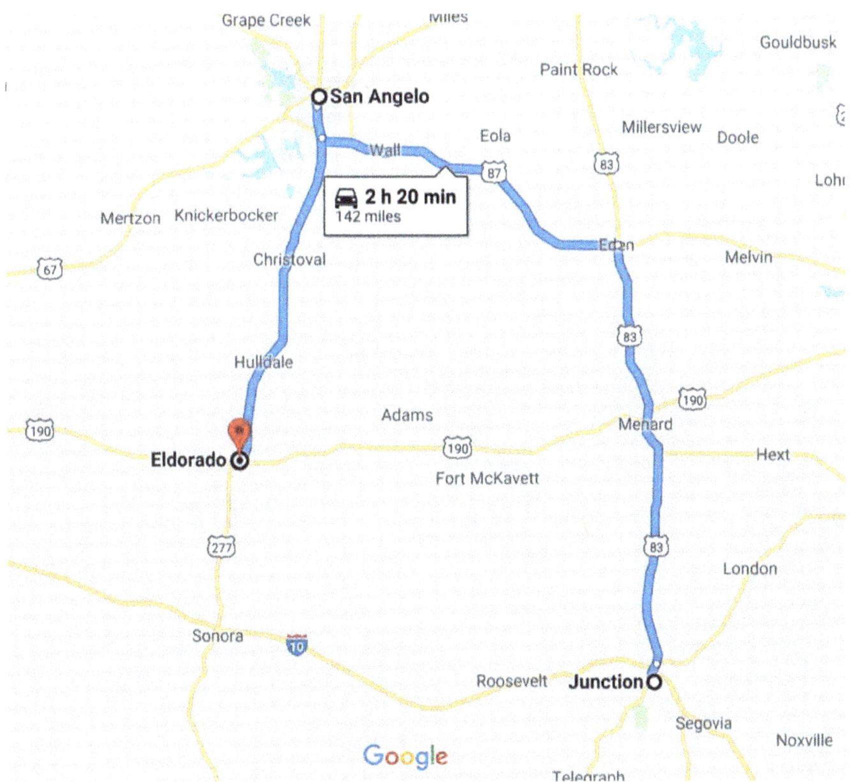

Junction to San Angelo to Eldorado

We woke to the gift of a hotel room for two nights—in San Angelo!

Wiping sleep from our eyes, we hit the road again.

We took two days off from traveling and sight-seeing. Our hotel room was one of those extended-stay suites, so I grabbed a few groceries from a nearby HEB, and we stayed in the room for every moment it was ours, keeping our feet propped up and doing much of nothing except sleeping. Tim got caught up on Andy Griffith episodes and game shows, and I got caught up on laundry and emails—almost.

I know there's a lesson in all of this. Even though we're not punching a time clock, we'd been working hard getting from one place to the next, pushing ourselves out of our comfort zones and staying on the move. We needed rest from all of it.

But after a nap or two, we were ready to hit the road again and explore.

San Angelo is known for murals around town, so we went in search of them.

One of my favorites—on the side of a hair salon, of course!

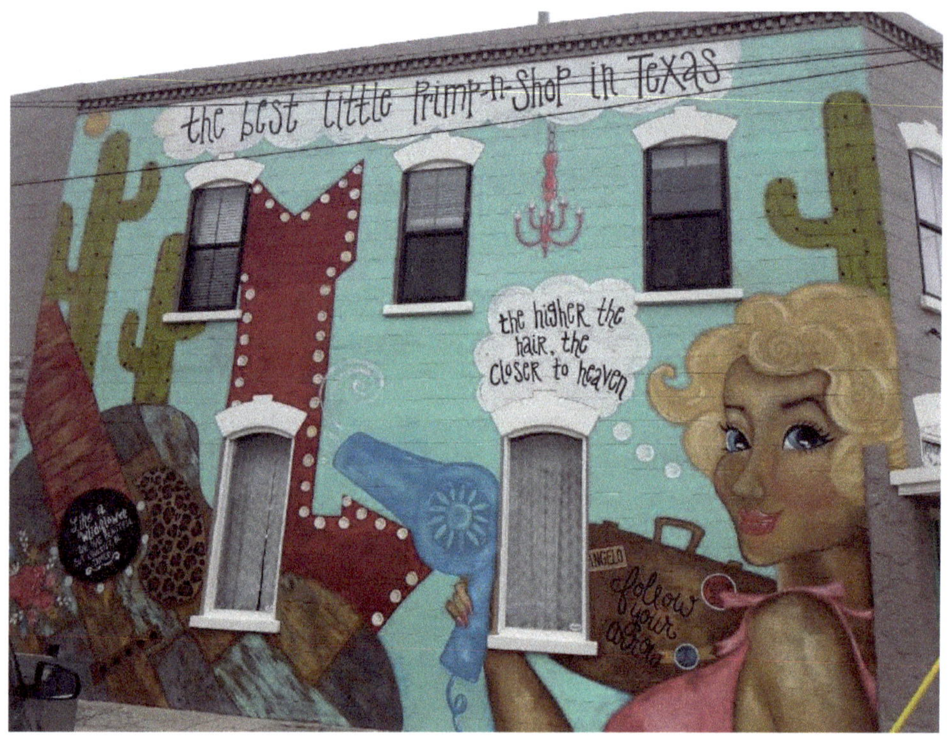

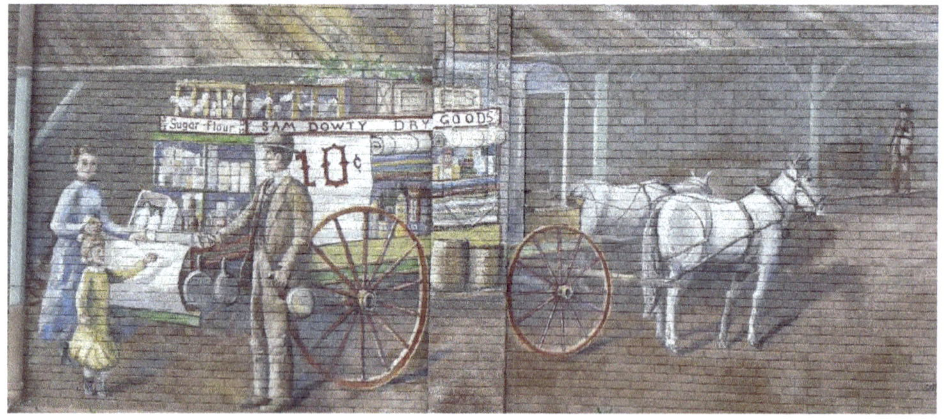

The mural below was so large, I had to divide it into several sections to take photos.

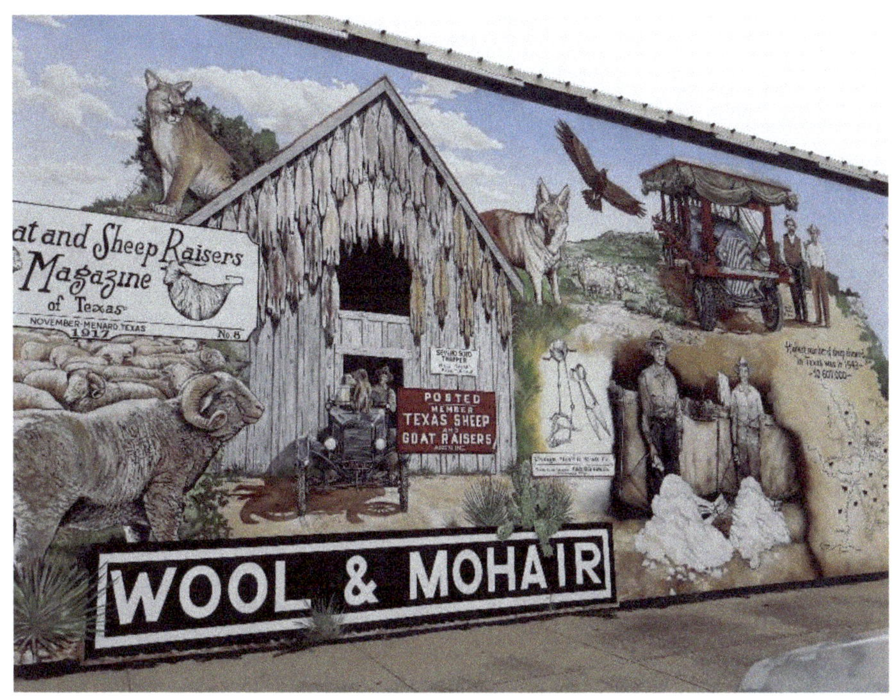

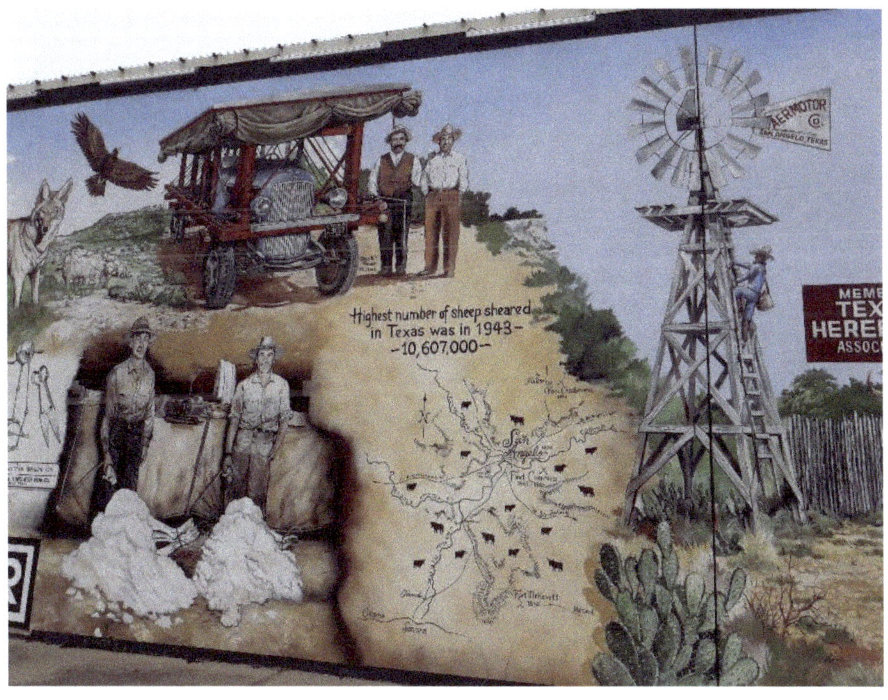

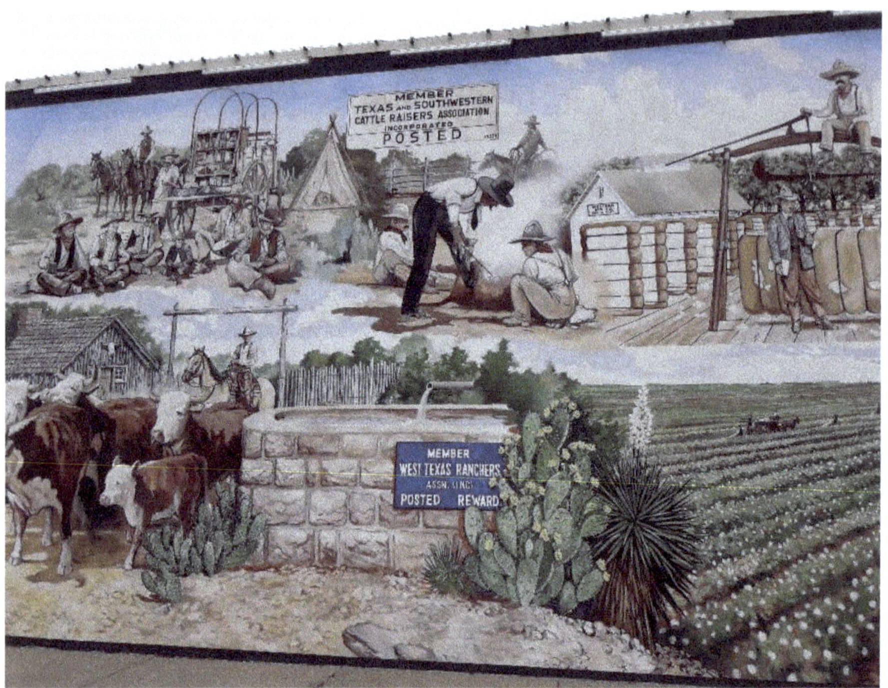

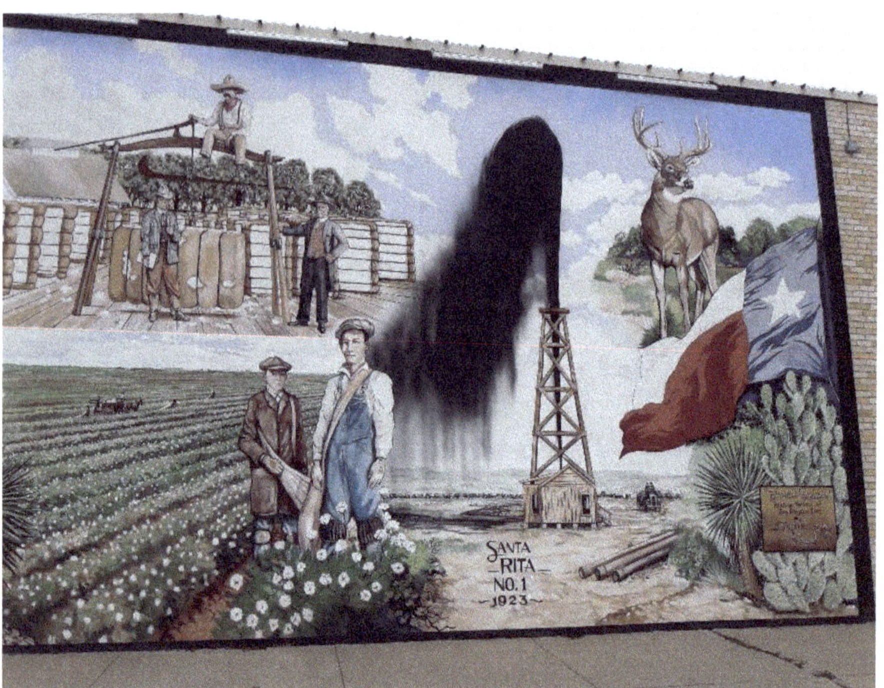

After chasing down all the murals, we turned on Waze to head toward El Dorado. But before we got out of town, we saw the "Best Burger" sign so we had to stop to check them out. The Lonestar Cheeseburger Company is a food truck that seems to have a permanent location. They've won awards and offer a fun dining experience.

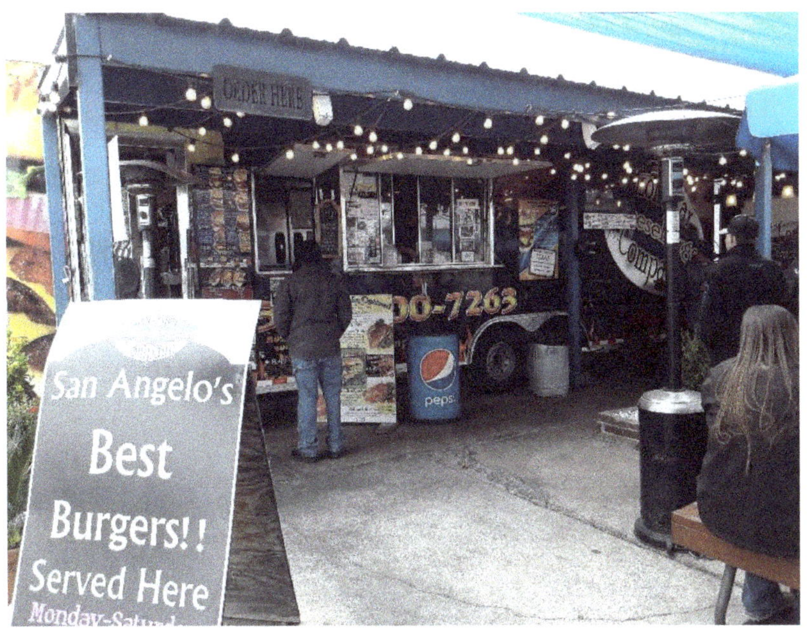

As regular readers of this #LeapFrog journey have already discovered, Tim is a huge western fan, so our travels through the southwest focus on different movies and characters. When we left San Angelo, El Dorado was our destination—Tim still on a search for John Wayne.

El Dorado the town was almost non-existent. We made a pit stop at a convenience store and asked the clerk about anything special in town that we should see. She told us, "Nothing. There's nothing here. What you see right here is it."

Tim was disappointed, but we drove around town anyway, and discovered a beautiful building.

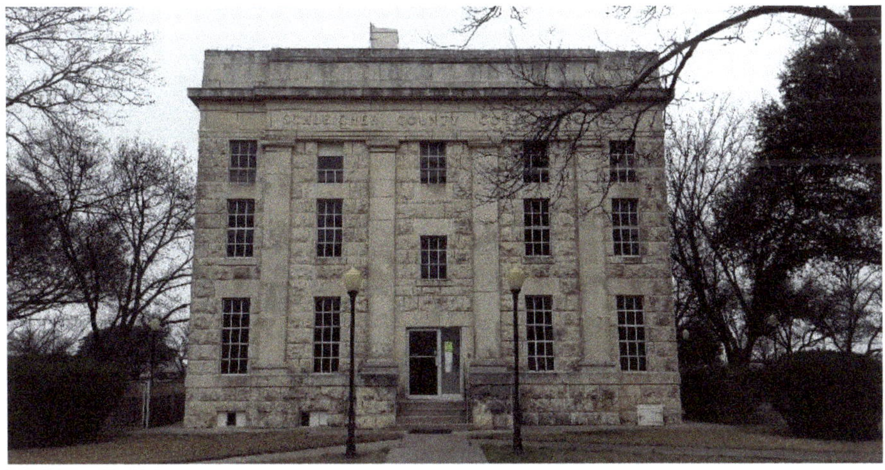

On one corner of the courthouse property, we found this tribute and reminder:

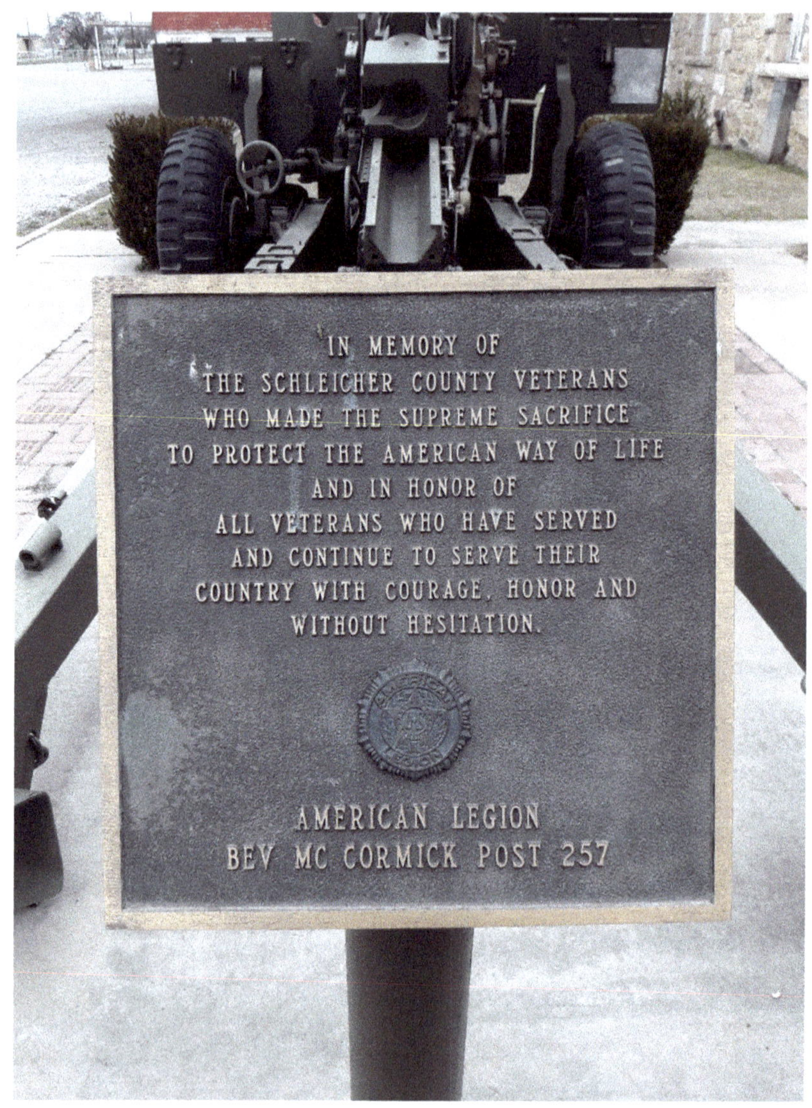

God bless our veterans for protecting our "American way of life."
We're grateful.

From the FROG Files:

It's currently 32 degrees - six degrees warmer than yesterday morning - but this morning, there's a layer of ice on the swimming pool we see outside our window.

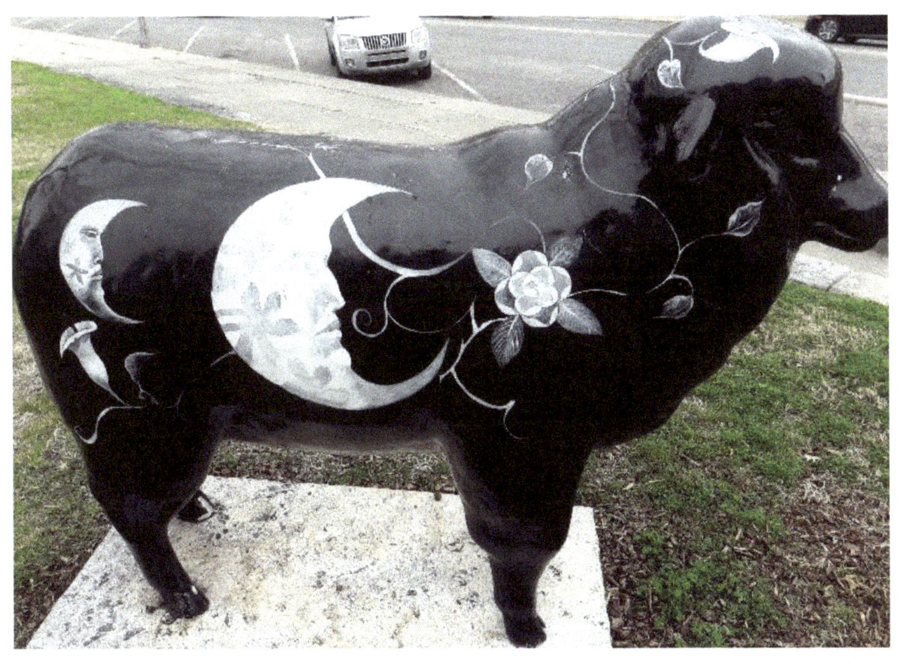

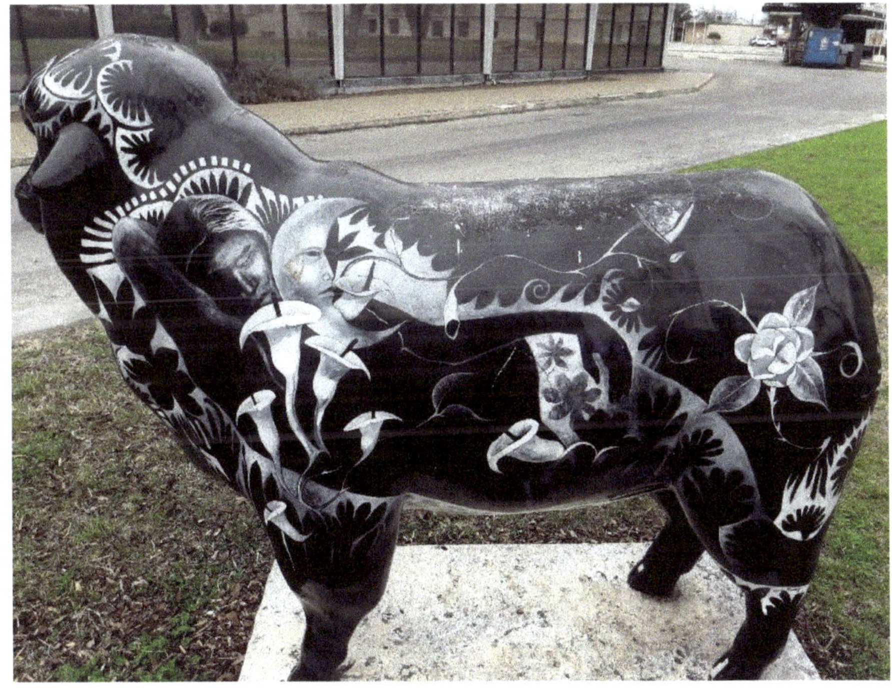

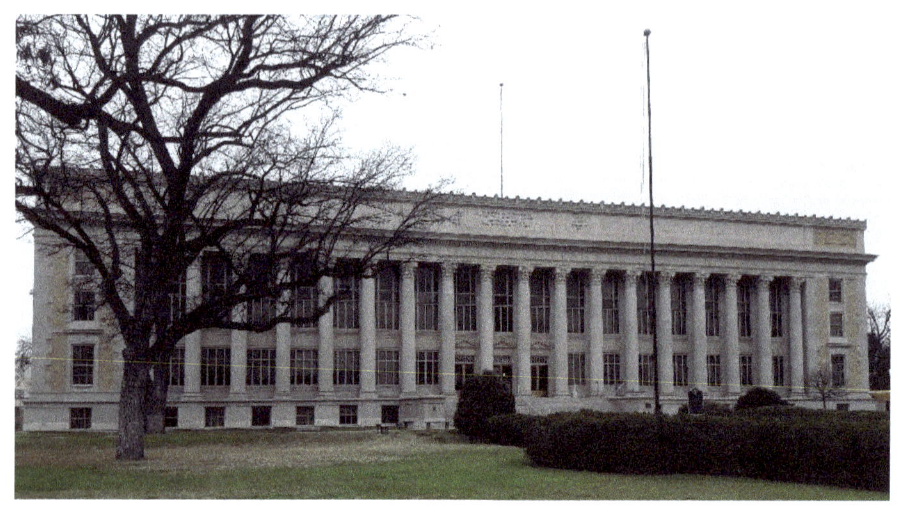

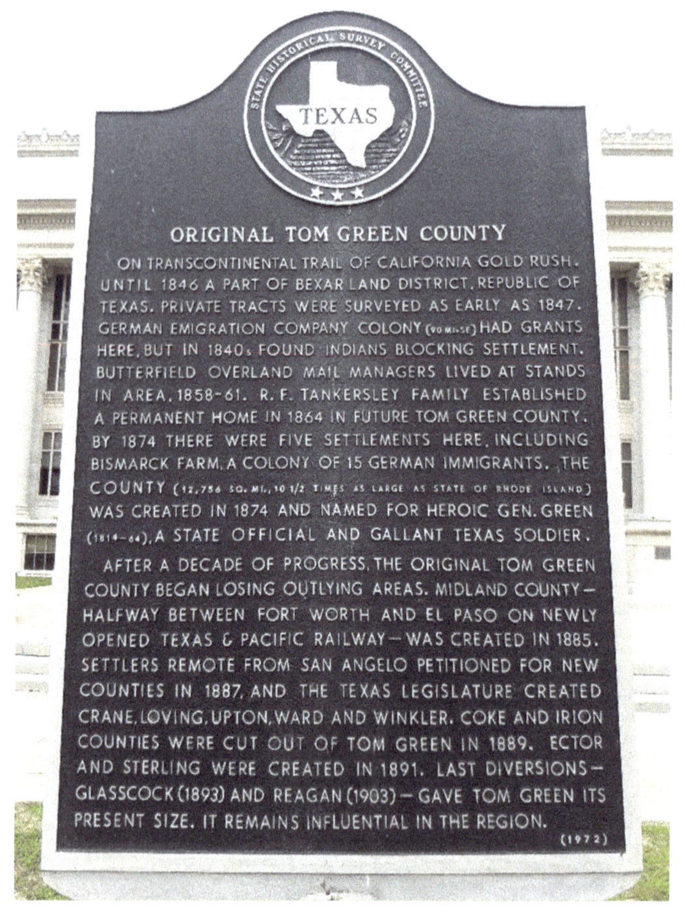

STATE HISTORICAL SURVEY COMMITTEE
TEXAS

ORIGINAL TOM GREEN COUNTY

ON TRANSCONTINENTAL TRAIL OF CALIFORNIA GOLD RUSH.
UNTIL 1846 A PART OF BEXAR LAND DISTRICT, REPUBLIC OF
TEXAS. PRIVATE TRACTS WERE SURVEYED AS EARLY AS 1847.
GERMAN EMIGRATION COMPANY COLONY (90 MI.-SE) HAD GRANTS
HERE, BUT IN 1840s FOUND INDIANS BLOCKING SETTLEMENT.
BUTTERFIELD OVERLAND MAIL MANAGERS LIVED AT STANDS
IN AREA, 1858-61. R. F. TANKERSLEY FAMILY ESTABLISHED
A PERMANENT HOME IN 1864 IN FUTURE TOM GREEN COUNTY.
BY 1874 THERE WERE FIVE SETTLEMENTS HERE, INCLUDING
BISMARCK FARM, A COLONY OF 15 GERMAN IMMIGRANTS. THE
COUNTY (12,756 SQ. MI., 10 1/2 TIMES AS LARGE AS STATE OF RHODE ISLAND)
WAS CREATED IN 1874 AND NAMED FOR HEROIC GEN. GREEN
(1814-64), A STATE OFFICIAL AND GALLANT TEXAS SOLDIER.

AFTER A DECADE OF PROGRESS, THE ORIGINAL TOM GREEN
COUNTY BEGAN LOSING OUTLYING AREAS. MIDLAND COUNTY—
HALFWAY BETWEEN FORT WORTH AND EL PASO ON NEWLY
OPENED TEXAS & PACIFIC RAILWAY—WAS CREATED IN 1885.
SETTLERS REMOTE FROM SAN ANGELO PETITIONED FOR NEW
COUNTIES IN 1887, AND THE TEXAS LEGISLATURE CREATED
CRANE, LOVING, UPTON, WARD AND WINKLER. COKE AND IRION
COUNTIES WERE CUT OUT OF TOM GREEN IN 1889. ECTOR
AND STERLING WERE CREATED IN 1891. LAST DIVERSIONS—
GLASSCOCK (1893) AND REAGAN (1903)—GAVE TOM GREEN ITS
PRESENT SIZE. IT REMAINS INFLUENTIAL IN THE REGION.
(1972)

Chapter Twenty

Change of Terrain and a Midnight Visitor

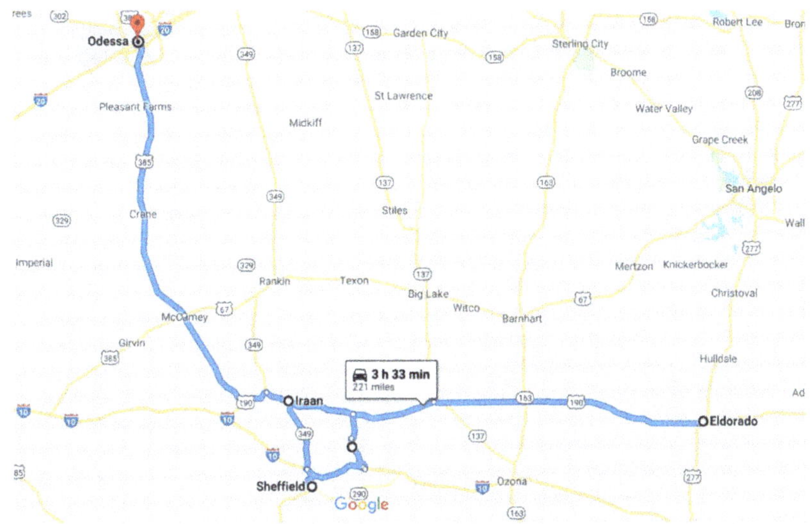

Eldorado to Iraan and Odessa

Once we got west of Austin, the Texas terrain became flat and sage-brushy. As we left San Angelo and El Dorado, the terrain was still the same, but somewhere along US-190, the horizon changed dramatically. I almost wrecked the car wanting to get a picture before it was too late.

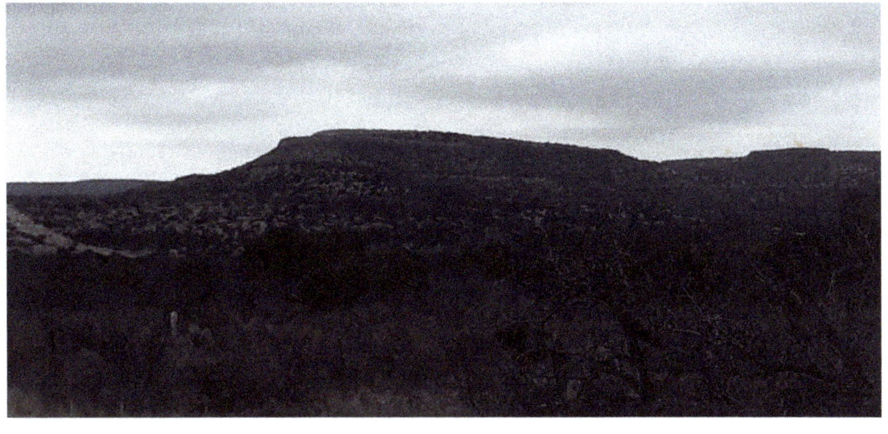

Mesa!

We'd never seen mesas before, and apparently, the state of Texas knew that, because almost immediately we found a picnic area where we could pull over safely to snap a few pictures. (Notice the clouds—still no sunshine!)

Unfortunately, that picnic area was loaded with drug paraphernalia, so we moved on.

We'd found an overnight rest stop on freecampsites.net, so we made way for I-10 in Iraan. The town is off the interstate a few miles, but we didn't realize that until we'd passed through and reached the interstate. It was still early, so we decided to gas up the car before settling in for the night—but there were no gas stations at that exit. We drove to the next town—going east toward Sheffield, which seemed to be pretty much a ghost town. We noticed residents getting into their car on the main road we were driving, so I rolled down my window and asked for the nearest gas station. She told me it was in Iraan—18 miles away!

Supply and demand pricing greeted us in our second visit to Iraan—gas was almost $3 per gallon—the highest price we'd seen the entire trip.

When we finally got back to the rest area, we were delighted to find this beautiful mesa as our view.

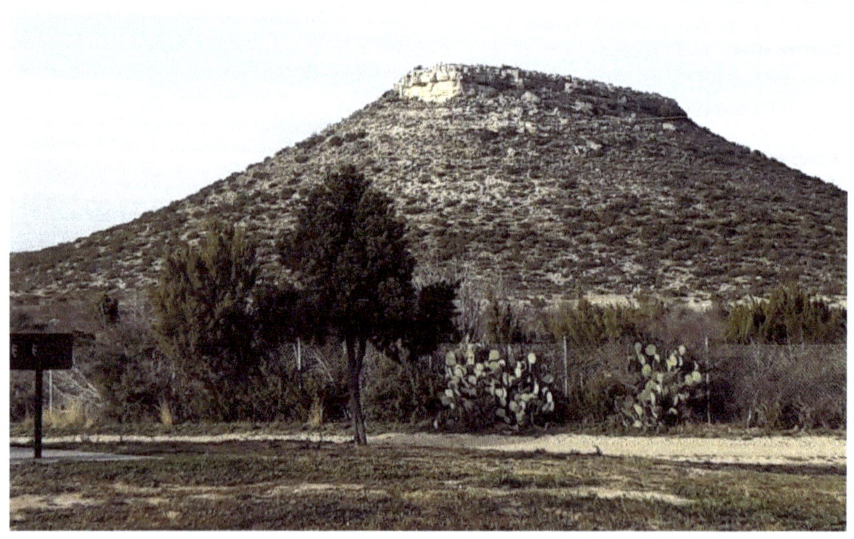

We cooked dinner then settled in for the night. The rest area wasn't busy, so it was a peaceful night.

Around midnight, Tim woke up and planned to use the restroom. He looked outside and decided to wait. A skunk was roaming around the grounds, sniffing at light poles and trash cans and car tires. Tim watched him for about an hour, then dozed off

again.

I knew nothing about the skunk when I woke up at six and

made my own trip to the restroom. Tim told me about it when I got back—I'm thankful I didn't discover it on my own!

We'd gotten a note from a friend overnight, telling us to check out Odessa so we took off.

On the way, we went through the small town of McCamey and found this beautiful tribute.

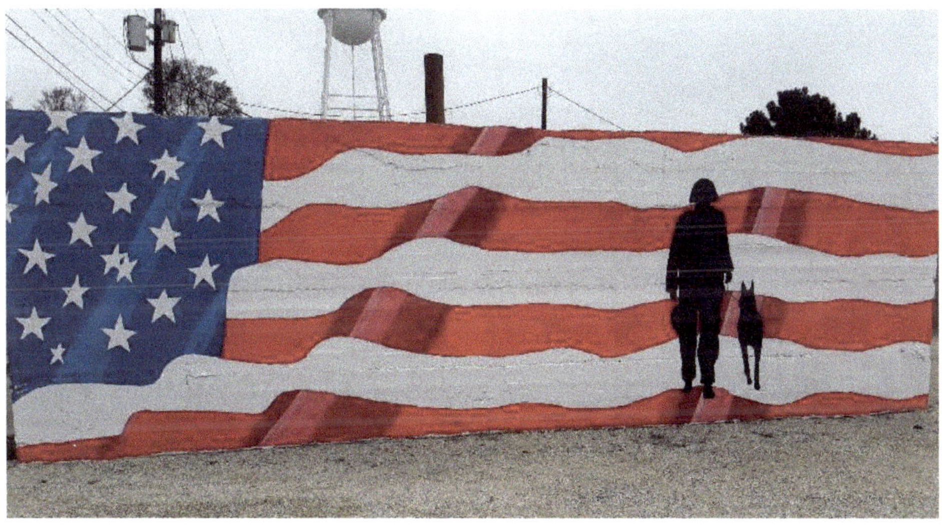

Further down the road, I had to stop to shoot this one:

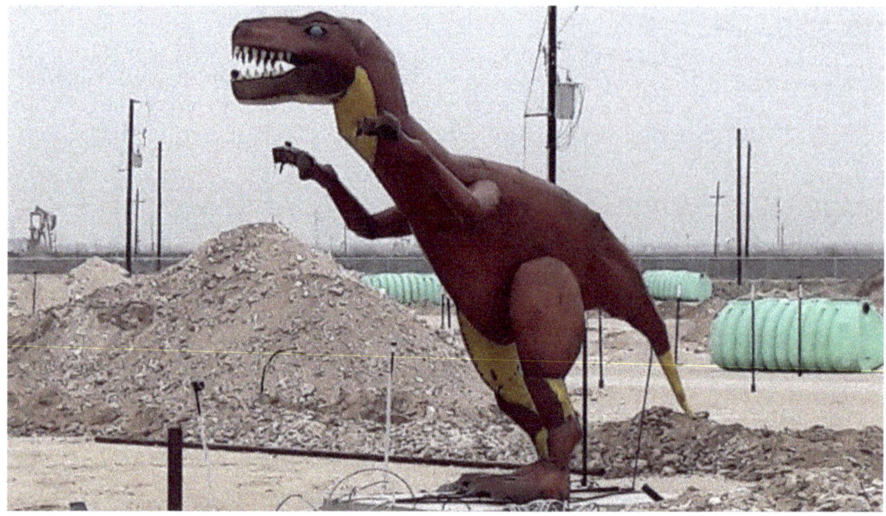

We weren't sure what awaited us in Odessa. My friend had told us to check out the Shakespeare Theater at the school, but that's all the information I had, so during a pit stop, I searched for other "must-sees" and learned about the Chris Kyle memorial.

The theater was closed when we arrived, so I could only snap photos from outside the gate.

The Chris Kyle memorial was a little harder to find because it first appears to be a rather odd location—in a busy retail location—but then when I saw the VA hospital right next door, it made more sense.

If you're wondering who Chris Kyle is, watch the movie *American Sniper*—he was a Navy SEAL and an American hero.

The first word I used to describe this memorial to my son was "intelligent"—it's a thought-provoking, thoughtful, intelligent site.

Our final stop in Odessa was a fun break.

From the FROG Files:

Temps are dropping tonight, down to 29. That's our coldest night out yet.

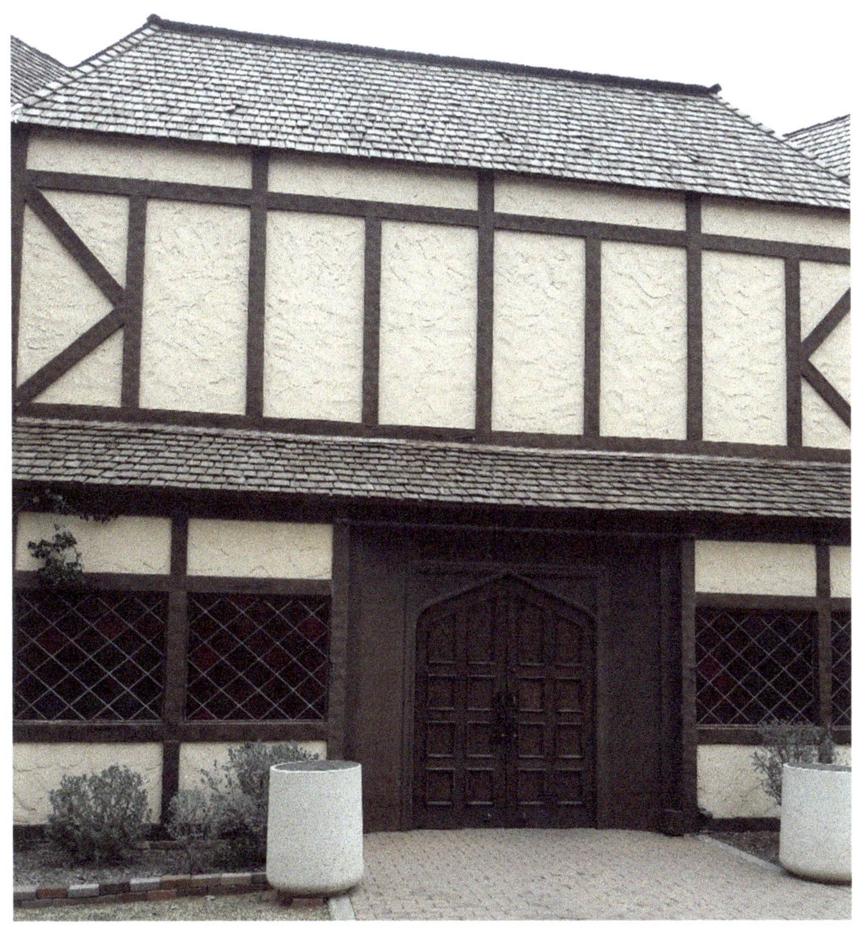

Above: Shakespeare Theatre; Below: Chris Kyle memorial

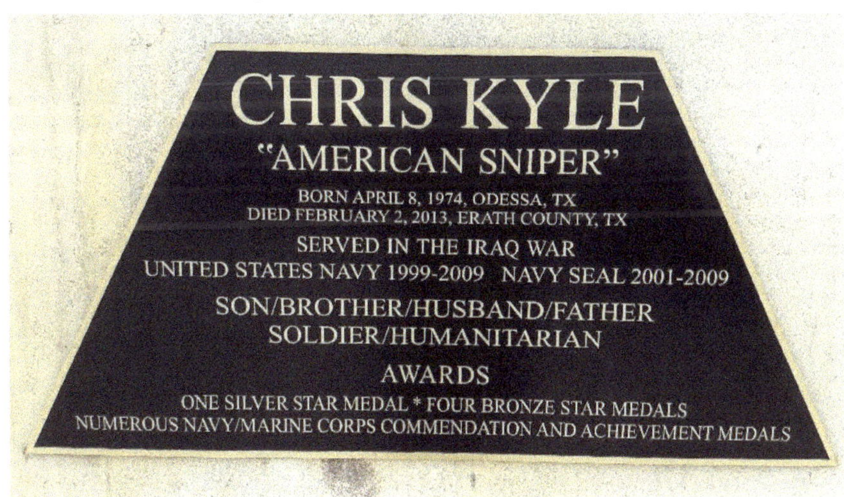

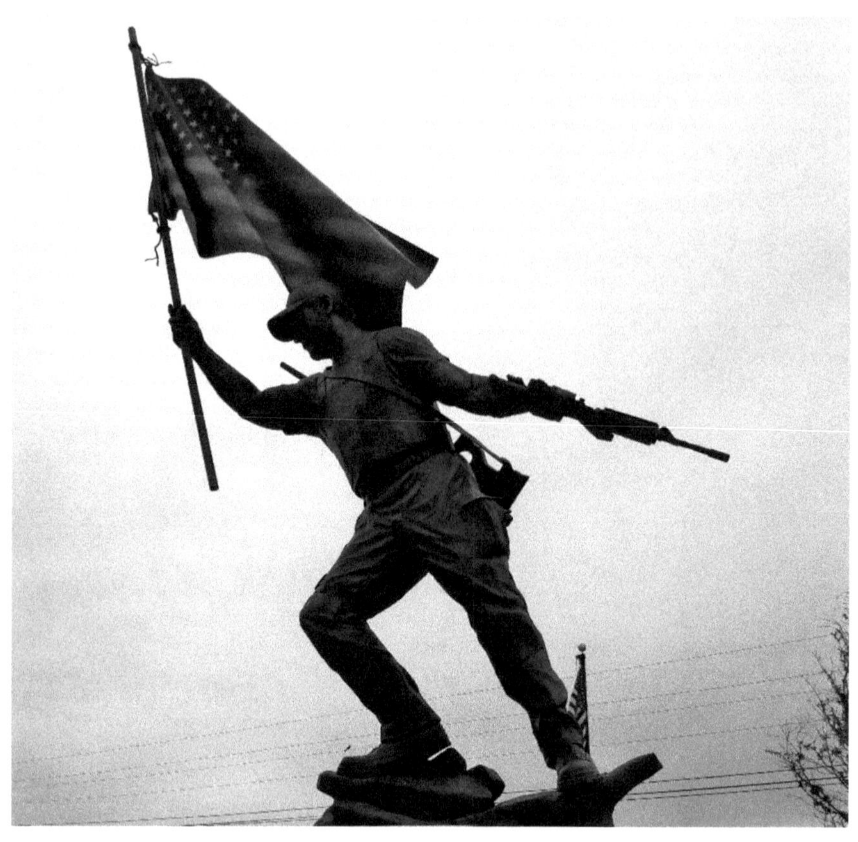

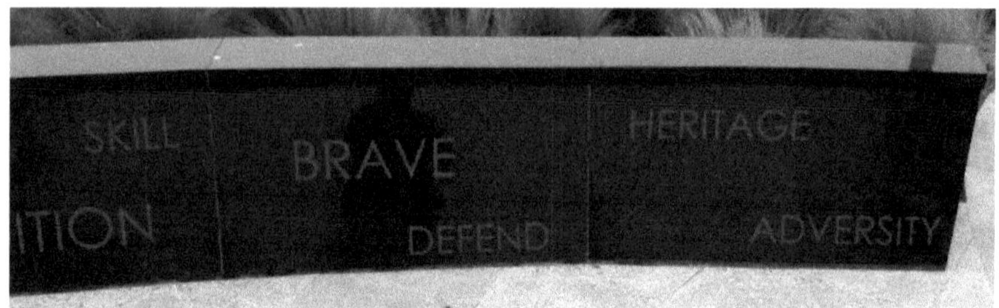
SKILL
BRAVE
HERITAGE
ITION
DEFEND
ADVERSITY

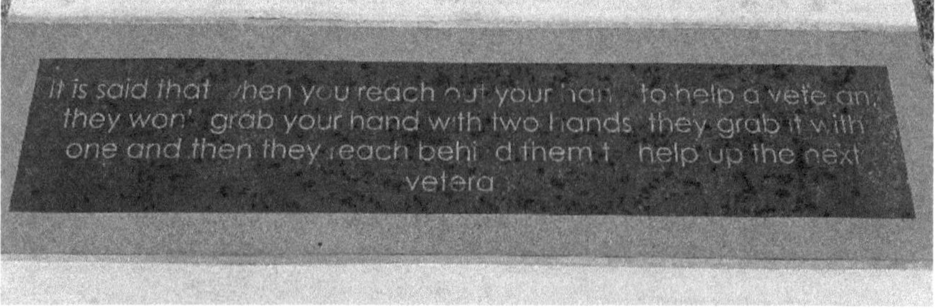
It is said that when you reach out your hand to help a veteran,
they won't grab your hand with two hands, they grab it with
one and then they reach behind them to help up the next
veteran

And then we discovered the Texas Stonehenge, and my very own Samson!

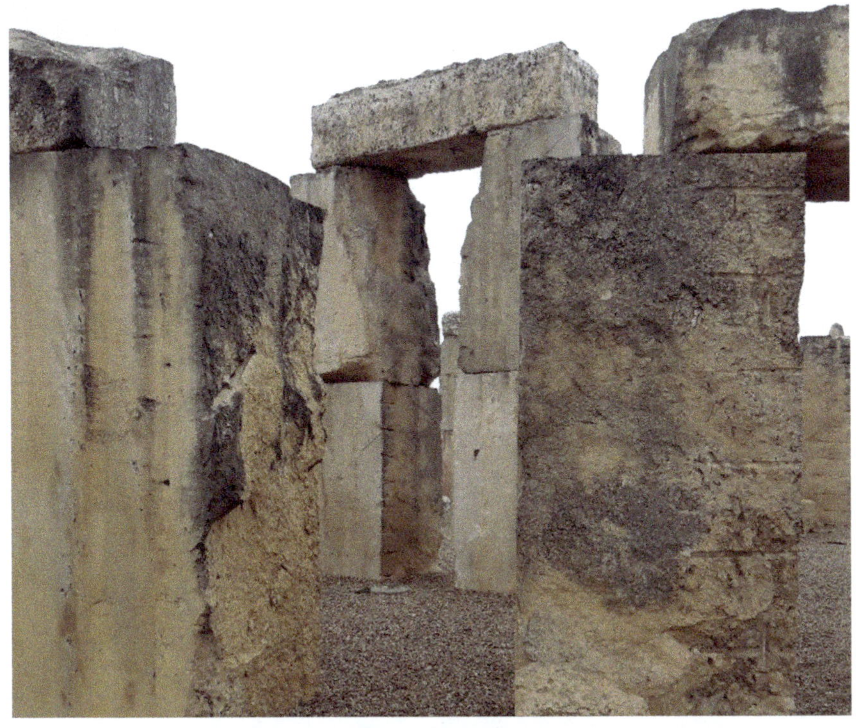

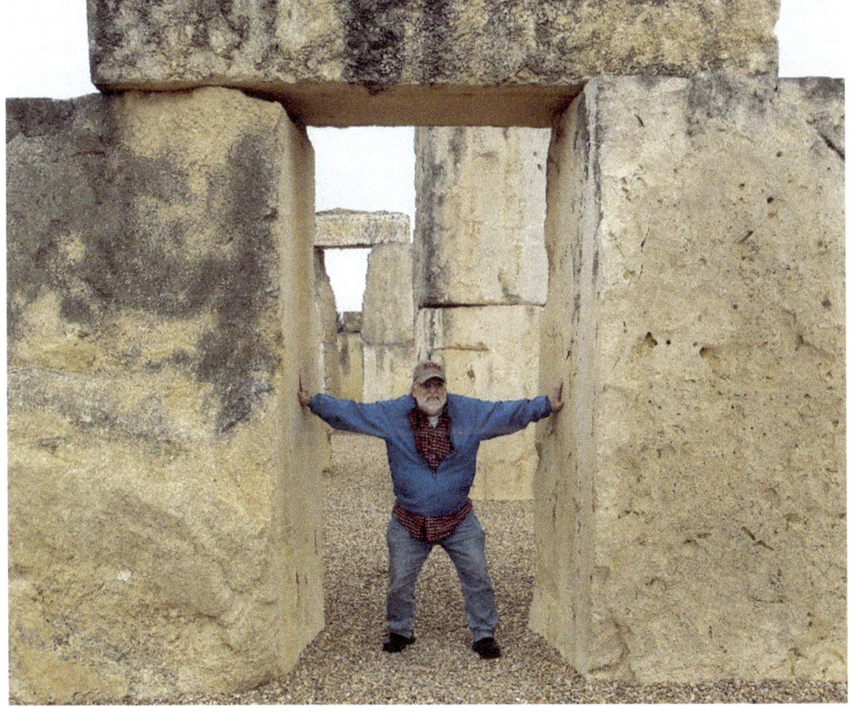

Sample Artwork:

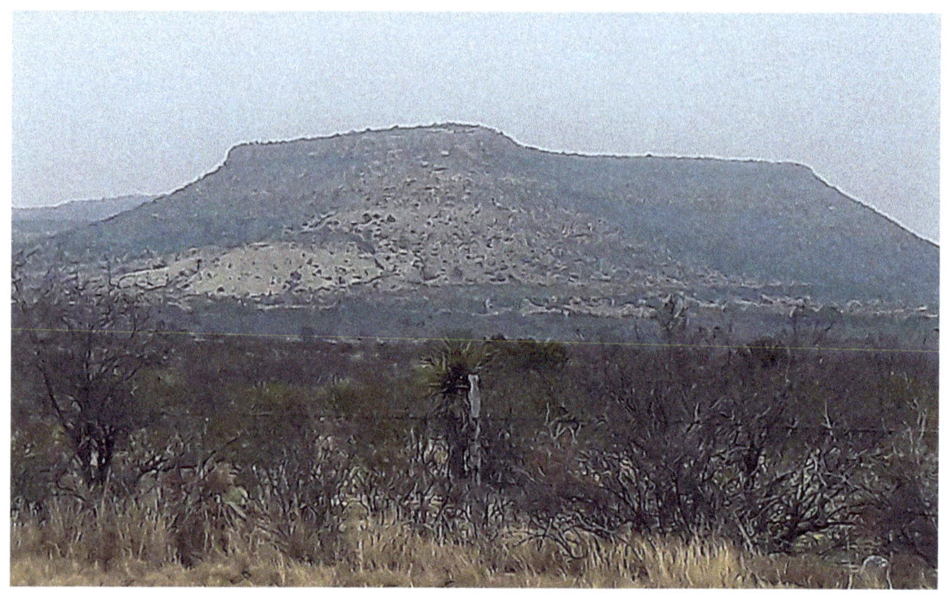

West Texas Mesa 

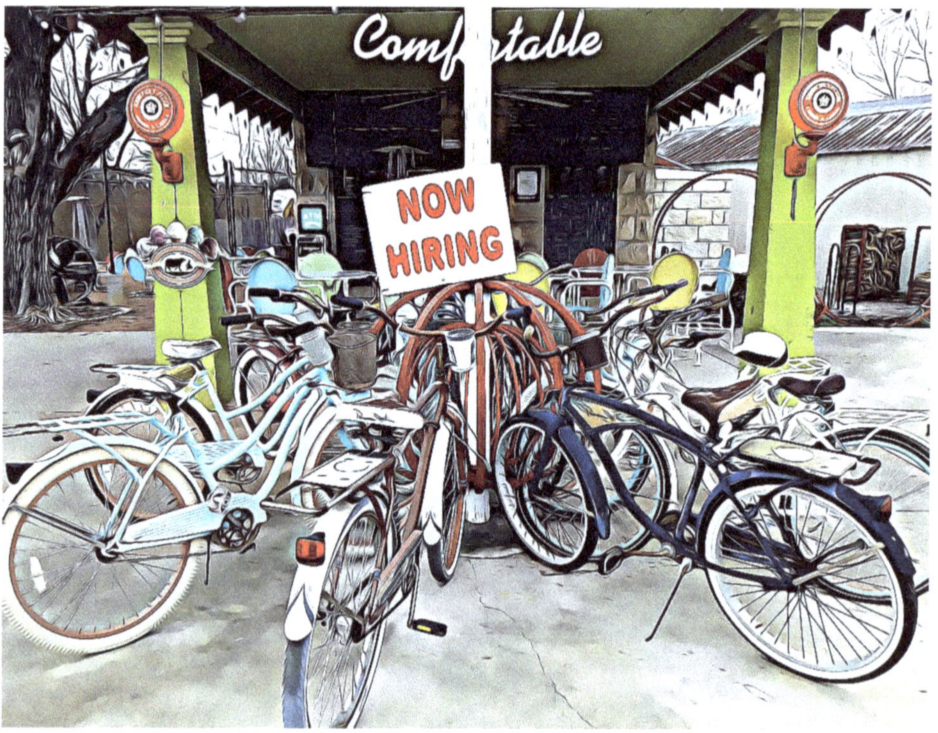

Bicycles in Comfort Texas

Chapter Twenty-One

Settling into New Mexico

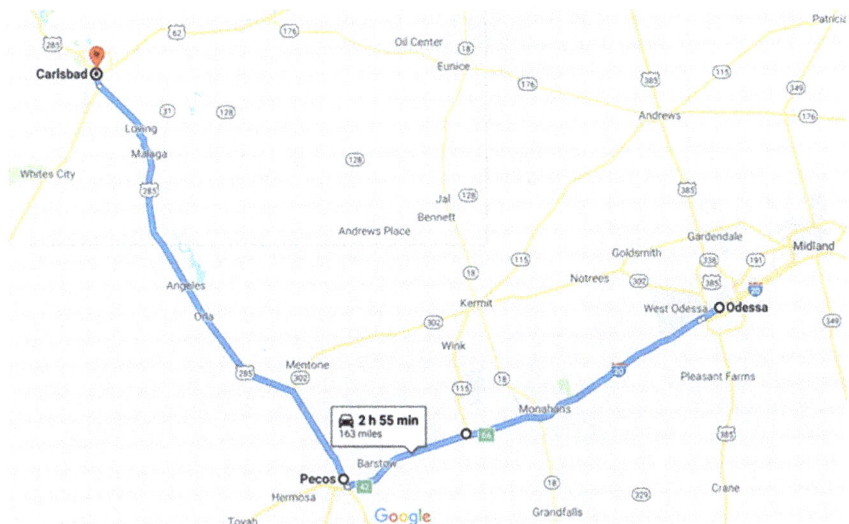

Odessa, Texas to Carlsbad, New Mexico

Feels like it took forever to get out of Texas. Confession: the night before we crossed the state line, I realized I was afraid of New Mexico. I have no idea where that fear came from—I've longed to go to Santa Fe forever, and I've never really been afraid to go anywhere else, so being afraid of New Mexico sure seems ridiculous. One of my friends teased that it was like entering a foreign country, and I recognized some of the same feelings I had the first time I went to Europe. I was experiencing fear of the unknown for the first time since we left home.

After roaming all over Odessa, we continued pressing west, stopping to car camp overnight at a rest stop in Pyote, TX. The rest area was pretty and quiet, but after the previous rest stop skunk, I was cautious about what we might discover. But this time, we had a different kind of visitor: bunny rabbits! My photos are too grainy to share, but we watched two bunnies play and hop and chase each other for about an hour in pure delight.

This rest area was a great one. They offered educational information in a fun way for families.

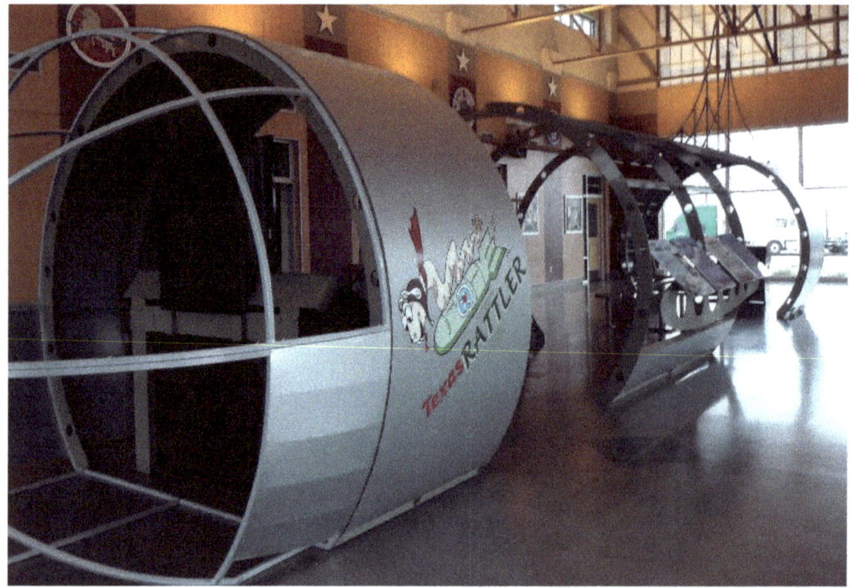

The next morning, we intended to explore Pecos a bit, but instead, we grabbed a quick breakfast, and started for Carlsbad.

Friends had told us we should enter the state from the northwest side, instead of the south, but since we were already south, we, unfortunately, didn't take their advice.

Oil fields surround Carlsbad. The land is scruffy, and the air reeks of oil and gas. The roads leading into Carlsbad from the south are under construction, so the first "face" of New Mexico was not a positive one for us. But we stayed in town for three days and discovered quite a few treasures.

But first we had a couple of maintenance issues we needed to address.

My phone—and camera—began giving me a lot of problems, and since it was an older phone, I was also running out of space. As soon as we got to Carlsbad, I found a Metro store, and upgraded my phone (for only the $15 activation fee, thanks to one of their great promotions!)

And tires. We sorely needed new tires. We'd left home shy of needing them, and after all the miles, it was time. We'd been told as long as we were at 5/32, we could hold off, but we knew the tread was less than that, so we shopped around and ended up at Walmart, where they changed them out within an hour. We had them check the old tires, and after measuring, they said the best tread we had anywhere on the tires was a 3/32, but that much was rare. They said most of the tires were at 2/32 or less—and that means BALD. So timing was perfect.

I also had work waiting for me, so we found the Carlsbad library and spent a couple of days there trying to get caught up. I also spent time hunting for free camping sites in the area, primarily through freecampsites.net.

We still hadn't purchased a new tent, so while we were waiting on our tires, we checked out their tent selection, and found one on sale that was much like the one we lost in Texas. We decided to give it another try, because we needed to be horizontal again.

After the car was ready, we drove out to one of the free campsites I'd found. It had a toilet and picnic tables, so I thought we were good to go. But once there, we discovered there were no wind barriers, and the camp sat on a small hill. With a windstorm coming in—and blowing sand—we decided not to stay. But I sure loved the way it looked.

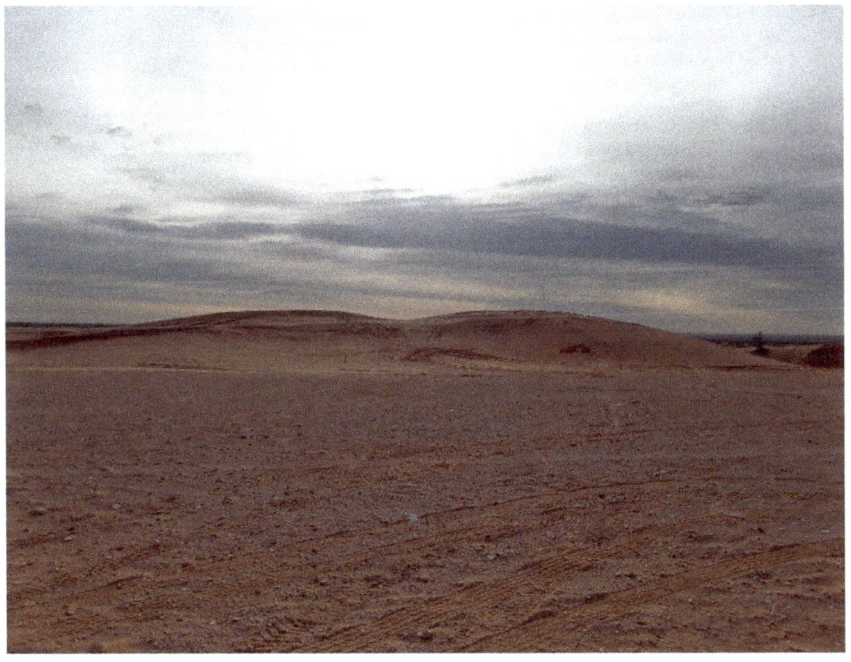

Grateful for the new tires when I looked back to see the tracks we made! Definitely not the Georgia red clay we're used to. This was pure sand!

We then went out to check out a nearby state park, but they were full, so we car camped during our stay in Carlsbad.

From the FROG Files:

We are in Carlsbad, NM - my first new state since we started this journey. I'm still not used to Central Time, so it will take a while to convert to the mountain time. Thankfully, the phones change for us, so that will help my brain adjust eventually.

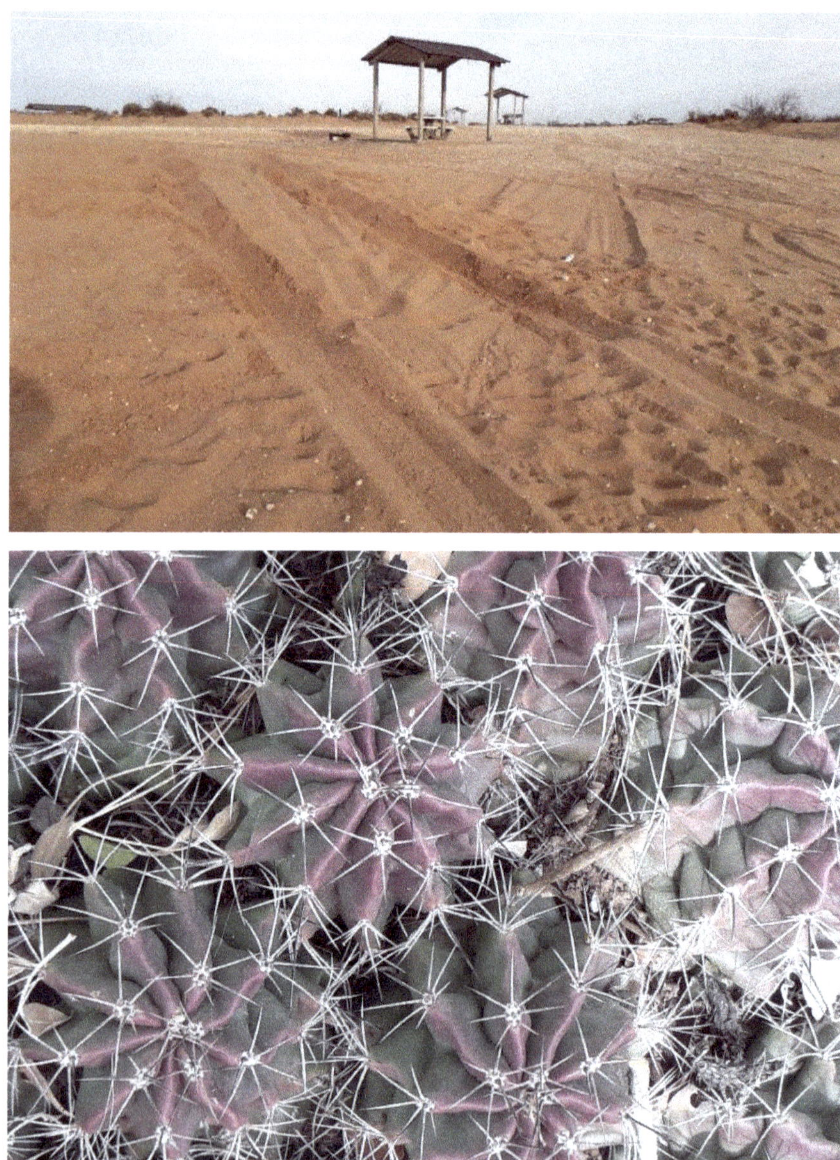

Chapter Twenty-Two

Exploring Carlsbad's Treasures

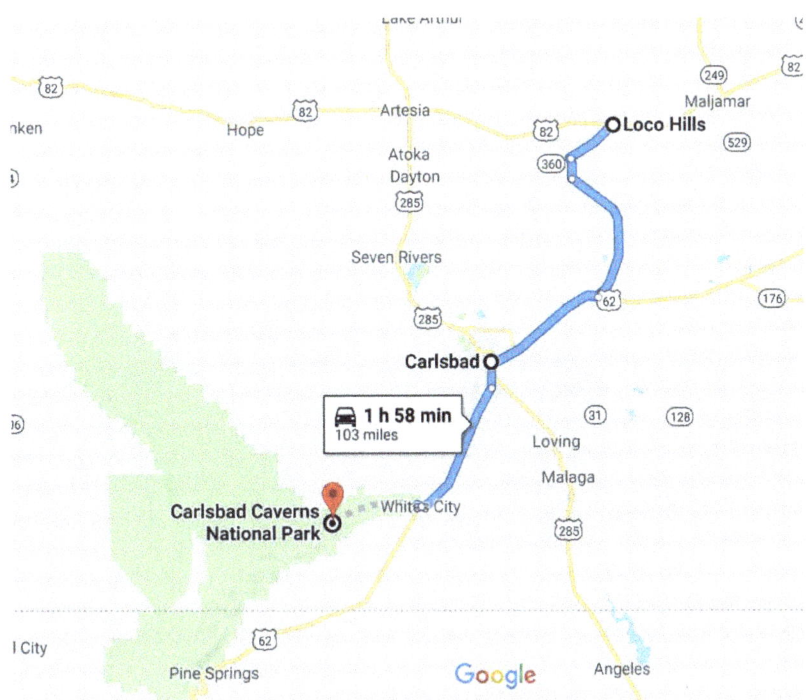

With Carlsbad base, trips to Loco Hills and Carlsbad Caverns

Our first impression of Carlsbad wasn't positive, but the more we explored, the more we found to love.

My favorite find was the Pecos River Village Recreation Center, which we discovered rather by "accident" (if you believe such a thing.)

We were in search of—and in desperate need of—showers. When I saw a sign for a rec center, we drove there to see what they had to offer.

In the parking lot, I was greeted by one of the employees and I asked if they had showers available. She said not at this facility, but there were showers in the bathhouses across the river from where we were standing—and still part of the city facilities. She then told me more about the Rec Center and invited us to come hang out any time we wanted. Later that afternoon, we did exactly that, and found the place to be an example of what other cities could/should offer. All generations use this rec center—young mother groups, exercise groups, elderly coffee clubs, teens, homeschool groups, homework clubs.

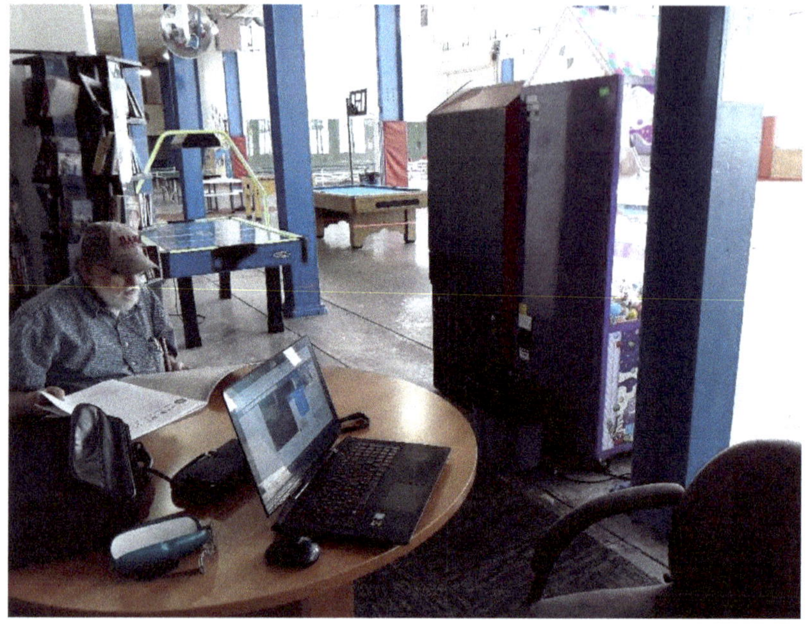

We located the bathhouses, and Tim found the showers for both of us. He'd found the men's shower, but I didn't turn enough corners in the women's restroom to find the single shower. When the restrooms were empty, he went in the women's shower as I stood guard outside and he found the women's shower for me. Ha!

Tim took a shower in the men's restroom—cold water—but I didn't feel comfortable doing so—there were no doors or curtains—just a shower tucked into the corner away from everything else. It probably would have been private, but I'm extremely self-conscious, and did not want to risk anyone walking in on me. (I don't want to traumatize anyone!)

Next to the bathhouses, the city offers a water park that looks like great fun for warmer weather. The whole area on both sides of the river were maintained well and quite beautiful, even in the middle of winter.

On one of our final days in Carlsbad, we finally drove out to the Caverns—a long drive, with hard, high winds fighting us the whole way, which made me start watching the weather again.

Carlsbad Caverns was immense, which was expected. I hadn't thought about how deep in the ground they are but learned moments before we got on the elevator to take us down.

Tim had been having more and more difficulty getting around, so I wasn't sure we could do the caverns at all, but I researched before we went, and learned that we could take the elevator down into the Big Cave, and could walk as much or as little as we wanted at that point.

We went as far as the shortcut, which took us about an hour to make the loop. Tim had to rest at several points along the way, with only one area that was challenging (a slight incline), but the rest was fairly easy to maneuver.

We both grew up in Alabama, going to Cathedral Caverns on field trips, and both of us had been (separately) to different caverns in Virginia, so the caverns themselves weren't as fascinating for us as they probably were for anyone who'd never seen caverns before. But the size amazed us both, and my imagination created all sorts of stories about past, present, and future generations getting trapped in there, and wondering how they'd work their way out.

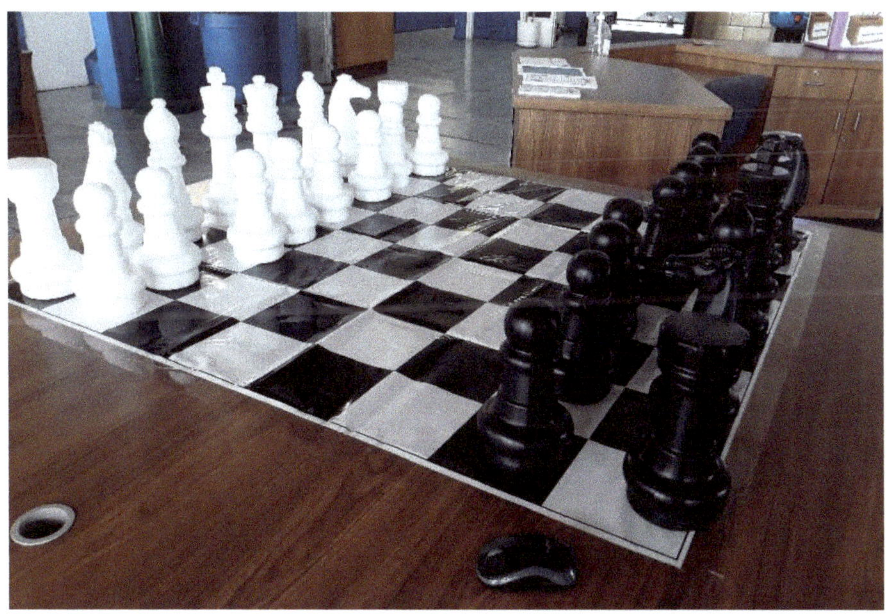

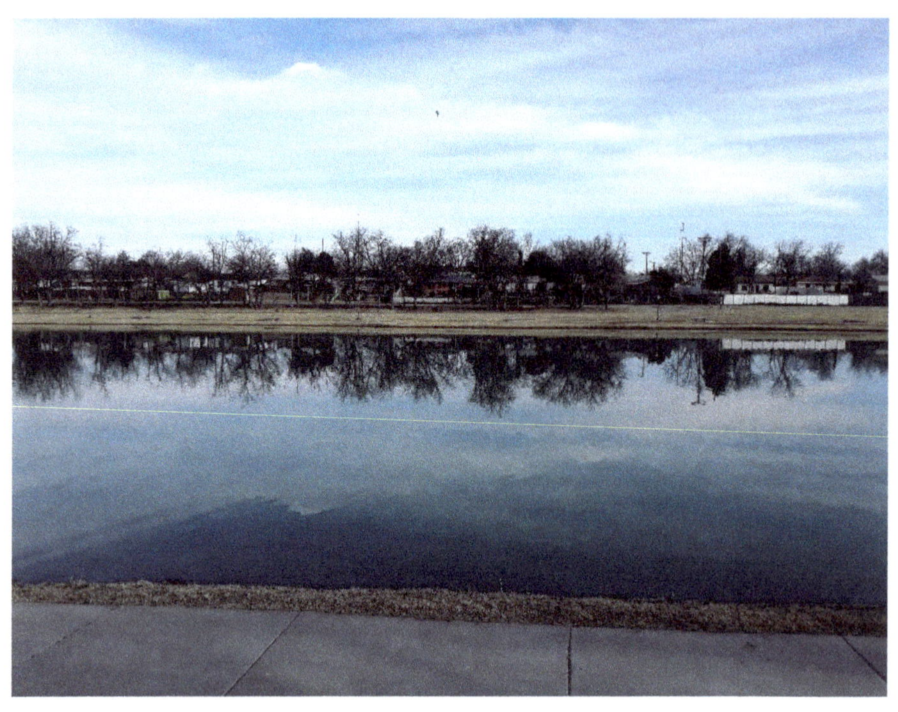

Above: The Pecos River; Below: Skate Park

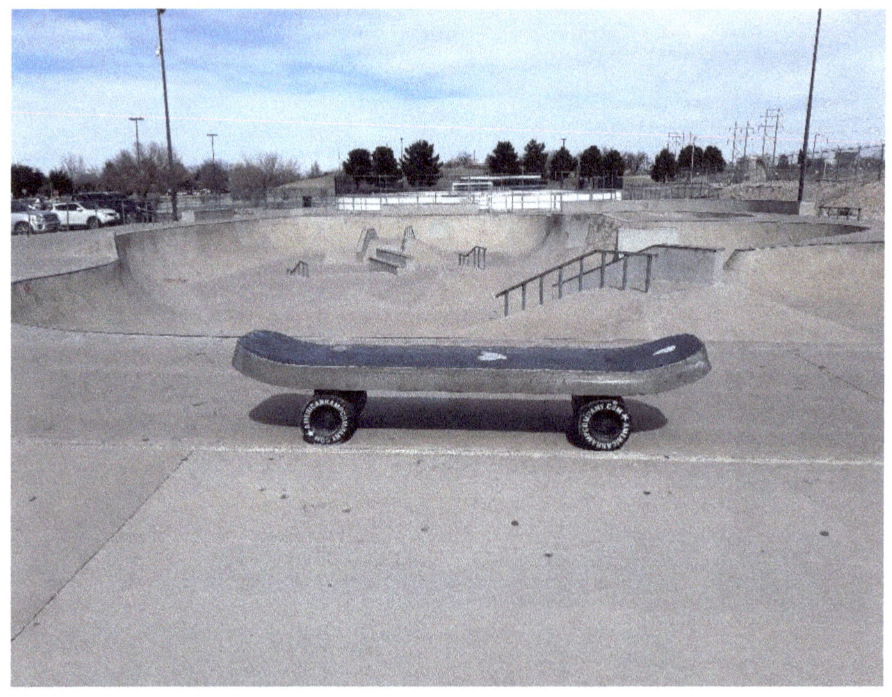

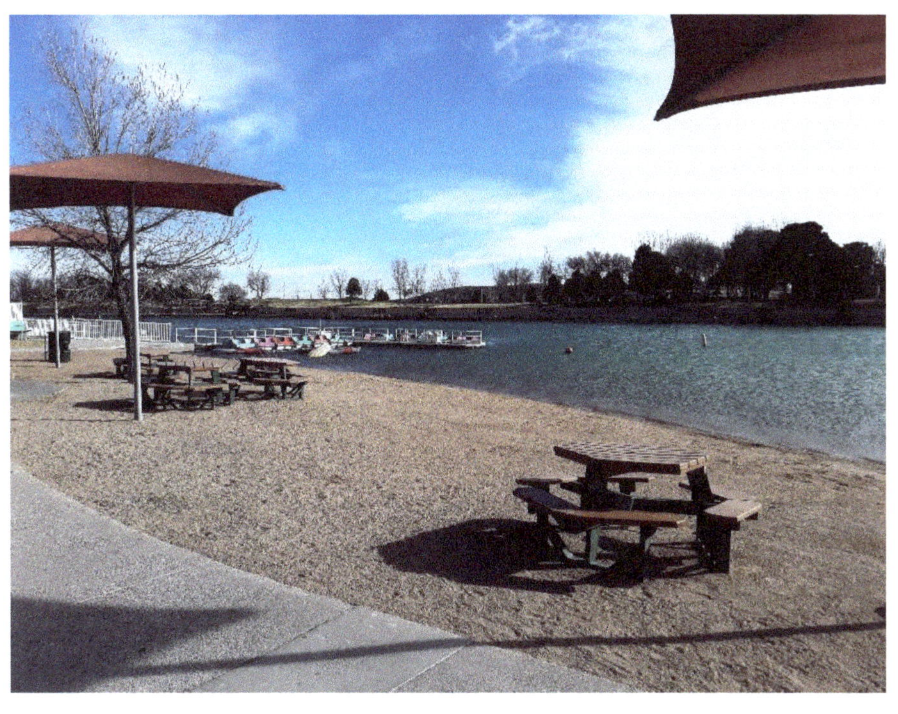

Above: Water park on the Pecos; Below: Recreation Center

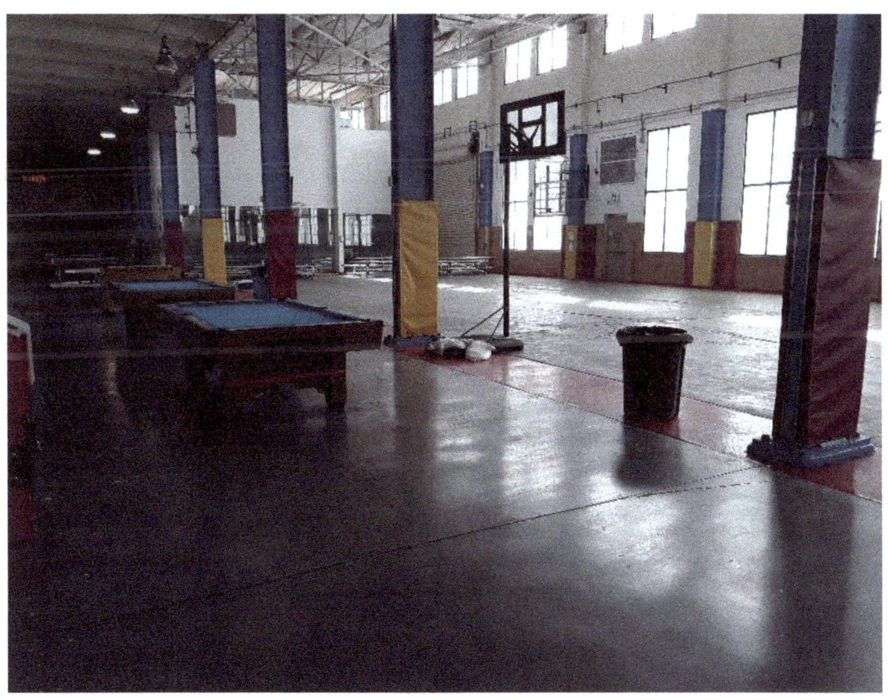

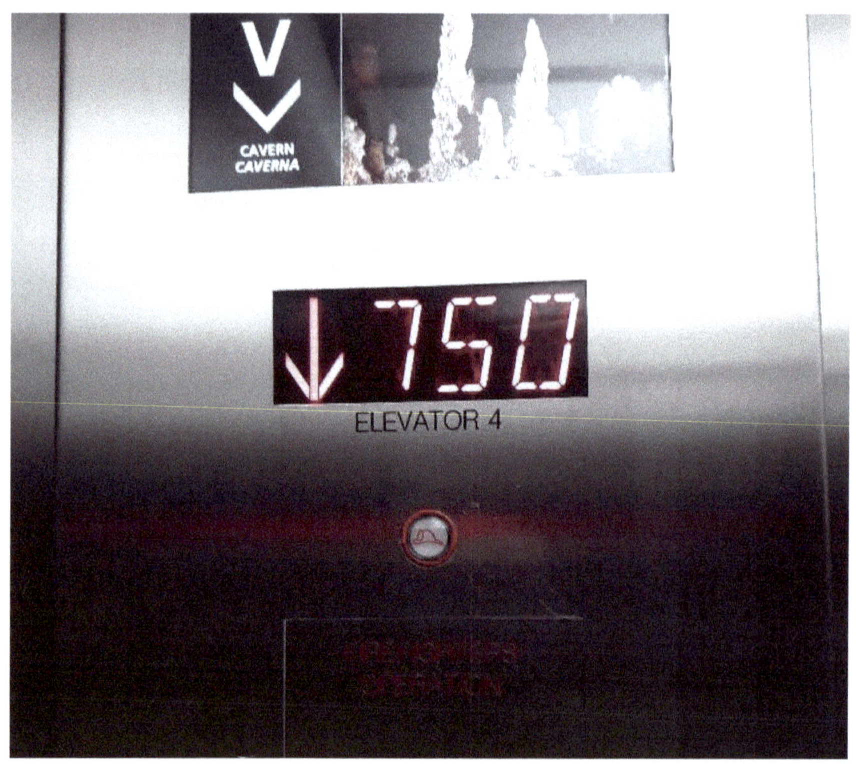

750 feet below the surface at Carlsbad Caverns

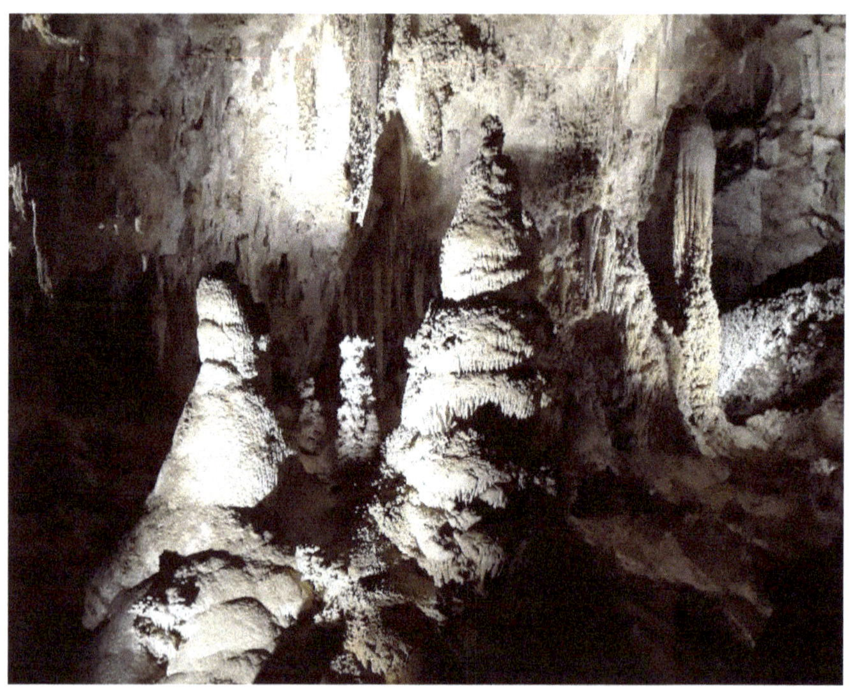

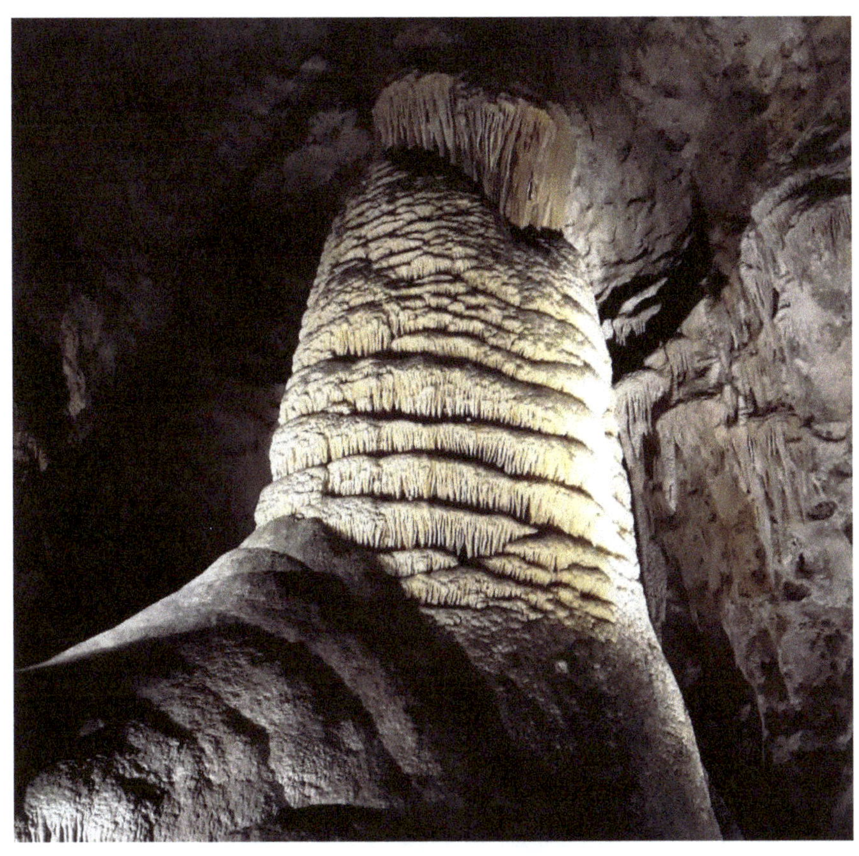

Carlsbad Caverns 📷

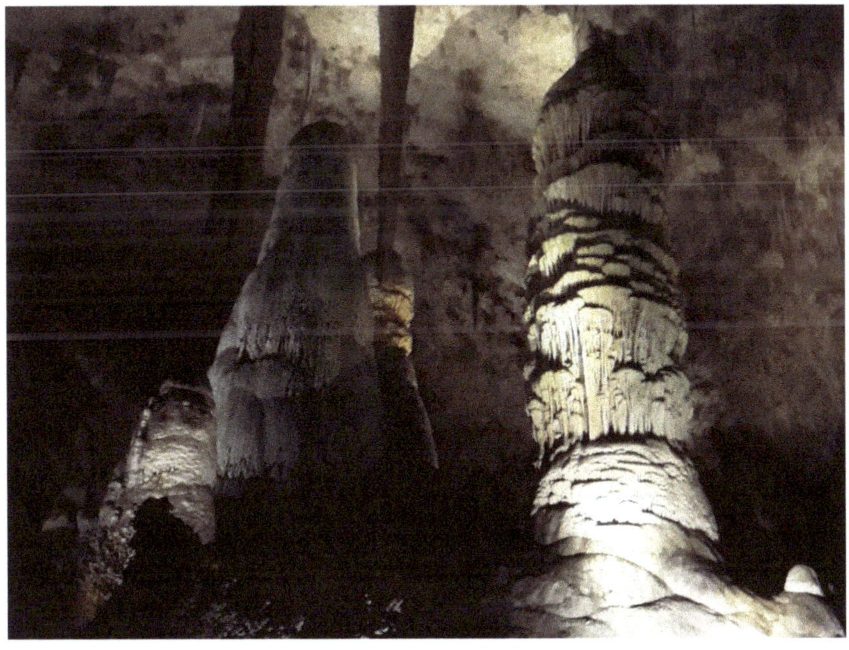

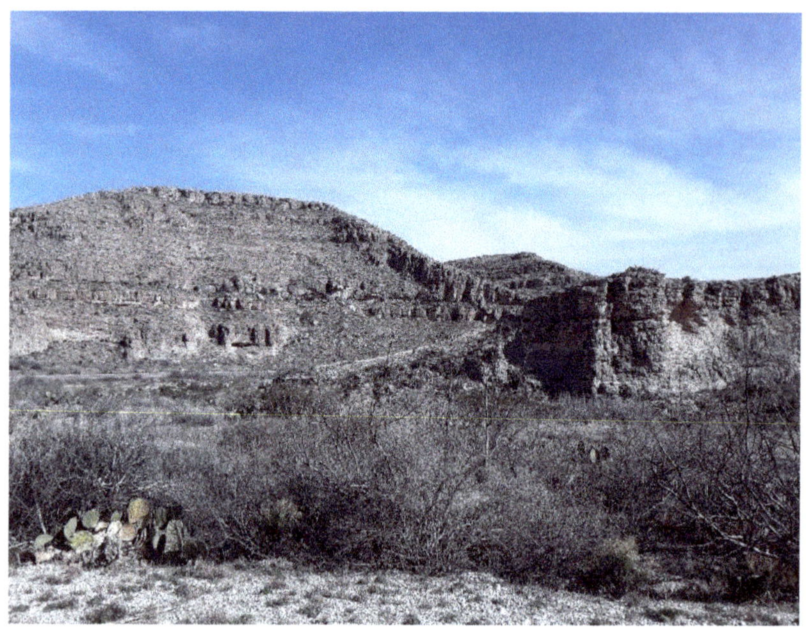

Along the road around Carlsbad Caverns

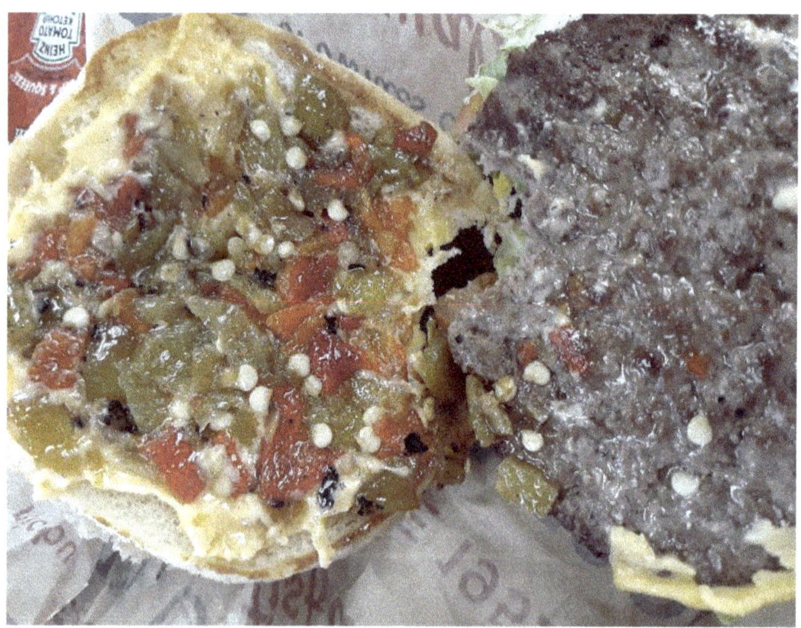

Hatch Green Chile burger – loved the flavors!

From the FROG Files:

We're watching the weather stuff and winds. I thought we were going to head to Guadalupe Mountain National Park, but the winds are supposed to get bad - with gusts up to 80 mph. And they're supposed to be bad for days.

Chapter Twenty-Three

A Desert Experience

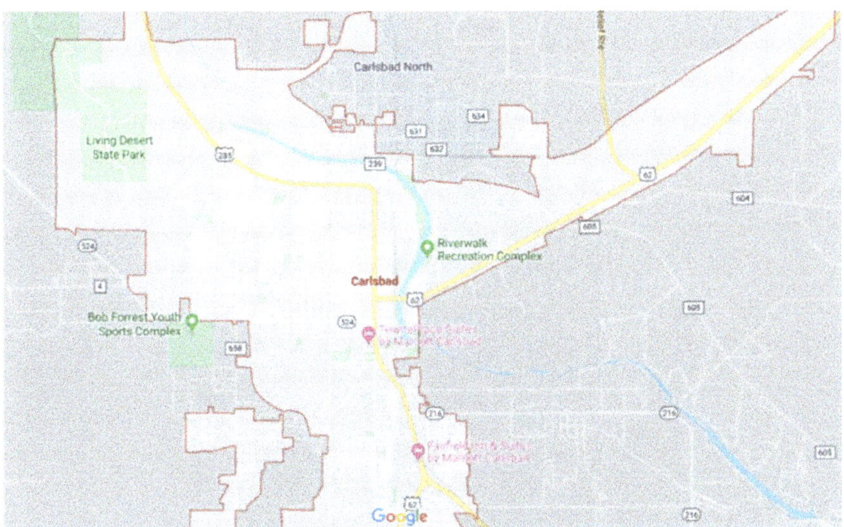

City of Carlsbad, New Mexico

With both of us being born and raised in Alabama and living most of our lives in Alabama and Georgia, the desert was a new experience for us, and our knowledge of the desert was limited.

One thing I most wanted to see as we approached the desert states was a saguaro cactus. I didn't know what they were called, but I knew I wanted to see one.

While we were in Carlsbad, I learned about The Living Desert Zoo and Gardens State Park, and on our last day, we paid a visit.

Temperatures had warmed up a little, and the sun shone for a couple of hours, but the wind was brutal. Tim was having a bad day, and I wasn't convinced we could explore everything, but the more we looked the more we wanted to explore. One of the volunteers answered questions for us, and I learned that saguaro cacti do not grow in the Chihuahuan Desert, which we were in, so I'd have to wait until later to see them.

The docent also told us we could rent Tim a motorized scooter for only $5 so we could explore outside, too, and I'm so glad we did

The paved loop led us around the living desert, where educational plaques taught us about the different types of plants and cacti.

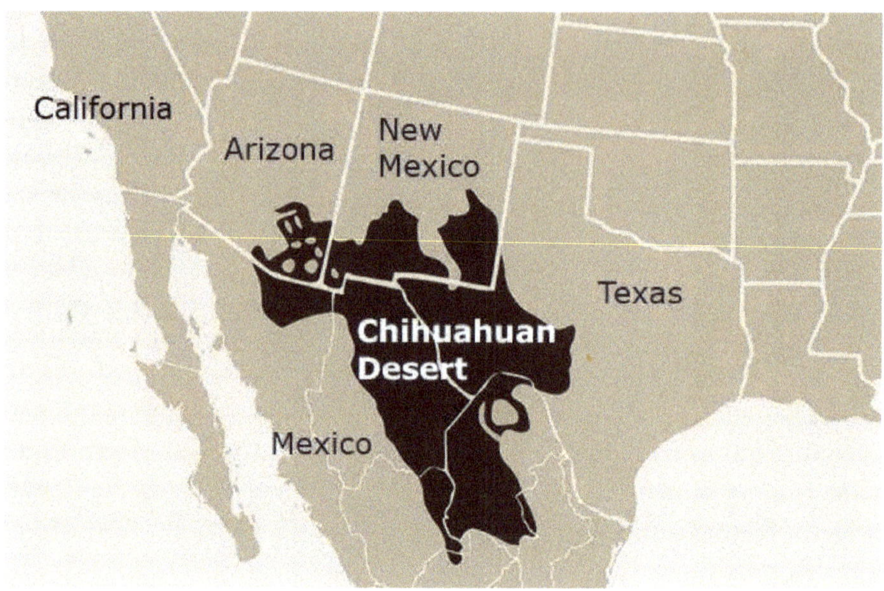

I'm not much of a zoo fan in general—I feel sorry for the wild animals held in captivity, even though I love having the

opportunity to see them up close.

The layout and design of this zoo added interest as we made our way through.

We're still laughing over one exhibit, with the wild cats.

We first saw a cage for bobcats but didn't see any. Then we passed a rock, and what looked like the same cage, but a sign for mountain lions. There were two up high in the rocks.

I was sharing our journey with Zach by text. I sent a photo of the Bobcat and Mountain Lion placards below, and a picture of the mountain lions, and he pointed out that those weren't bobcats. I told him they were all in the same cage, and he insisted I was wrong. Then he pointed out the diet of the mountain lions.

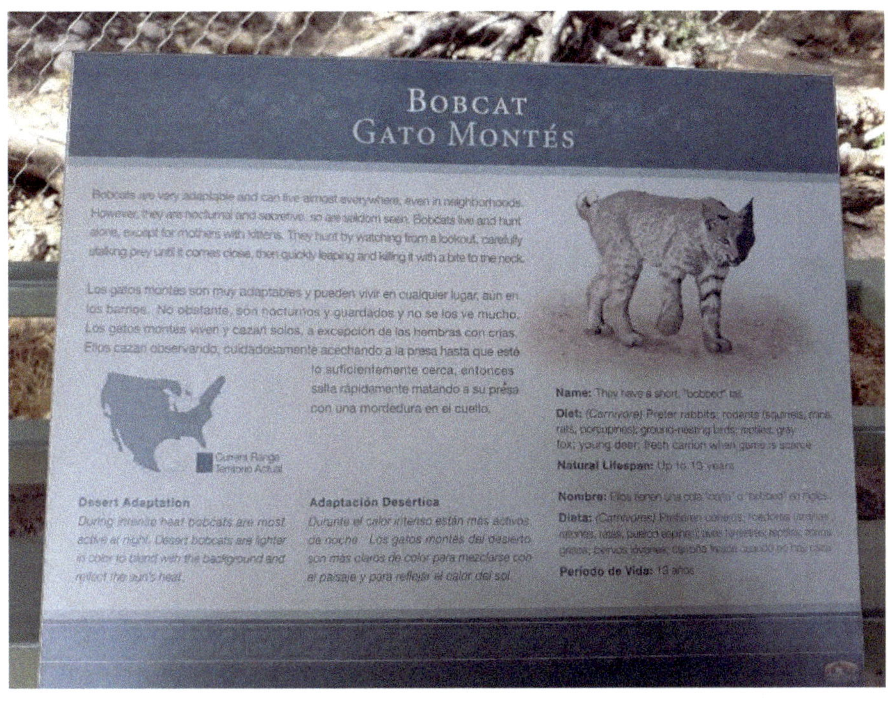

BOBCAT
GATO MONTÉS
Bobcats are very adaptable and can live almost everywhere, even in neighborhoods. However, they are nocturnal and secretive, so are seldom seen. Bobcats live and hunt alone, except for mothers with kittens. They hunt by watching from a lookout, carefully stalking prey until it comes close, then quickly leaping and killing it with a bite to the neck.
Los gatos montés son muy adaptables y pueden vivir en cualquier lugar, aún en los barrios. No obstante, son nocturnos y guardados y no se los ve mucho. Los gatos montés viven y cazan solos, a excepción de las hembras con crías. Ellos cazan observando, cuidadosamente acechando a la presa hasta que esté lo suficientemente cerca, entonces salta rápidamente matando a su presa con una mordedura en el cuello.
Current Range
Territorio Actual
Desert Adaptation
During intense heat bobcats are most active at night. Desert bobcats are lighter in color to blend with the background and reflect the sun's heat.
Adaptación Desértica
Durante el calor intenso están más activos de noche. Los gatos montés del desierto son más claros de color para mezclarse con el paisaje y para reflejar el calor del sol.
Name: They have a short, "bobbed" tail.
Diet: (Carnivore) Prefer rabbits; rodents (squirrels, mice, rats, porcupines); ground-nesting birds; reptiles; gray fox; young deer; fresh carrion when game is scarce.
Natural Lifespan: Up to 13 years
Nombre: Ellos tienen una cola "corta" o "bobbed" en inglés.
Dieta: (Carnívoros) Prefieren conejos; roedores (ardillas, ratones, ratas, puerco espines); aves terrestres; reptiles; zorros grises; cervos jóvenes; carroña fresca cuando no hay caza.
Período de Vida: 13 años

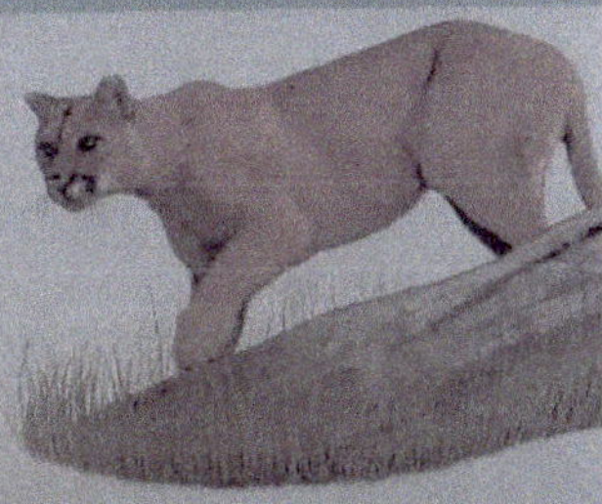
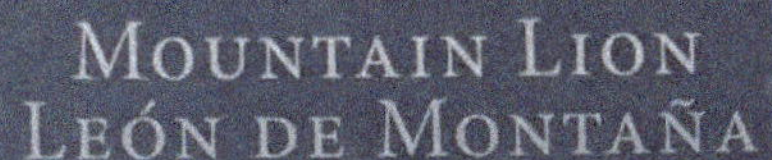
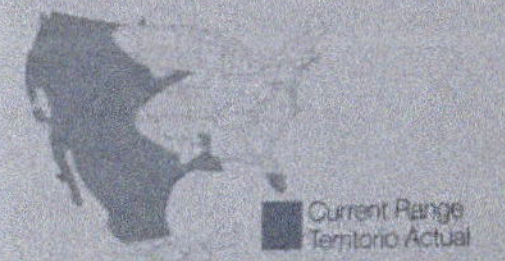

MOUNTAIN LION
LEÓN DE MONTAÑA
Mountain lions once roamed throughout the Americas. Territorial and solitary, they only pair for two weeks to mate. Females breed every other year, spending more than one year teaching their spotted kittens to hunt. These athletic predators stalk prey noiselessly until close enough, then leap up to 20 feet and kill the prey with a bite to the neck. They hunt night or day in the wild but are typically nocturnal in more urban areas.
Los leones de montaña alguna vez vagaban por todas partes de las Américas. Territoriales y solitarios, sólo se aparean por dos semanas para procrear. Las hembras procrean cada dos años, enseñando por más de un año a sus crías a cazar. Estos atléticos depredadores acechan a la presa sin hacer ruido hasta que se acerca lo suficiente, entonces saltan hasta 20 pies y matan a la presa con una mordedura en el cuello. Cazan de día o de noche, pero son estrictamente nocturnos en la presencia de los humanos.
Current Range
Territorio Actual
Desert Adaptation
During intense heat they are most active at night. Desert mountain lions are lighter in color to blend with the background and reflect the sun's heat.
Adaptación Desértica
Durante el calor intenso ellos están activos por la noche. El color de los leones del desierto es más claro para mezclarse con el paisaje y para reflejar el calor del sol.
Name: They live in mountains and resembled lions to e
Diet: (Carnivore) Prefer deer; elk; rabbits; rodents; po raccoons; birds; large insects (grasshoppers); smaller (coyotes, bobcats)
Natural Lifespan: Up to 13 years
Nombre: Ellos viven en las montañas y a los antiguos exploradores les parecían leones.
Dieta: (Carnívoros) Prefieren ciervos; alces; roedores; puerco espines; mapaches; aves; insectos (saltamontes); carnívoros pequeños (coyotes, ga
Período de Vida: 13 años

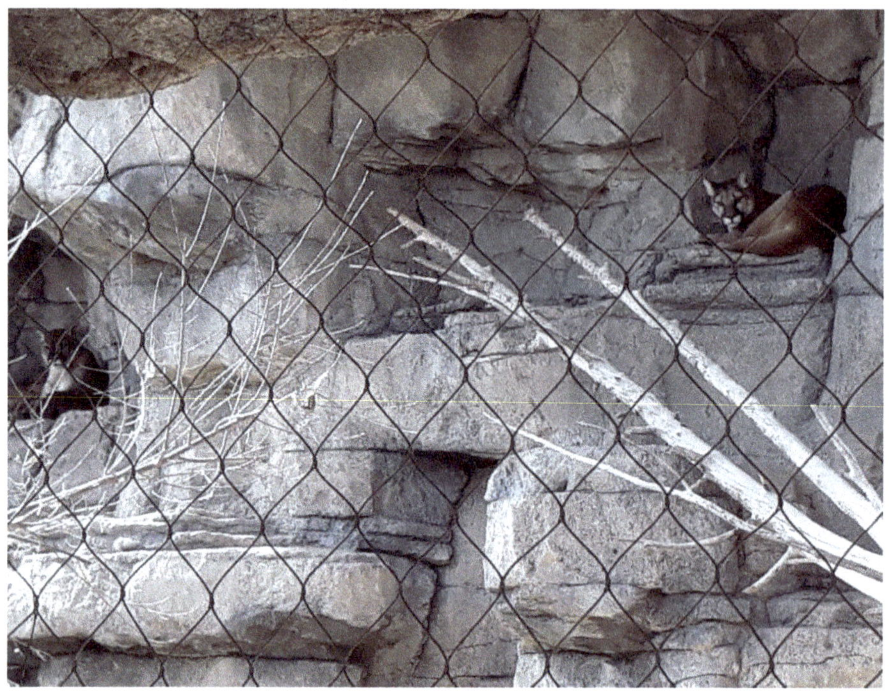

That day, the bobcats were either in hiding or the mountain lions were napping after a feast. (No, I didn't go back to see if they were in separate cages, but I'm sure they were.)

The Javelinas were a delight. I'd never seen any before, and they ended up being so playful, I tried to capture a short video. I wanted to take one with us! (View the video on my blog: https://tracyruckman.blogspot.com/2019/03/leapfrogs-desert-experience.html)

The Mexican wolves were enormous and seemed to keep watch over the park.

I saw my first roadrunner, too. (Seeing it in captivity helped me recognize it a few days later when one ran across the road in front of us!)

This wall summed up our visit as we went back inside the visitor's center:

The Living Desert was a great introduction.

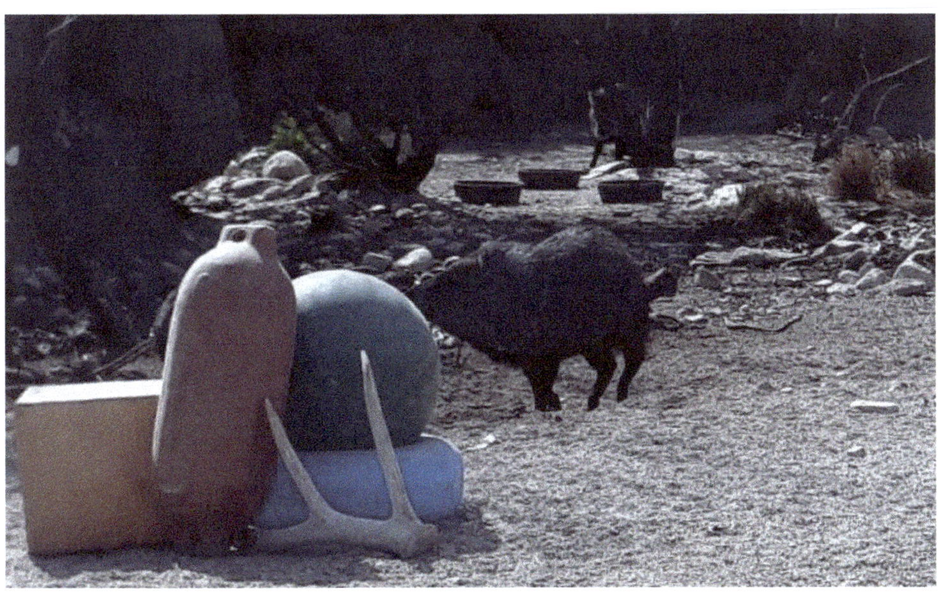

Our first encounter with Javelina. Aren't they cute?

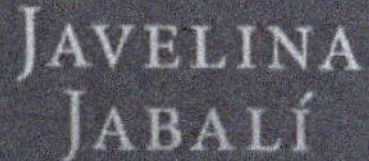

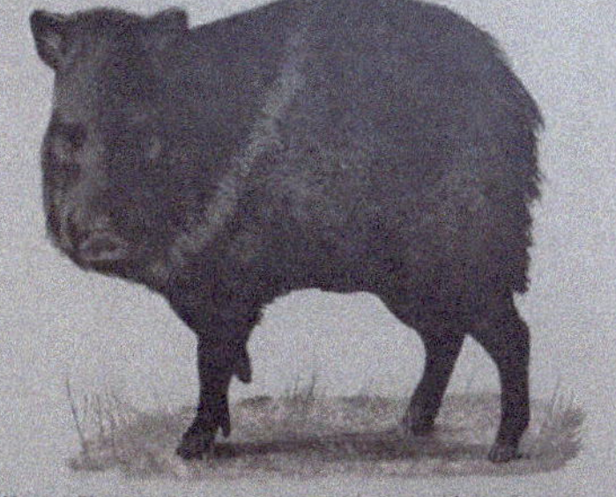

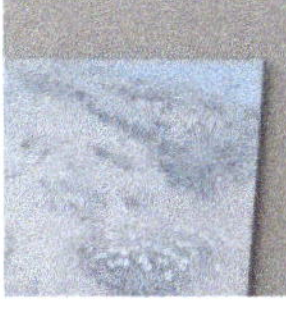

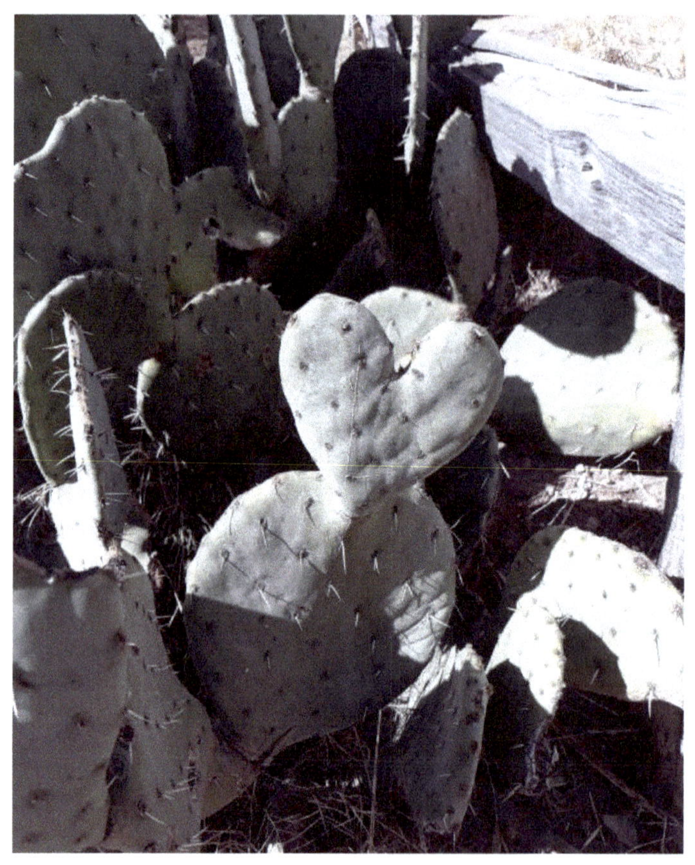

Above: Cactus; Below: Selenite

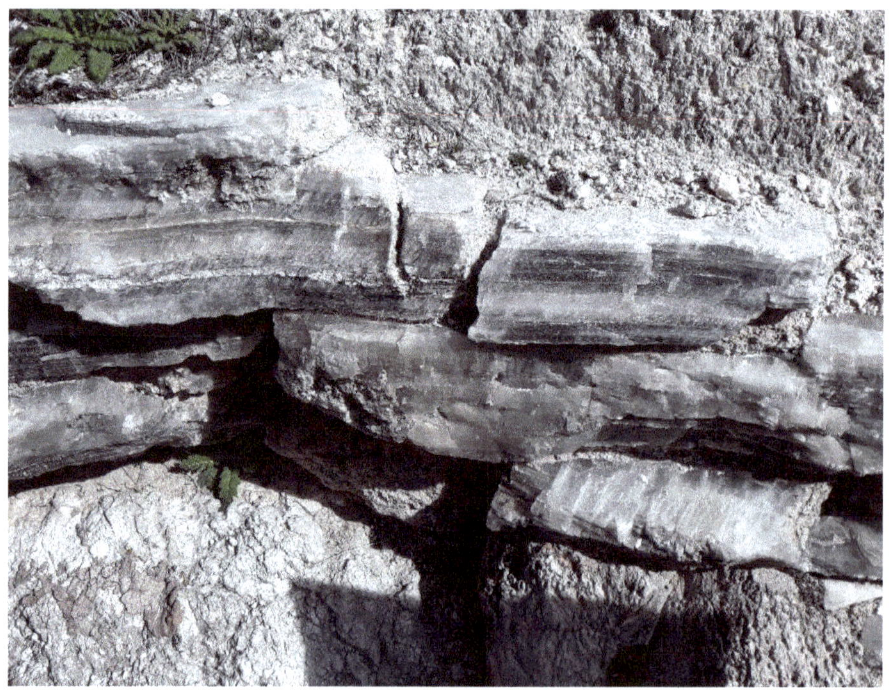

Chapter Twenty-Four

A New Town Filled with Art

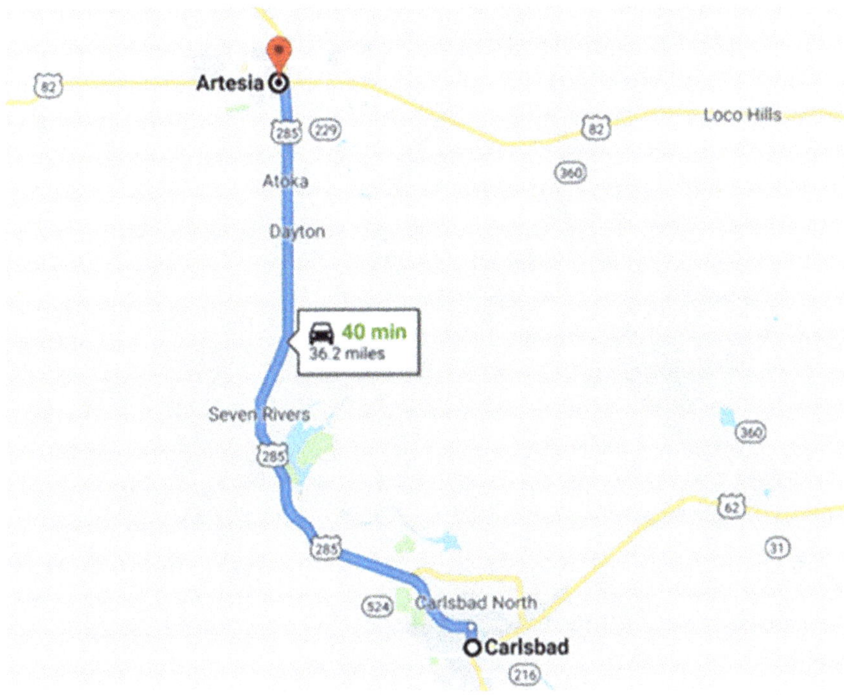

Carlsbad to Artesia

While we were in Carlsbad, we explored our next route and destination. We'd originally planned to continue west, but after the Living Desert experience, I found a fun listing on RoadsideAmerica.com about statues in the town of Artesia and wanted to check them out.

I fell in love with this town. Everywhere we turned, there was something new that seemed to connect with some aspect of our lives.

Art, architecture, books, history, westerns—everything seemed to fit.

One of my favorites was this sculpture by artist Vic Payne that shares the story of the oil company these two friends formed over the hood of a Ford truck. So lifelike—I felt I could hear their conversation as I studied them.

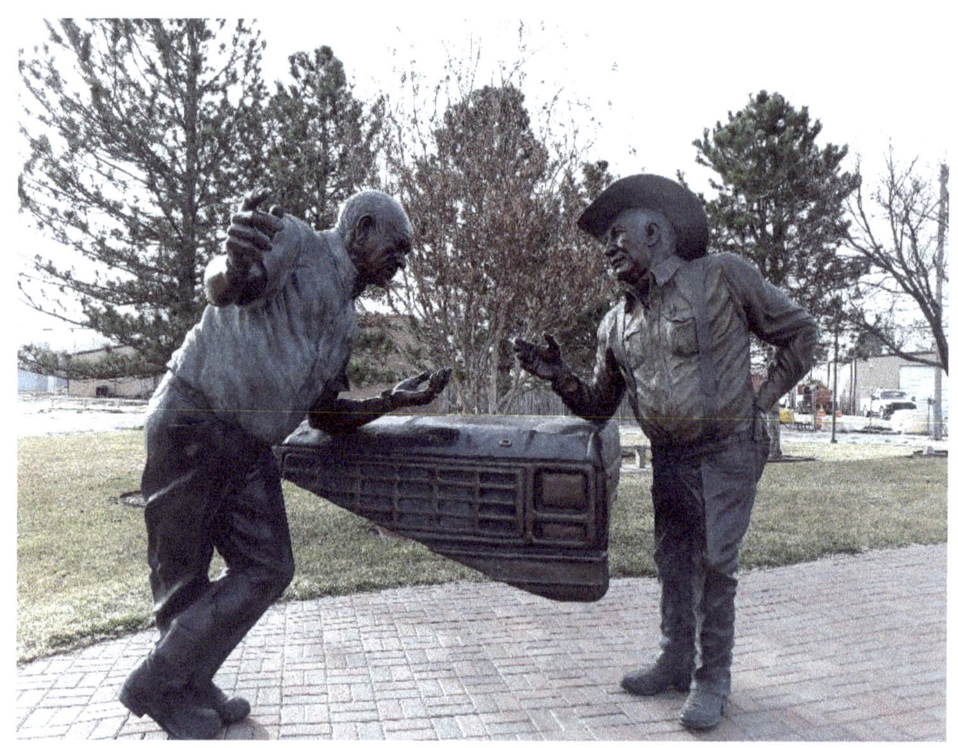

On our drive to the library, we discovered this massive sculpture in the middle of the street. I was awed by sculpture as a whole, but when I got out and looked at it up close, I burst into tears—literally.

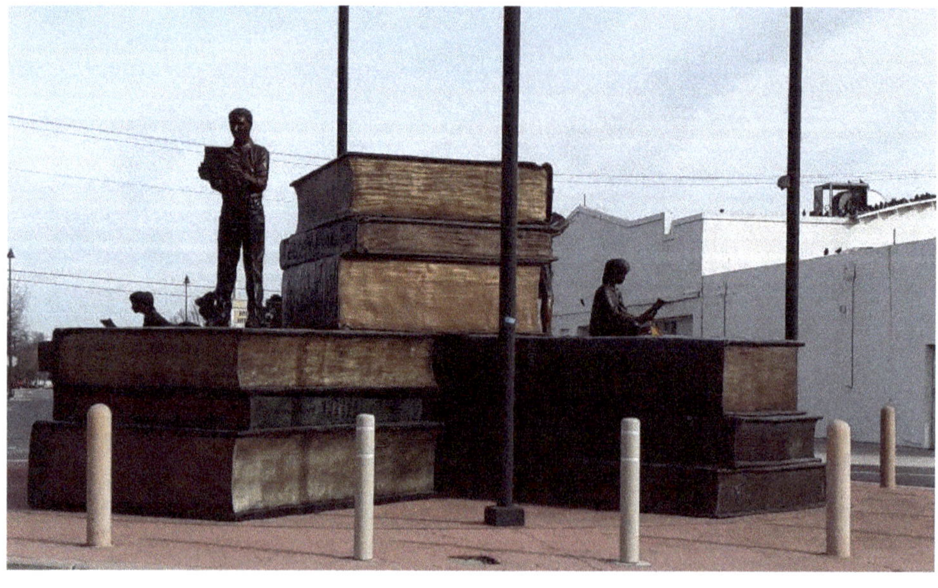

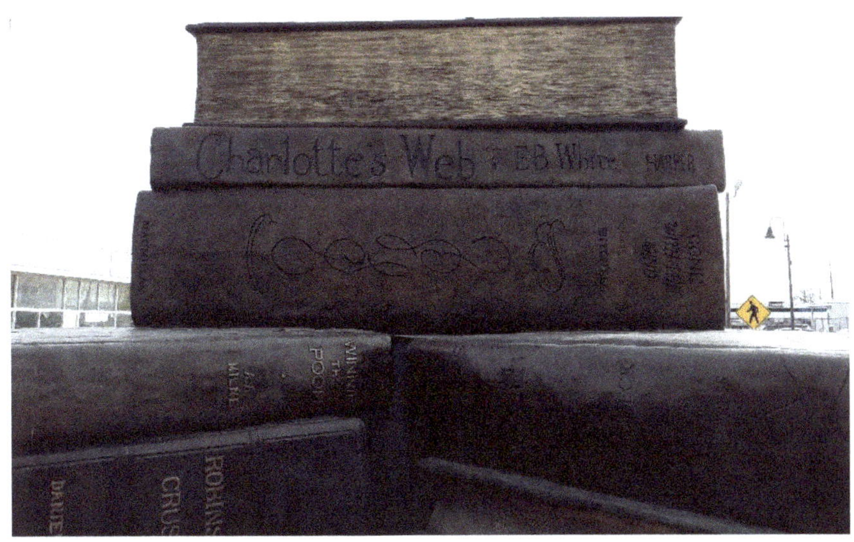

The fact that the town honors books and encourages reading this way touched me deeply, but then to find that each of the books was a book I've read—well, that's when the waterworks started.

When I saw the young girl above, I wondered whether the book she was reading was a real book, too, so I got closer. When I saw the title of the book, I sobbed with joy and amazement.

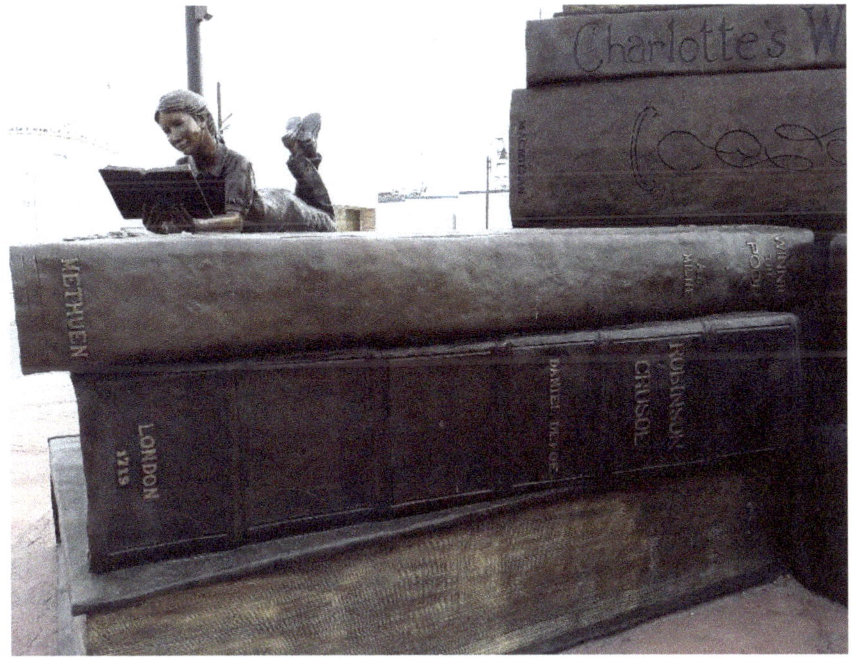

Redeeming Love by Francine Rivers.

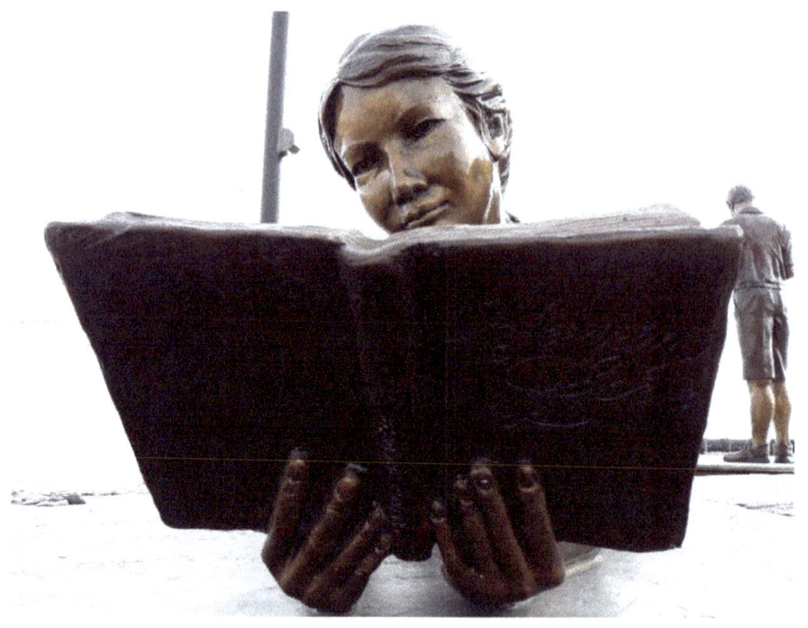

Thank you, Artesia, for honoring writers and encouraging readers in such a beautiful way!

Then we discovered El Vaquero.

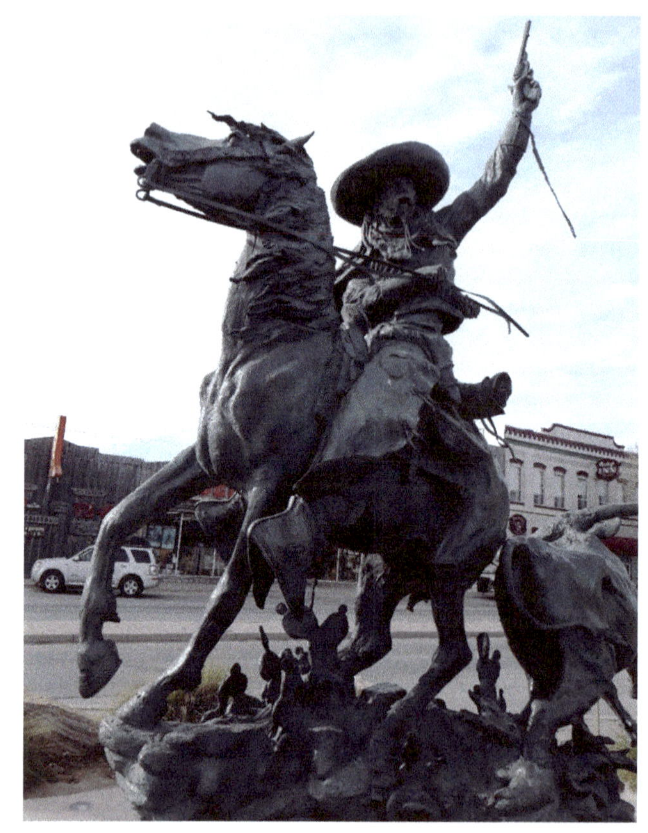

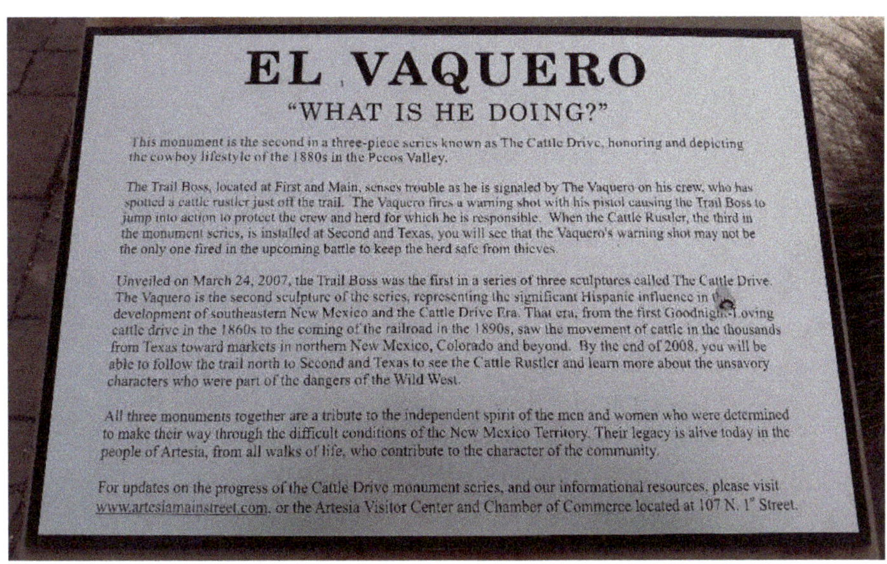

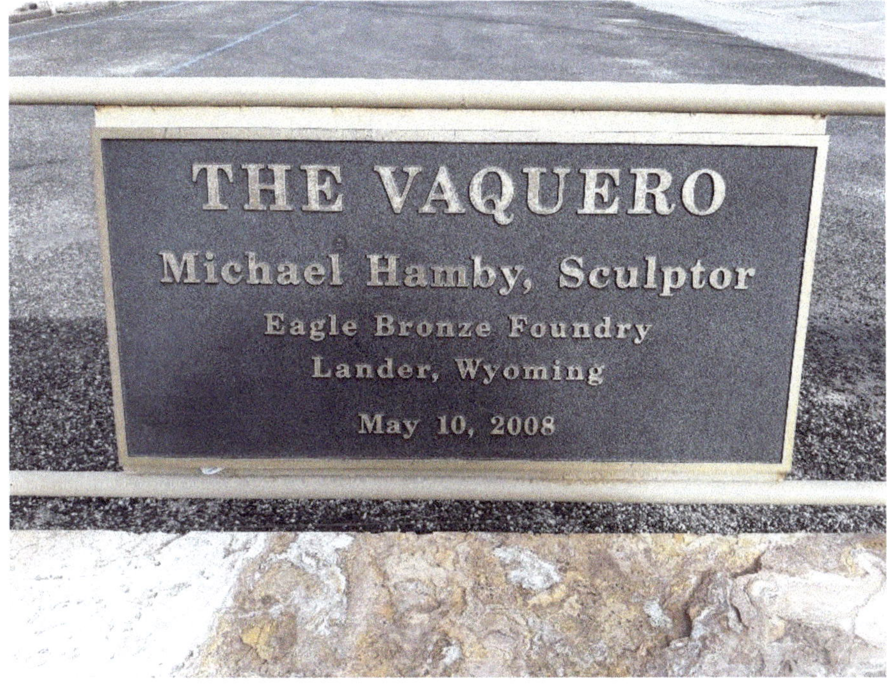

We continued roaming around town and discovered another statue on a corner that created more waterworks for me.

This statue in Artesia continued our *Lonesome Dove* experiences!

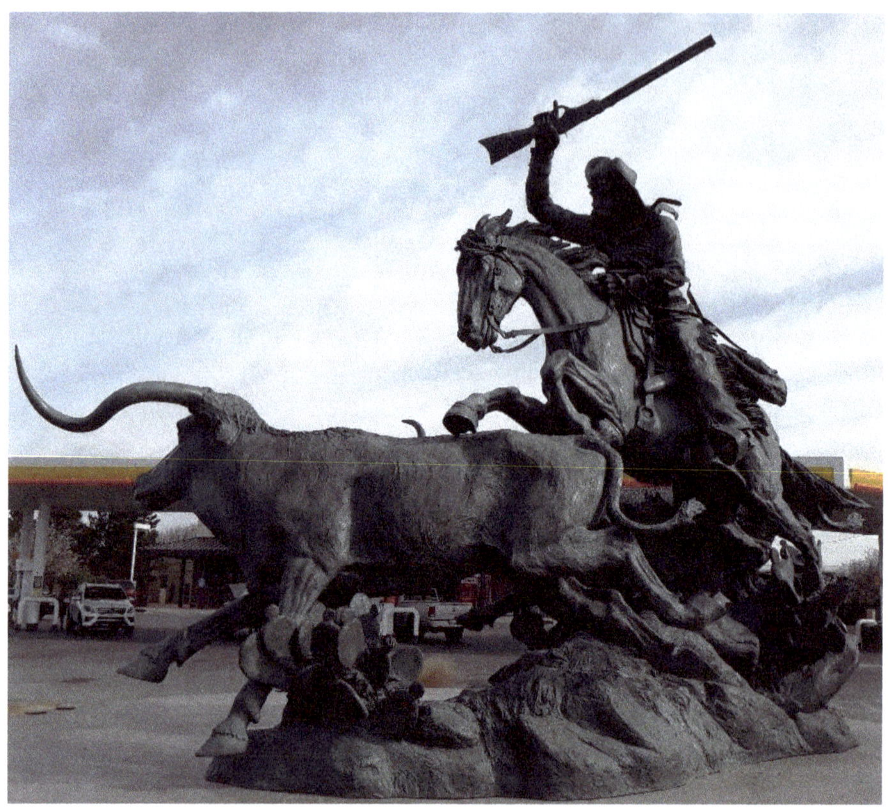

THE GOODNIGHT-LOVING TRAIL

In the mid 1860s, an increasingly dangerous Comanche Indian presence threatened cattle drives heading directly north out of Texas. Because of the danger and hoping for cattle markets at US Military Forts along the eastern front of the Rocky Mountains, Charles Goodnight and Oliver Loving decided to take a different route. They planned to go southwest across barren, dry lands to the Pecos River and then strike 300 miles north along the Pecos to Fort Sumner, in the New Mexico Territory, and to markets further north. In June 1866, they left the Brazos River in North Central Texas with 2000 head of Longhorns. Forty days later, having lost 400 head to quicksand and a lack of water, they arrived at Fort Sumner where they were able to sell half of the remaining herd for $12,000. Their success led to the naming of the route the "Goodnight-Loving Trail." Many others followed in their footsteps, but not all were successful—many lost their lives or their herds and horses to thirst, alkali poisoning, quicksand, drowning, floods, stampedes or Indian raids. The trail later had competition from the railroads (1894 into Artesia), and ceased altogether with barbed wire fencing in the very early 1900s.

"TAKE ME BACK TO TEXAS"
LONESOME DOVE

Although Lonesome Dove author Larry McMurtry does not contend that his 1985 best-selling book is an actual account of historical events, the story offers an accurate portrayal of life on a nineteenth-century cattle drive in the southwest. In fact, many similarities exist between the Lonesome Dove main characters Augustus McCrae and Woodrow Call and those real-life history makers Oliver Loving and Charles Goodnight, who forged the Goodnight-Loving Trail that passed through this area.

The fictional fate of Augustus McCrae was that, in real life, of Oliver Loving. As history states in 1867, on the third Goodnight-Loving cattle drive, Loving and another cowboy were ahead of the herd when they were ambushed by a group of Comanche Indians about 40 miles south of here, near the present day town of Loving. Oliver Loving was wounded and sent his partner to retrieve Goodnight, who was about seventy miles further down the Pecos with the herd. Goodnight arrived days later at the ambush site with no sign of Loving. Goodnight then rode up the Pecos to Ft. Sumner, where he was pleased to find Loving, who had escaped the ambush. Despite desperate efforts to save his life, Loving died due to complications related to surgery. Honoring Loving's last request, Goodnight took his partner's body back to Texas for burial.

During the night, our phones alerted us that we were under a high wind warning again. Weather forecasts for area towns are showing "Blowing Dust" as the day's description, where we normally expect it to say "Rainy" or "Sunny" or "Mild." I'm seriously considering tying a bandana around my neck in case I need it.

Weather this morning also shows the temps are not going to hold steady warm like I'd hoped. Cold, snow, and ice are now moving in all around us Monday night.

We have to figure out a shelter for us to stay put for a few days - I don't drive in snow or ice.

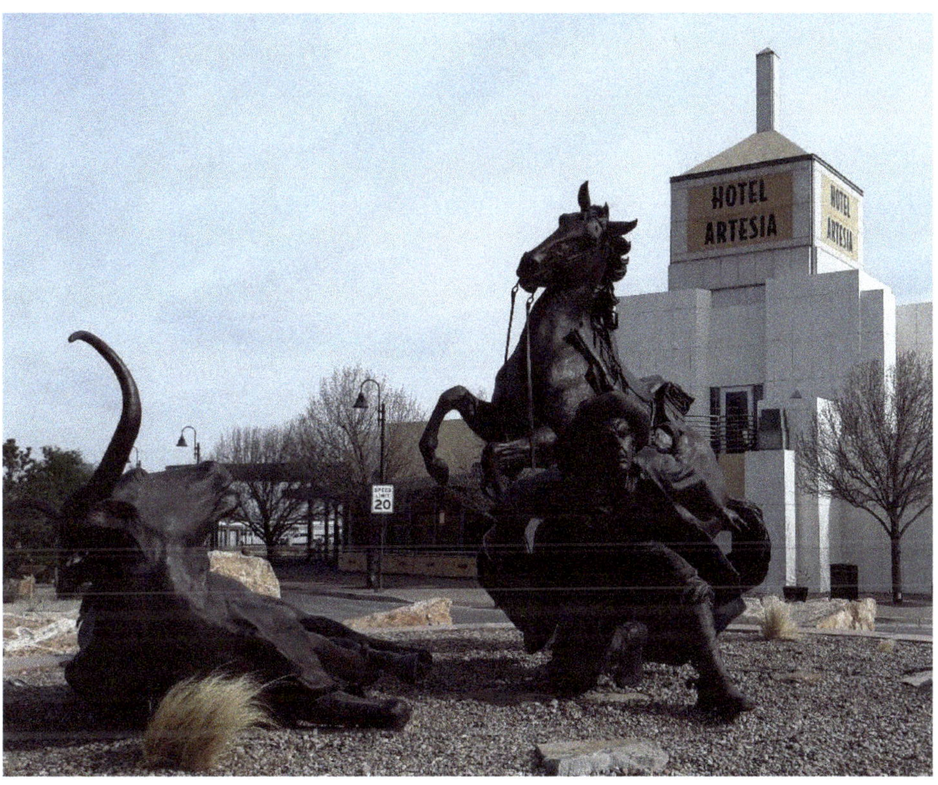

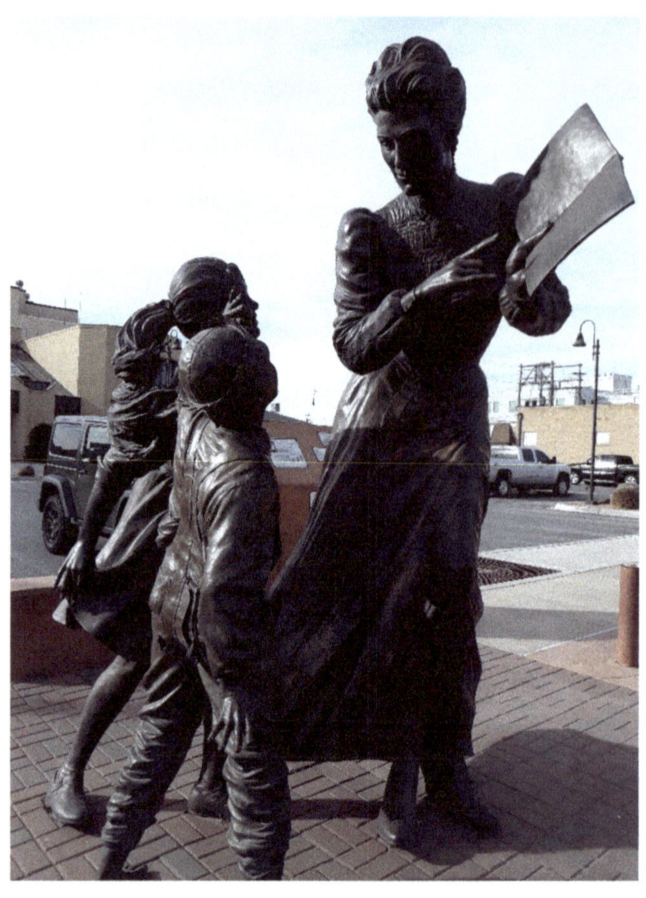

Above: First Lady of Artesia; Below: Library mural

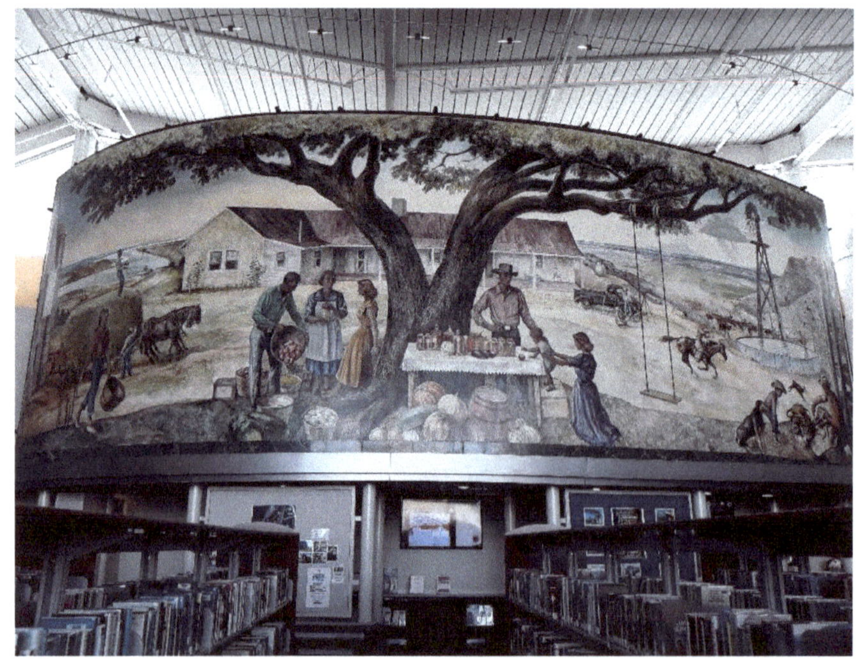

Chapter Twenty-Five
Running from the Weather

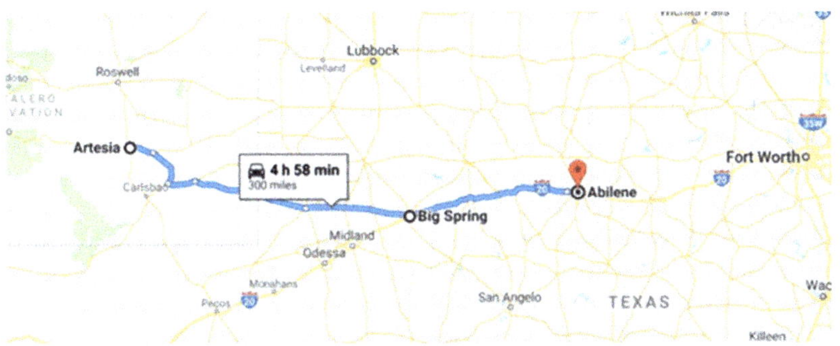

Artesia, New Mexico to Abilene, Texas

On our last night in Artesia, we learned that the weather was rapidly changing and was likely to get bad in southern New Mexico quickly. I checked weather reports for every direction and found a small cone of an area that was going to be relatively unscathed by the coming storms. We made the unexpected decision to head back into Texas to ride out the storms.

Once we made the decision to change directions, we were both too antsy to sleep, so we decided to start moving to get ahead of the storms. I don't enjoy driving at night, but we felt we almost didn't have a choice if we were going to get away from the snow and ice in time. (I'm a Bama girl—I don't do ice and snow, remember?)

The cone I mentioned earlier included several towns in Texas we'd not yet visited, so we set out, not sure where we'd stop as we went. I planned to drive as long as I could before parking somewhere overnight, then we'd figure out a better plan the next day.

Along the way, we checked a few of our camping apps, and found a Walmart that had overnight parking in Lamesa, TX, but when we arrived at that address, the Walmart had closed down and a police car sat in the lot monitoring it, so we decided to drive down to Big Spring. There, we found a Walmart and crashed for a few hours.

Unfortunately, when I woke the next morning, I was sick to my stomach and felt miserable, but we moved on. We stopped for breakfast so I could try to put something in me that would settle my stomach, and then we set off for Abilene.

One of my dearest friends has ties to Abilene, but that's the only connection I had to the town. And I honestly knew nothing about it, so I pulled up RoadsideAmerica to see what I could find. I was delighted to discover so much variety.

They love children's books. We found a Dr. Seuss park with low-to-the-ground statues so children can interact with characters from the books.

The town has a "Storybook Sculpture Hunt" app that parents can download then take their children around town on a scavenger hunt for all the different statues. (They provide directions on how to do an audio tour, too!)

As we drove around town, we discovered several other delightful sculptures that made me wish my kids were little again so I could share the town with them.

Somewhere along the way, I discovered that one of the sculpture gardens features sculptures based on the artwork of Garth Williams. I instantly recognized the name, because he is the artist who illustrated all the Little House books I cherished in childhood. But I never followed his career, and had no idea he also illustrated so many other favorites, including one I read to my boys again and again:

Our delight with Abilene didn't end with the storybook sculptures, though.

The Jacob's Dream sculpture garden shares the story from Genesis 28, and it is quite breathtaking. I would have enjoyed spending more time there, but because of the wind and cold, Tim stayed in the car while I snapped a few photos and retreated.

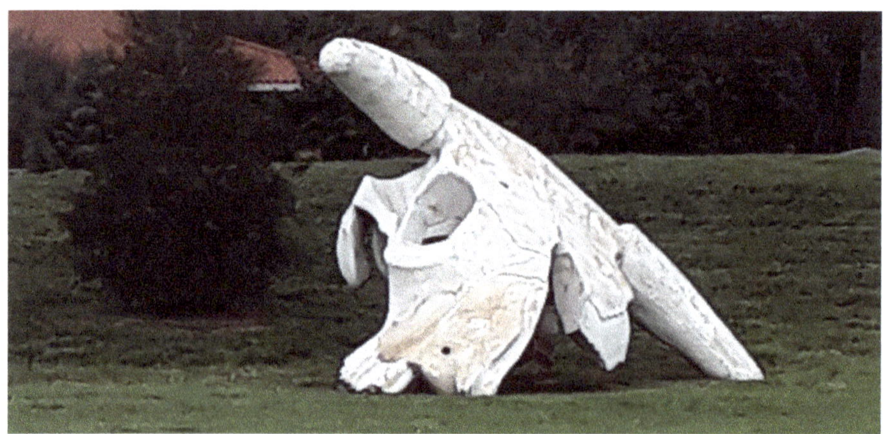

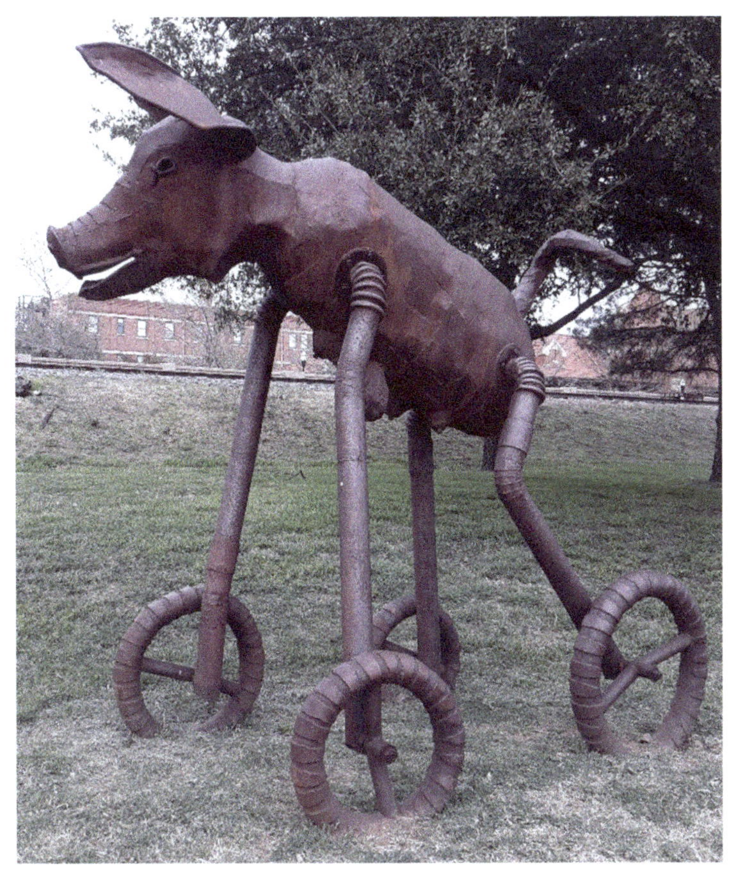

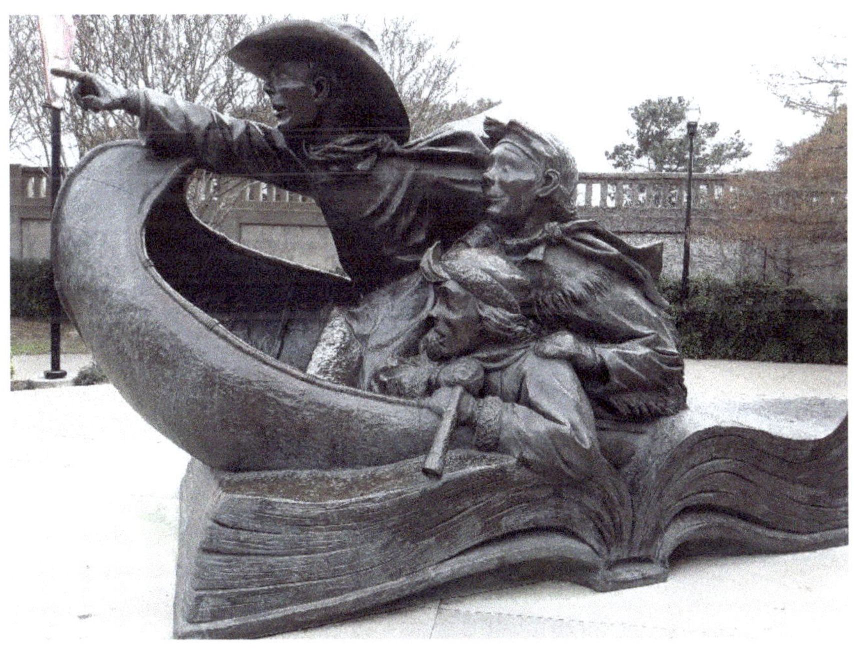

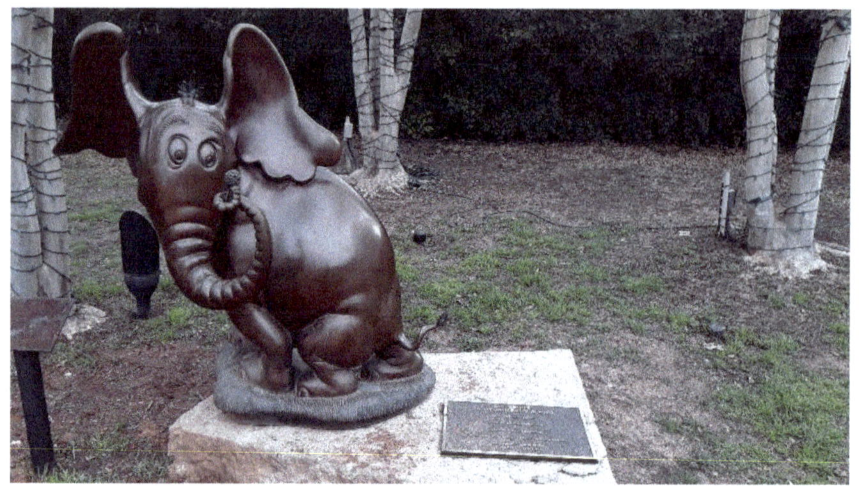

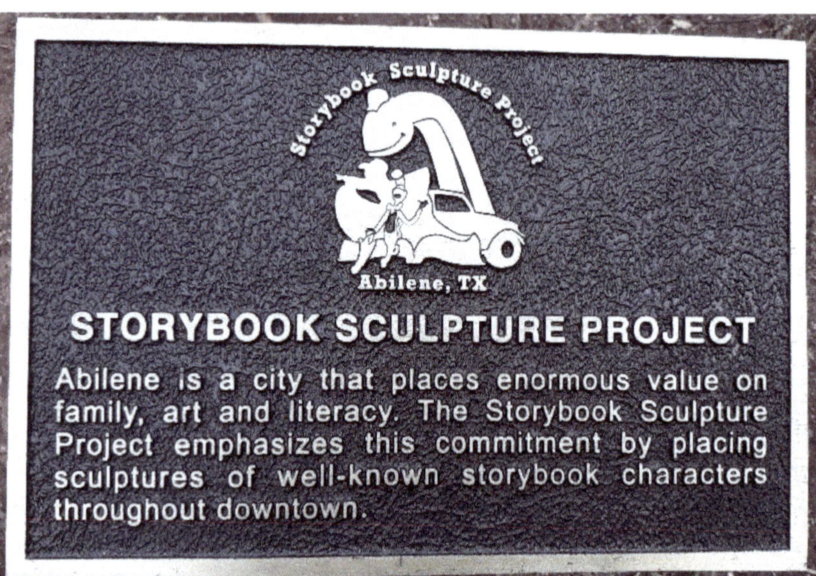

Storybook Sculpture Project
Abilene, TX
STORYBOOK SCULPTURE PROJECT
Abilene is a city that places enormous value on family, art and literacy. The Storybook Sculpture Project emphasizes this commitment by placing sculptures of well-known storybook characters throughout downtown.

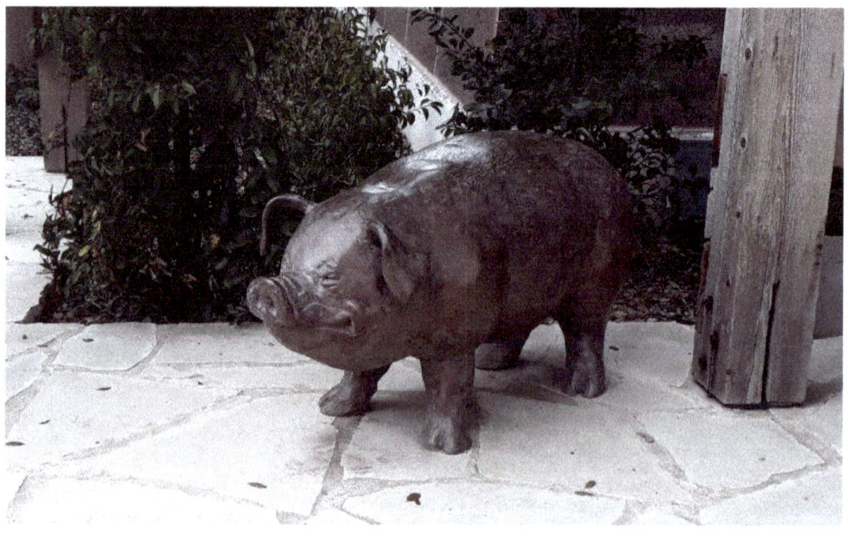

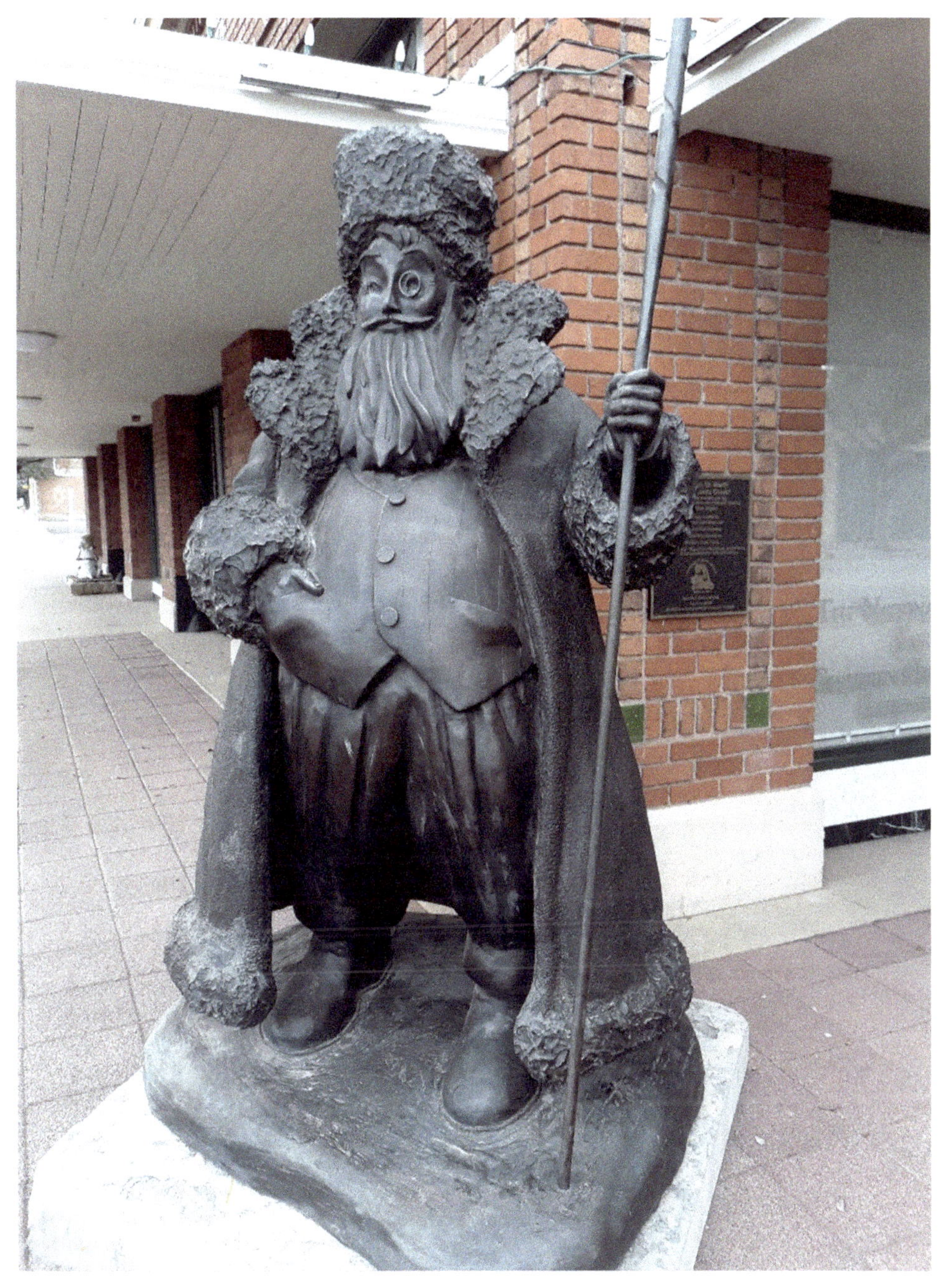

Could he be related to Tim?

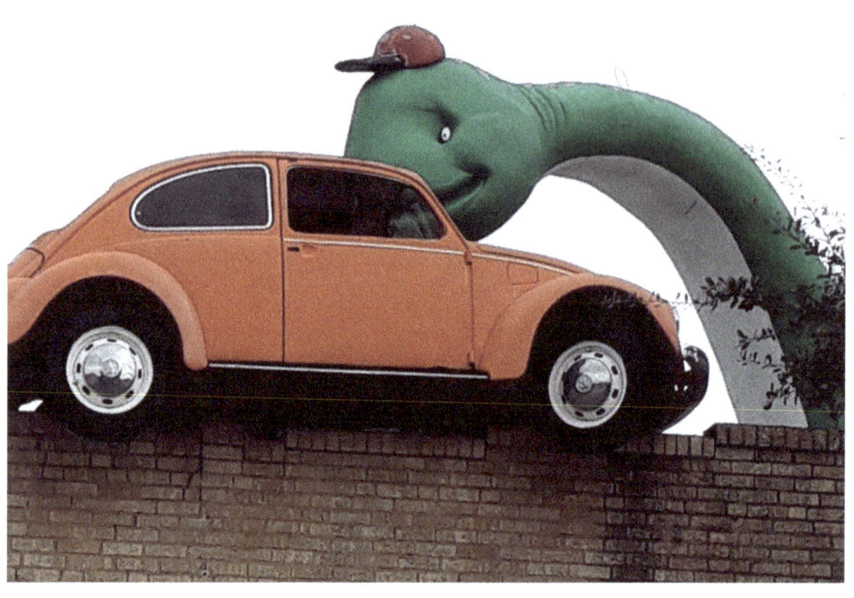

Above: Yes, on top of a building!

Below: Little Library filled with children's books.

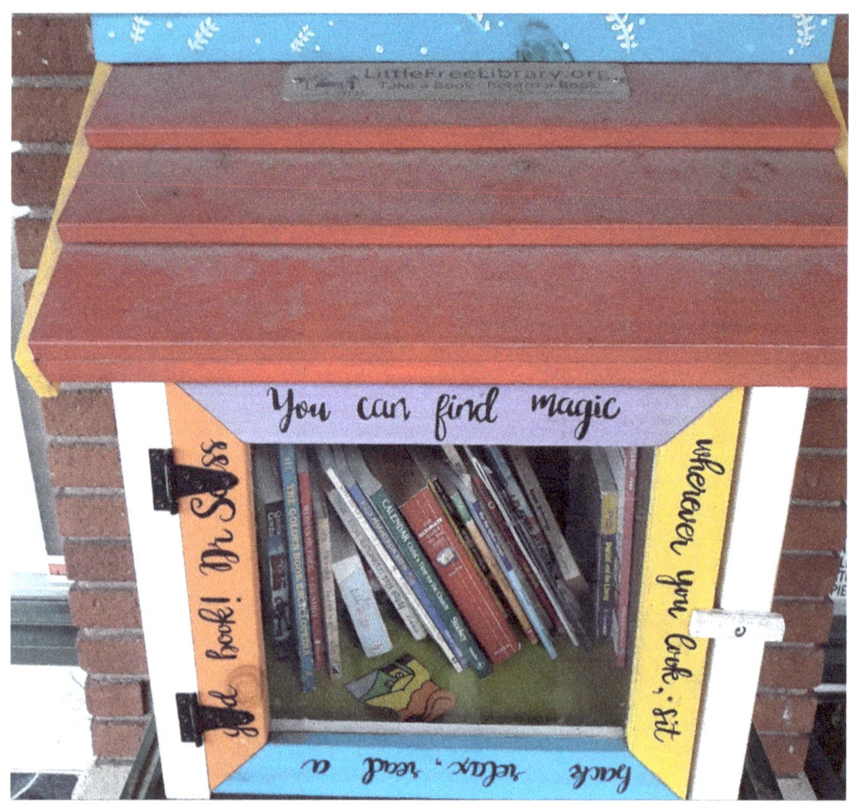

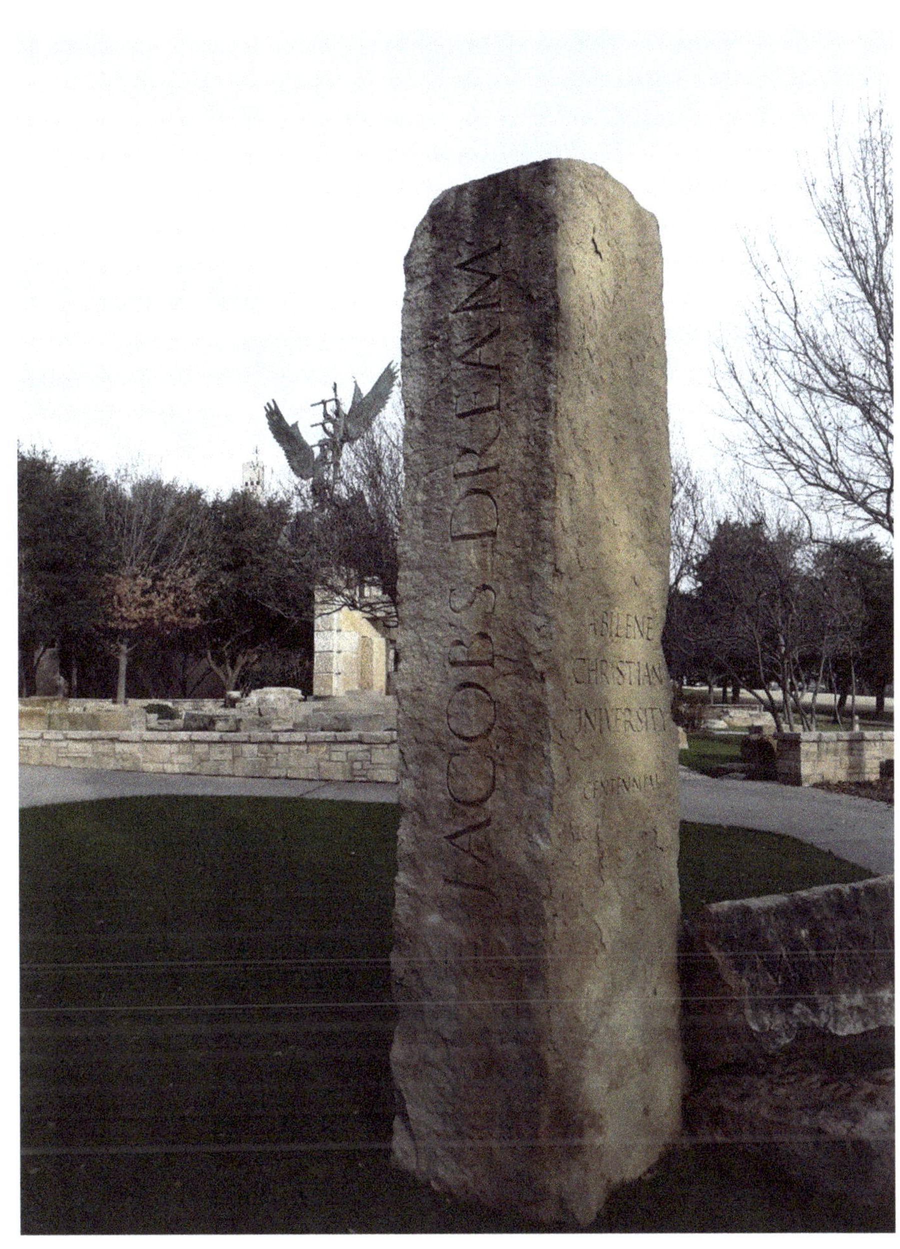
JACOB'S DREAM
ABILENE
CHRISTIAN
UNIVERSITY
CENTENNIAL

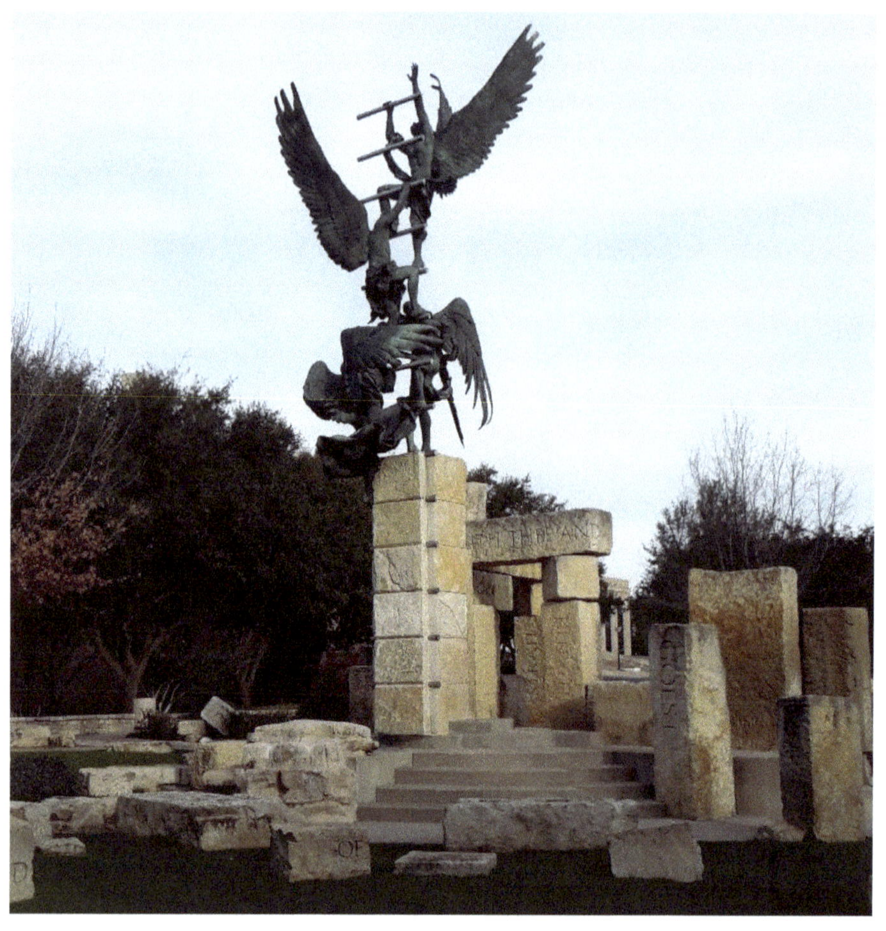

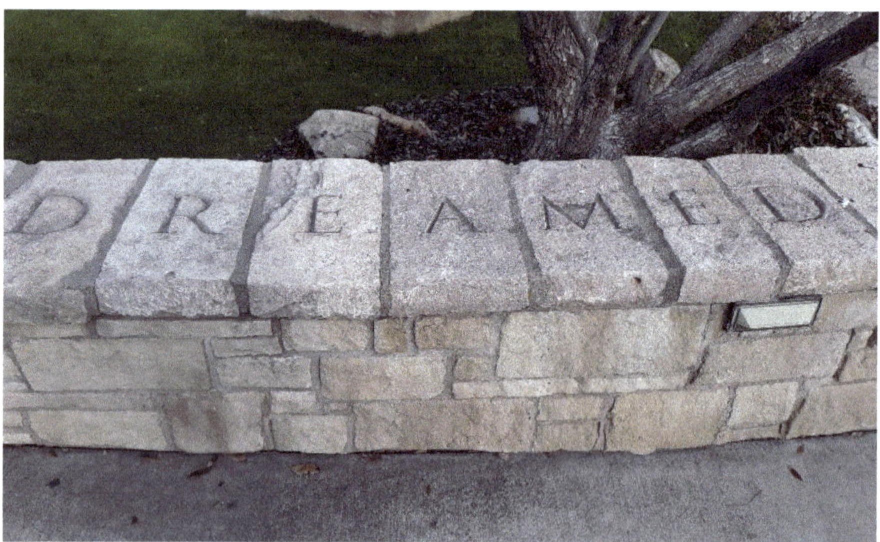

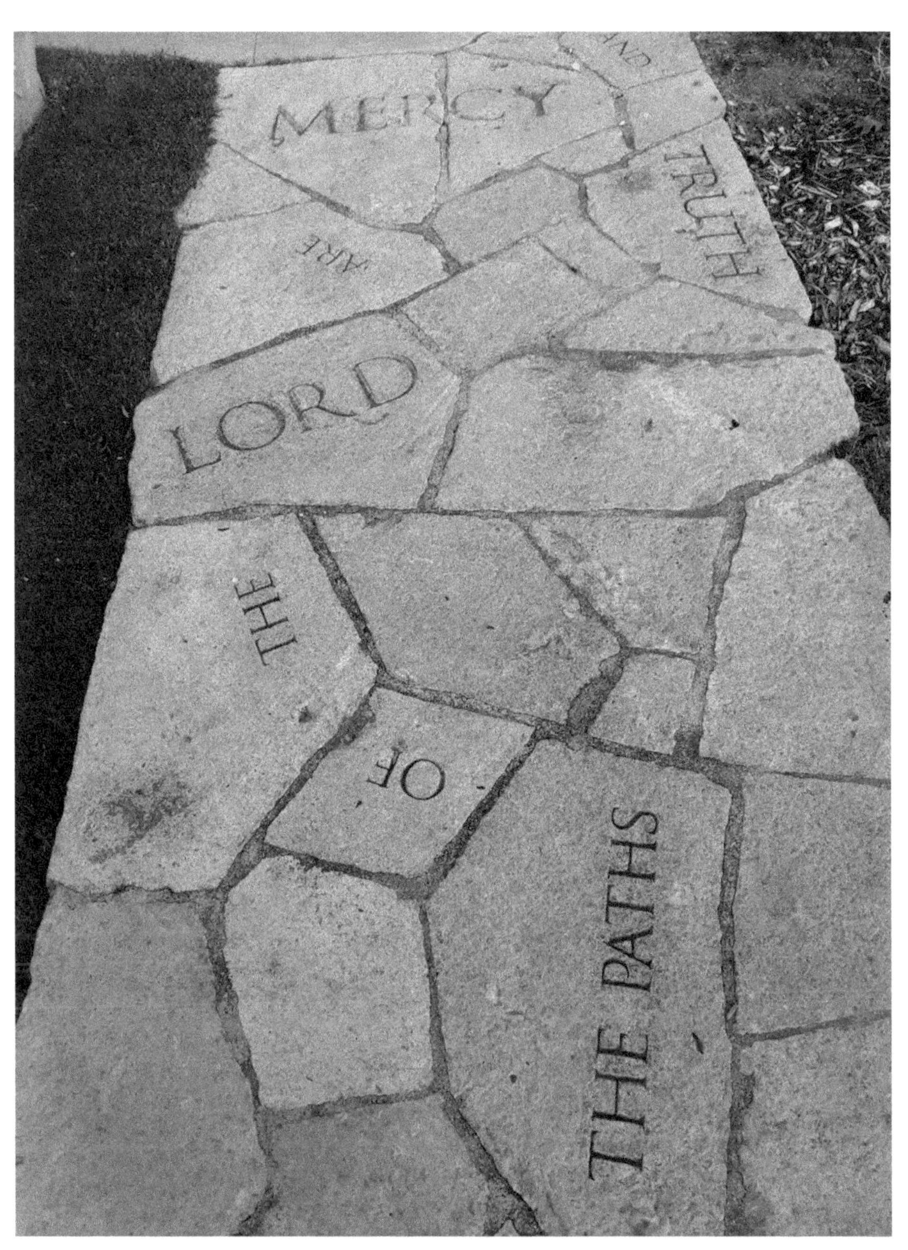

MERCY
TRUTH
ARE
LORD
THE
OF
THE PATHS

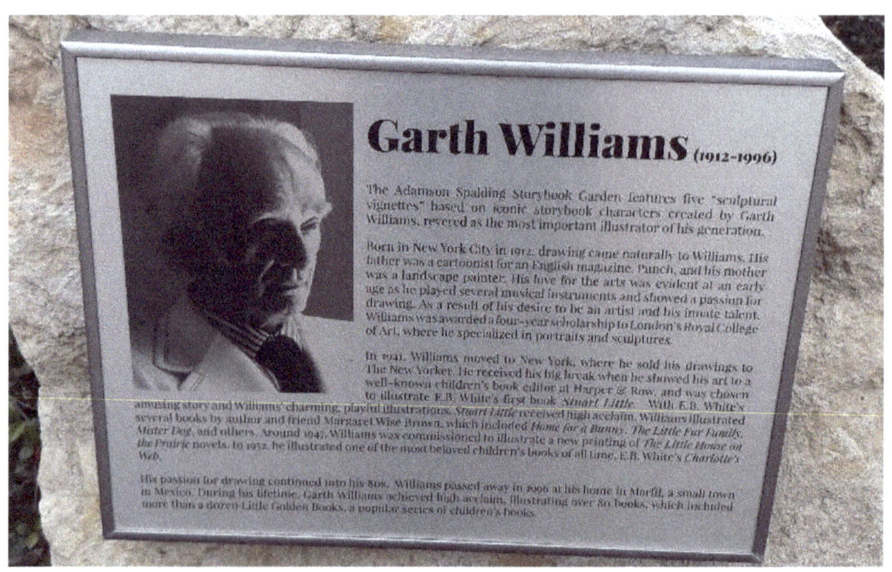

Garth Williams (1912-1996)

The Adamson Spalding Storybook Garden features five "sculptural vignettes" based on iconic storybook characters created by Garth Williams, revered as the most important illustrator of his generation.

Born in New York City in 1912, drawing came naturally to Williams. His father was a cartoonist for an English magazine, Punch, and his mother was a landscape painter. His love for the arts was evident at an early age as he played several musical instruments and showed a passion for drawing. As a result of his desire to be an artist and his innate talent, Williams was awarded a four-year scholarship to London's Royal College of Art, where he specialized in portraits and sculptures.

In 1941, Williams moved to New York, where he sold his drawings to The New Yorker. He received his big break when he showed his art to a well-known children's book editor at Harper & Row, and was chosen to illustrate E.B. White's first book, Stuart Little. With E.B. White's amusing story and Williams' charming, playful illustrations, Stuart Little received high acclaim. Williams illustrated several books by author and friend Margaret Wise Brown, which included Home for a Bunny, The Little Fur Family, Mister Dog, and others. Around 1947, Williams was commissioned to illustrate a new printing of The Little House on the Prairie novels. In 1952, he illustrated one of the most beloved children's books of all time, E.B. White's Charlotte's Web.

His passion for drawing continued into his 80s. Williams passed away in 2006 at his home in Marfil, a small town in Mexico. During his lifetime, Garth Williams achieved high acclaim, illustrating over 80 books, which included more than a dozen Little Golden Books, a popular series of children's books.

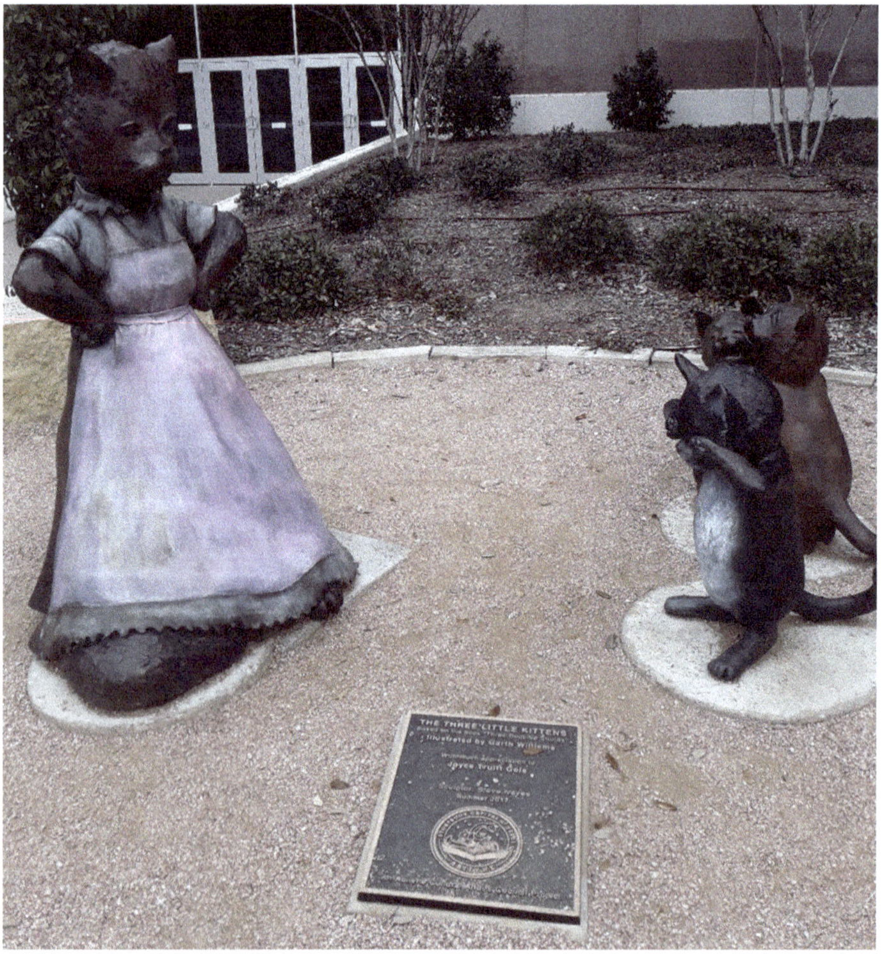

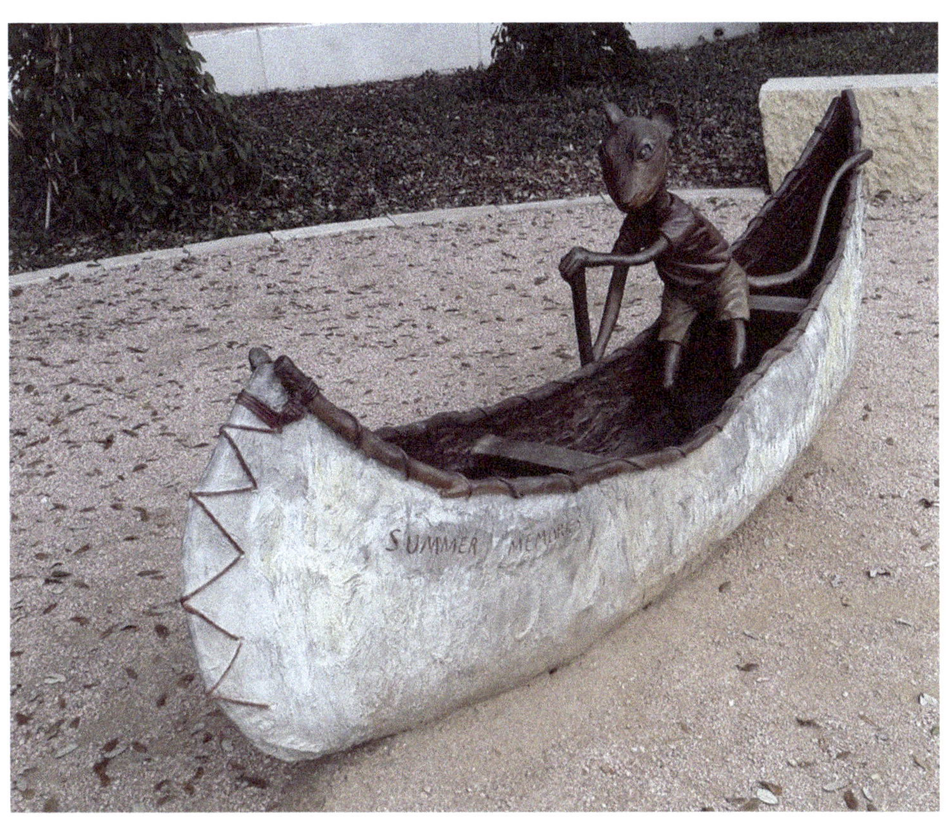

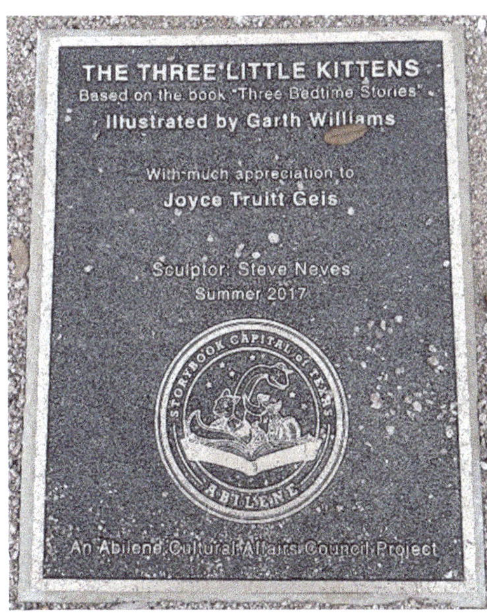

THE THREE LITTLE KITTENS
Based on the book "Three Bedtime Stories"
Illustrated by Garth Williams

With much appreciation to
Joyce Truitt Geis

Sculptor: Steve Neves
Summer 2017

STORYBOOK CAPITAL of TEXAS
ABILENE

An Abilene Cultural Affairs Council Project

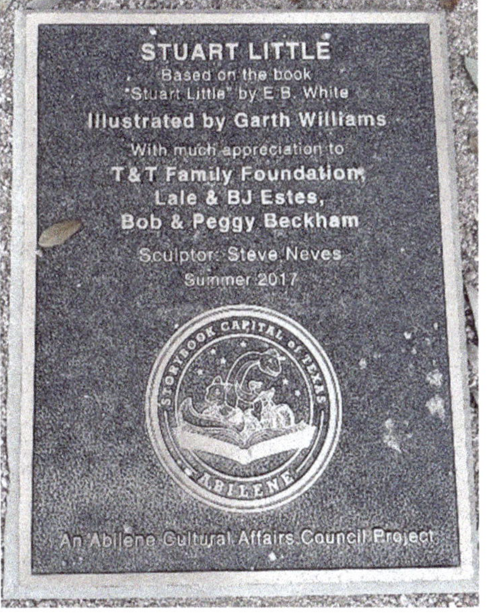

STUART LITTLE
Based on the book
"Stuart Little" by E.B. White

Illustrated by Garth Williams

With much appreciation to
T & T Family Foundation,
Lale & BJ Estes,
Bob & Peggy Beckham

Sculptor: Steve Neves
Summer 2017

STORYBOOK CAPITAL of TEXAS
ABILENE

An Abilene Cultural Affairs Council Project

They also had the cheesy: I convinced Tim we had to pose. He wasn't thrilled, but we both did it. I was laughing so hard, I almost fell off, and no, I'm not sharing that photo.

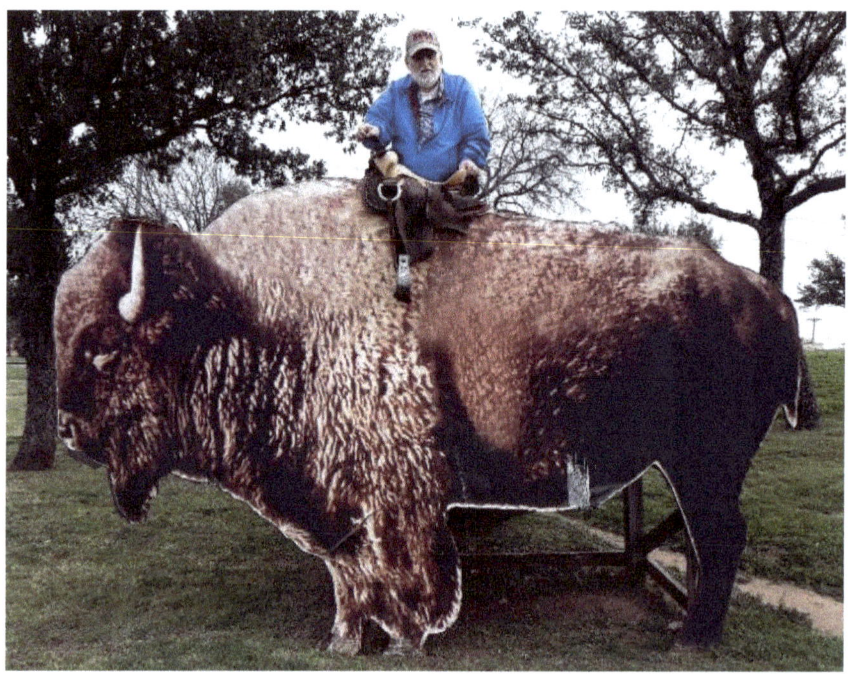

From the FROG Files:

I must have picked up a 24 hour stomach bug or something - I felt yucky for a few hours yesterday morning, and had one hard round of vomiting, but after I added a dose of Advil on top of the Excedrin Migraine - and after I sent out the prayer request - I began feeling better and by evening, I was almost back to normal. (ha - me, normal!?)

We thought we were escaping the weather, but it seems to have caught up with us. Sigh. Temps were only supposed to go to 35 last night, but instead dropped to 30, and now sleet and "ice on the roads" is called for tomorrow morning with temps about the same for the next couple of days. Waah.

I know our schedule and route makes no sense to anyone - not even us at times - but every time we do something different than what we originally planned, I discover some delight I never expected to find - like all the wonderful things here in Abilene.

Chapter Twenty-Six

A New Tent and a Little Time to Breathe

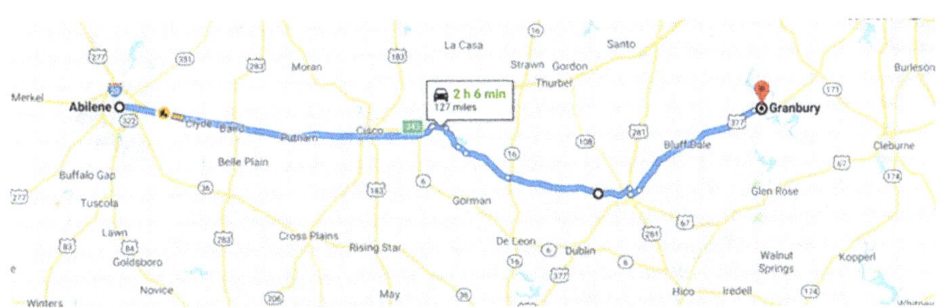

Abilene to Granbury

Somewhere along our journey, another dear friend told me how much she and her husband loved Granbury, Texas. I searched and discovered a free camping site so when we left Abilene, we pointed toward Granbury.

I fell in love with this town. It's about the size of my hometown in Alabama, which is also a lake town, so it felt comfortable and homey from the moment we arrived.

The Rough Creek City Park offers a boat ramp with large parking lot, a couple of docks, and a great area for pitching tents. They also have a couple of drive-through or back-in spots for RV boondocking, but no hook-ups. When the weather warms up, they also offer public restrooms, but while we were there, they were locked up tight. Thankfully, the city provided porta-johns, and we brought our own water, so we were set.

(TIP: A water and ice station is across the street from the park, so you can bottle your own water for only 25 cents per gallon or restock ice for $2/bag.)

When we got to town, we stopped in at Walmart to get supplies and walked through the camping department. We discovered that a tent we'd had our eyes on had been drastically reduced, so we decided to exchange the tent we'd bought in Carlsbad, but still hadn't used or even opened, for the bigger, better one—and it was cheaper, too!

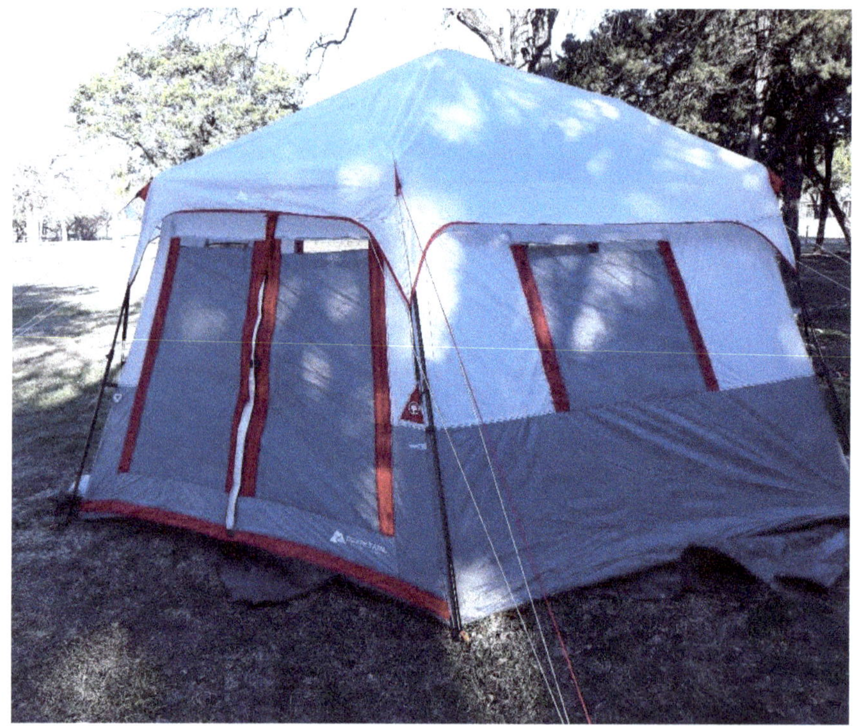

I love our new goofy hexagonal tent! It's large enough to feel like a living room when we're inside it, so that's a bonus. The first time we set it up was a challenge—one of the legs had been bent backwards (at a joint), so trying to figure that one out took a few minutes—but now, we're able to set it up in about ten minutes.

The wind knocked down one of the arms one day, and we provided plenty of entertainment for the residents across the street trying to get it back up, but the next morning, we added extra guy line support and haven't had any problems. No leaks either. Whew!

A special word of thanks to the kind neighbors who heard all the laughter from the other neighbors and came over to offer tools, help, support if we needed it. Your kindness surprised and blessed us.

I finally got a cot, too!

The campground was peaceful, with only a couple of campers. Weekends get busy because of the boats, but we were far enough away that it didn't bother us. I loved being on the water, and occasionally catching a whiff of lake water made me happy.

Tim got happy, too, when I introduced him to Braum's ice cream. He said it was the first time he'd ever had a banana split with hand-dipped ice cream instead of soft serve. (And if you've never had Braum's ice cream, try the strawberry—best in the world.)

Our time in Granbury was spent more on taking a breather from the road and on taking care of necessities like getting an oil change, installing a hitch for the car (and then a cargo carrier), and on getting a 20 lb propane tank for our heater and camp stove (instead of spending a fortune on the 1 lb cylinders). But we did explore the area and visited the town of Weatherford, too. (Ranch land between the two towns was some of the prettiest we've seen!)

Somewhere along the way, before we got to Granbury, I developed a rash on one of my ankles that gave symptoms of poison oak. I hadn't been around the stuff, so I'm not sure how I got it, but began treating it with Calamine while we were camped. Thankfully, it didn't spread, and the Calamine dried it up in about ten days.

We couldn't have campfires in the city park, but we were able to cook on our camp stove, so I was glad to have home cooking again. We finally found a percolator so we could have good (and hot!) coffee, too.

Planning took another turn while we were in Granbury. Weather continued to play a role in all our decision-making, and the storms (and cold weather) seemed to follow us east.

Our last night in the park, winds hit hard. We hurriedly packed, but before we could finish, it began sleeting. We finished loading the car, then checked into a hotel for the night. The next morning, I went to the car and discovered ice on the door handles. A friend gifted us with a second night at the hotel so we could stay put until the cold blew through.

We debated directions, and finally decided, as ridiculous as it seems, to head west again.

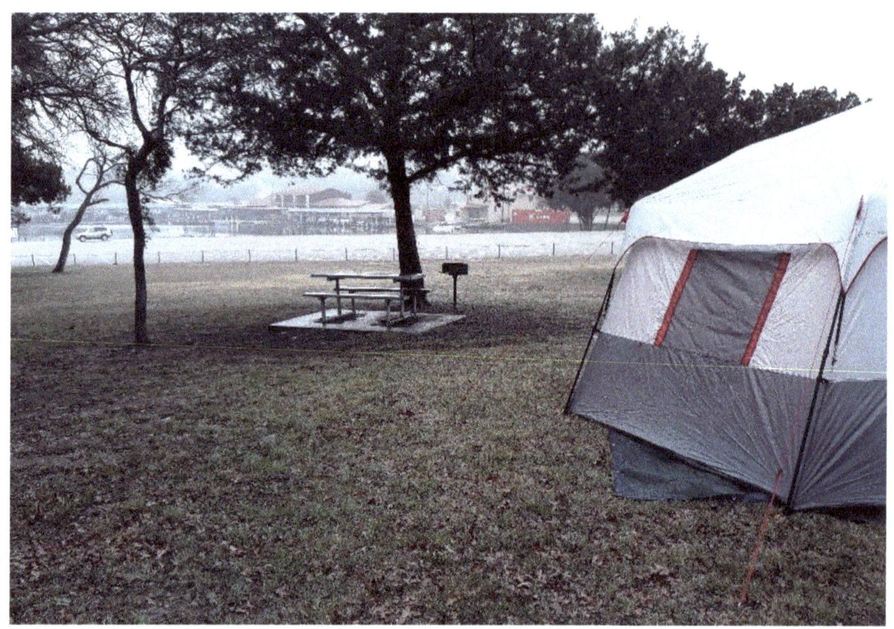

Above: Weekdays in the park were quiet.

Below: Glowing on our first night with our new
built-in LED lights inside our tent.

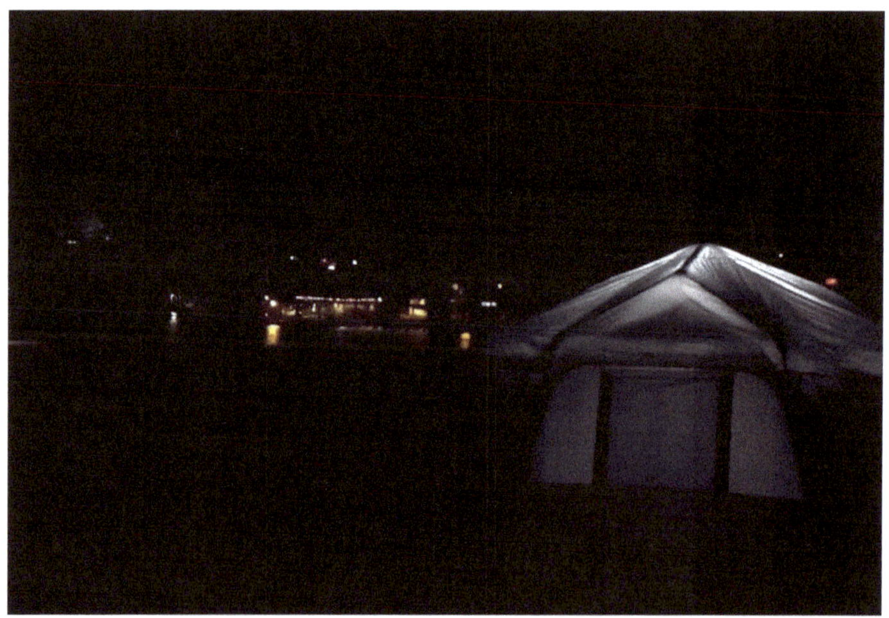

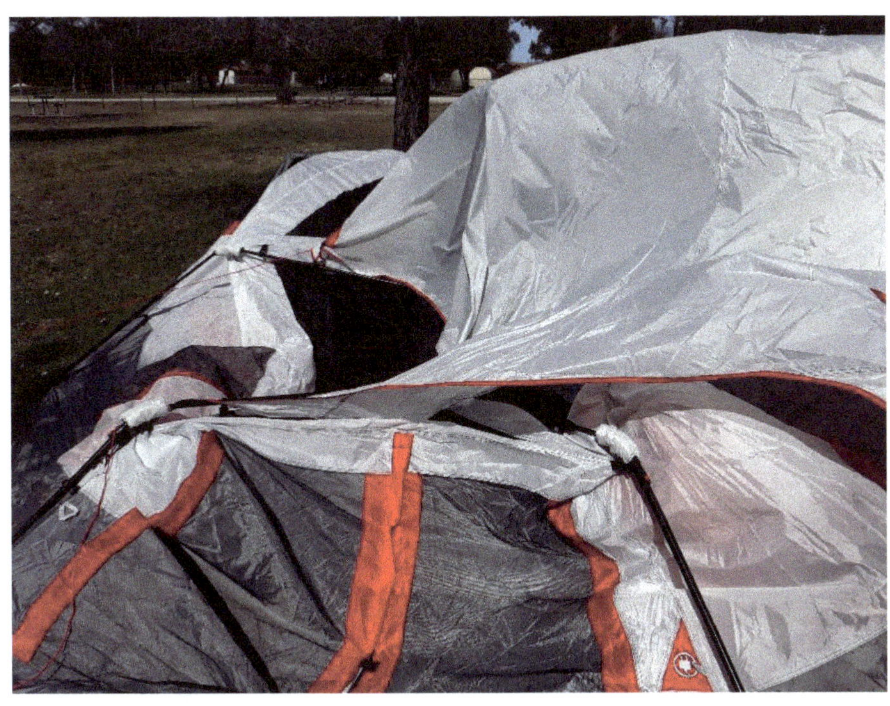

Above: Collapsed, before we added additional guy lines

Below: New towing package installed, and cargo carrier attached.

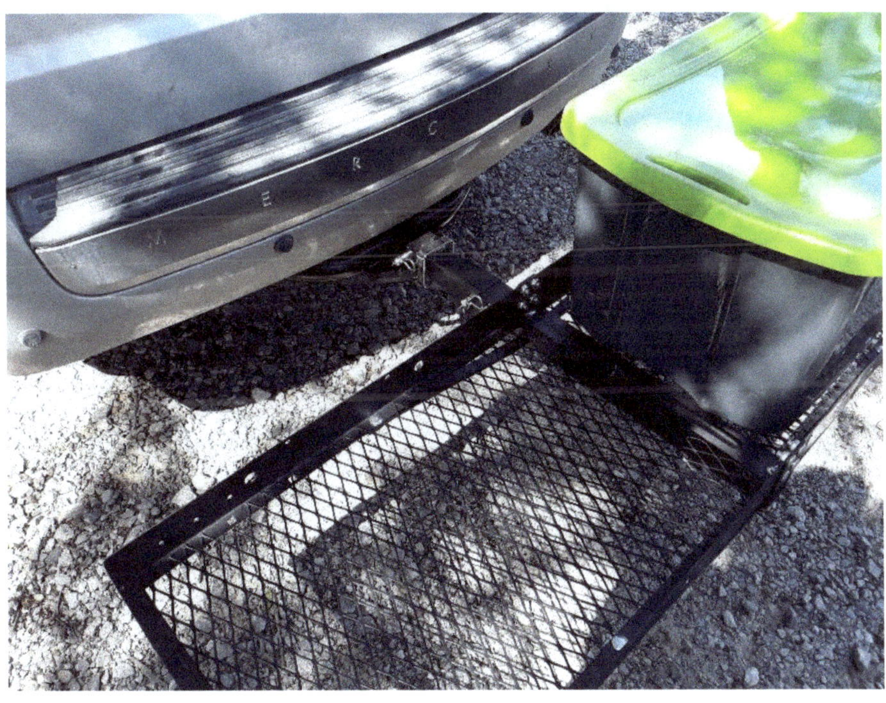

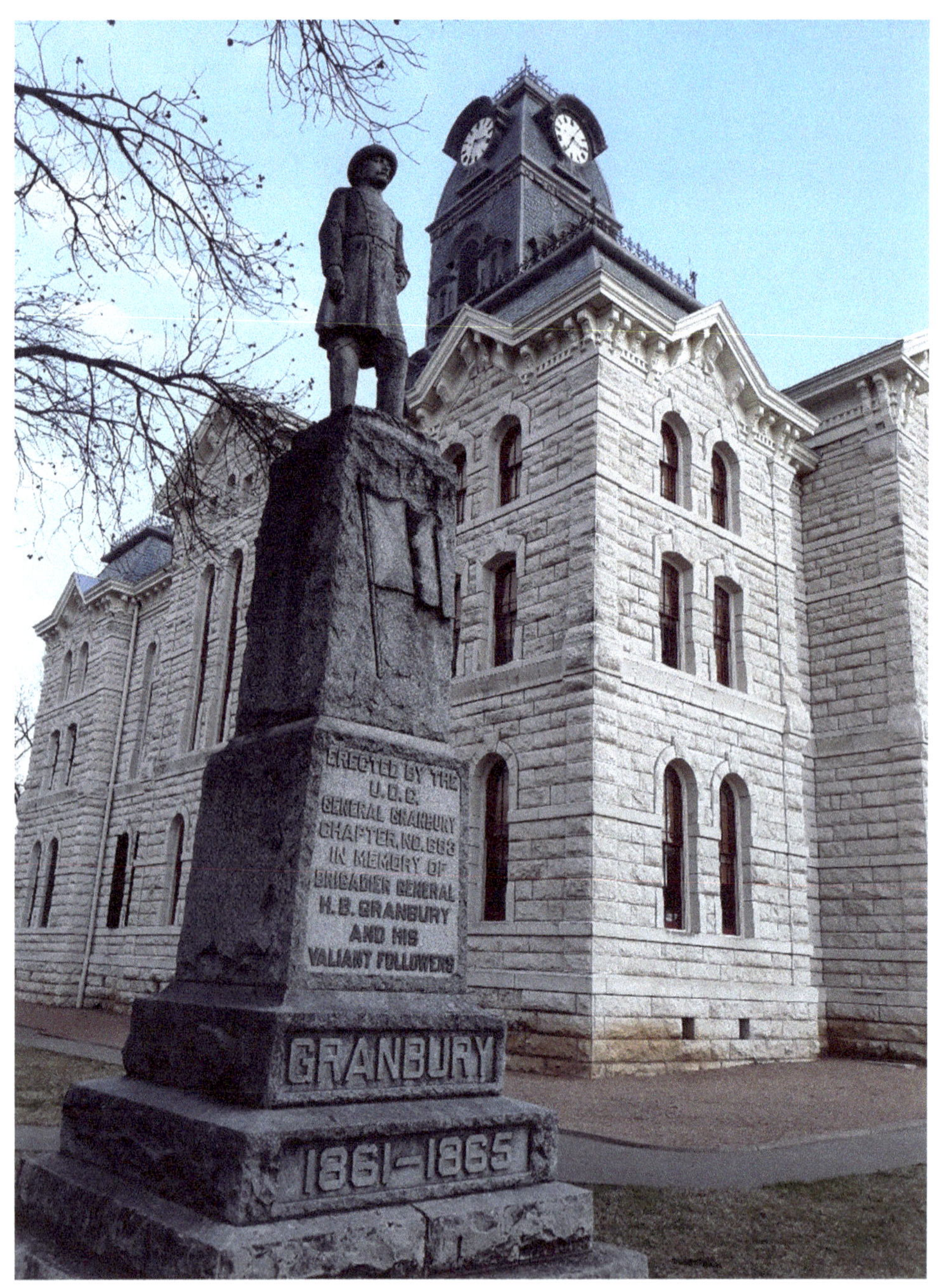

Historic Hood County Courthouse

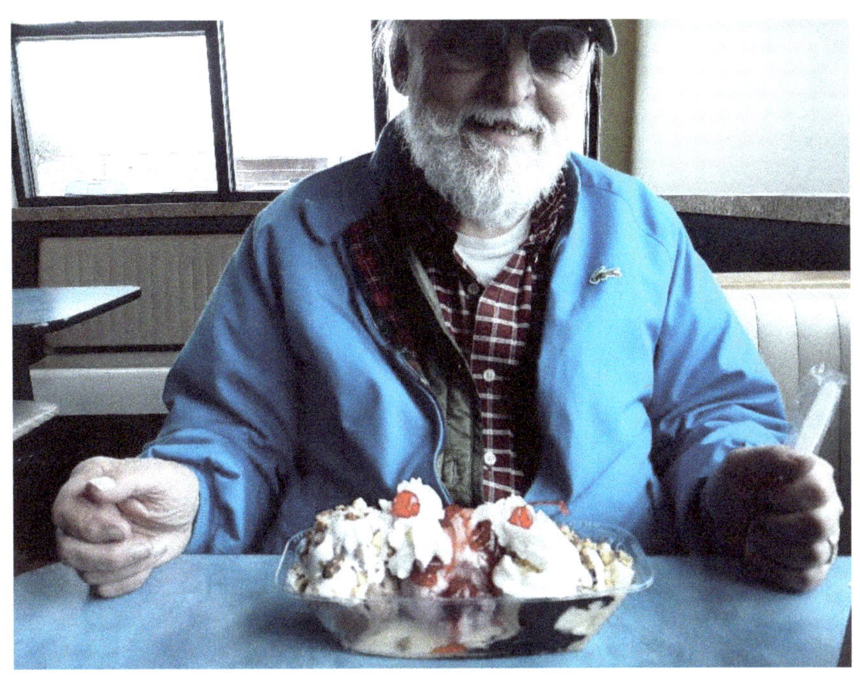

Above: Braum's Banana Split

Below: Houston Street Park, Granbury

(Also known as Shanley/Bicentennial Park)

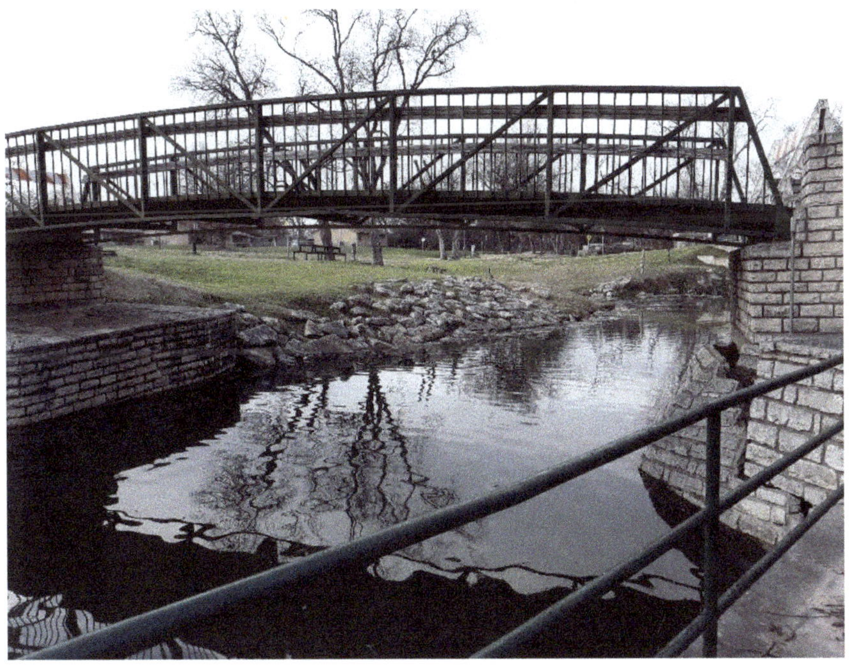

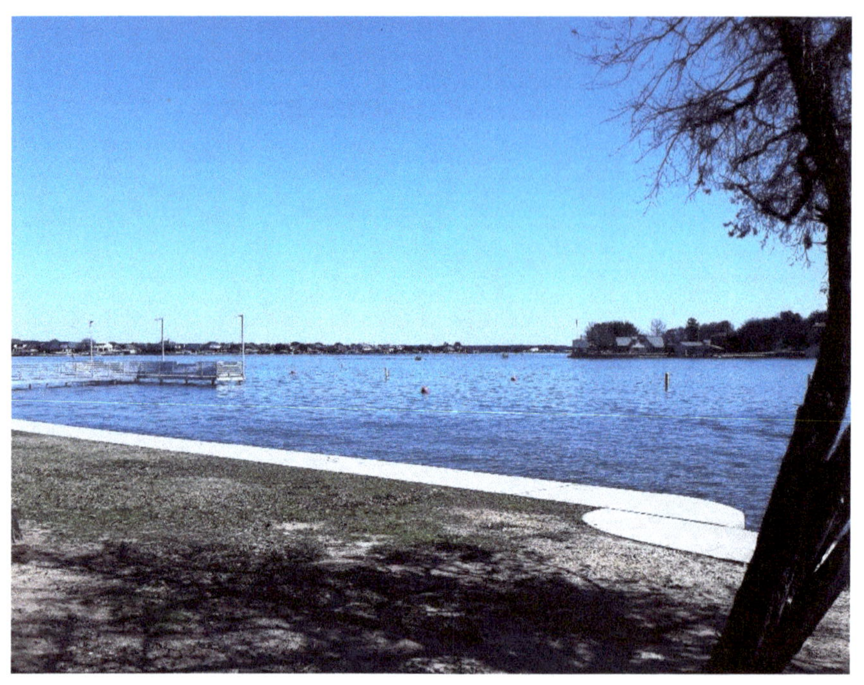

Above: View of Rough Creek / Brazos River

Below: Clean Laundromat even offered free detergent if needed.

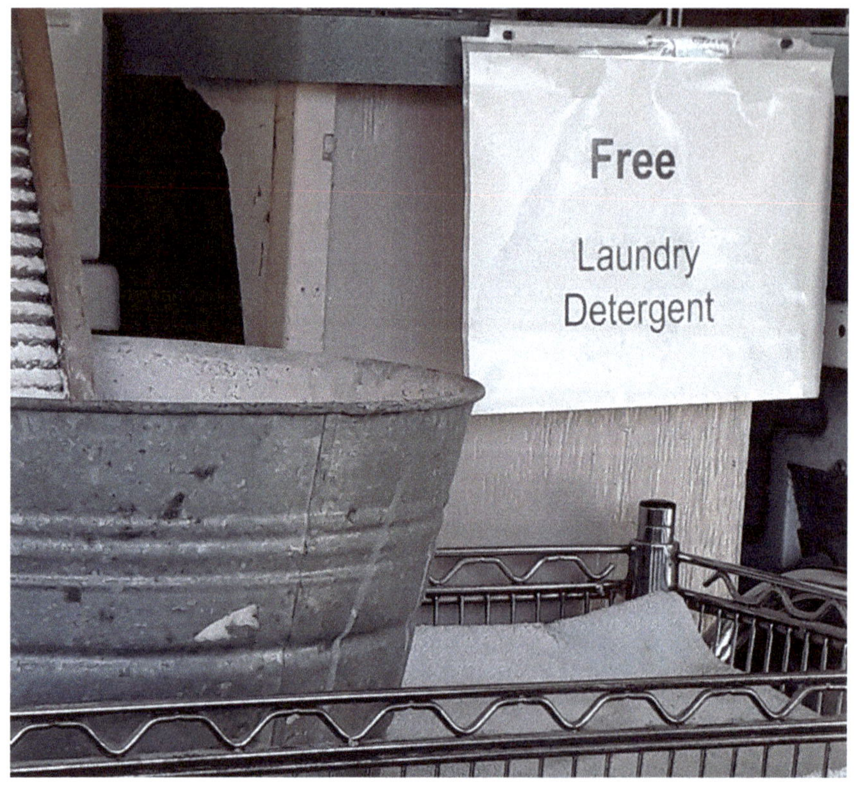

From the Frog Files

(We were in Granbury for several days, so the snippets below are taken from letters spread out over that time.)

We've tried to avoid winter, but it seems to be chasing us. I just checked the weather channel and saw news of two massive storms that will impact most of the country over the next ten days, or longer.

We left Abilene today just as sand trucks began pouring out on the interstate there. The temps were 32 and dropping as we left.

We're now parked at a gorgeous lake in Granbury, TX, but it's too wet to set up camp, so we'll car camp again tonight and see what tomorrow brings. It's currently 39 degrees, going down to 32, but only briefly, with tomorrow hopefully reaching 61.

We were able to locate a community center in Abilene that offered showers, so at least we're clean and fresh smelling.

The sun is shining gloriously this morning, but I made the mistake of looking at the weather to see how long it was going to last. Sigh. Windy today, with a high of 61, and thankfully dry for the next three days but temps start dropping again, then snow moves in here on the fourth. We're leaving here on the 30th, but right now, I'm not sure which direction. To the east - north and south - severe storms are blanketing almost everywhere; to the west - north and south - weird winter storms are everywhere. We seem to be sort of in a pocket.

I'm sorely tempted to just drive to FL. I'm so tired of fighting the weather. And I know it's only a matter of a couple of weeks when things will turn to spring, so it's probably foolish to even consider at this point. But I'm ready for sun and warmth.

It's currently 30 degrees, with a windchill of 21. We are under a winter weather advisory and it is sleeting, even as far north as Dallas, which is the direction we're planning to head after trying to get some bluebonnet photos.

Thankfully, I am writing this update from a hotel in Granbury.

Last night, as the winds and misty sleet continued, we kept packing the car. I checked Hotwire and decided to use some gift money to get a hotel for $50. We rushed to finish the car as some drug-induced young people arrived and began harassing us. It took us 2 hours to get warm after we checked in. I'm grateful the heater went to 80 degrees. Lol!

This was an extravagance so we can't stay. I requested a late checkout, but they have another arrival, so we must leave by noon.

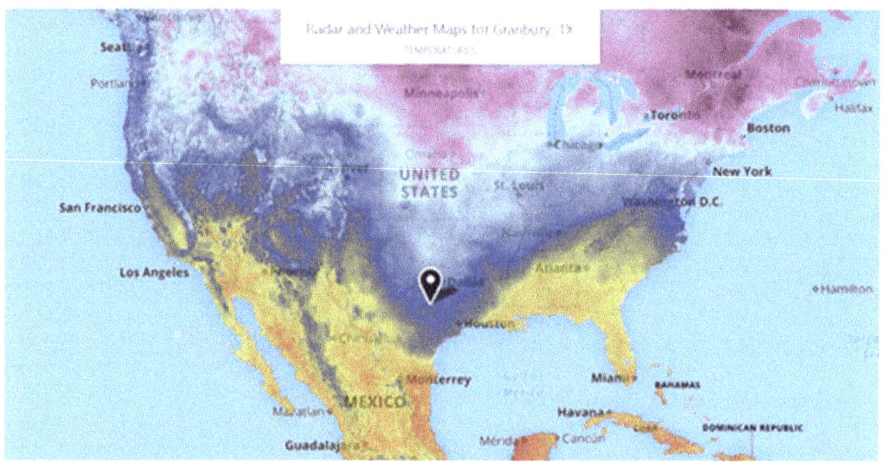

Above: The blue is the cold front settling in, white is snow.

Below: Sleet crunchies on the car door handle.

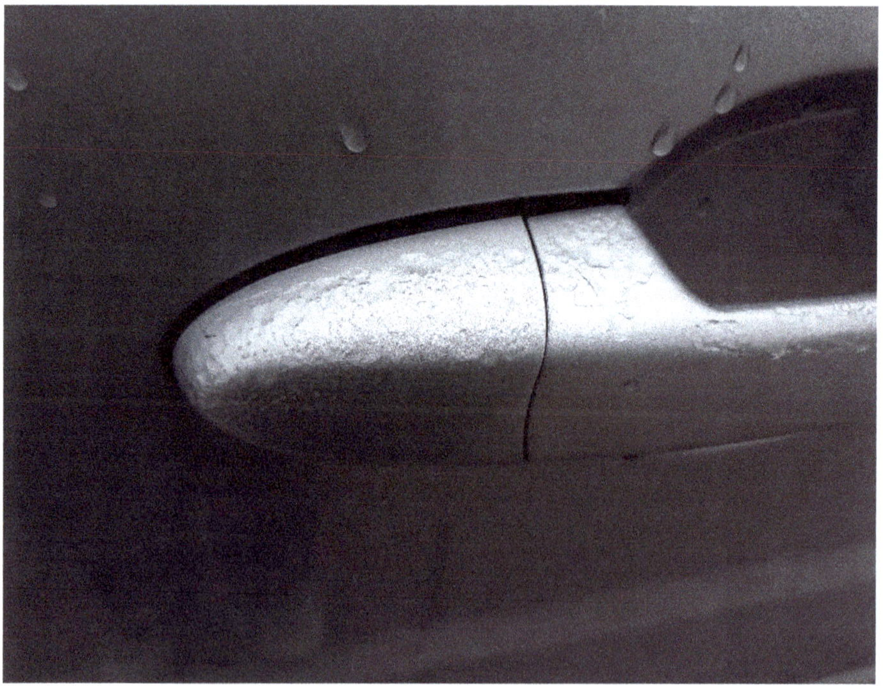

Chapter Twenty-Seven

Speeding West Again

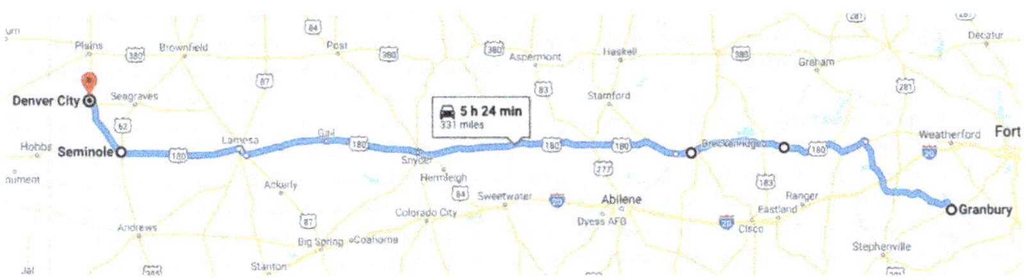

Granbury to Denver City, Texas

During our extended stay in Granbury, Texas, I kept an eye on the weather and battled my own inner doubts about continuing our journey. We had a choice to make—either head back home and settle into a quiet, normal life again, or continue traveling. (No choice for some of us, right?)

After much prayer and many discussions, we knew there really wasn't a choice— we wanted to keep traveling and had to make a few adjustments to make traveling work for us instead of against us.

The weather appeared to be clearing up out west, so we decided to make the Grand Canyon our next goal, with a few stops on the way. Once we had that on our radar, I began deeper research and plotted our route.

When we packed the car in Granbury (in wind, sleet, and darkness), we couldn't figure out how to fold up our new hexagon-shaped tent, so we stuffed it in the car, intending to fold it later. as we approached the state line, we found a great city park outside Seminole, TX, where we could car camp overnight, and we pulled out our tent there, then figured out how to fold it up and get it back in its bag. Whew!

Somewhere along the way, we passed an interesting house with some familiar characters hanging out in the yard, so we turned around to snap a shot!

We're currently sitting at a picnic table in the shade of glorious, warm sunshine and very gentle warm breezes. Temperature is 79 degrees, and it feels like Heaven.

We're car camping tonight in a city park located between Seminole and Denver City, Texas. The places we thought we would be staying in Seminole were not good, so when we found this park with great reviews, we decided to drive a bit north to check it out. I'm so glad we did. It's beautiful.

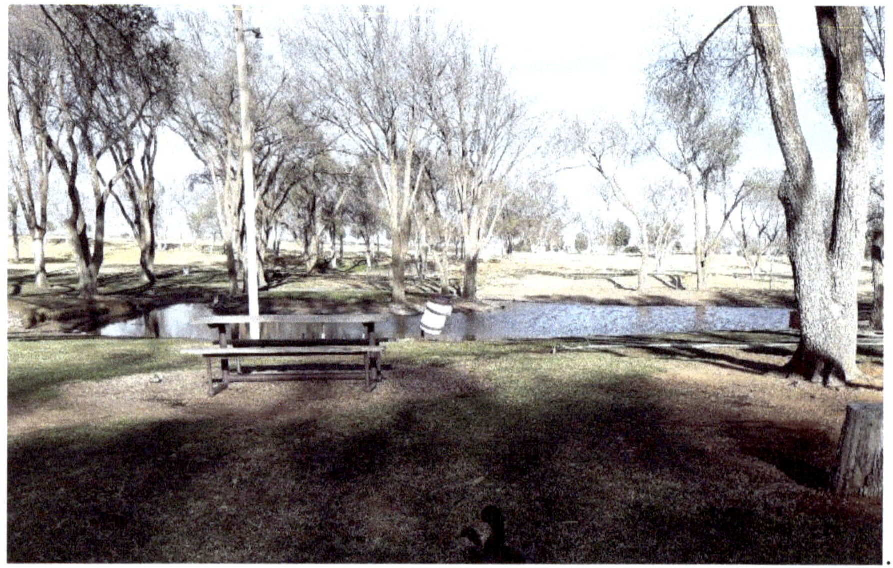

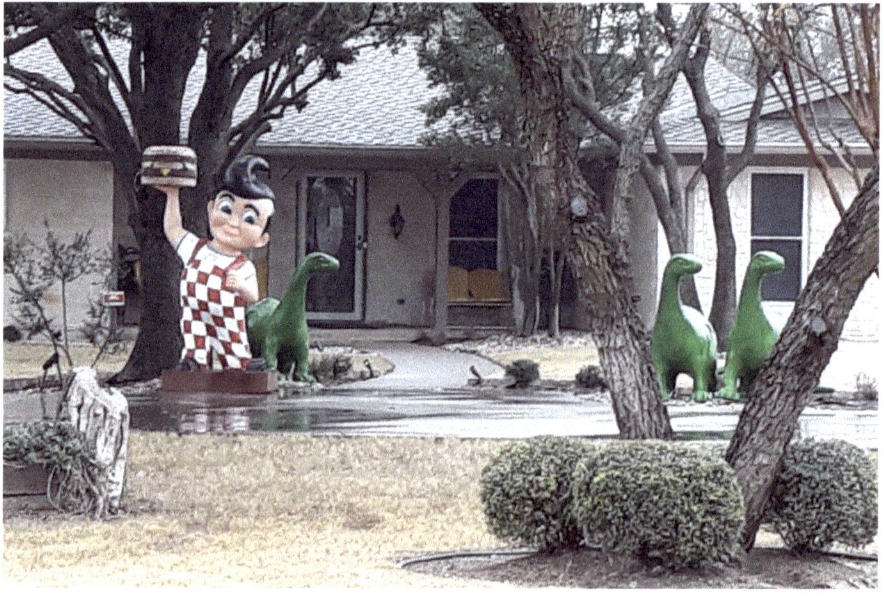

Chapter Twenty-Eight

Speeding Through New Mexico

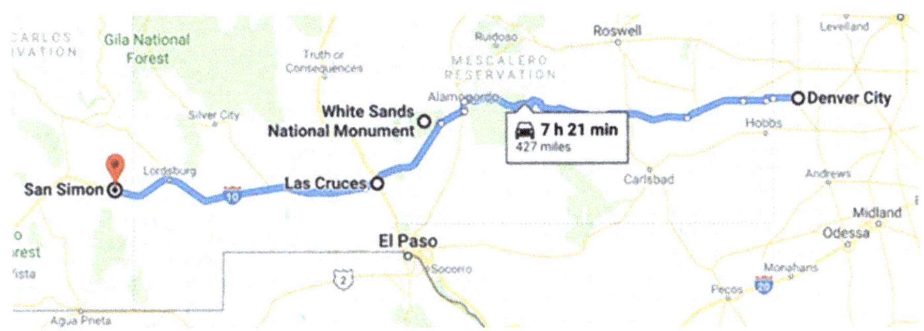

Denver City, Texas to San Simon, Arizona

We tried not to backtrack in any area we'd already been but couldn't avoid it completely. We went through Artesia again, traveling the same road we'd left from there in the dark, and discovered we hadn't missed much the first time.

But from Artesia on, we were in new territory. And back in the mountains. And my mountain fears seemed to be increasing.

We learned something important on this leg of the journey—with the new hitch on our car, we realized it probably could not handle towing a pop-up camper at all. The SUV struggled a great deal through the mountains of Cloudcroft, New Mexico, with an elevation of 8,668'.

I was focused on getting to the NM/AZ state line before nightfall, and we wanted to see White Sands, so we didn't hang around Cloudcroft, except to refuel. We could sense the altitude difference—both of us were extremely thirsty. Snow was still on the ground, too. I loved seeing all the evergreen trees in the area—a new and refreshing site.

And then—White Sands!

Pulling into White Sands National Monument, I wasn't really sure what to expect. Driving through the entrance gate wasn't that impressive—just looked like a little white sand here and there, and we've seen plenty of that on beaches. But the further we drove into the park, the more white sand there was—and when you realize all this sand is constantly blown about by winds, and yet remains, it's quite incredible and beautiful.

You'll notice sunshine in the pictures, too. A rare sight in our travels thus far, and not one we took for granted. Such a beautiful day!

On the drive from White Sands to Las Cruces, we encountered something new—a dust storm! Tim snapped a photo while I continued driving. The storm wasn't severe enough to make the truckers stop driving, so I followed their lead and kept moving, too.

(Interestingly, we encountered the dust storm BEFORE all the warning signs informing us what to do in case of a dust storm!)

After all the struggle the car had with the mountains, and after the dust storm, when we got to Las Cruces, I decided we should replace the air filter. I'm glad we checked it—it was filthy and heavy. While we were at the Auto Zone, I discovered the town had a Sportsman's Warehouse, so I checked their website and found a case for my fly rod—FINALLY! We hit the road again, determined to get close to the state line before nightfall.

Since I was doing all the driving, Tim served as shot-gun photographer and snapped this cool tunnel outside Alamogordo.

Just before sunset, we arrived at a rest stop in San Simon, and was amazed at how the terrain was changing once again.

Tomorrow, we begin exploring Arizona!

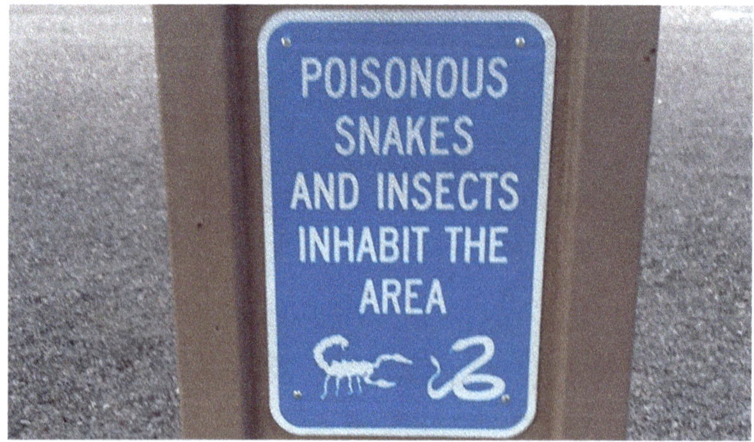

Above: Tim's photo of the dust storm as I kept driving.

Below: Inside White Sands National Park

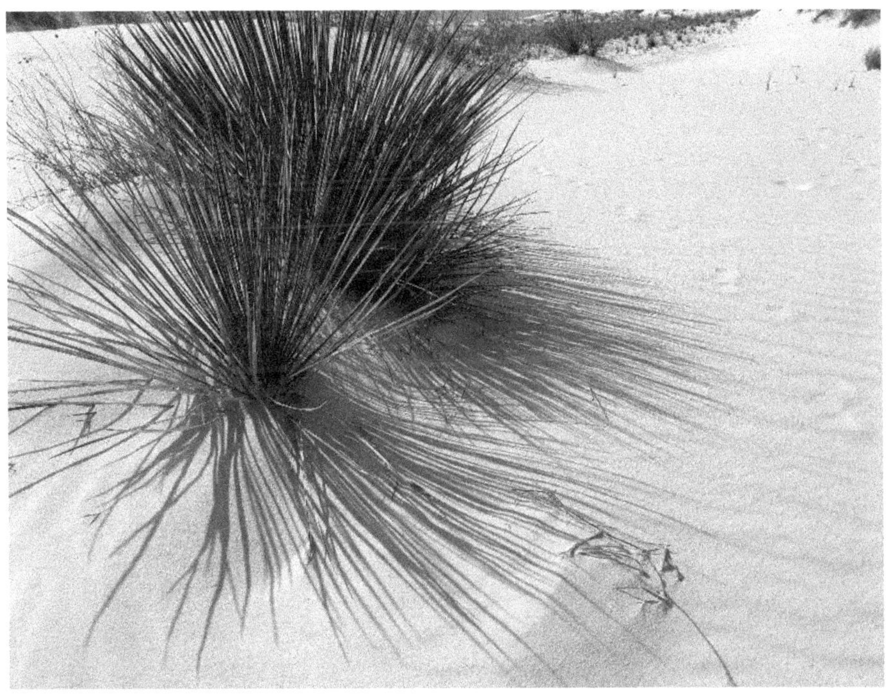

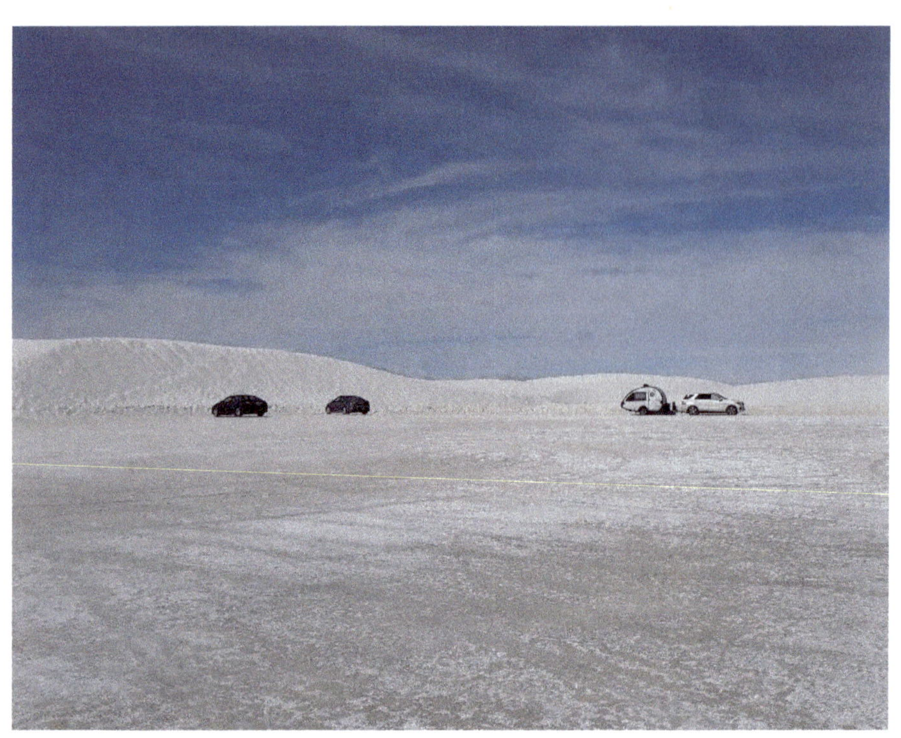

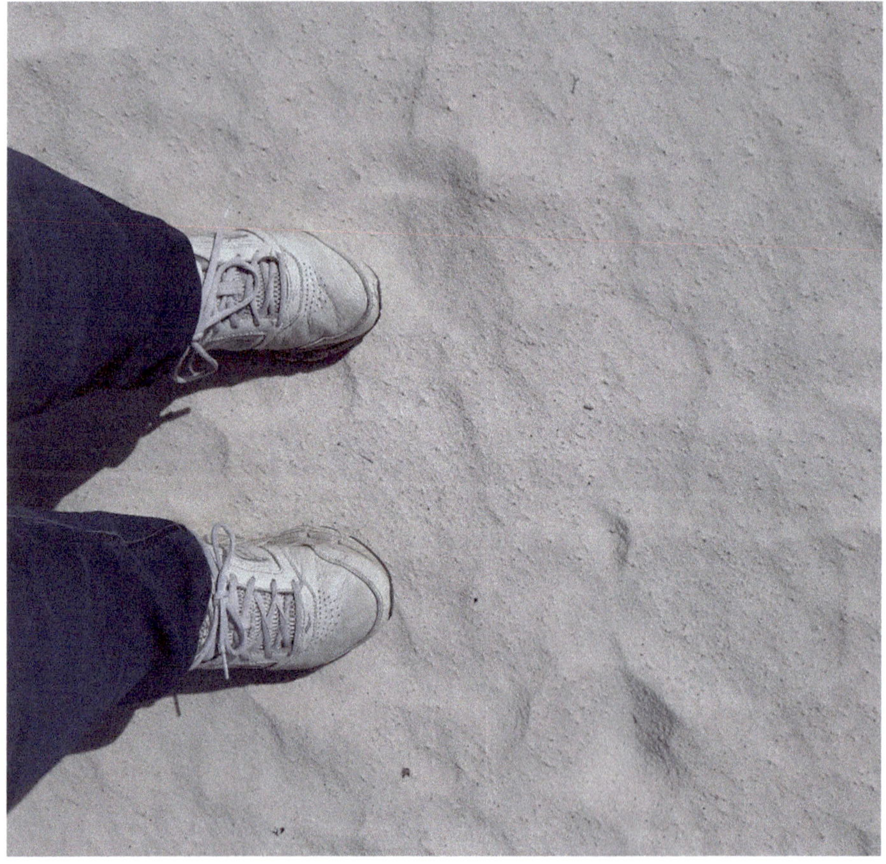

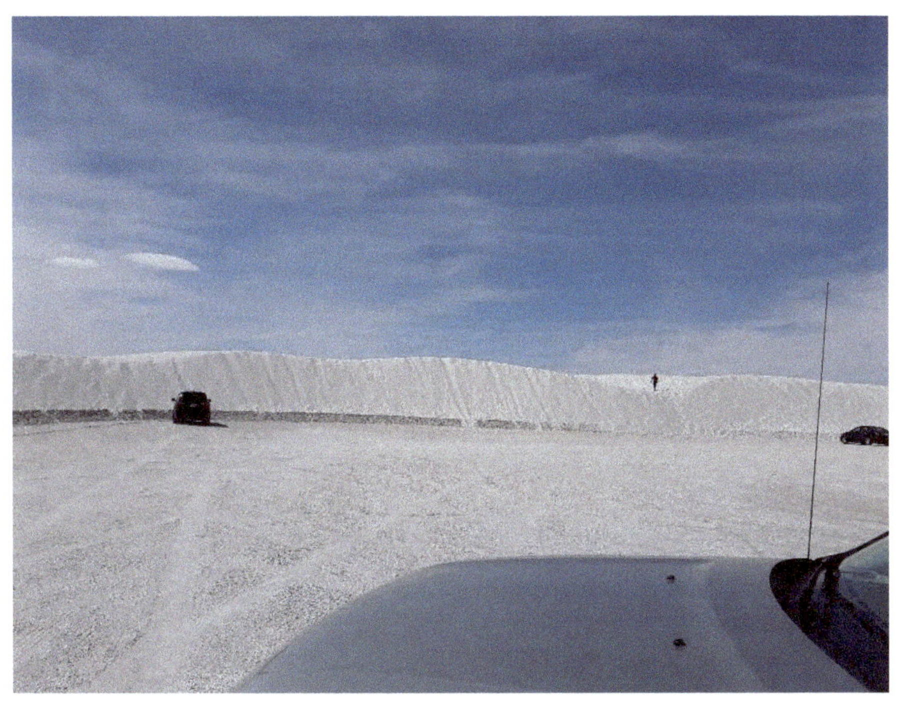

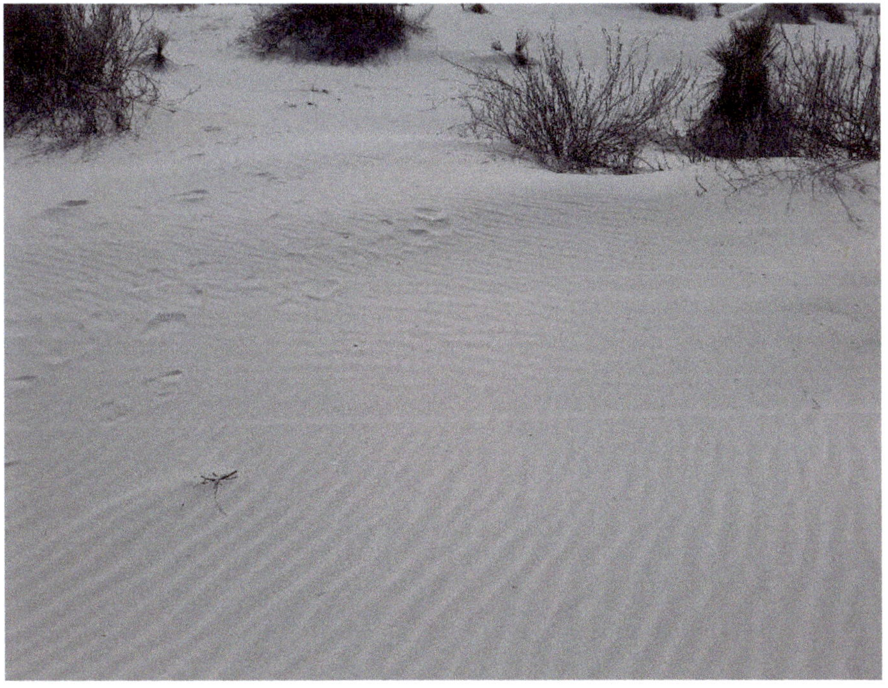

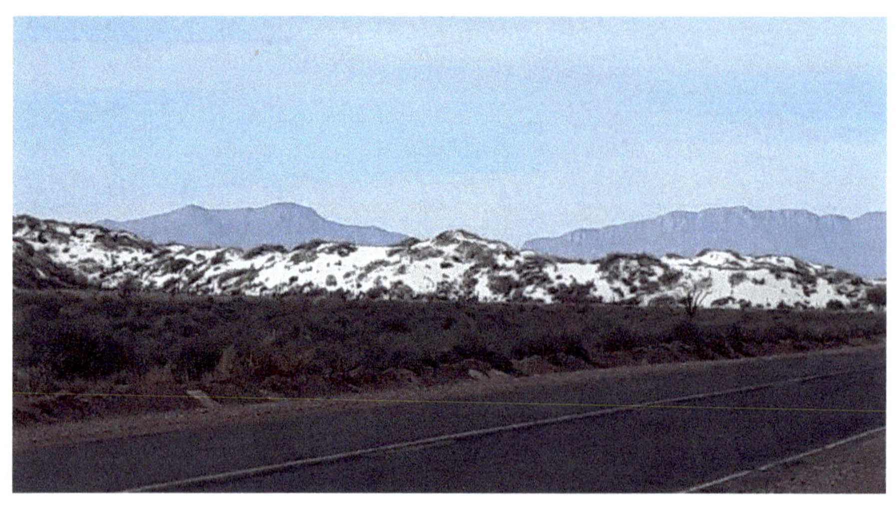

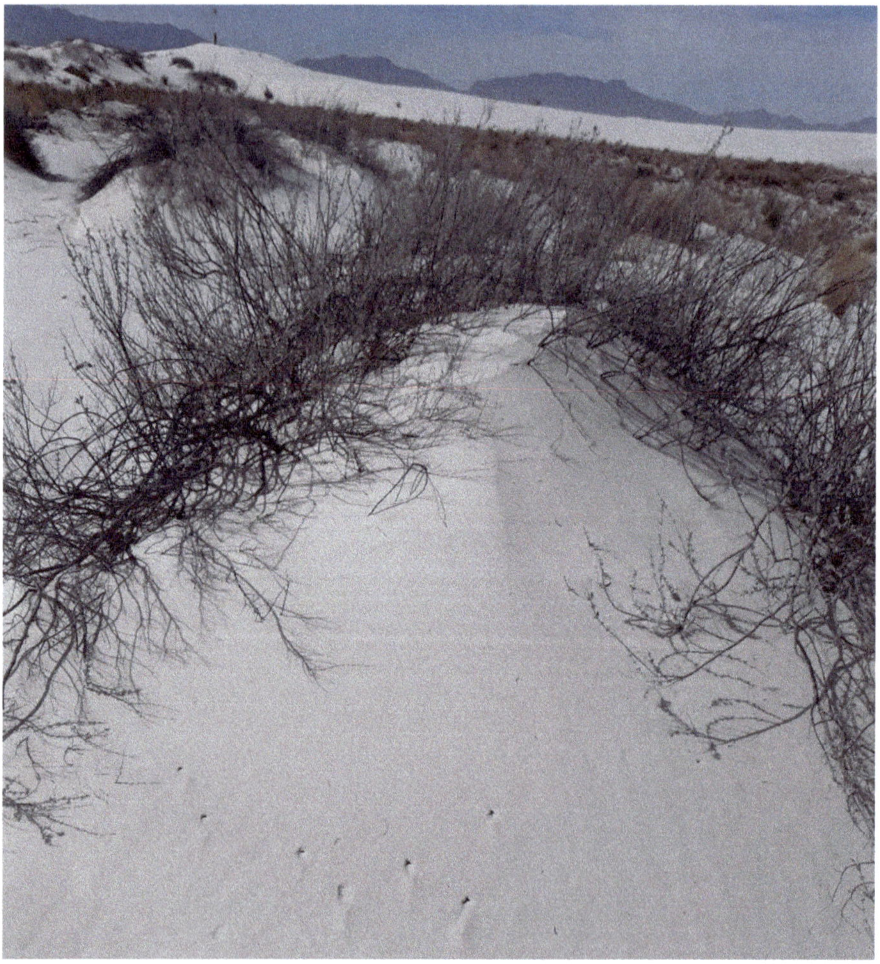

Chapter Twenty-Nine

On to Arizona

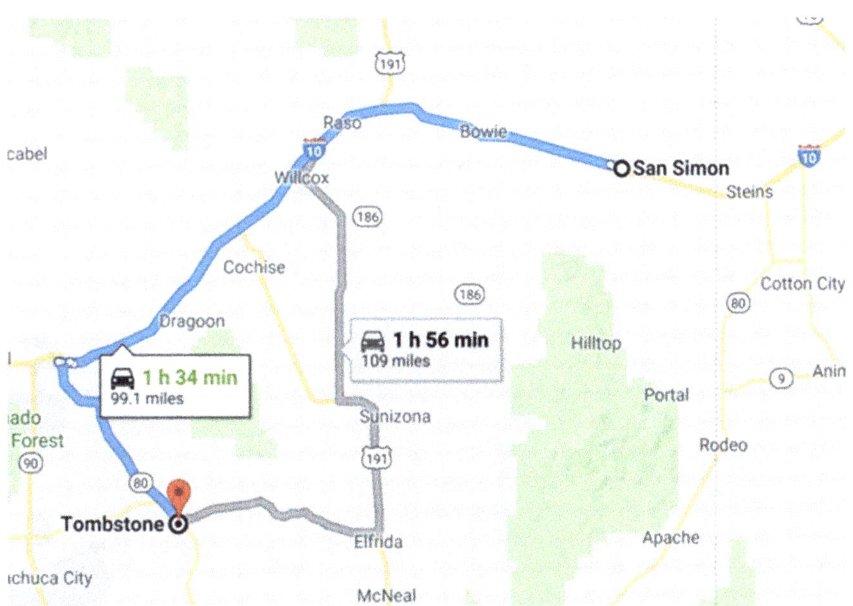

San Simon to Tombstone

Excited to be in Arizona—my second "new" state, and Tim's third. We had a peaceful night in the San Simon rest stop after speeding across New Mexico, and the morning dawned bright and clear! Sunshine!! As we started driving, clouds hovered over the mountains in the distance. I had to pull over to snap a picture.

While we were pulled over, we decided to grab a cup of coffee from the convenience store, but it was too early, and they weren't opened. We weren't exactly sure where we were when we pulled off the interstate, but this window educated us quickly.

Next up: Tombstone, Arizona. I wanted to find my huckleberry and Tim was gearing up for shoot-out.

I'm not sure what I expected, but Tombstone was much more touristy than I like. I was afraid we'd not be able to experience the best parts—because of budget—but was surprised to learn that the OK Corral offered a ticket to several events and products for only $10.

The town is like a movie set, and a lot of fun. The main streets have wooden sidewalks and dirt streets. Storefronts fit the period, and cowboys and saloon girls walk the streets like any busy western town of old. Cross streets are regular traffic, so stagecoaches drive the main drag, as Spyder motorcycles and Smart cars cruise the side streets.

Our tickets included the shootout at the OK Corral, cheesy but fun and educational, and the actors were great.

I'd seen the next attraction referred to as "the blob" on review sites, so I wasn't sure we'd care for the Historama (you can see photos on RoadsideAmerica), but I loved it. If you've ever seen Atlanta's Cyclorama, telling the story of the Civil War, the Historama is much like that, except in "blob" shape. It's more of a volcano shape that rotates, with different parts moving as the story unfolds. We learned the sad (and victorious?) history of the town of Tombstone. The story is told through the historama and through film, narrated by Vincent Price. Photos were not allowed, but I was a good girl and didn't try to sneak any, unlike others
sitting near us.

Our ticket also included admission to the museum attached to the OK Corral, and to the newspaper museum down the street and around the corner (and a free newspaper to commemorate our day!) With a newspaper background and ink in my blood, I loved this one!

The town doesn't take itself too seriously, and that made it even more fun. Notice the last item on the menu board picture.

On the way to Tombstone, I'd seen a cross on the side of the road but had traffic behind me so I couldn't stop. As we left, I decided we'd try to find it again—and we did. The Holy Trinity Monastery.

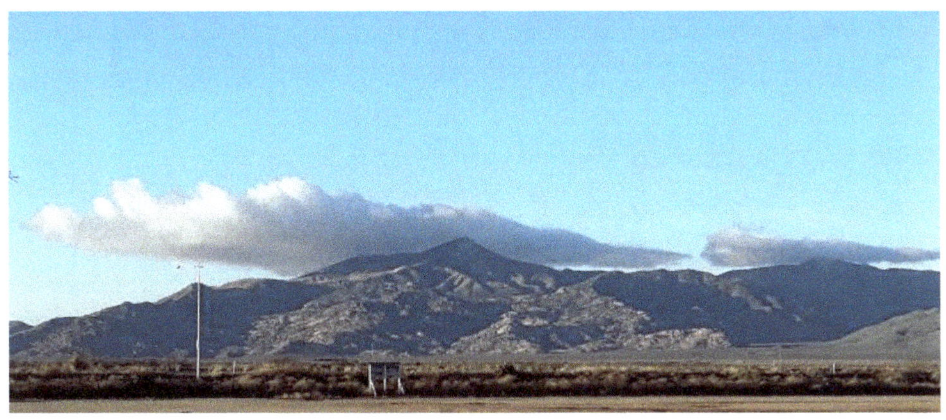

Bowie, AZ, Hometown of Rambo

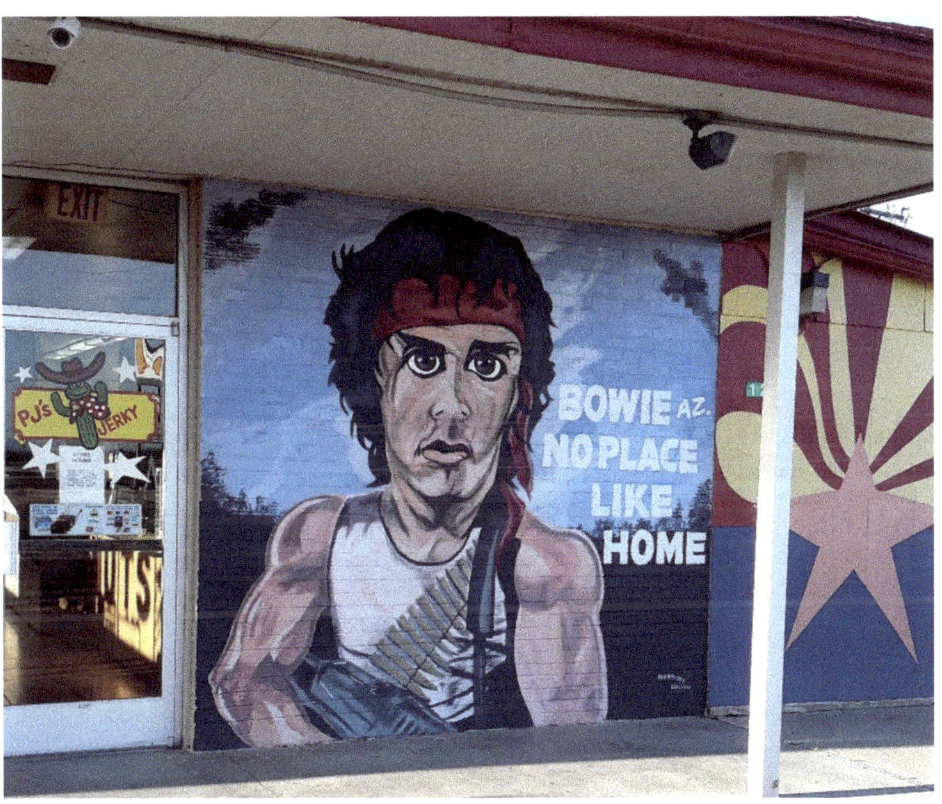

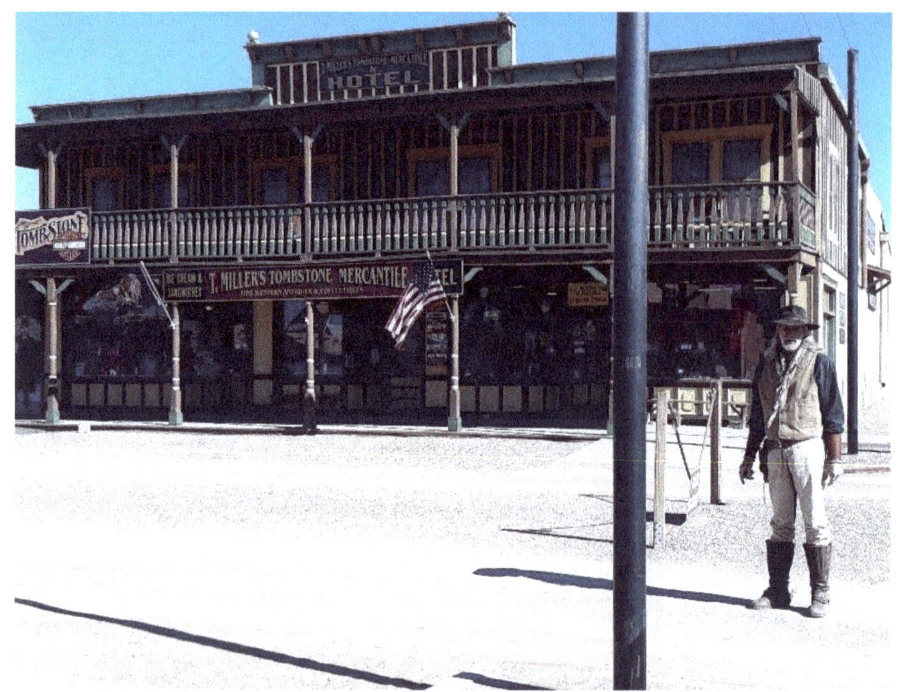

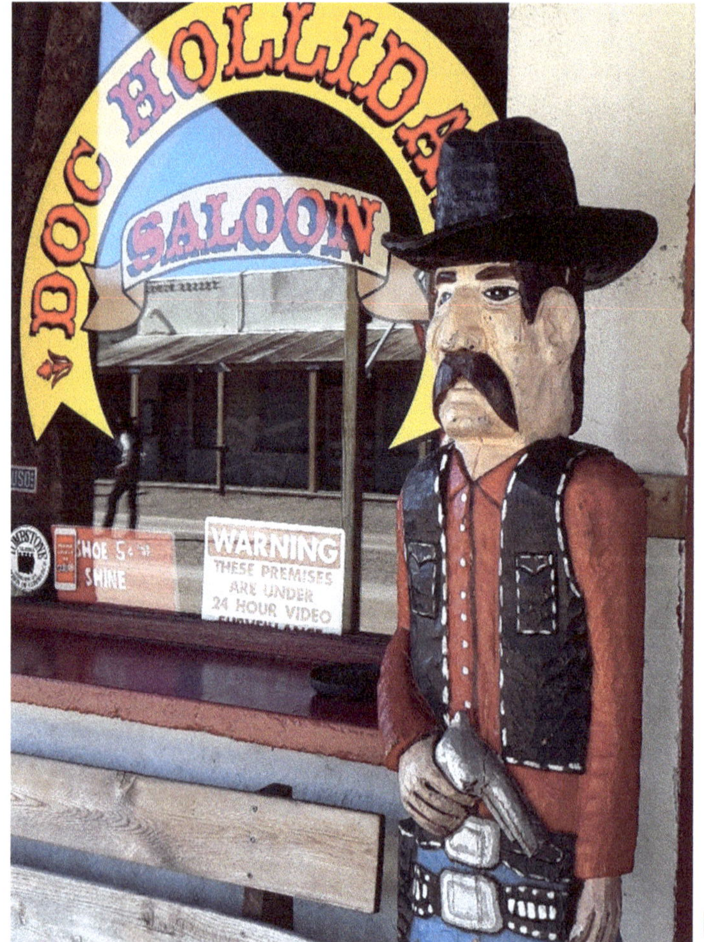
DOC HOLLIDAY
SALOON
WARNING
THESE PREMISES
ARE UNDER
24 HOUR VIDEO
SURVEILLANCE
SHOE 5¢
SHINE

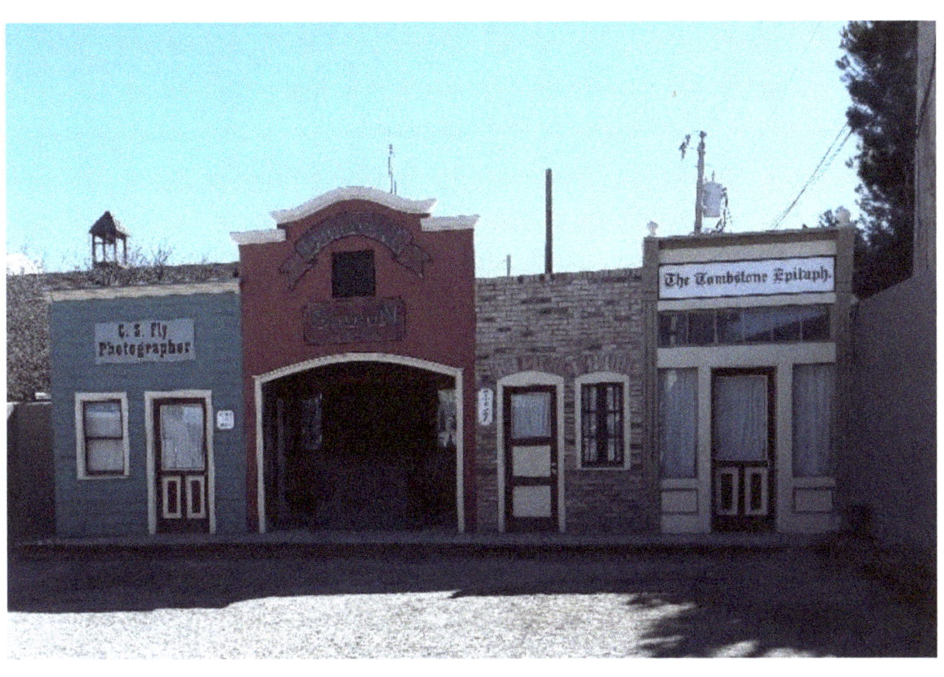
C. S. Fly
Photographer
The Tombstone Epitaph.

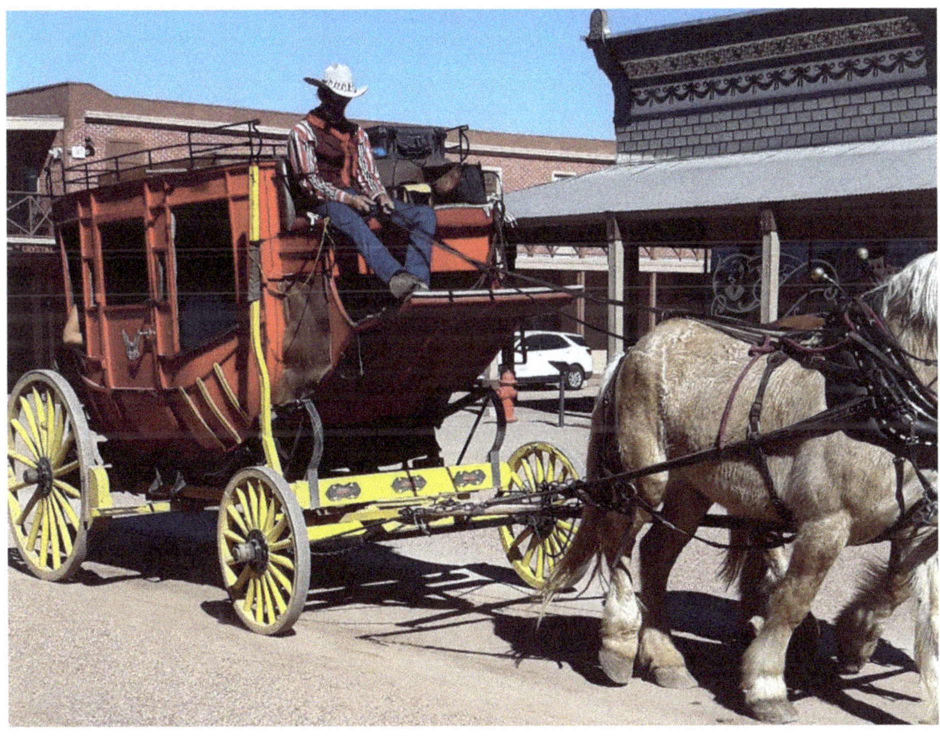

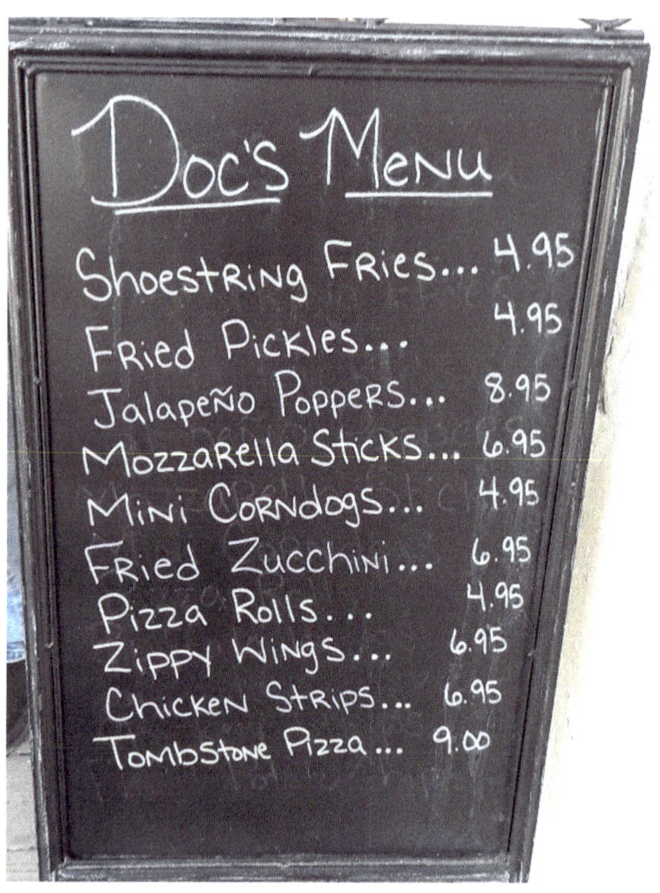

Doc's Menu
Shoestring Fries... 4.95
Fried Pickles... 4.95
Jalapeño Poppers... 8.95
Mozzarella Sticks... 6.95
Mini Corndogs... 4.95
Fried Zucchini... 6.95
Pizza Rolls... 4.95
Zippy Wings... 6.95
Chicken Strips... 6.95
Tombstone Pizza... 9.00

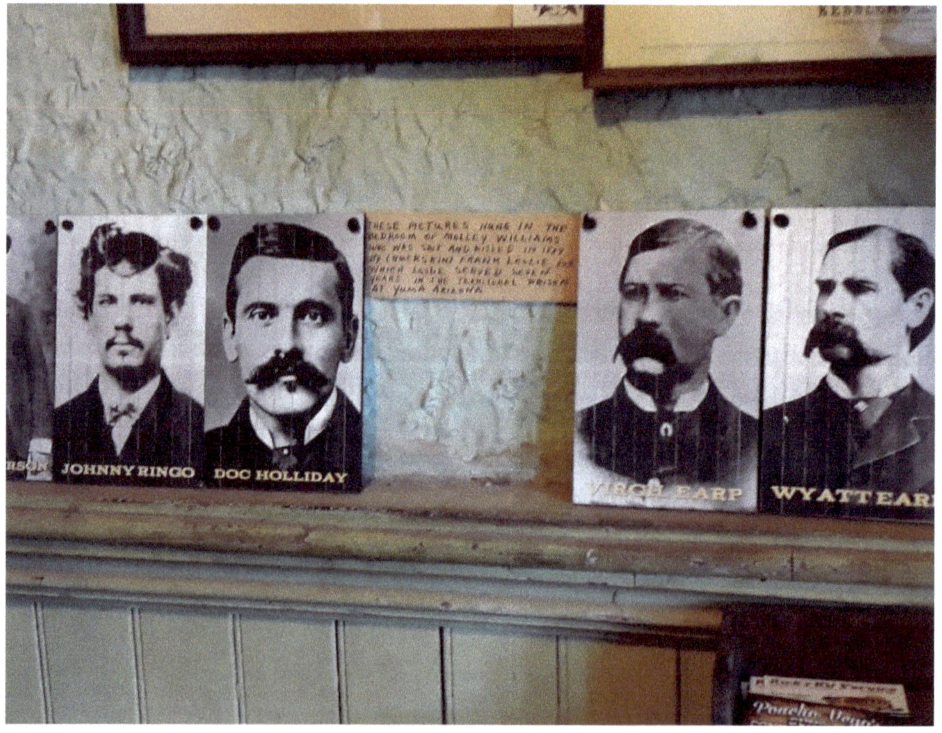

JOHNNY RINGO
DOC HOLLIDAY
VIRGIL EARP
WYATT EARP

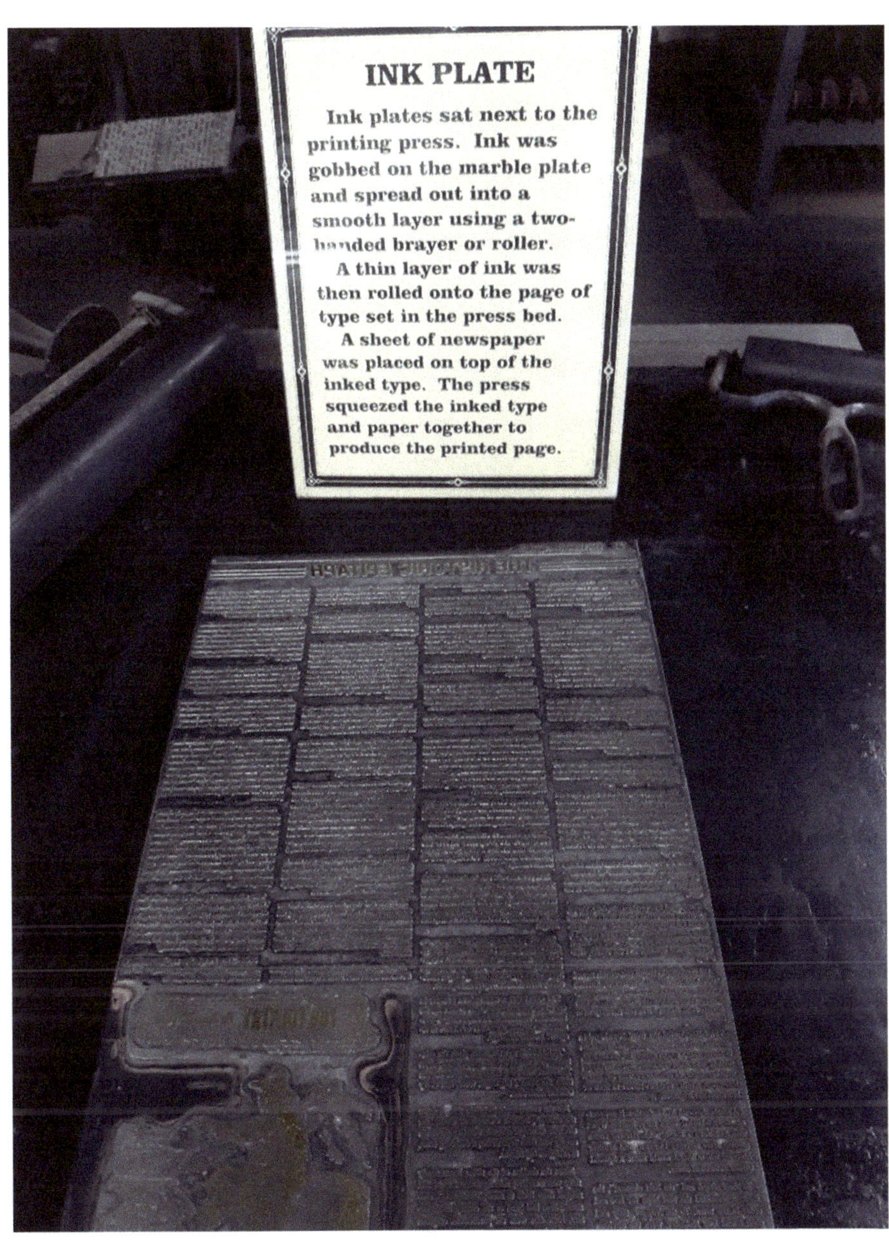

INK PLATE

Ink plates sat next to the printing press. Ink was gobbed on the marble plate and spread out into a smooth layer using a two-handed brayer or roller.

A thin layer of ink was then rolled onto the page of type set in the press bed.

A sheet of newspaper was placed on top of the inked type. The press squeezed the inked type and paper together to produce the printed page.

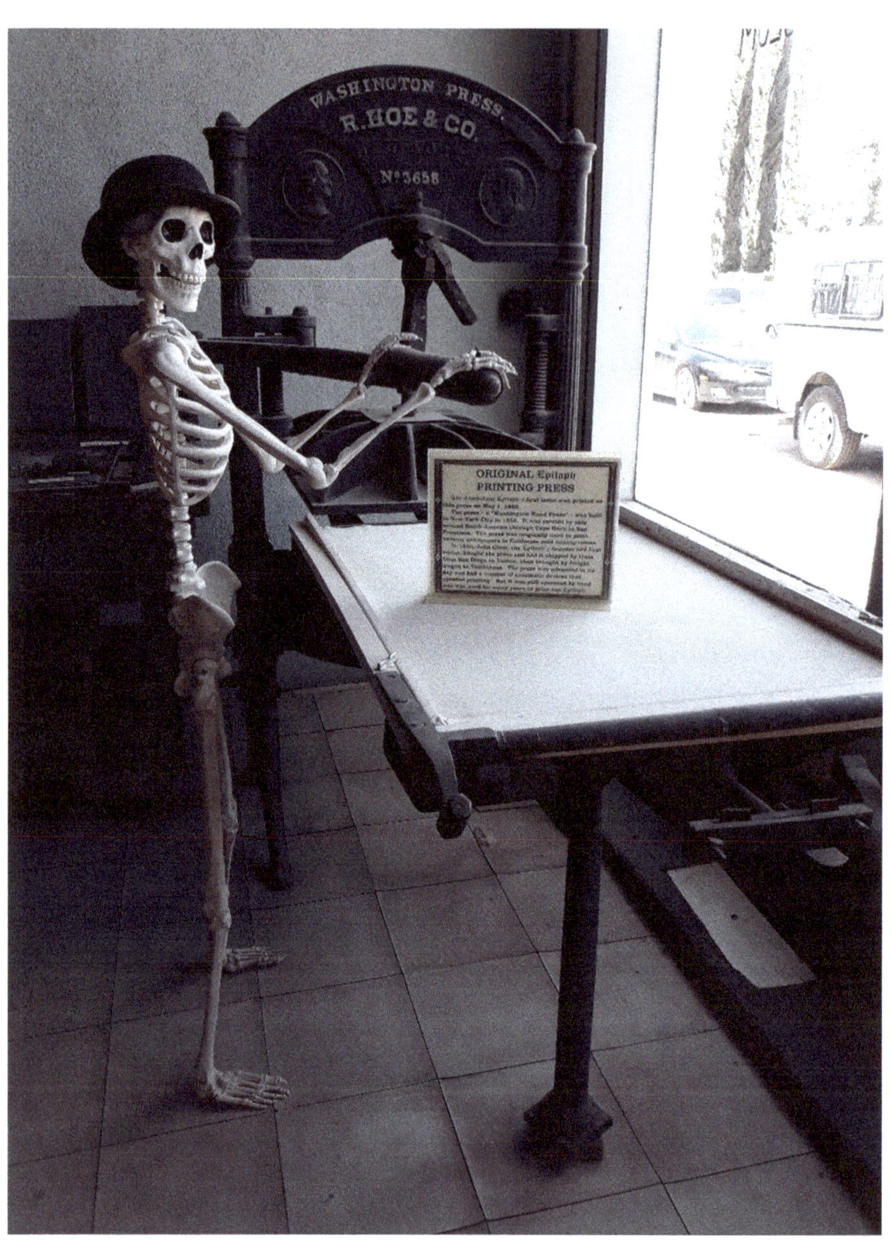
WASHINGTON PRESS.
R. HOE & CO.
No 5658
ORIGINAL Epitaph
PRINTING PRESS

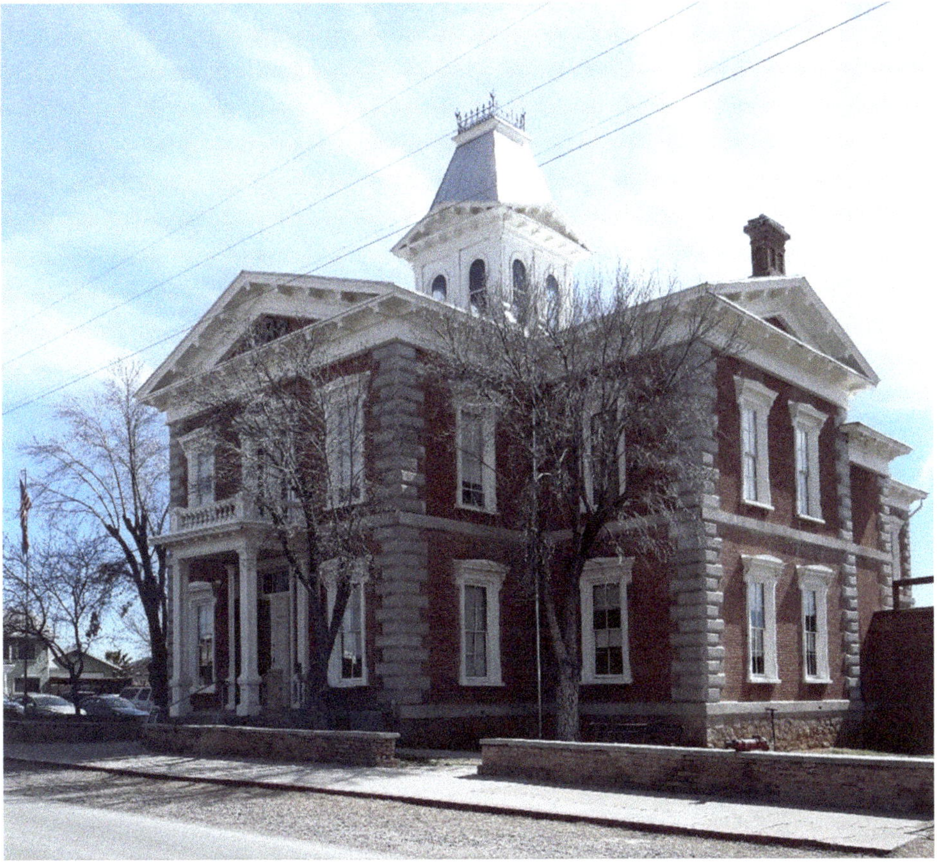

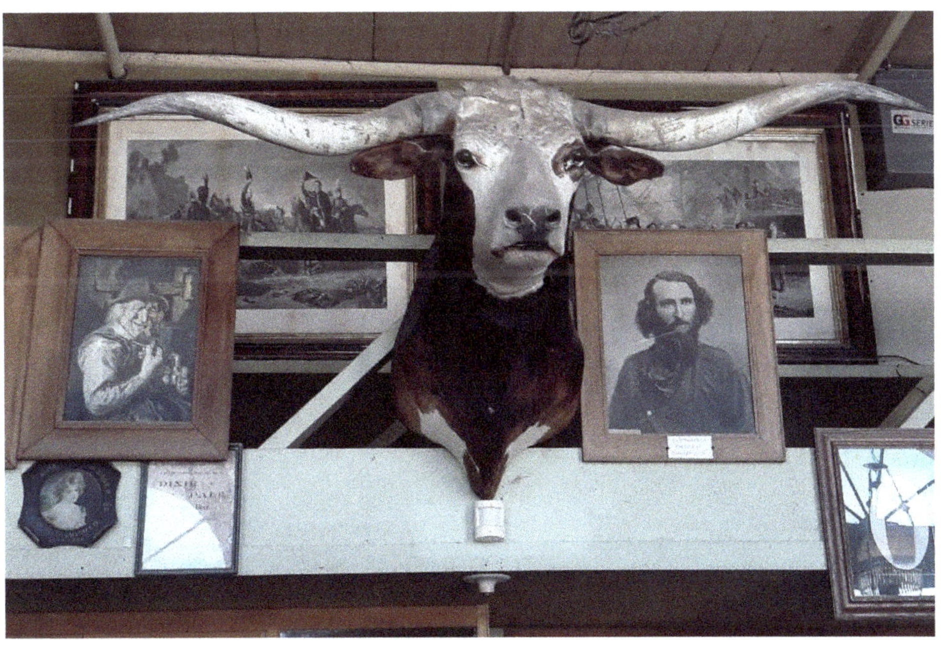

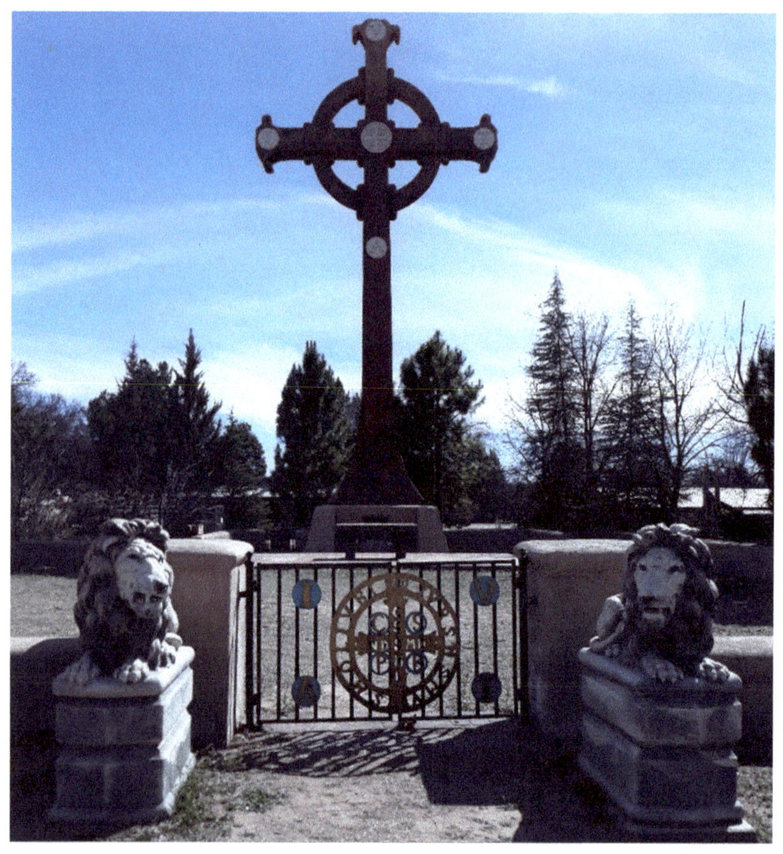

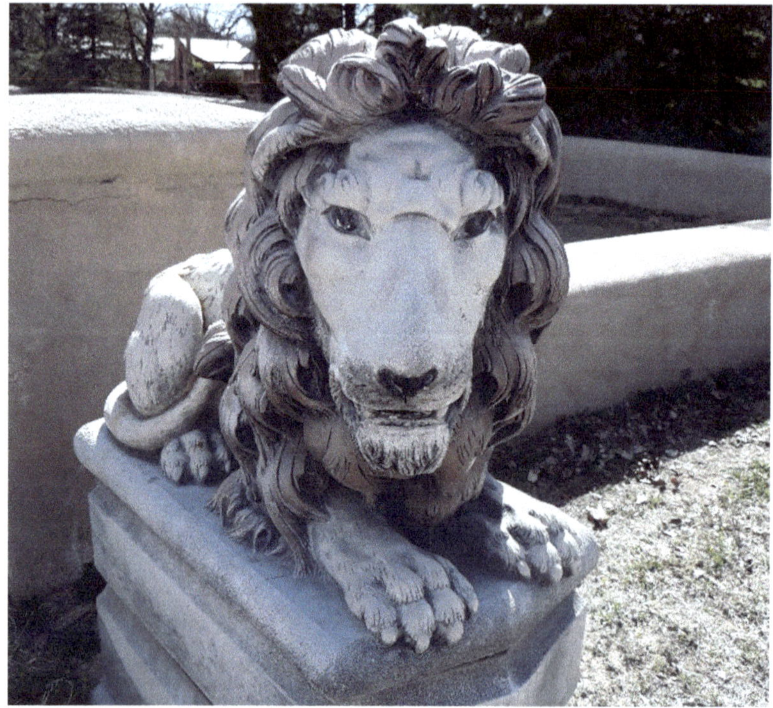

Chapter Thirty

Mountain Fears and the Saguaro

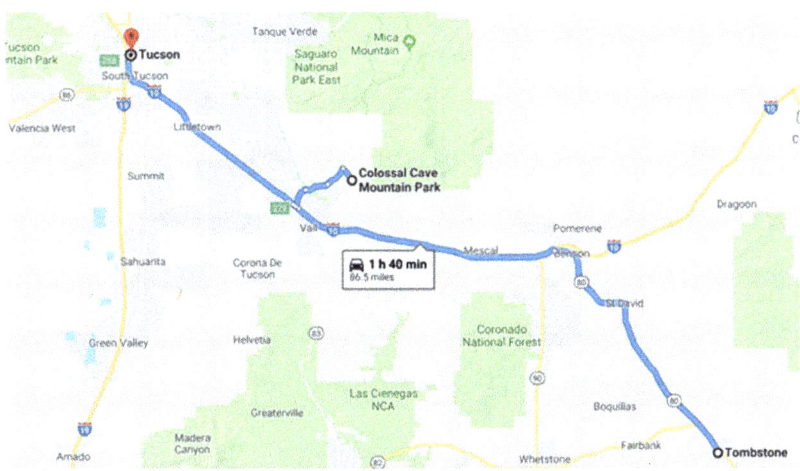

As we neared the desert, I began longing to see something I didn't know anything about—not even its name! At the Living Desert in Carlsbad, I learned the cactus with arms was a saguaro, and that they did not grow in the Chihuahuan desert, where Carlsbad is located. I had to wait until we got to Arizona to see them.

Driving from Tombstone to Tucson, we kept our eyes peeled, waiting and watching to see these cacti. We were heading for the Saguaro National Park, but I hoped to see them before we got there. And we did!

We'd learned of a camping area as we traveled, so I called to learn if they had sites available and was told they had only a couple but if I came right then, they'd probably still be there.

We told them we were about 20 miles away, and although they don't hold sites, they said they'd see us soon.

As we turned off the main road going toward the camp, we spotted saguaro growing freely on a hillside! I was so excited, because they were everywhere, like I'd hoped they would be.

The drive to the camp got me though. The road split, one side leading up the mountain, the other side down. The closer we got, the narrower the road got. Regular readers of my blog will already know where I'm going with this—my mountain fears took over as we drove. Gravel was falling down the edges as we went up, up, up. By the time we got to the top, where the office sat perched on the side of the mountain, my hands were firmly locked around the steering wheel. When I climbed out of the car, my legs were shaking.

I made my way inside, through a beautiful rock entryway lined with teen and young adult hikers. The guy I spoke with on the phone was behind the desk, remembered me, and had the paperwork ready for us to take a site. As I paid the $7 fee, he said, "Spots aren't designated, so if this area is full, try the overflow." I took the pass he offered, listened to the directions (back down the mountain), and went back to the car.

Going down the mountain proved worse than coming up—sharp, narrow turns on a steep grade. We finally made it to the campsites, and all those teens and young adults I'd seen going in were in every site, and the overflow area was full, too.

By this point, my nerves were shot. I refused to drive back up the mountain for a refund, so we left. Even though money was tight, losing that $7 was the better option. Maybe they'll put it in a fund to widen the roads for future guests.

We ended up car camping that night and the next morning, we arrived at the Saguaro National Park before the office opened. The entrance gate was manned though, so we could enjoy the early morning exploring.

The Saguaro National Park is actually divided into two districts, one east of the city of Tucson and the other west. One entry fee covers both districts. We chose the east side for this trip but hope to visit the west side in the future.

The visitor's center hadn't opened when we arrived, but the gate attendant was already at work, letting drivers into the eight-mile loop as the sun rose.

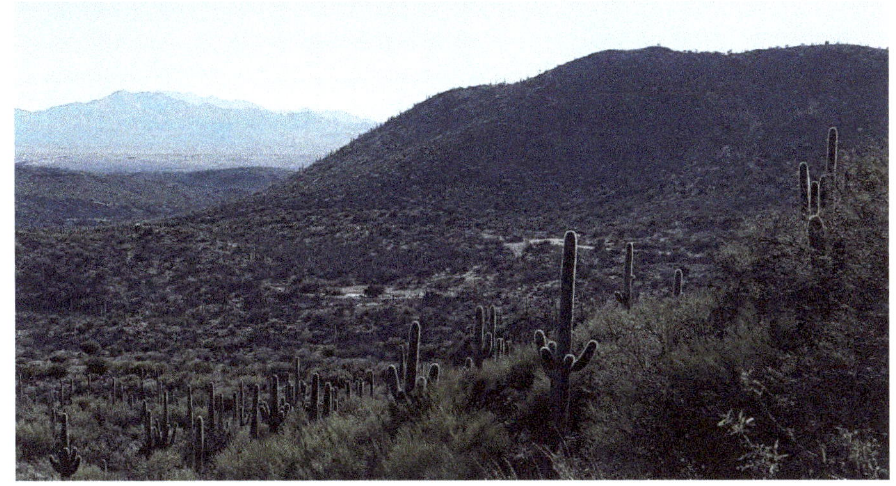

Above: First saguaro sightings!

Below: Cholla cactus Inside Saguaro National Park

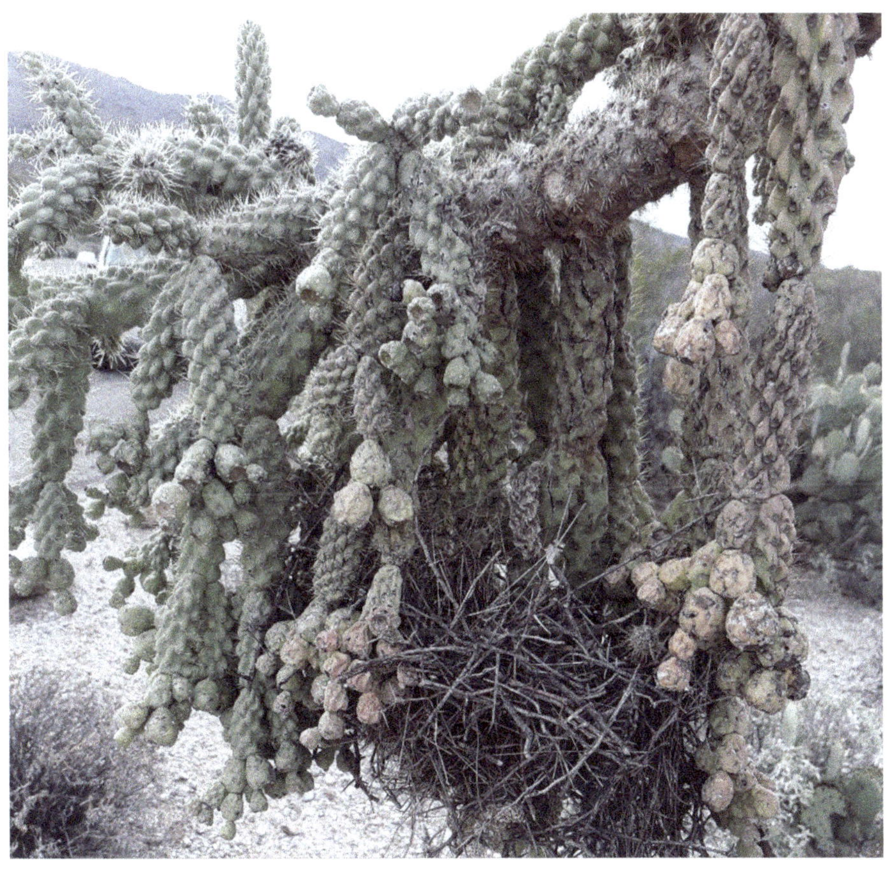

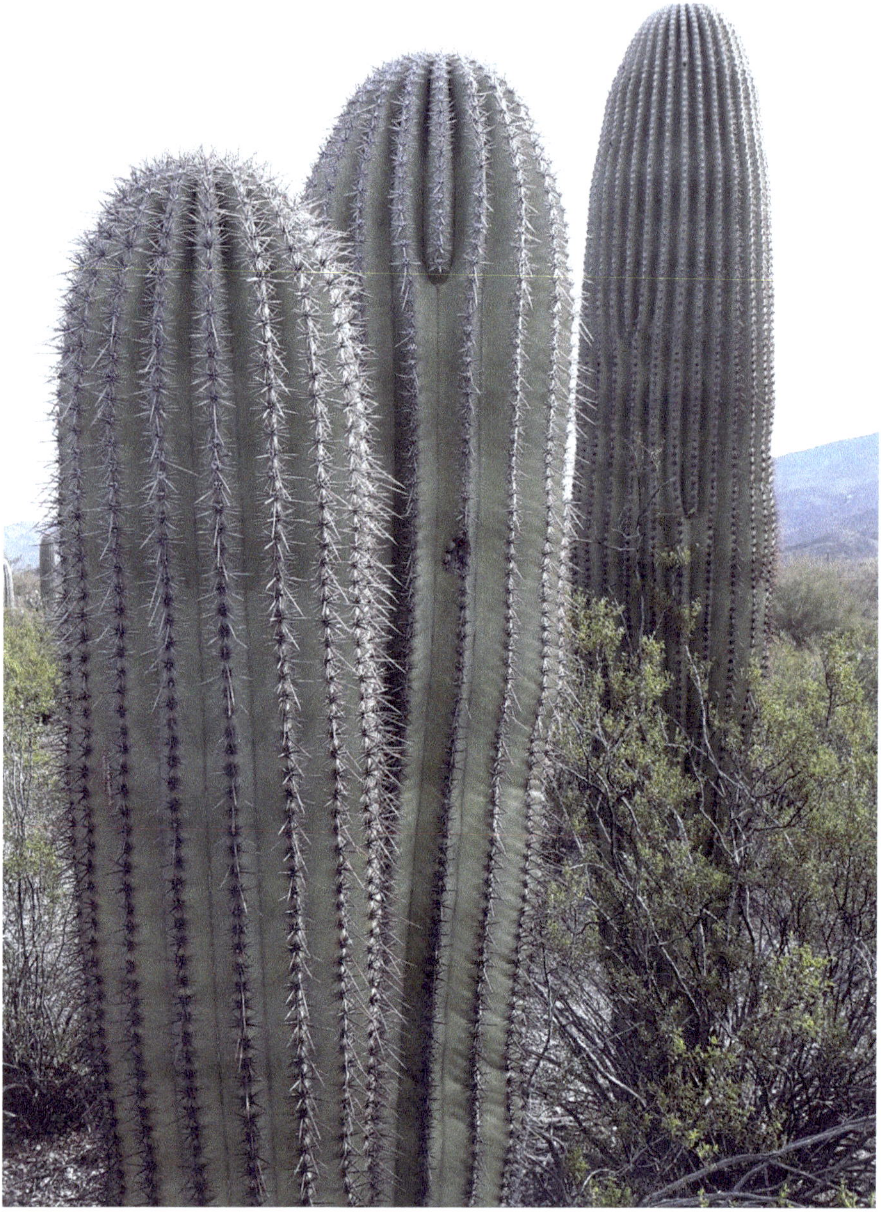

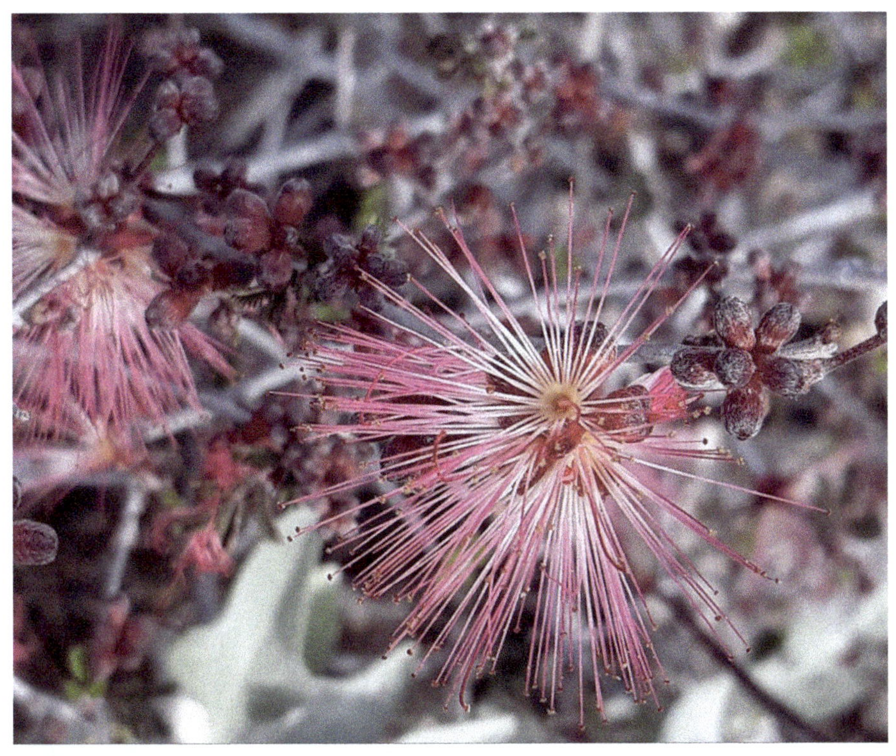

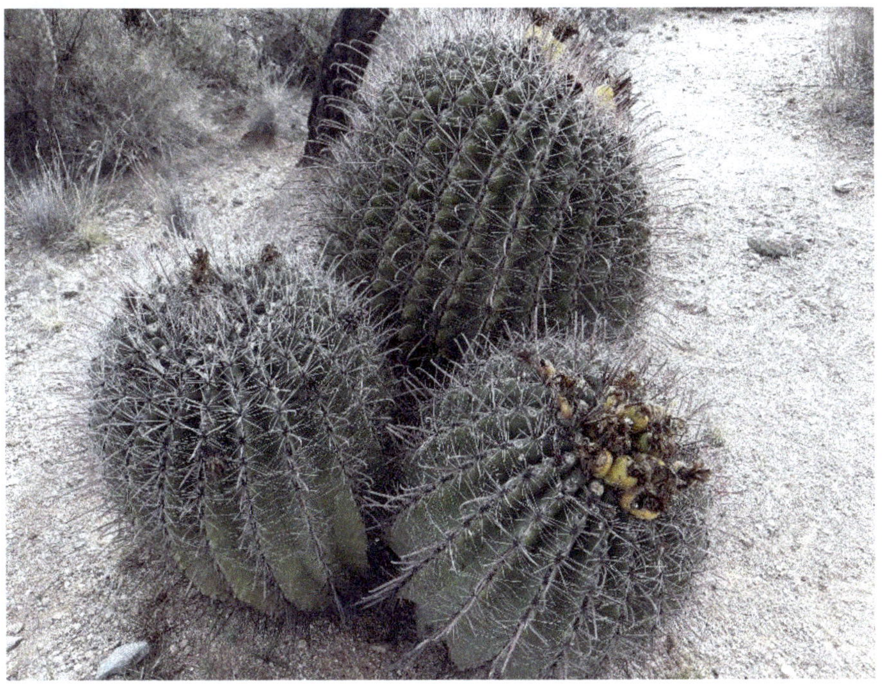

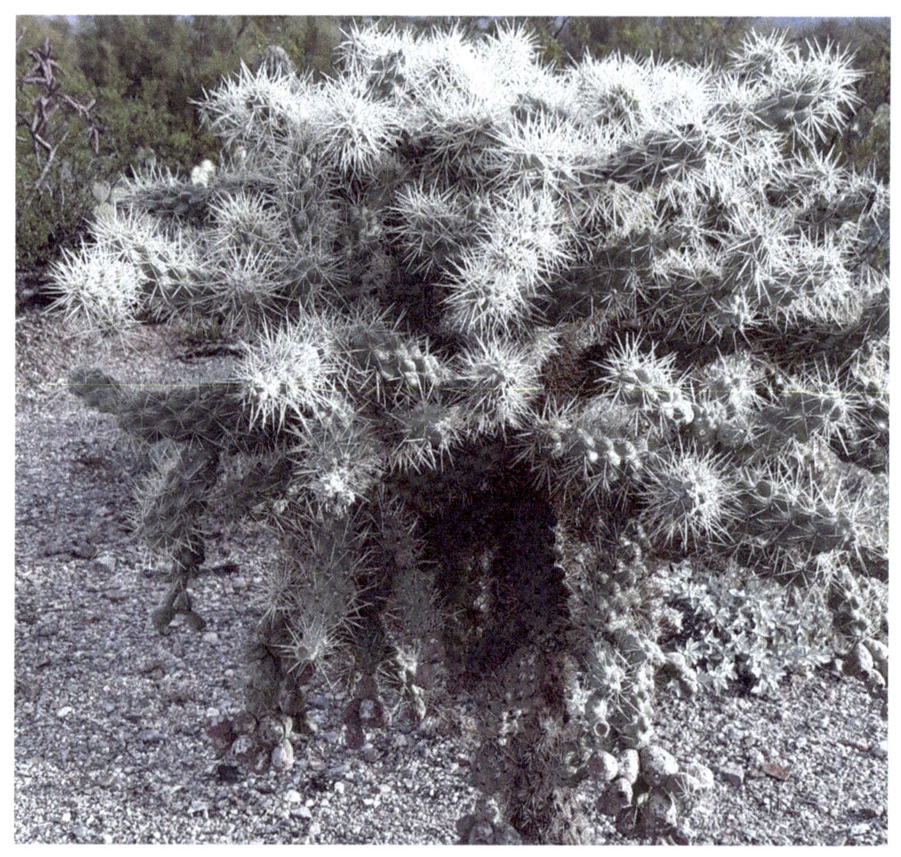

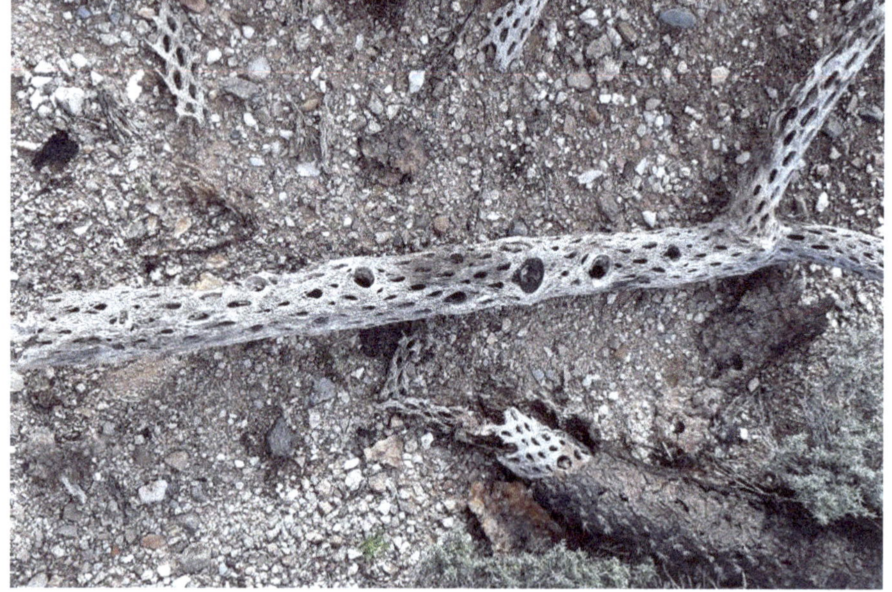

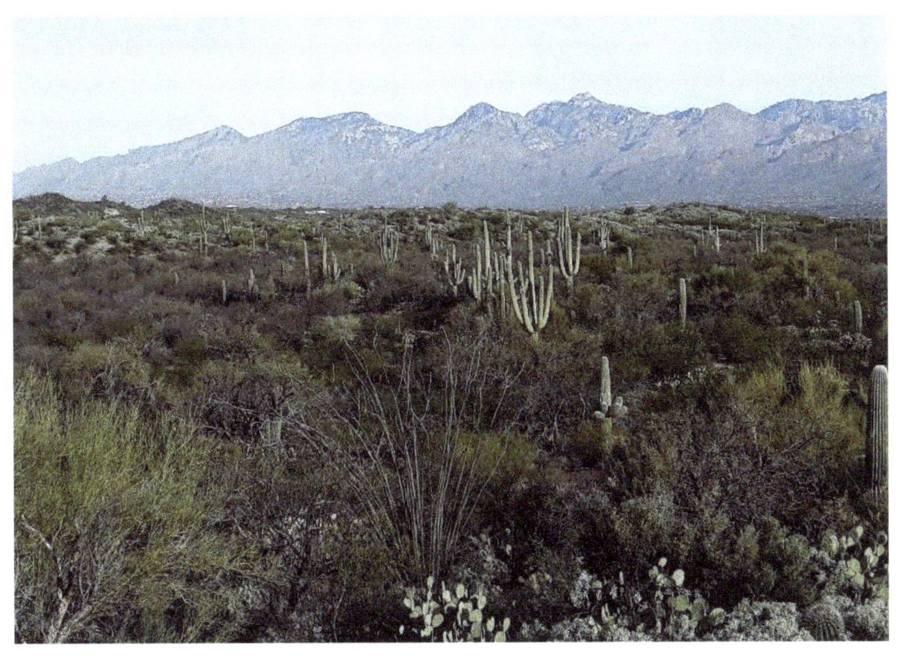

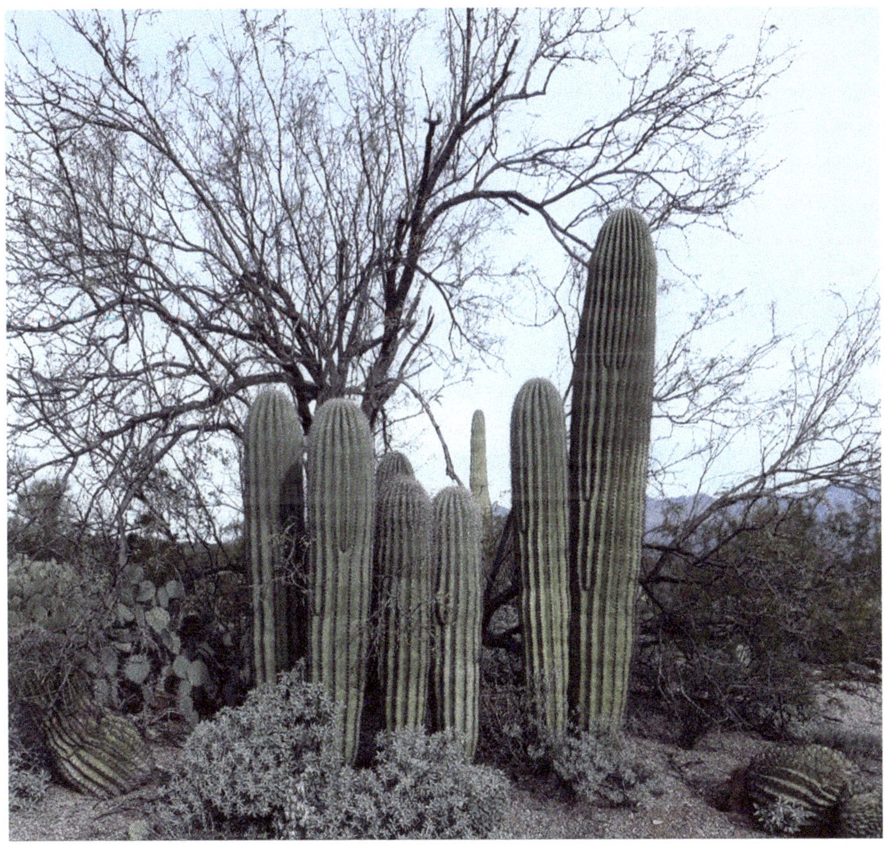

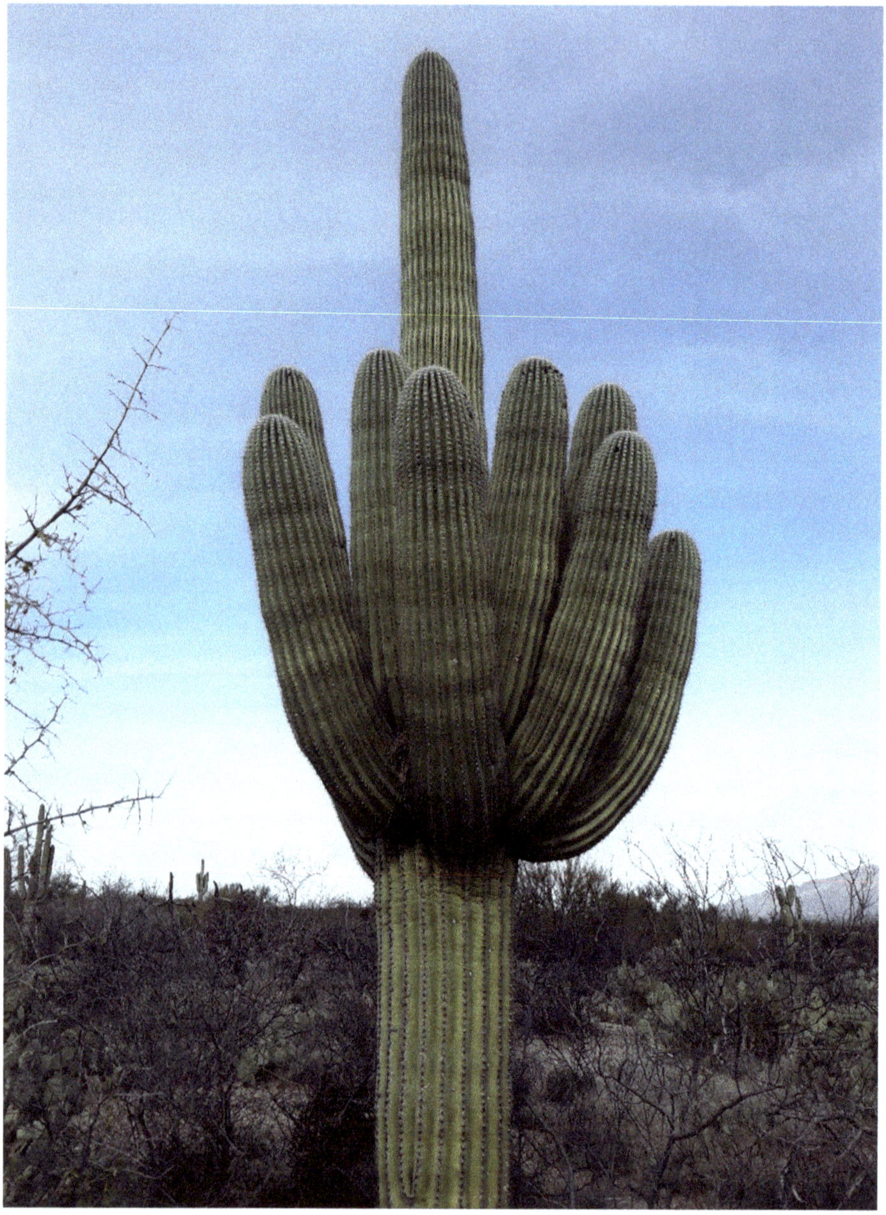

Chapter Thirty-One
Grand Canyon Bound

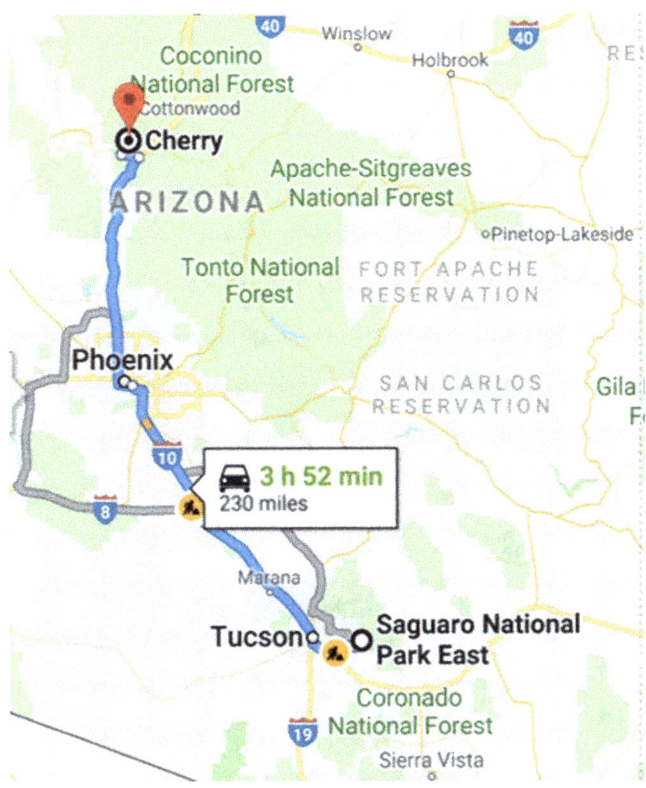

Tucson to Cherry

When we left the saguaros, we drove north to the Prescott National Forest. I'd found a free campsite calling our names and I was ready to rest for a few days. When we arrived, we found the vault toilets—and SNOW!

The area was remote and we had no cell service. Coyotes howled all night. One other family was there, and a gentleman who seemed to serve as "gatekeeper," but he said this was public land, to make ourselves at home.

The frogs and I loved the peacefulness, but Tim, not so much. During the night, it got much colder than forecast, so by morning, we'd decided to move on.

[NOTE: As this book was being published, the Forest department announced closure of the primitive camping in this area for the next two years, due to abuse of the land by littering and extended stays. Sad to hear, but after our experience, I understand their reasoning.]

Temps dropped dramatically overnight, and the coyotes had disturbed Tim too much, especially without cell service, so we packed up and continued northward.

One mistake I've made repeatedly on this trip is not having numerous plans for each leg of the journey. I've always thought of myself as being spontaneous and flexible, but I've discovered I really need to plan to make the most of our journey. And thus far, I've not had a plan, except to GO.

This far into our trip, I'd also not had any down time to do research to get ahead of us on the road. I'd been fortunate to find all that we had, but we missed so much. And on this leg of the journey, I was too tired to do any research at all.

Unfortunately, that created a huge problem and a huge gap in our story, because I wasn't prepared for the beautiful and unique town of Sedona.

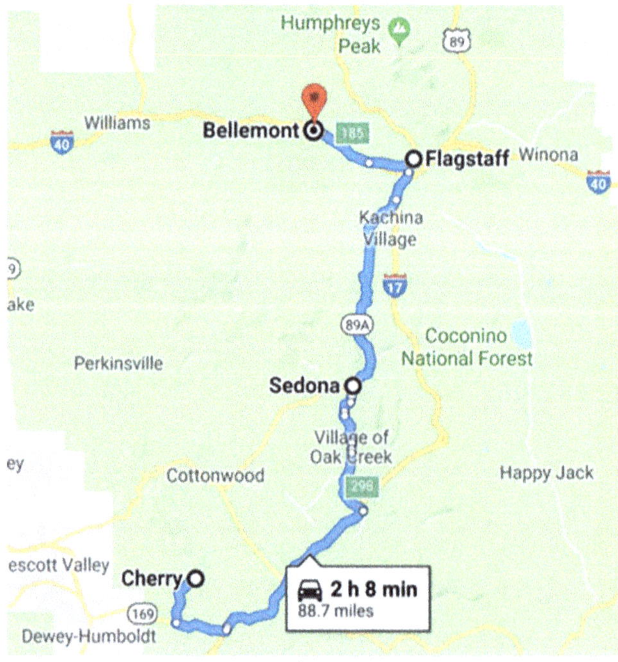

Cherry to Sedona, Flagstaff, and Bellemont

We packed up camp and continued north. I saw the signs to get off the interstate to go to Sedona, so I made a sudden decision to do so. We were driving along, and suddenly, the landscape changed dramatically.

I knew nothing about Sedona and what was coming. The closer we got to town, the heavier the traffic, and the roads were not designed to pull over—until we found all the pull-over sites. And they were all full. We circled every one of them, but there wasn't a single space to park.

I got frustrated, not being able to find anywhere to stop to capture all I was seeing. We went from one roundabout to the next, wanting to stop, but forced to keep moving on.

Tim wasn't inclined to snap photos at the moment, so we didn't capture the unique storefronts.

Sedona is a missed opportunity, but we will be back.

We kept moving on, taking what seemed to be the only road out of town—89A. (I later learned this is one of the most scenic drives in the country—and I might agree with that if I'd taken more time to enjoy it.)

We ended up in Flagstaff where we stopped in at a fun diner. Tim was thrilled they served breakfast all day. I ended up not eating. (Let's say I'd recommend the breakfast over the regular menu.)

While Tim ate, I realized how incredibly tired I was, and I found a cheap hotel rate on Hotwire for only $23! I splurged, not knowing what we'd find, and honestly, not expecting much. But the Days Inn in Bellemont was fairly new and had hired a young man, Michael, who was personable and friendly, knowledgeable about the area, and seemed to care about the guests. Rooms were on the smallish side (reminded me of European hotels), but clean and new. Huge bargain and a great stay.

Just what we needed before heading into the Grand Canyon!

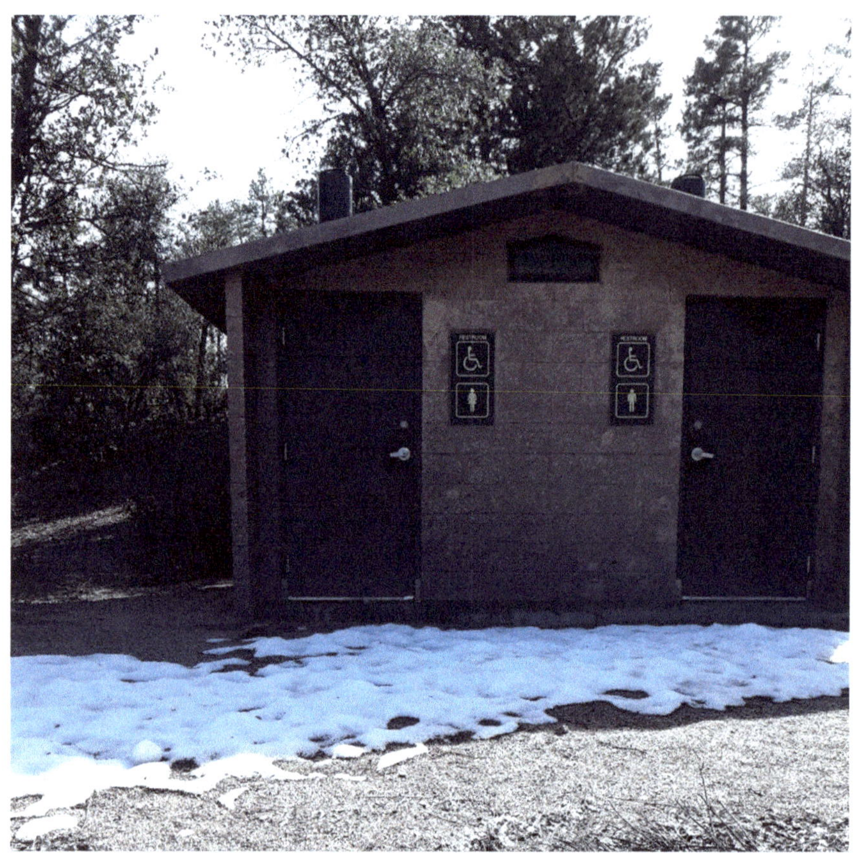

Above: Nice vault toilets in remote campground.

Below: First sighting of Sedona.

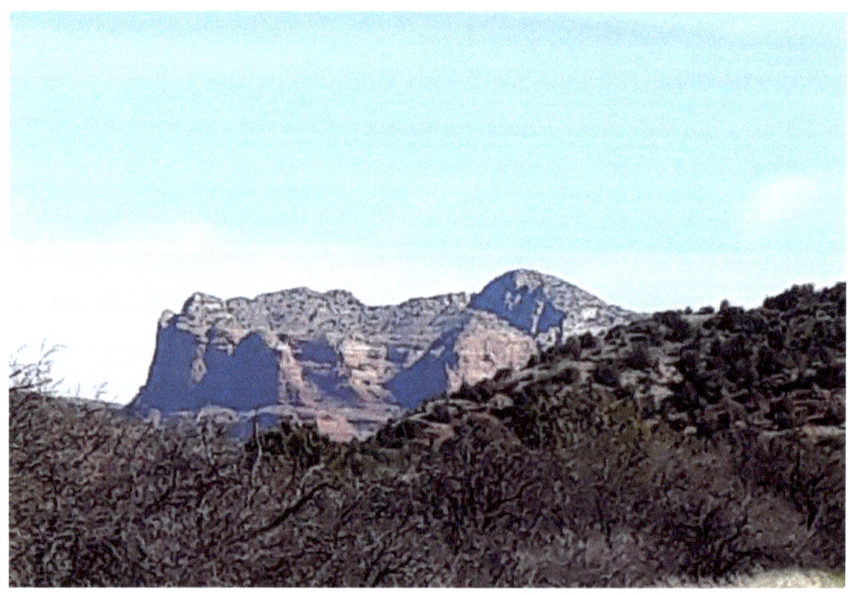

Chapter Thirty-Two
The Grand Grand Canyon

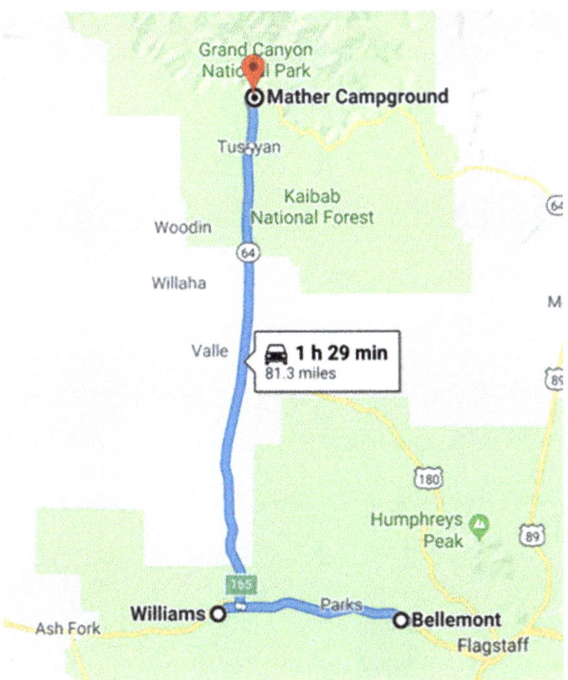

Bellemont to Grand Canyon National Park

Before we left Granbury, Texas, I made reservations for three nights at the Mather Campground in the Grand Canyon. While we'd been stationary in Granbury, doubts plagued us about continuing our journey but after a little rest, we shook off those doubts, knowing there was so much more to see. Making the reservations gave us more of a plan than we'd had in weeks, and a goal to work toward to keep us moving forward.

After our great night's stay (cheap!) at the Bellemont Days Inn, we trekked toward the Grand Canyon.

Tim wasn't feeling well, and not getting around well, so we weren't sure of our plans once we got there. I'd checked the weather forecast and it kept changing, getting colder every time I checked.

A special guest was waiting to greet us as we arrived at the Mather office: Mama Elk. And yes, snow still on the ground, too!

The campground employees were helpful and kind. When they saw Tim was having trouble getting around, they changed our campsite to one near a restroom to make it easier on him. The campground was great—peaceful, spacious, beautiful. The restrooms were clean and well-maintained. Because it was still early in the season, not all the restrooms in the camp had been opened yet. The park also had pay shower and laundry facilities in a building close to the office.

Once we saw our campsite, Tim suggested we start sight-seeing before the weather got too bad, and we decided we'd car camp for the night. We put our nametag on our site post, then went to the Marketplace where we could park to catch one of the shuttles.

The shuttles allowed us to see so much in a short time. Tim could handle getting off and on the buses okay, but not much hiking. The winds were brutal, which also made it a little more difficult for him.

Side rant: One thing that amazed me during our visit—people's sheer stupidity. The wind was blowing so hard, everyone was having a hard time walking along the paths. We saw several folks unsteady on their feet, and if the wind was powerful enough to knock ME about, you know it's a strong wind. Yet, at every stop along the way, someone—different each time—had to take a selfie or have a picture made with them in a precarious position. One man balanced on his toes on a rock outside the guardrails, so his partner could take a photo of him "in" the Grand Canyon. At the same stop that the wind almost knocked me off my feet on flat ground. So when you read about the deaths at the Grand Canyon—of people falling over and dying—this should give you a clue. Rant over.

My favorite part of the Grand Canyon South Rim was Hermit's Rest. The history behind the building—since 1914—was amazing, and the views were incredible. The fireplace was a welcome sight, and hard to leave once we were there.

We traveled every loop the shuttles took us, and explored many of the stops, but continued fighting the wind.

Once we'd made the full journey, we took refuge in front of a fire in the Yavapai Lodge lobby where I was able to get online and check the weather.

Notice the clouds and haze in a few of the photos. That was snow moving in.

Once we've finished the trolley loops, we checked out the market and scored a whole roasted chicken (delightfully warm and fresh) for only $4 and took it back to camp for our dinner.

While we ate, we discussed all the possibilities, our current needs, and a timeline. And decided we'd take off the next morning to try to outrun the snow once again. The park refunded the remainder of our stay when we checked out, so that was a blessing. We hope to return to the Grand Canyon again someday—hopefully, in warmer weather.

From the FROG FILES:

Wind has been fierce, so we've decided to car camp tonight. Snow is coming in Friday - some bus drivers think it will actually arrive early. I'm also not feeling well. Likely altitude issues, probably mixing with stress. I have the shakes pretty bad.

Internet service here is very limited. We're currently hanging out in a lodge in front of a fire. Tim asked if they'd notice if he pitched the tent here.

Because of the incoming snow, we may not stay here until Saturday morning. I'm ready to get out of mountains and cold.

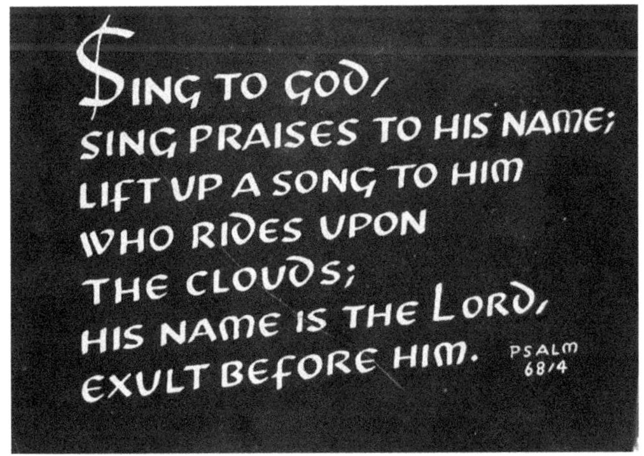

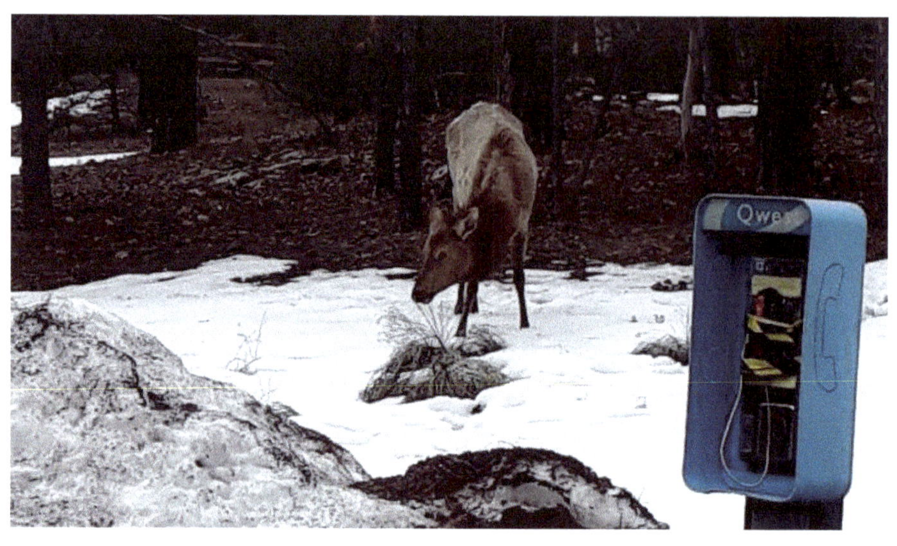

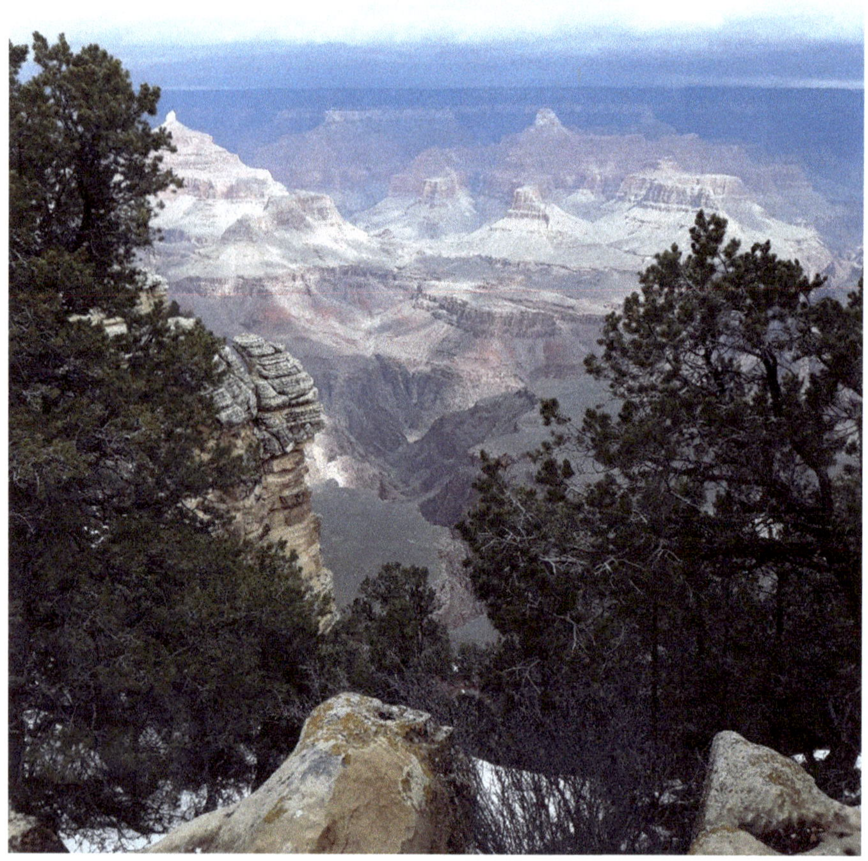

(Several Grand Canyon art pieces available)

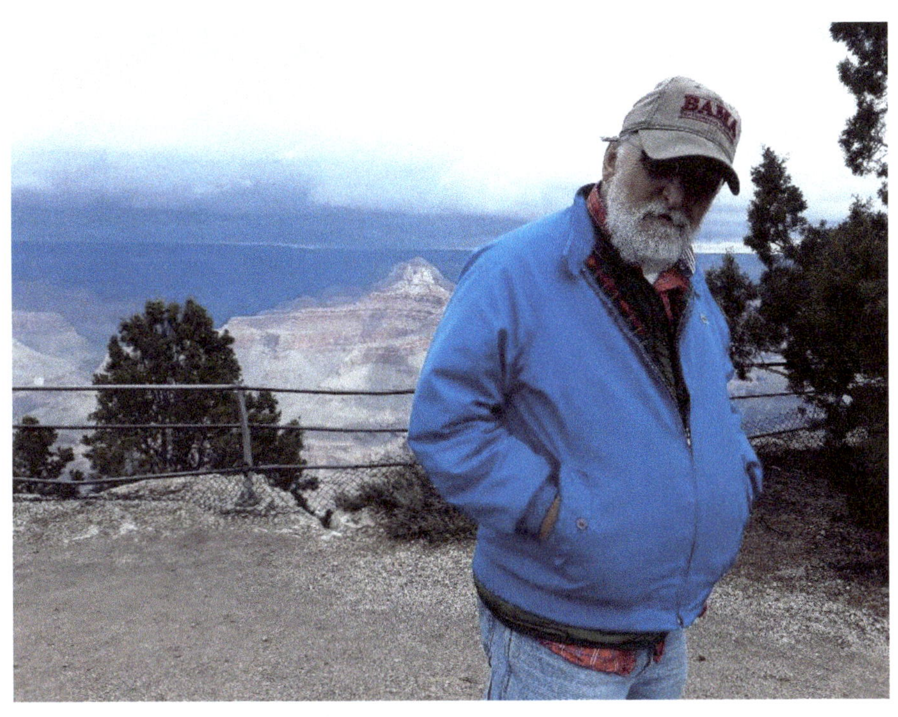

Fighting the bitter wind, with snow in the distance

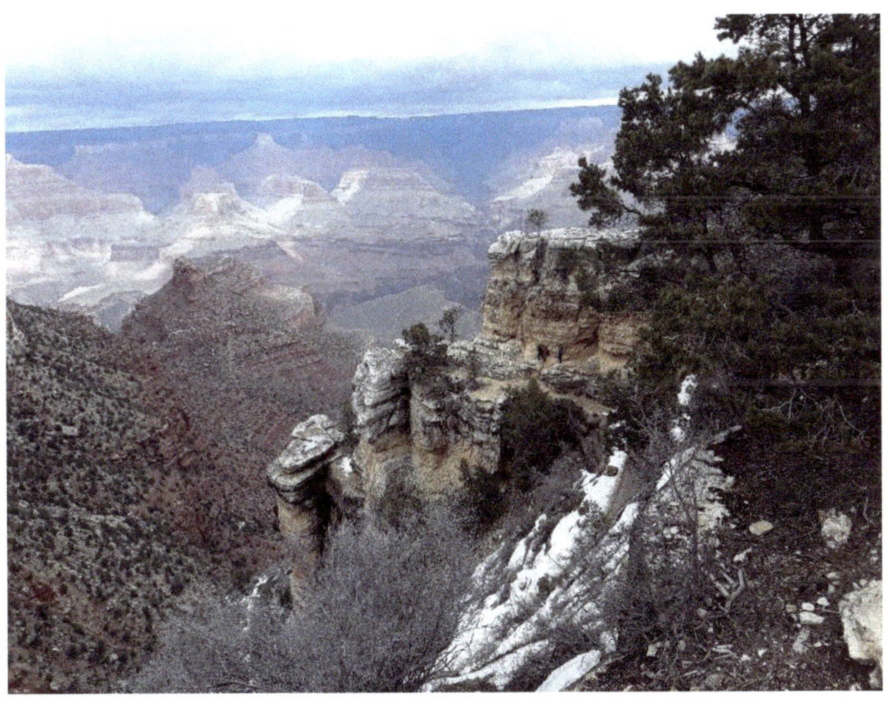

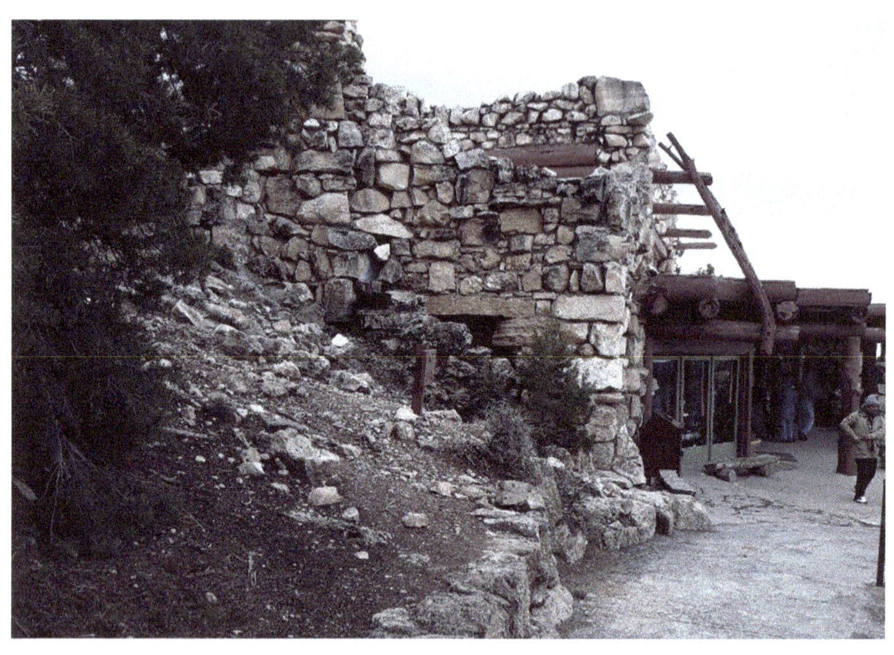

A nice refuge at Hermit's Rest

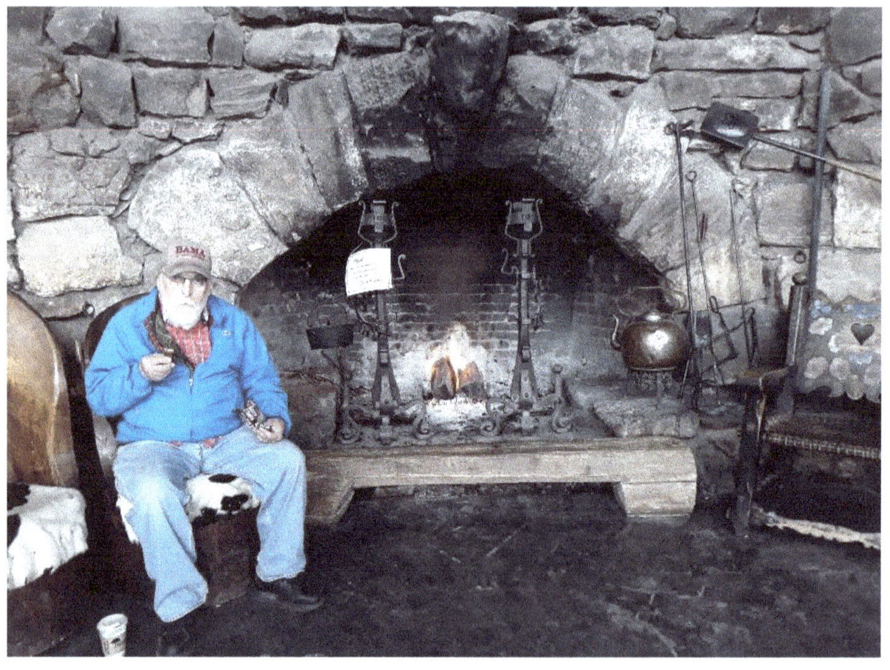

HERMITS REST

A decade before it became a national park, the Santa Fe Railway planned the construction of a rest house eight miles west of their railway station at the Grand Canyon's South Rim. The rest house was part of a larger plan for tourist development which included the eight mile road to its site, a trail descending into the canyon, and a tourist camp on the trail to the river. Construction of Hermits Rest began in 1914 at the cost of $13,000.00

Designed by renowned architect Mary Jane Colter, this one- story stone building had the appearance of a natural stone outcropping from the hill to the south, the effect of which was originally aided by an earth and stone roof covering. Composed of random rubble and hewn unfinished logs, the Hermit's Rest was well suited to its environment, perched on the rim of the Grand Canyon.

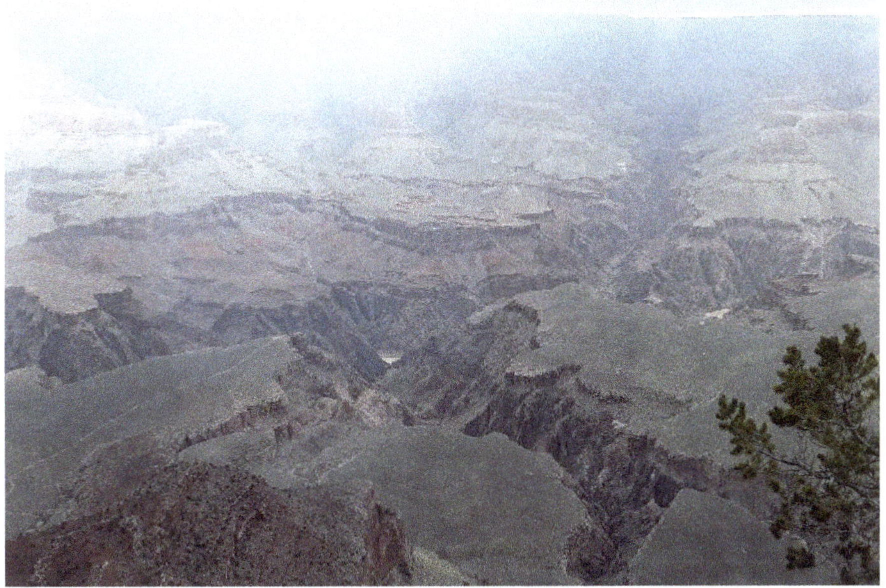

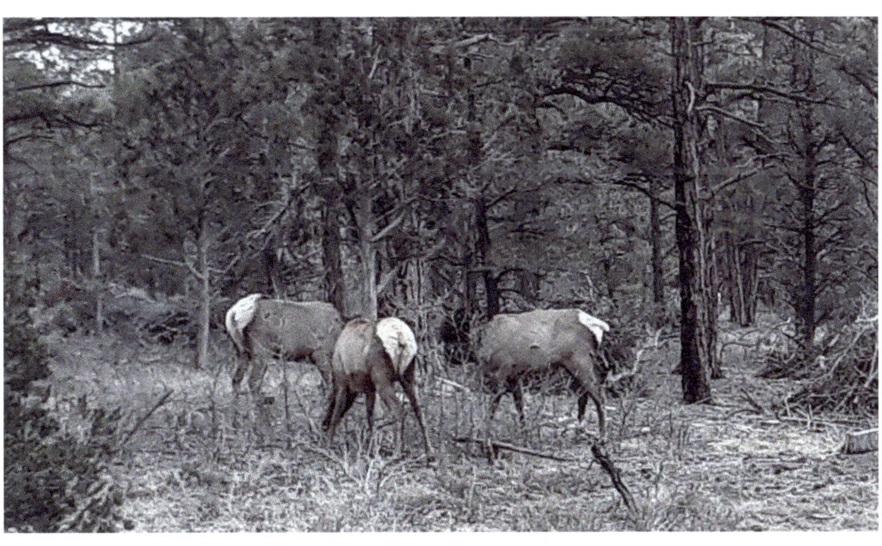

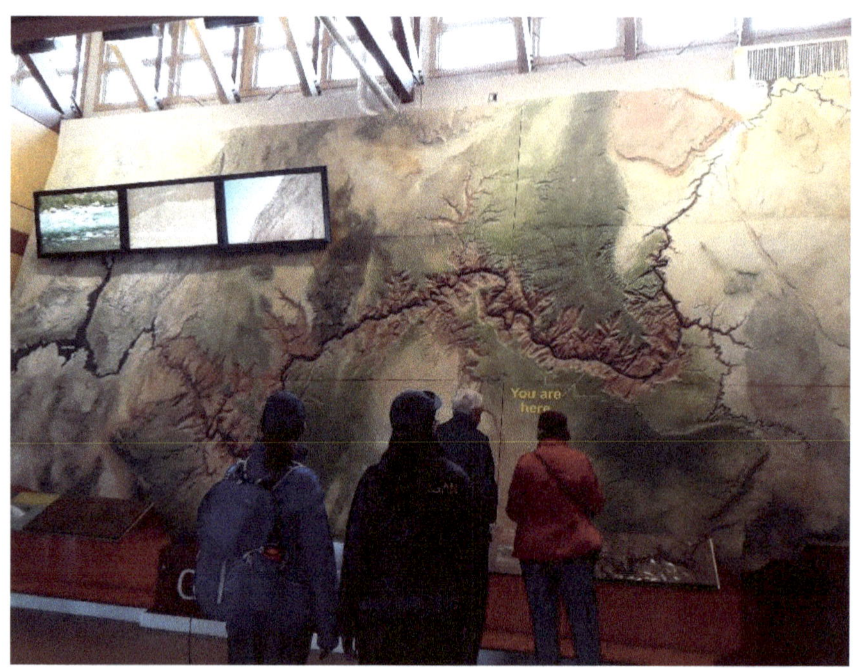
You are
here

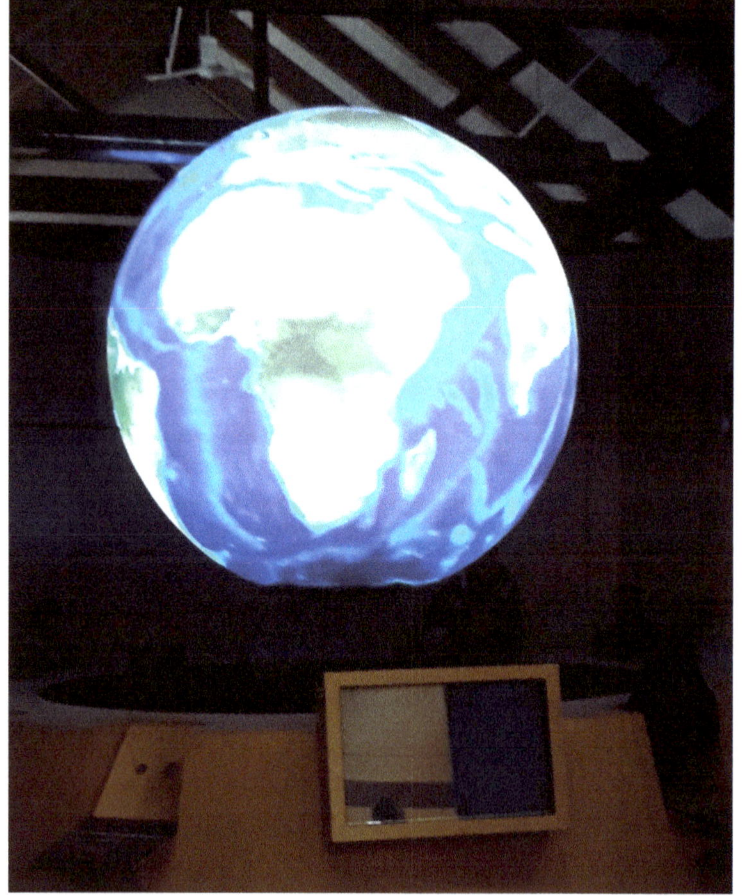

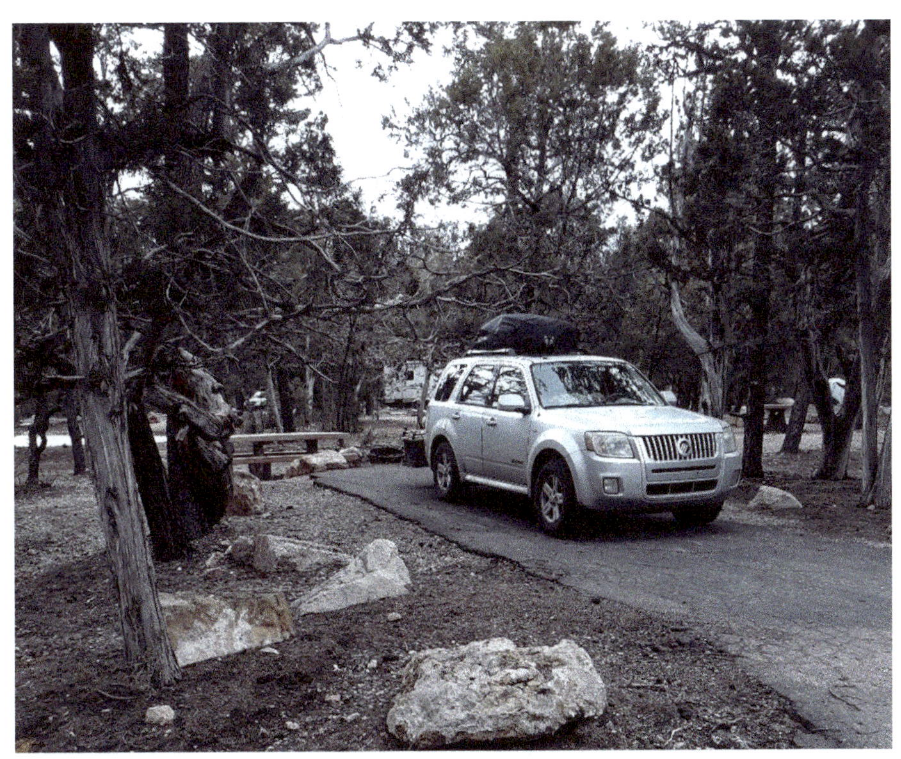

Mather Campground

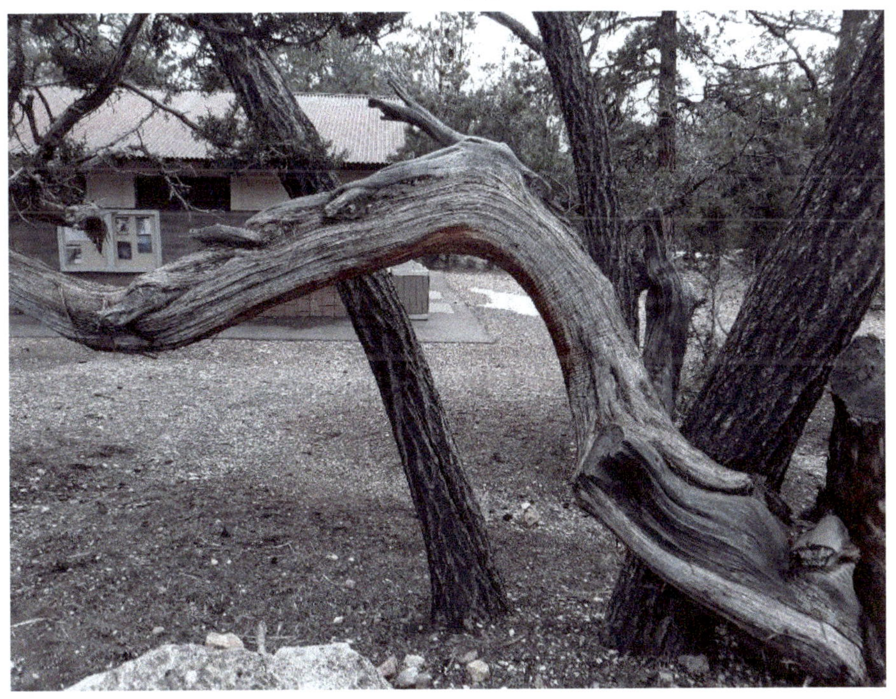

Sample Artwork:

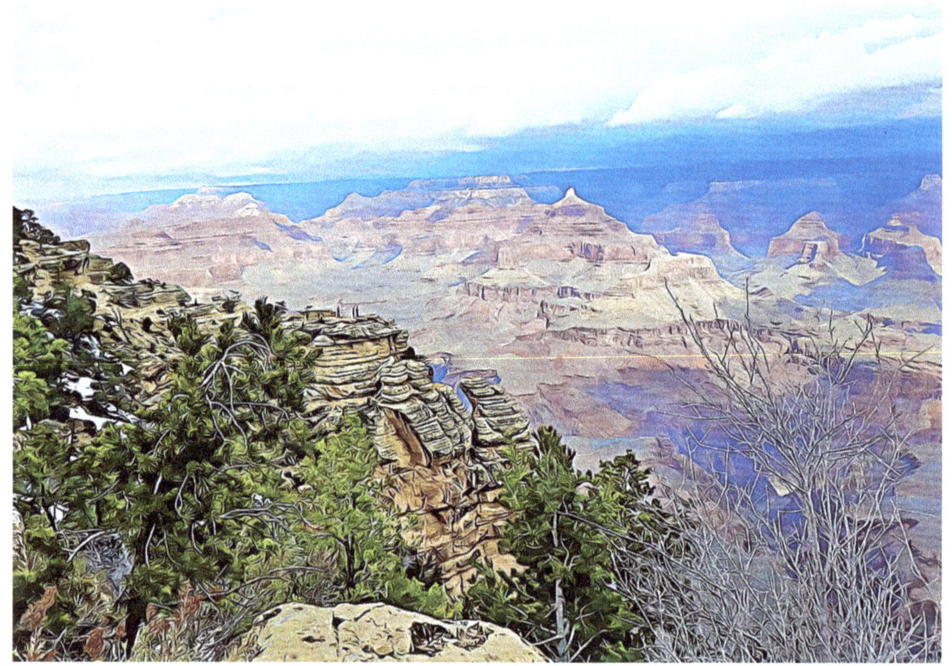

[Majestic Grand Canyon](#) 📷

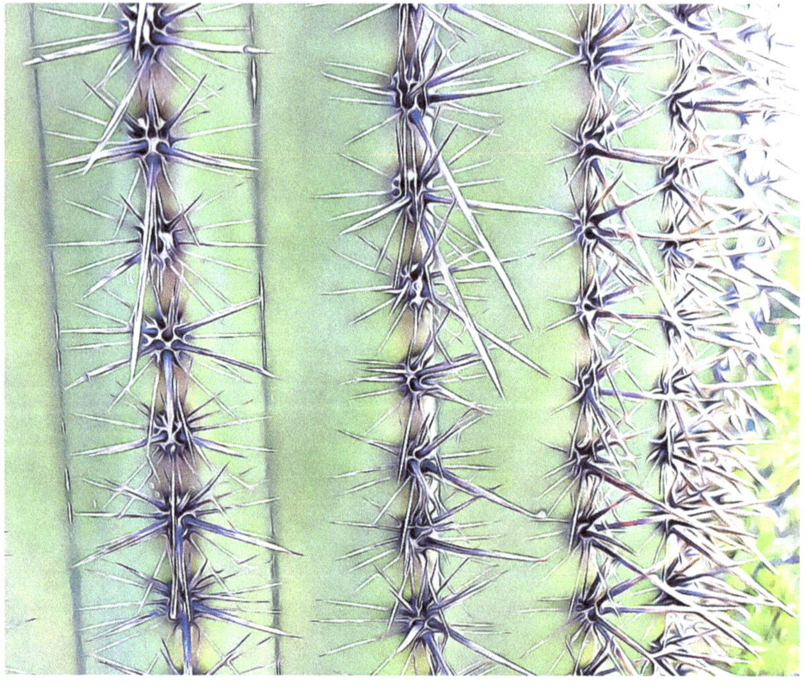

[Saguaro Closeup](#) 📷

Chapter Thirty-Three

Discovering Arizona

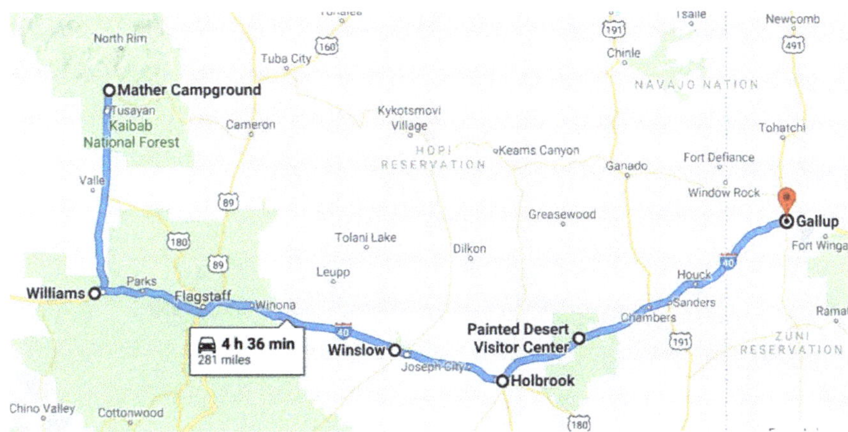

Grand Canyon to Gallup, New Mexico

As we left the Grand Canyon, we began the trip back east once more. We'd decided the previous night that we needed to get Tim back home for a doc visit, and I needed time to work and think where we weren't constantly on the go. Although we were going to make a quick trip getting back to Alabama and Georgia, we knew there were several towns we wanted to visit along the way—several of those "roadside attraction" kind of places that make each state unique.

But before we got too far, there was one place I had to see in Williams, AZ.

Zach reminded us about Bedrock City when we first arrived in Arizona, and we passed it on the way to the Canyon but didn't

stop so that was a priority on our way out. Somewhere in between Zach's reminder and the day of our actual visit, I learned that the property had closed down, and that it was up for sale for a cool $2 million. I know there's someone out there who could make this campground a success! And what fun it would be doing so!

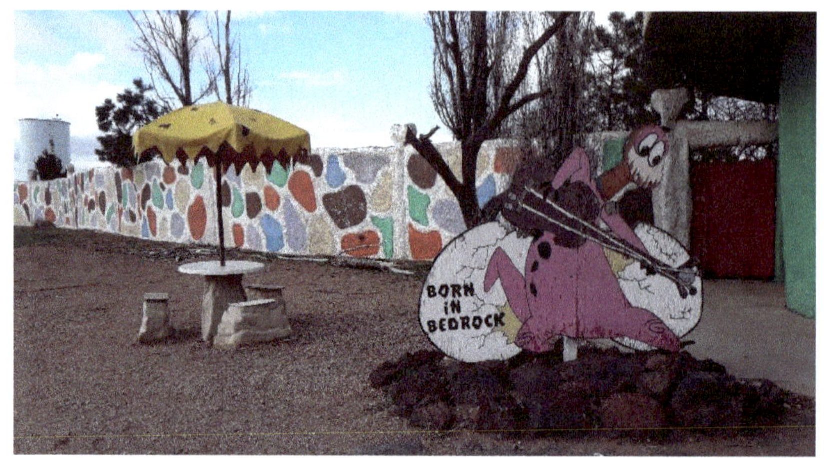

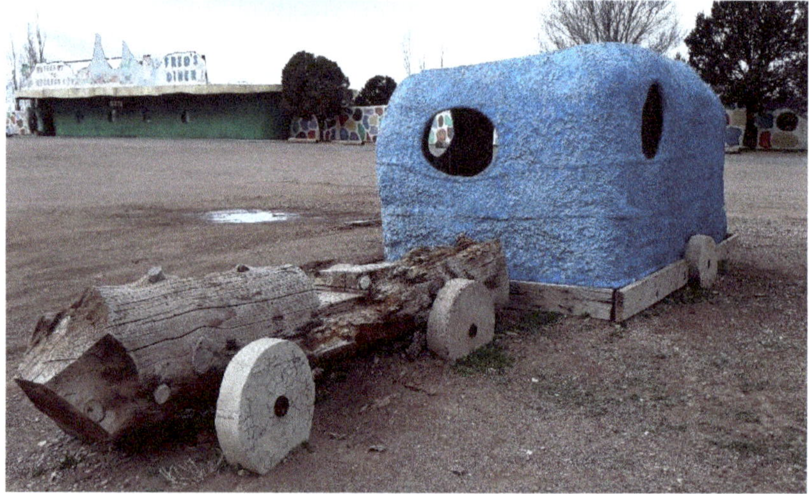

Next up, Winslow, and of course, standing on the corner.

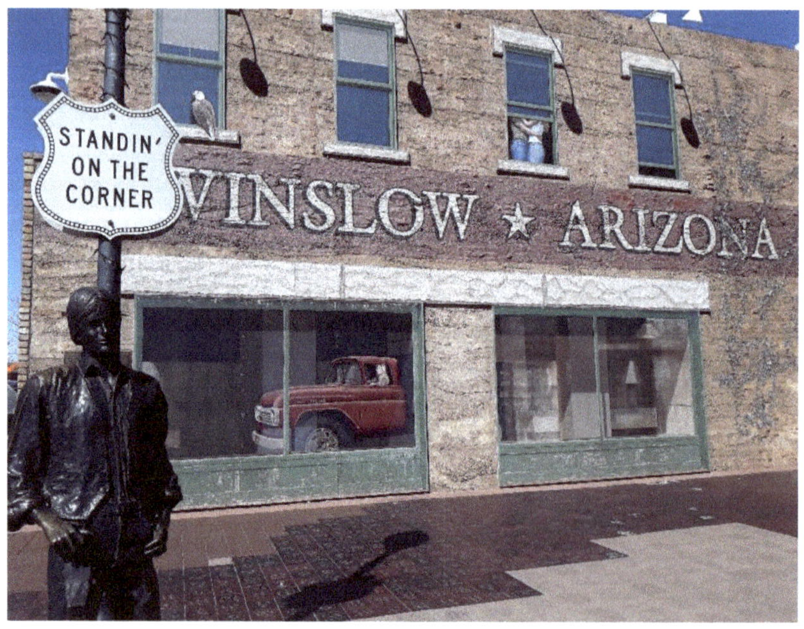

In Joseph City, we stopped at the famous Jack Rabbit Trading Post, which earned its reputation during the glory days of Route 66.

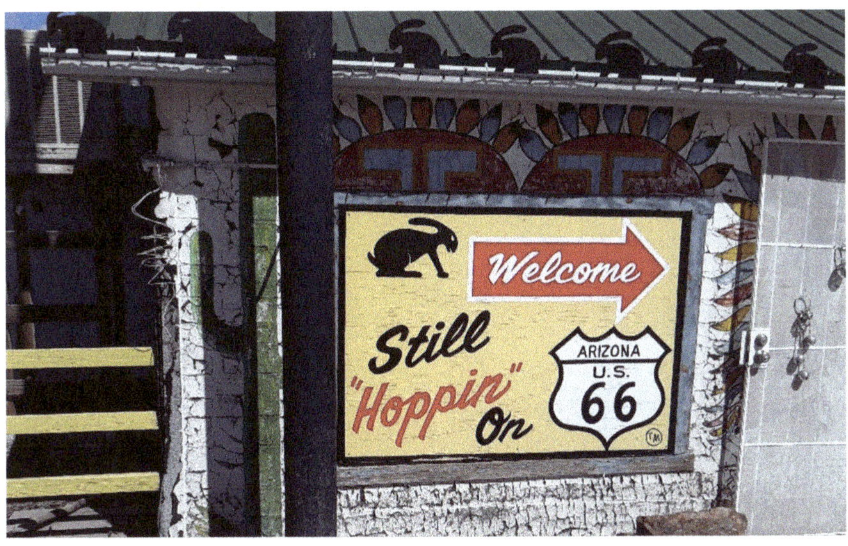

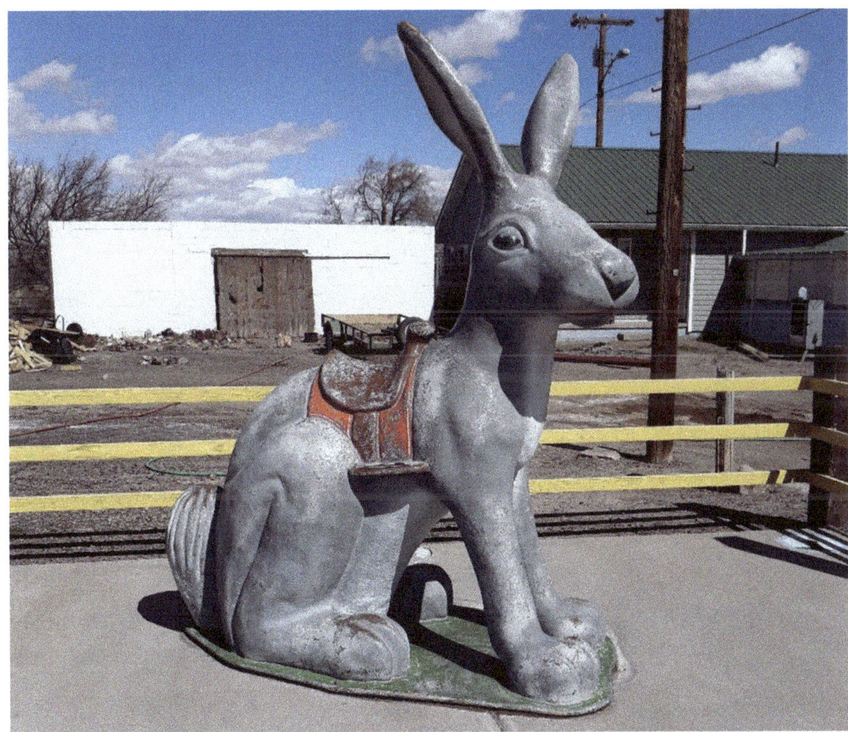

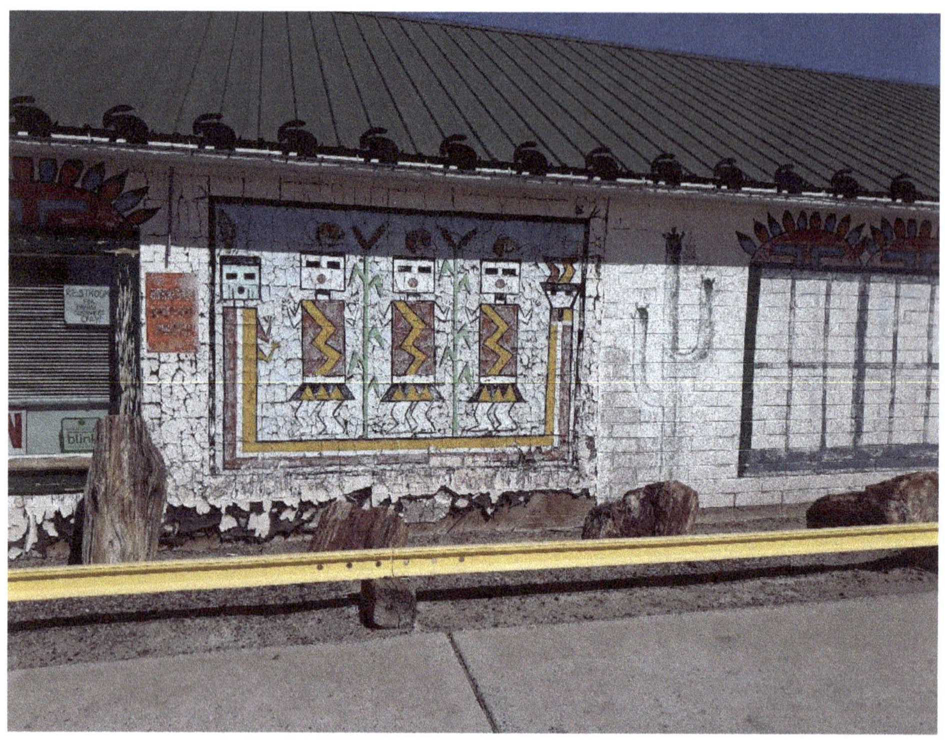

And then Holbrook. I knew there were a couple of things in Holbrook I wanted to see but couldn't remember them when we arrived until I saw one:

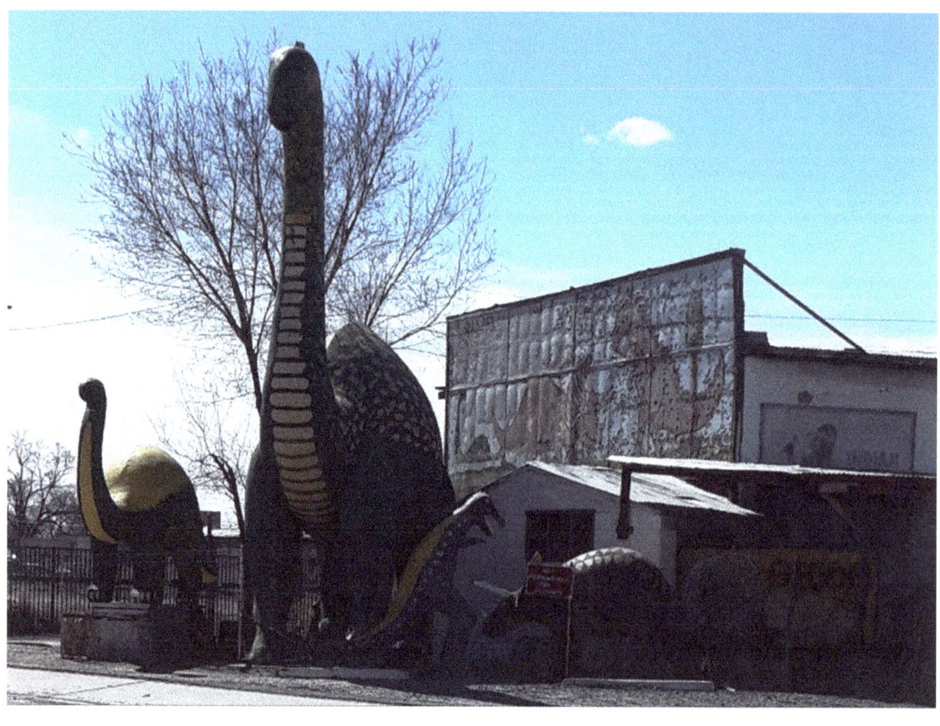

Holbrook is surrounded by dinosaurs in all shapes and sizes. I think we could have spent an entire day tracking them down all around the area. But the weather was pressing down on us, so we stayed focused.

Then I found the other!

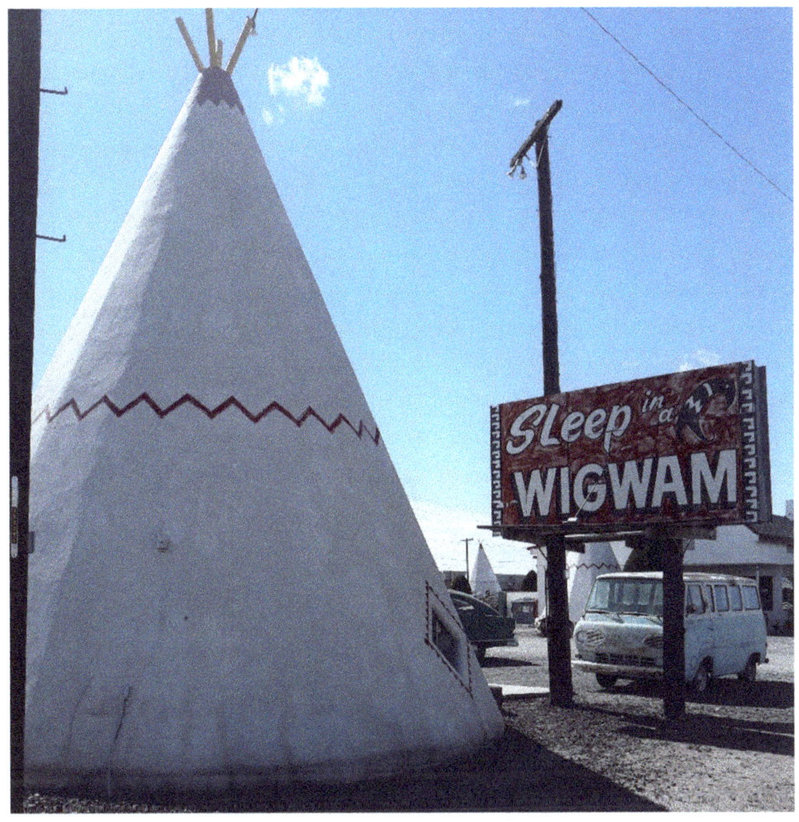

All the wigwams have classic cars parked in front of them, but you can park there, too. Wigwams are rented like hotel rooms, for less than $100 per night, at time of publication.

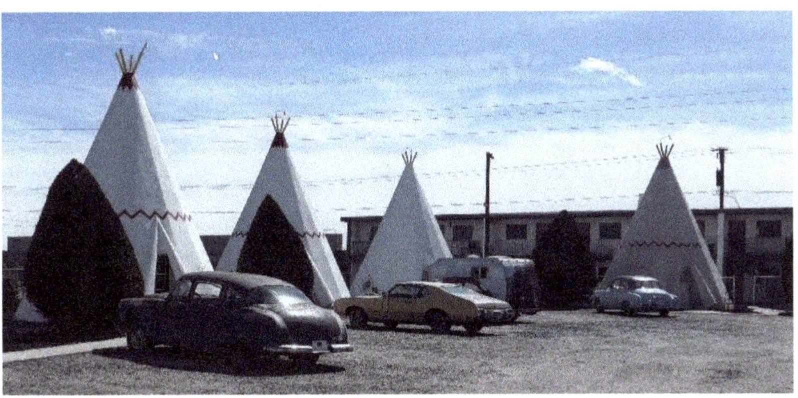

One food I didn't want to miss introducing to Tim was an Indian Taco. When I lived in Oklahoma, one of the civic organizations in our town held periodic fundraisers selling Indian Tacos—taco style ingredients served on top of delicious fry bread. One of my favorite foods that I've missed since we left OK.

Somewhere along the way, searching for Indian Tacos, I learned they have a Navajo origin, so I thought perhaps we'd find them once we entered Navajo country, and Holbrook is where we found them.

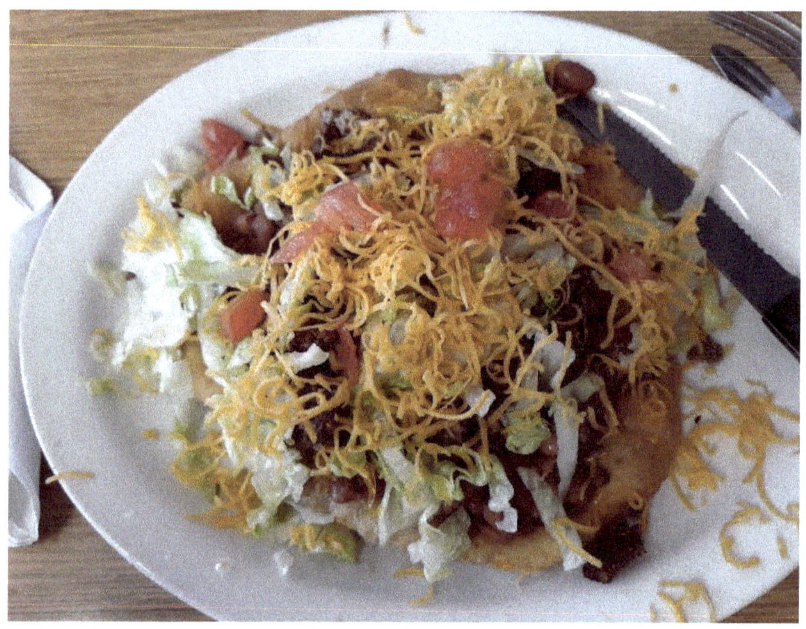

The cafe where we landed was recommended on several websites as having the best fry bread around, so we thought we were safe. But I found something in my water glass when she refilled it, and it was so gross, she comped our ticket without us saying a word, and we left. But by that point, we'd already eaten. So, we had our Indian taco (it lacked any seasoning at all, so not my favorite, even before the water glass incident, but Tim covered his with all sorts of sauces and thought it was great) and it was free. But at what cost? Thankfully, we suffered no ill effects.

As we left Holbrook, we kept seeing signs for the Painted Desert National Park. Even though it wasn't on our original plans, we decided to stop, and I'm glad we did.

This place had never even been on my radar. What a sight we would have missed!

We were sad to leave Arizona—so much more to explore. We had a few days of sunshine while we were in the state, and that always improves the state of mind, doesn't it?

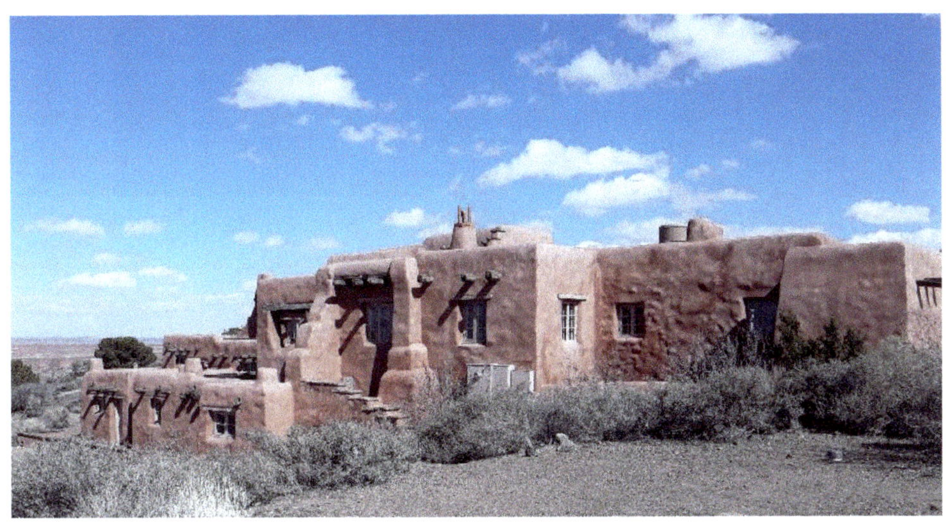

Painted Desert Inn

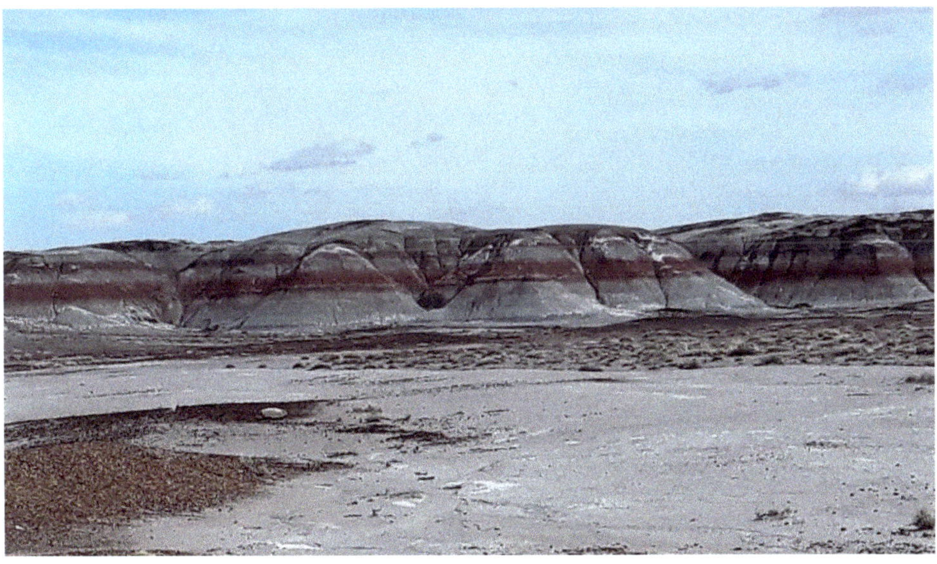

The Painted Desert

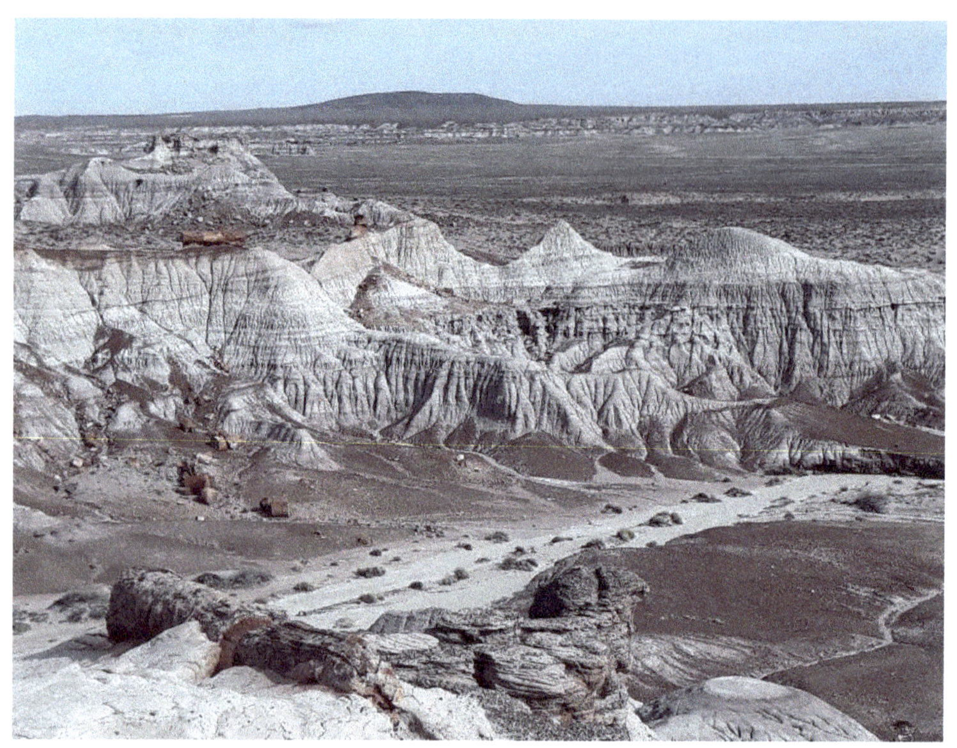

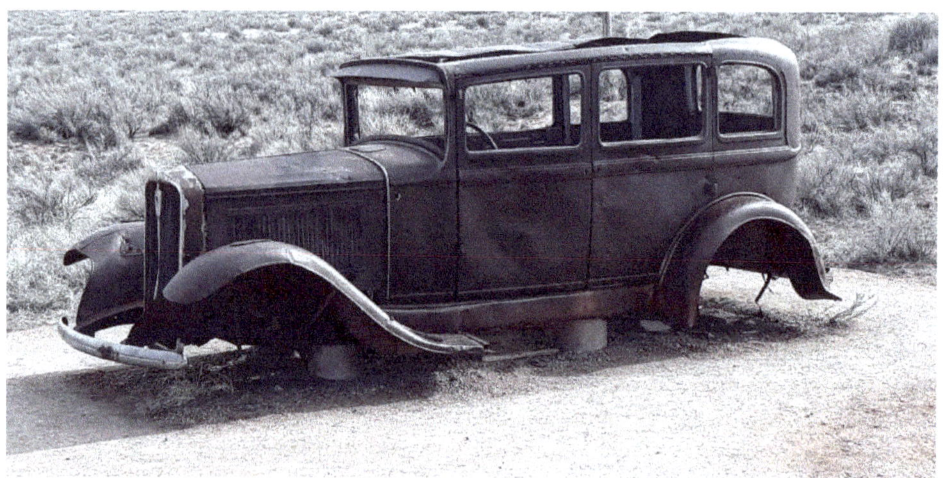

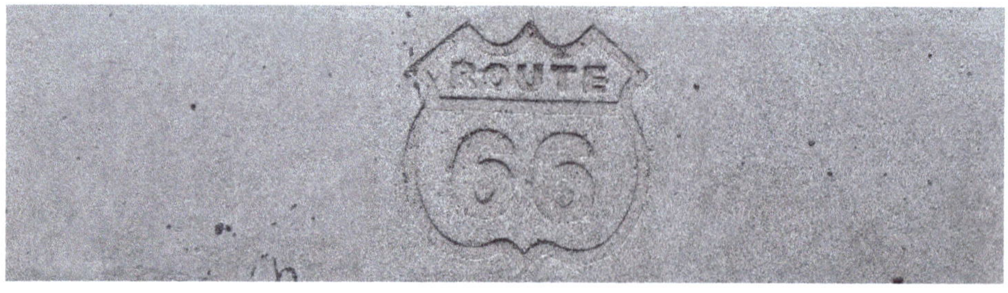

ROUTE
66

The weather here is turning for the worst. We learned last night we can get a refund on the rest of our stay, so we're pulling out as soon as the campground office opens.

We're not quitting our journey, but we are taking a break and heading for home base.

There were several towns of interest we planned to visit, so we will make brief stops along the way.

While we're stationary, I will focus on work. We will also explore Class C RVs to begin Part 2 of the Leap Frogs Adventures.

Some have suggested we settle down; others suggest we keep going. Our hearts and minds want to keep moving, but we need to make some adjustments and build more income to make that happen.

I'll write more as we go. I'm sending this from the now-closed Bedrock City in Williams. Fred Flintstone says hello.

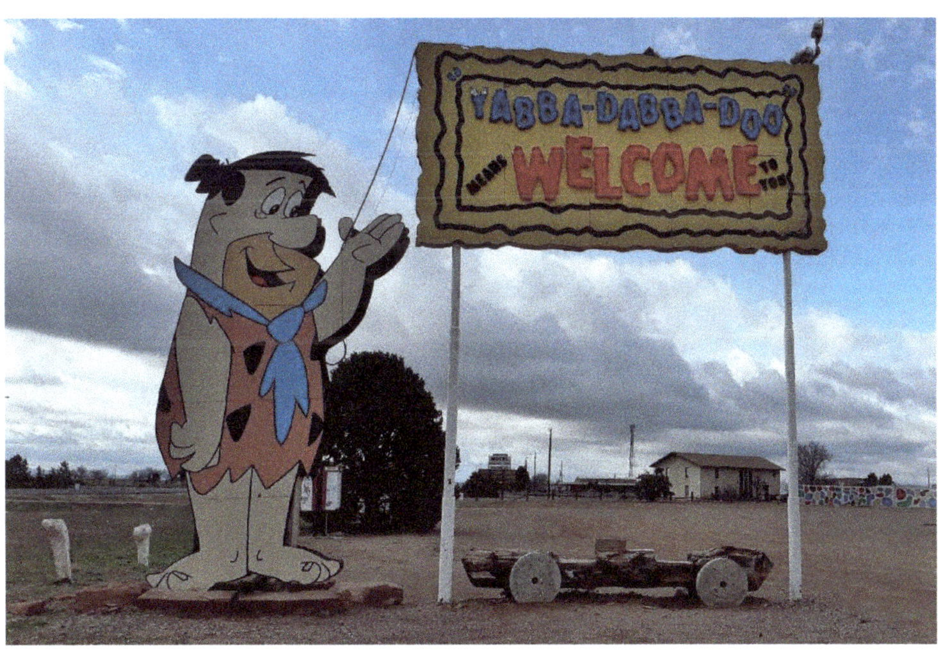

<h1 align="center">Sample Artwork:</h1>

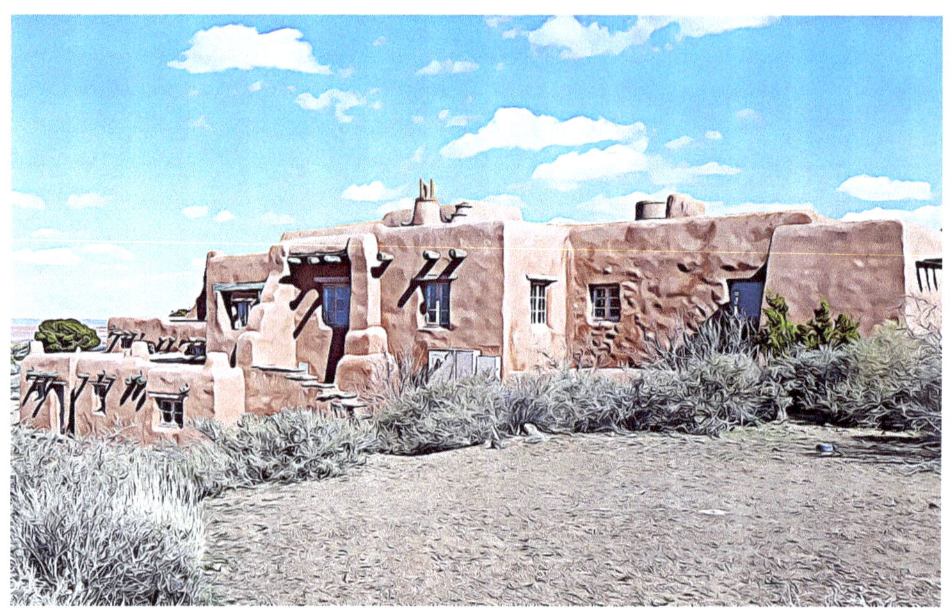

Painted Desert Inn 📷

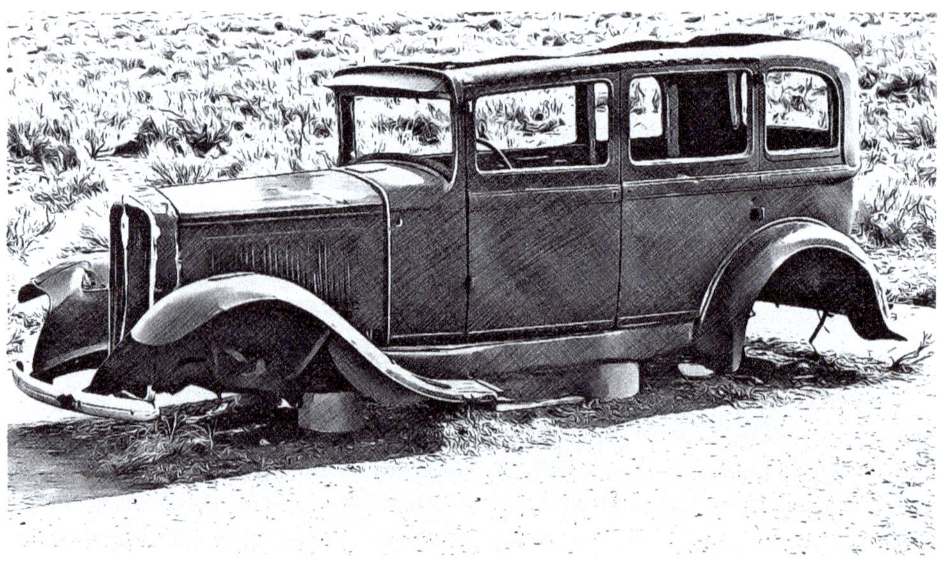

Little Piece of Tin 📷

Chapter Thirty-Four

Wacky Experience in Albuquerque

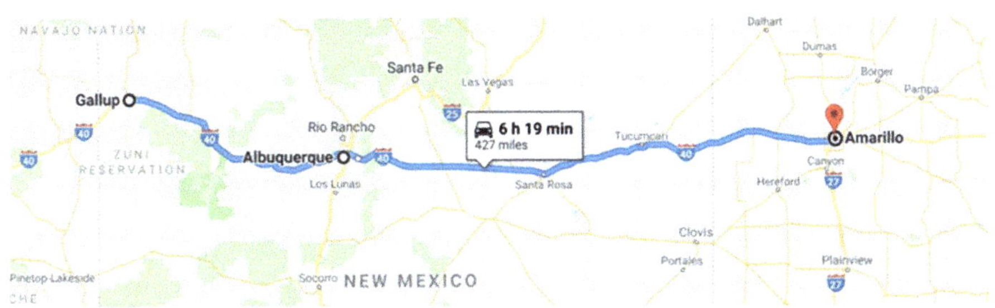

Gallup, New Mexico to Amarillo, Texas

After such a beautiful day in Arizona, it's hard to believe we were still trying to get ahead of the weather. Snow and cold were barreling down on us, so we were trying to get east first, and then south, so we'd cover more unexplored territory yet get us closer to home base.

We stuck to the interstate after we left the Painted Desert and kept pushing. A loved one gifted us with a night's hotel stay and dinner, so I made reservations (again through Hotwire), for a hotel in Albuquerque. We arrived around eight p.m. bone weary after driving for almost 400 miles. But when we pulled into the hotel parking lot, we sat at full alert.

I went to the office to check in, and the door was locked. The clerk motioned me around to the night window (at eight p.m.?) and when I told him I was there to check in, he motioned me
back to the door and met me there to unlock it, then locked the door behind me after I entered.

The smell of pot and meth almost knocked me over. The clerk was spaced out and could hardly function. Because we were both so tired, I went ahead and checked in and got our key. I asked who delivered food, and he shrugged and pointed out the window, drawing out, "Denny's?" like he was asking me. I also asked when breakfast was served and he said, "No breakfast."

Tim and I decided to go to Denny's before we lugged stuff to our room on the third floor. As we walked across the lot, a guy in a pickup truck was calling out to a woman standing on the hotel's sidewalk. I didn't pay attention to their conversation at first, but then he said, "$50? Okay, be at my room in half an hour."

After we ate (attentive and hilarious server—he's been with the company 19 years!), we grabbed our backpacks and found our room. I went to the bathroom and flicked on a switch. The light fixtures in both the bathroom and the sink area blinked on and off. Intent on using the facilities, I didn't think anything of it at first, but noticed the room had no toilet paper. Thankfully, I noticed ahead of time.

There was also only one towel in the room.

When I tried the other light switch next to the first one, the lights again blinked, but this time, something sizzled. I quickly turned them both off.

I went to the phone—Tim was still standing by the door, backpack in hand. I think he was already escaping the place in his mind. When I picked up the phone, I discovered noisy static. I dialed '0' anyway, and heard the clerk pickup, but could not hear a word he said, and couldn't even hear myself speak because of all the static. I called Hotwire while still in the room.

I explained the entire situation—no breakfast (which was advertised), the sizzling wires, no toilet paper, the meth/pot smell, and the parking lot characters, etc. He put me on hold for several minutes, then confirmed that the hotel did not offer breakfast like advertised (no one was concerned about sizzling wires!), so they would refund my money in several days.

We left the parking lot frazzled, tired, and without another plan, so we kept moving east. We ended up car camping at a rest area between Albuquerque and Santa Rosa.

We made a quick stop in Amarillo, for one specific purpose: Cadillac Ranch.

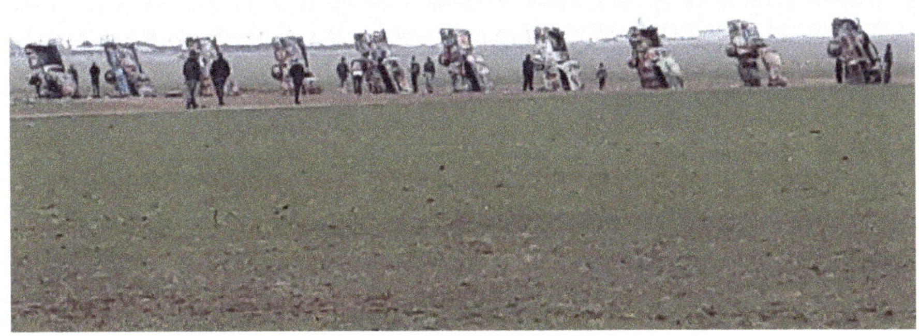

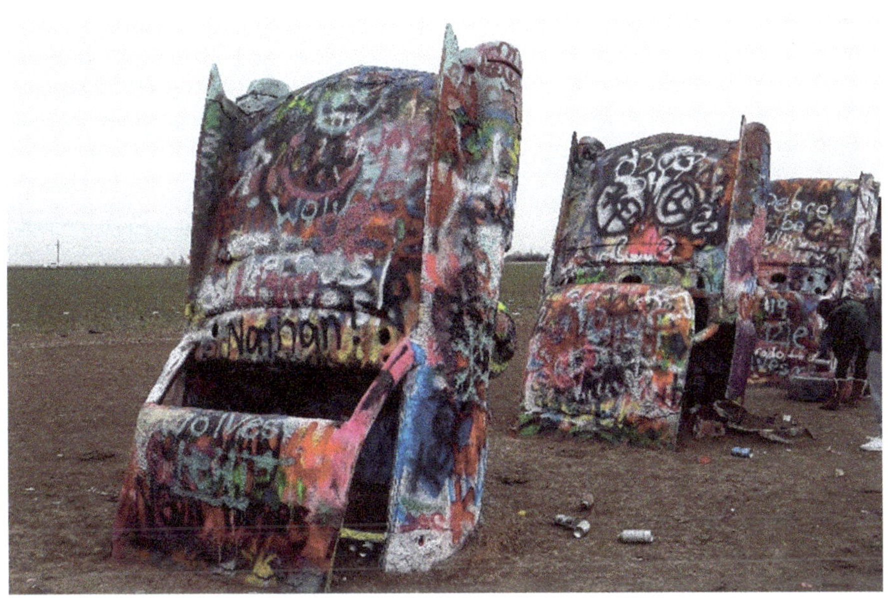

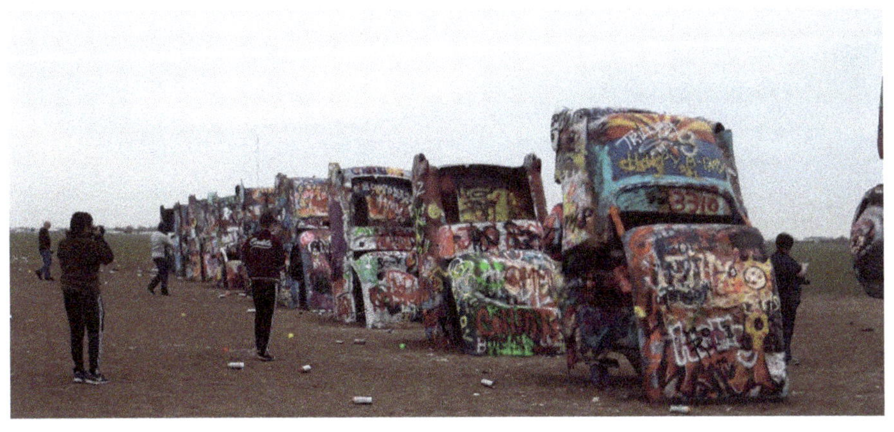

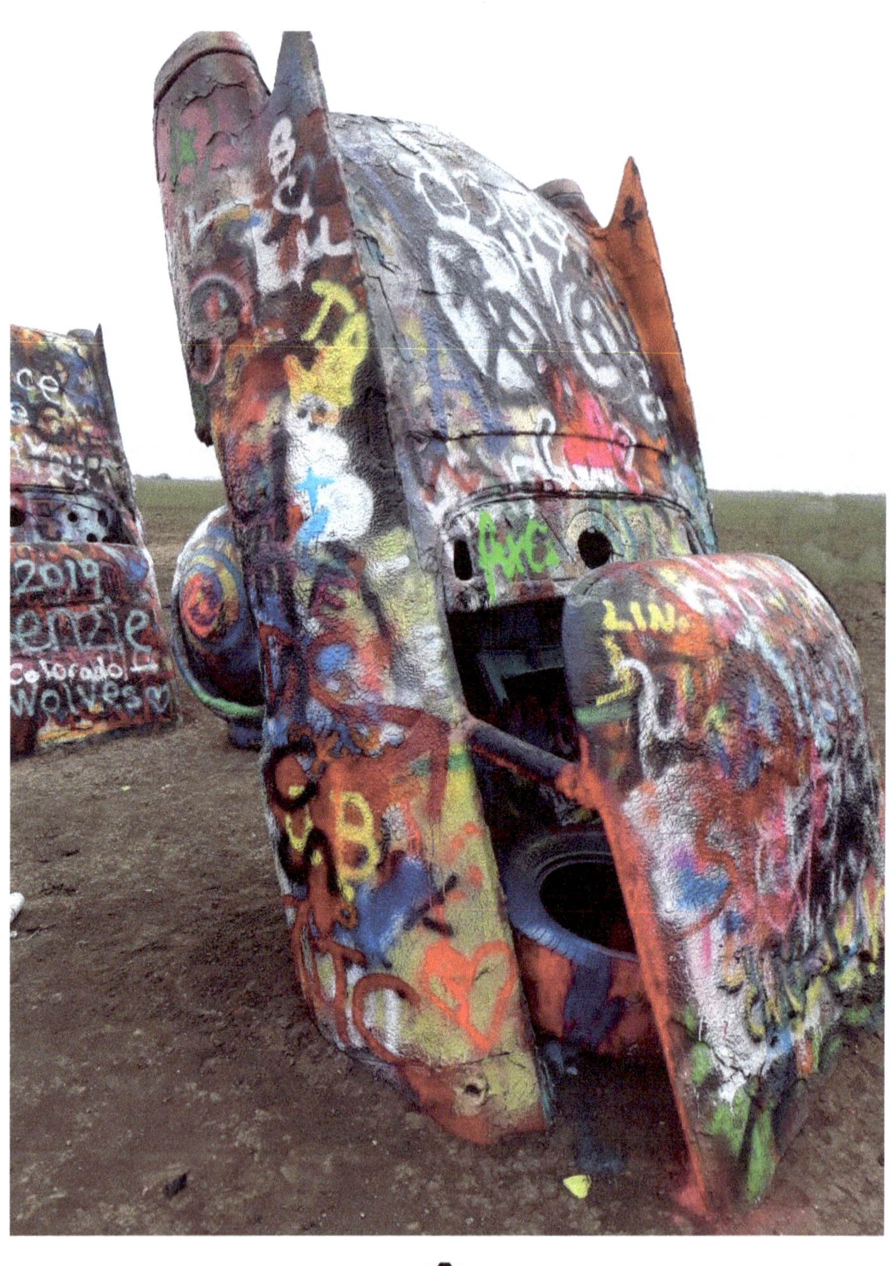

From the FROG Files:

We are nearing Winslow. Wind is fierce. Trucks are stopped, waiting it out, I guess.

Chapter Thirty-Five

Revisiting the Past

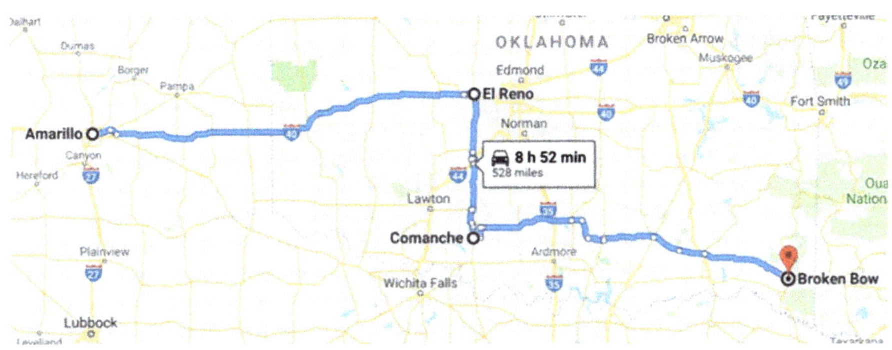

Amarillo to Broken Bow

From Amarillo, we drove to El Reno, to head south through Oklahoma on Hwy 81. In El Reno, we met a kind couple who invited us to share their table in a crowded diner. We learned they cotton-farmed 1,000 acres and that his wife is a teacher. They are the heart of our beautiful America, and it was such an honor and delight to visit with them.

This Oklahoma route was personal. Years ago, in another life, I lived there, and my children grew up there. We haven't been back in 24 years, so this part of the trip was a bit emotional for me, as I showed Tim farms and businesses I used to own, and the hospital where Jonathan was born, the schools Zach and Jonathan attended, the houses we lived in before we moved back to GA. Memories flooded my heart town to town.

We made the decision to cut through Arkansas instead of Texas to get back to my sister's house, where we planned to stay a few weeks to work, schedule, plan, visit doctors, etc. We stopped for the night in Broken Bow, Oklahoma, thanks to the gift of another loved one (money from the first fiasco was still tied up with Hotwire.)

I mention Broken Bow for two reasons. The Microtel we stayed in there had a sweet desk clerk. We asked her for food recommendations, and she told us about a convenience store down the street. I laughed and asked why she'd recommend a convenience store. She said it was her favorite place, with some of the best country cooking anywhere, and they had great prices.

We went to our room (with a huge smoky mirror the length of an entire wall—sort of creepy!) and finally, growling stomachs sent me to get our dinner at Bunch's Convenience Store. Along with everyone else in town!

The store was basically gutted of regular convenience store shelving (the coolers were along the walls, with a couple of small shelves of snacks to one side of the large room). A long hot bar stood along one wall, manned by several busy workers. Several tables were around for anyone choosing to dine in, but most everyone was taking their food to go. The menu included a meat-n-two option—choose one main entree, two sides, plus a choice of cornbread or hot rolls to go with it. The entrees changed daily, but that day included fried chicken, chicken tenders, goulash, fried fish, chicken fried steak, ribs, and Indian tacos. Sides included potatoes served several different ways, fried okra, mac & cheese, greens, corn, green beans, coleslaw, and baked beans. The selection was great, and the price even better—only $6.29 a plate! But the food went fast. I was stunned at how busy they were and took my time ordering—letting a couple of people go ahead of me as I tried to figure out what we wanted to eat. By the time I was ready to order, the fish and chicken fried steak were already wiped out. But the food really was that good, and it was all homemade. Definitely a must stop if you're in the area.

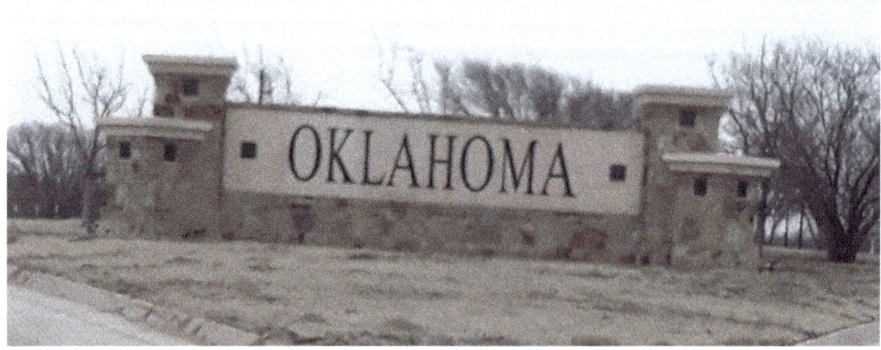

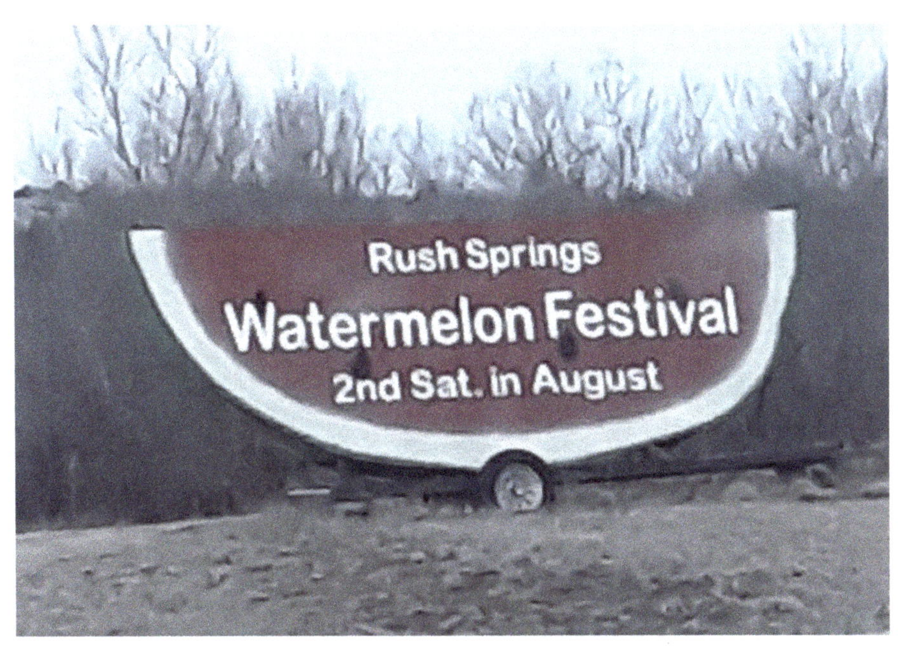
Rush Springs
Watermelon Festival
2nd Sat. in August

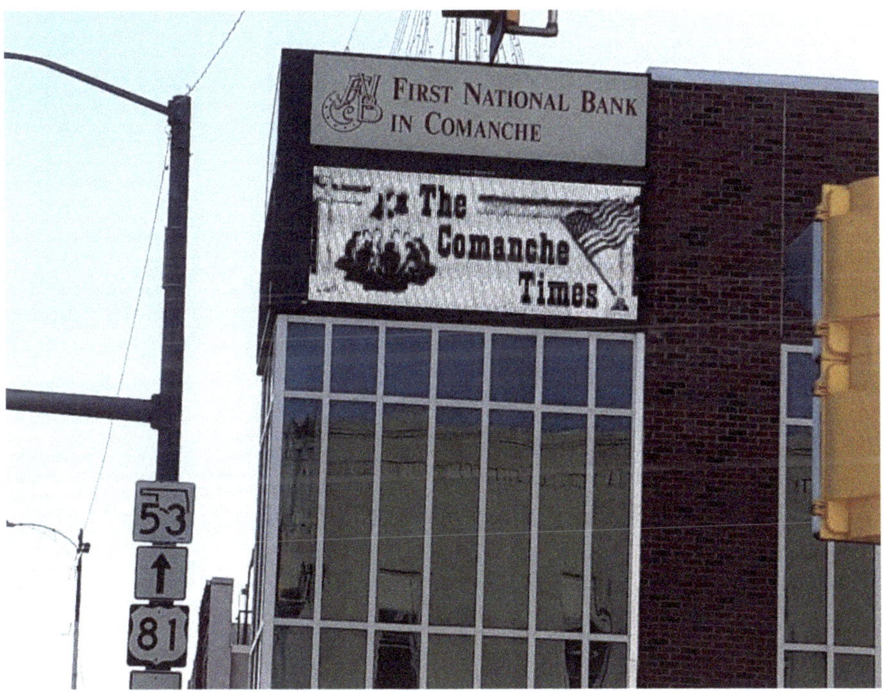
FNB FIRST NATIONAL BANK
IN COMANCHE
It's The
Comanche
Times
53
81

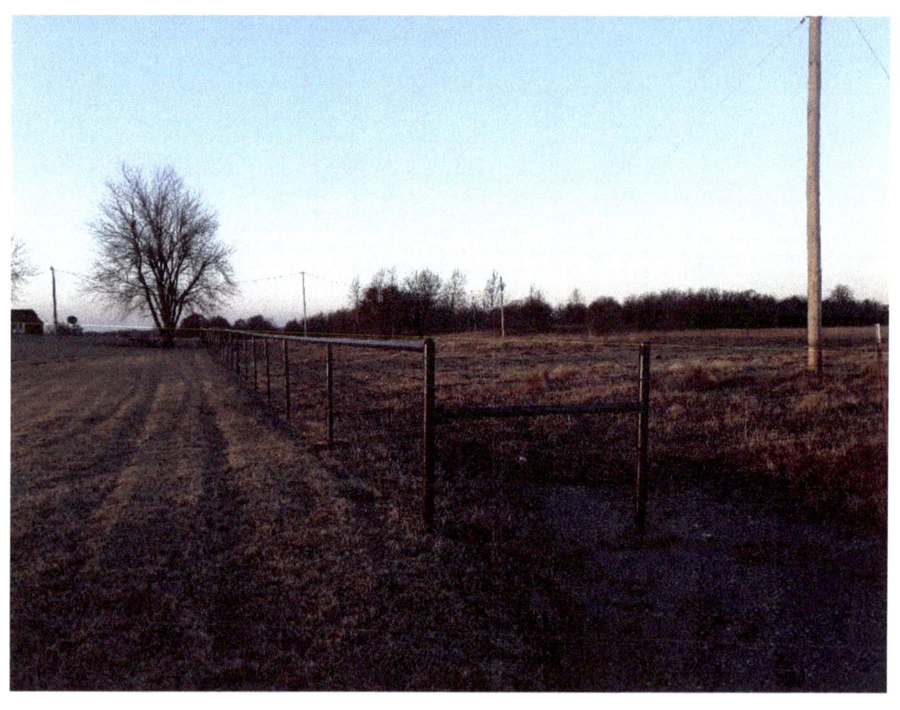

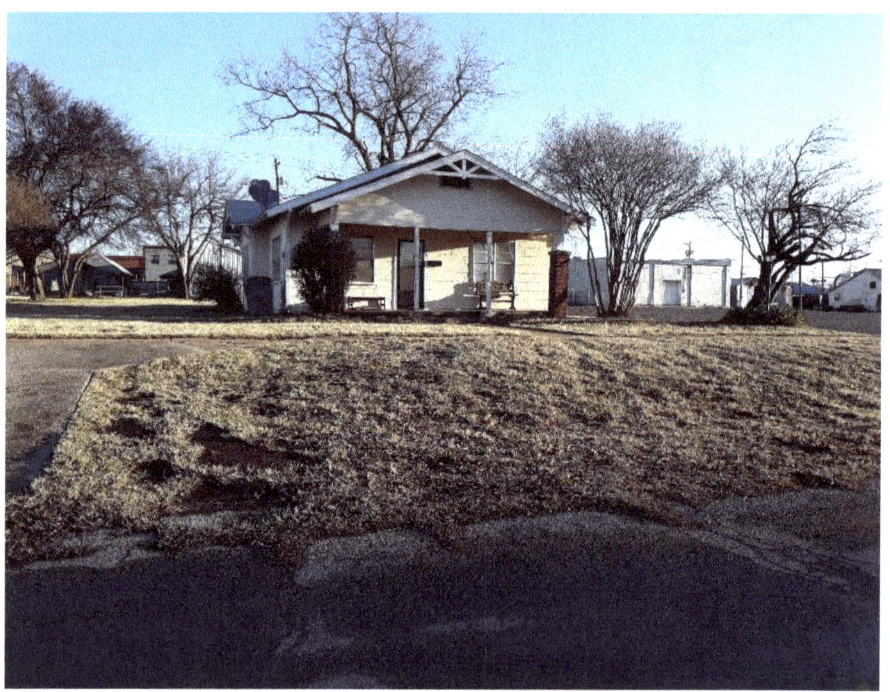

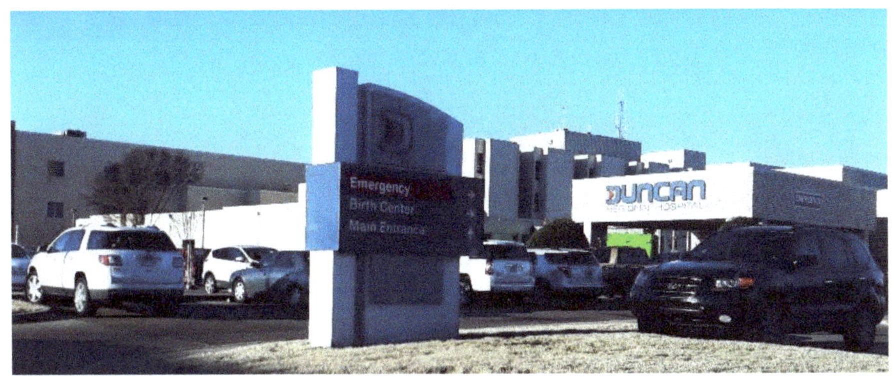
Emergency
Birth Center
Main Entrance
DUNCAN
REGIONAL HOSPITAL

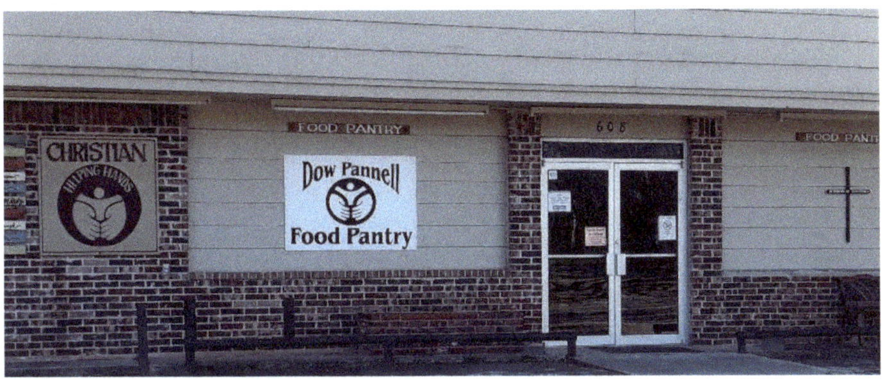
CHRISTIAN
HELPING HANDS
FOOD PANTRY
Dow Pannell
Food Pantry
605
FOOD PANTRY

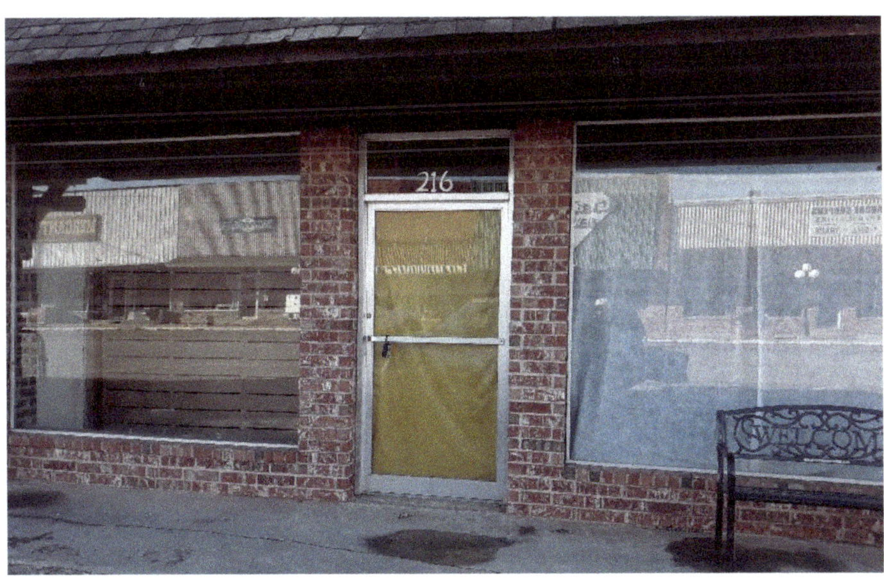
216
WELCOME

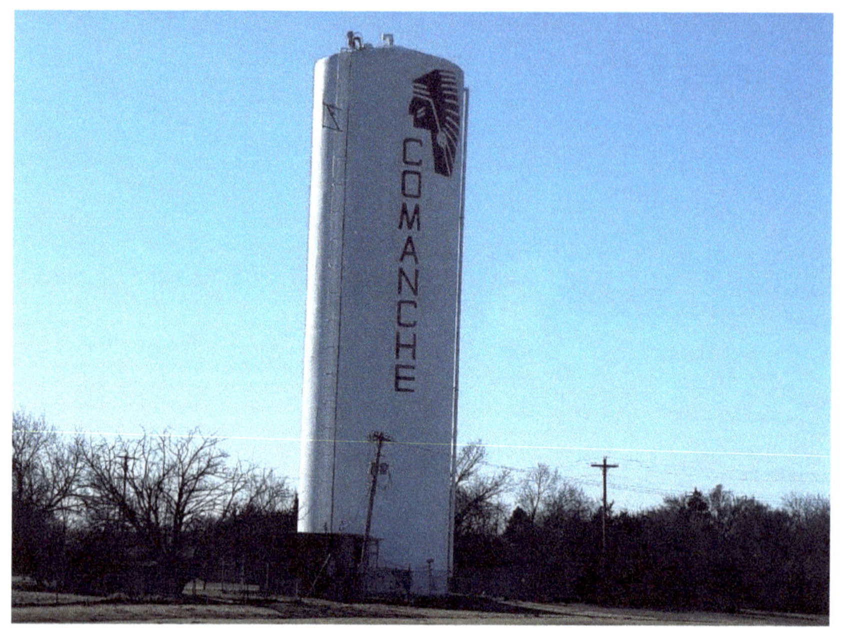

THE COMANCHE INDIAN

FIERCE WARRIORS OF THE SOUTHERN PLAINS

THE COMANCHE INDIANS NOMADS OF THE NORTH AMERICAN
SOUTHERN PLAINS ROAMED OVER THE COUNTRY IN
COLORADO KANSAS OKLAHOMA AND TEXAS

THE COMANCHE PEOPLE CALLED THEMSELVES "NUMUNUH"
WHICH MEANS THE PEOPLE

IT IS BELIEVED THE COMANCHE WERE THE FIRST
PEOPLE OF THE PLAINS TO USE HORSES
IN THEIR TRAVELS AND CONQUESTS

ONE WIDELY RECOGNIZED COMANCHE CHIEF WAS
QUANAH PARKER

THE CHISHOLM TRAIL

ON APRIL 1 1866 A HERD OF 1 800 LONGHORN CATTLE
LEFT CUERO TEXAS ON A 728 MILE TREK
TO THE RAIL HEADS IN KANSAS THEIR ROUTE
HAD BEEN LAID OUT BY JESSE CHISHOLM THE PREVIOUS YEAR

IT CROSSED THE RED RIVER AT DOAN'S STORE AND
FOLLOWED A ROUTE ALONG THE U S HIGHWAY 81 CORRIDOR

OVER 4,000,000 HEAD OF CATTLE MOVED OVER
THE CHISHOLM TRAIL

Chapter Thirty-Six

On to Tupelo and Beyond!

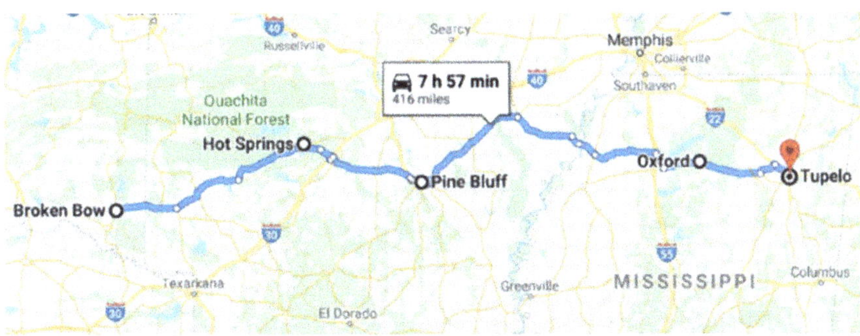

Broken Bow, Oklahoma to Tupelo, Mississippi

Our goal by this point was to get "home." We still wanted to explore as we traveled, but we only had one stop in mind between Broken Bow, OK and Alabama. We also chose to drive through the countryside of Arkansas, instead of sticking to interstates.

We learned one important lesson almost as soon as we crossed the state line: apparently, skunks like Arkansas but drivers do not like skunks. We passed at least a dozen skunks in less than 20 miles—it was awful, but in an odd way, funny too. (At least we didn't hit one ourselves! Whew! Phew!) What a memory to have of southern Arkansas.

We had finally escaped enough south to avoid the coming storm (the next day, we heard it called the Bomb Cyclone Blizzard! Grateful we weren't anywhere near it!) but we pressed onward. We drove through Hot Springs but did not stop to visit. The town had an interesting layout and looks like a place I'd like to return in the future for an in-depth visit.

We arrived in Tupelo ahead of a rainstorm, and Tim finally got to shake Elvis' hand.

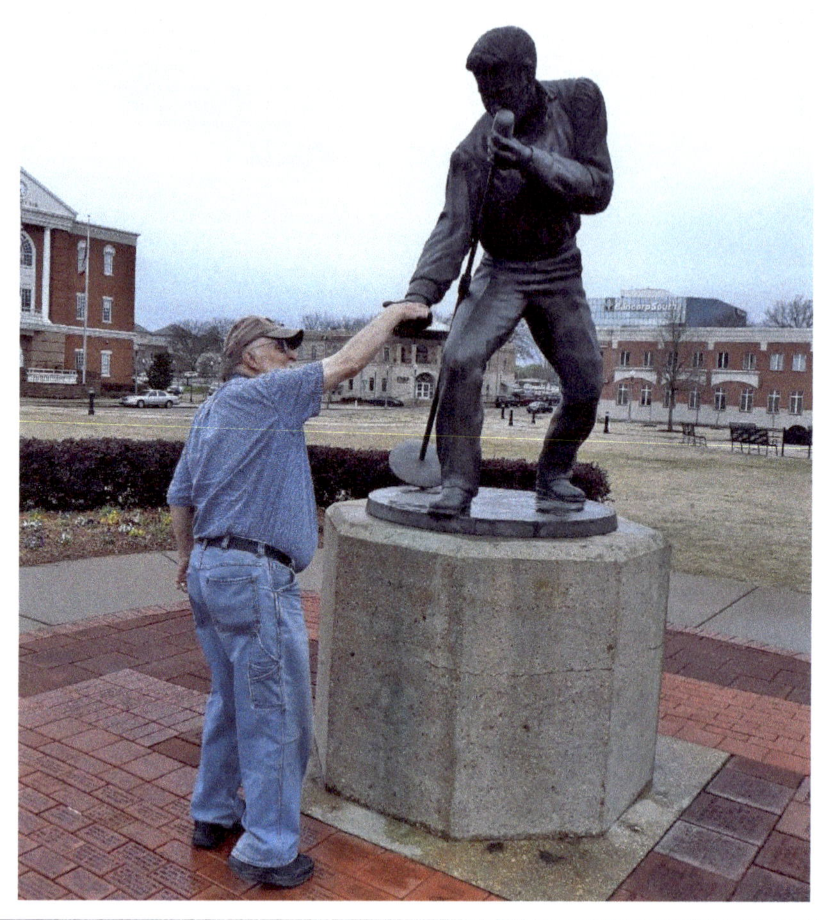

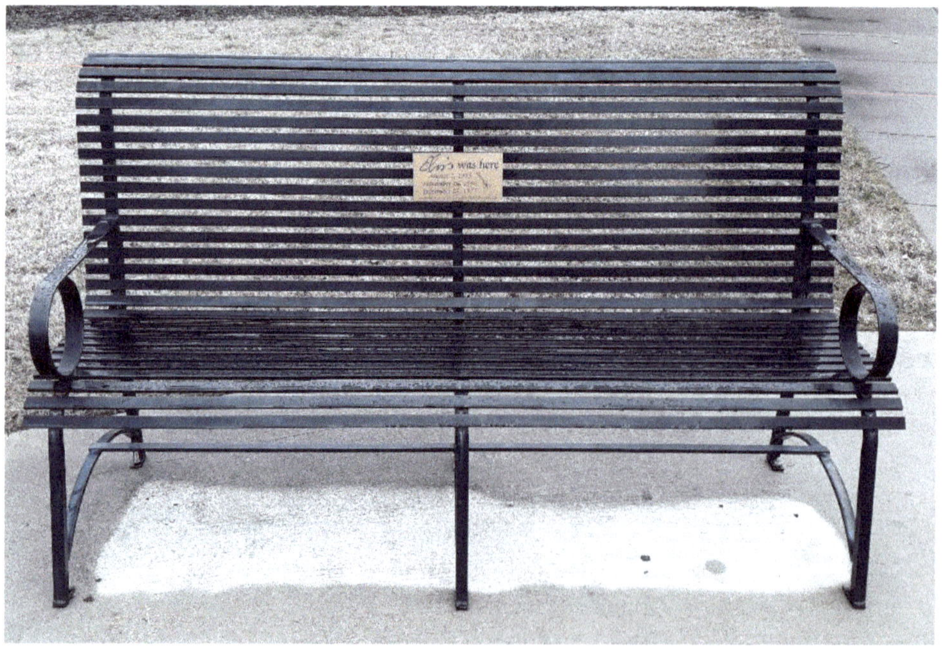
Elvis was here

Chapter Thirty-Seven
Toward a Brief Hiatus

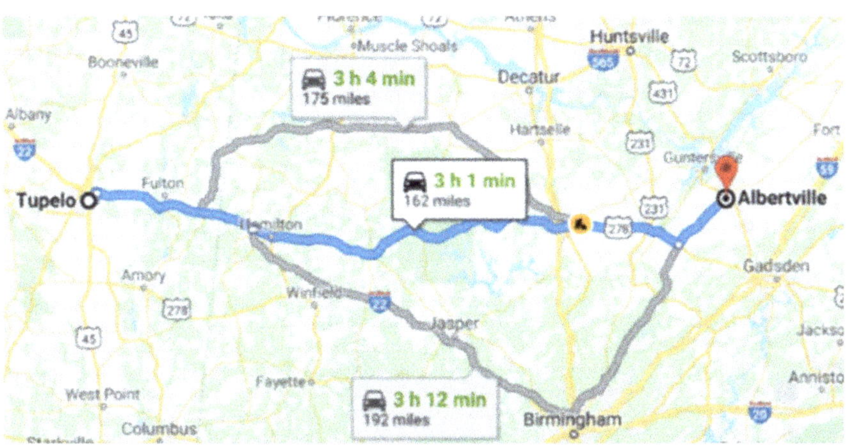

From Tupelo, it was a quick trip to our home base in Alabama.

Several have asked if this is the end of the #LeapFrog's journey, but I'm happy to say it is not. As this goes to press, we've completed our second leg of the journey (for a total of 189 days on the road), which may be detailed in a later book. The second leg was a bit different from the first one, so I'm not yet sure about the content for a book.

Tim got a clean bill of health from the doc and learned that he'd lost 14 pounds on our journey (the bum!) The doc said the travel seemed to agree with him, because all his blood work and tests showed he was in better health than before! (Doesn't give us answers for several things, but ... I'm glad to have the good report!)

Now that the second leg is complete, we spent the last half of 2019 recuperating and trying to decide whether and how to continue our travels. If we continue, we need a Class C RV to solve most of the problems we faced on both trips (and we realize it could create its own set of other types of problems). But we have to make that happen, and we're not there yet.

Stay tuned to my blog (www.TracyRuckman.com) or my Facebook author page (https://www.facebook.com/tracyruckmanauthor/) . I'll update there with any future developments.

If you're on the fence about taking a journey like this yourself, do it! I look back now and can't believe we did all that we did, saw all that we saw.

Would we do anything different? Lots! But the main one is not waiting – we should have started this journey many years before we did.

At the end of this book, I've included a few pages with details about the equipment we took with us. I've also recently published the Jot it Down Camping Journal to help you plan your own camping adventures.

Thank you for traveling along with us.

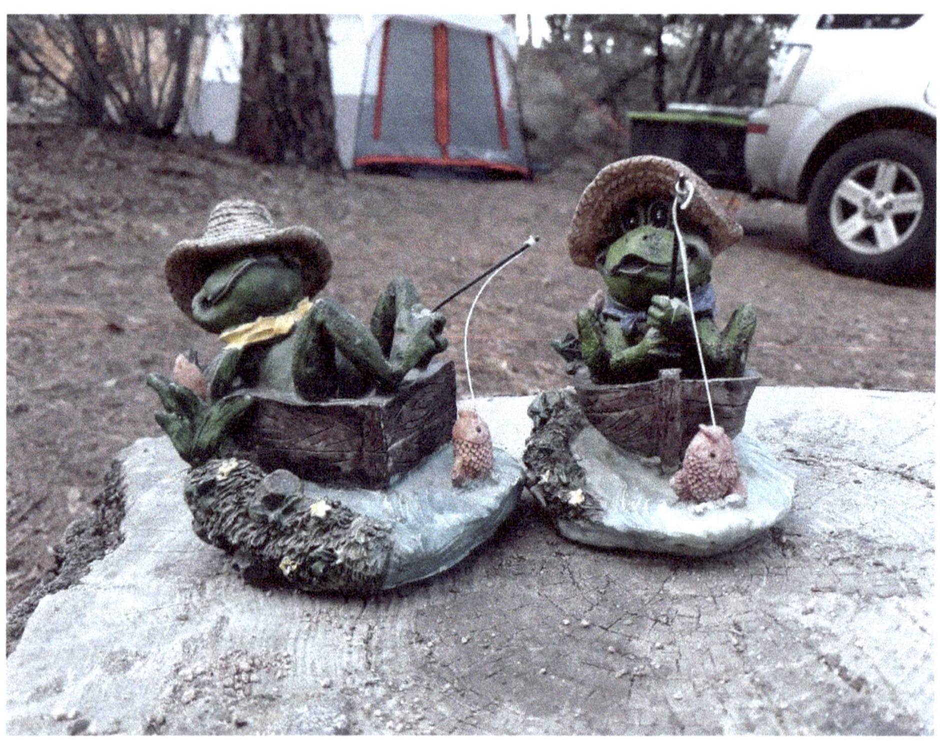

Tracy's Travel Art

I've used several of the images in this book to create a variety of art, from canvas and photographic prints to merchandise.

As we prepared this book for press, I made some significant changes in the availability of my artwork, and I'm happy to announce that all of my art can now be purchased on FineArt America and Pixels (one company, two different websites, with different products on each.)

To view and/or purchase any of my artwork, visit:

https://fineartamerica.com/profiles/tracy-ruckman/shop

Or visit one of my collections:

Featured Art

Travel Art

Water

Bridges

Beach Life

Churches and Courthouses

Black & White

Our Equipment

The equipment and gear we travel with always generates a lot of questions and fellow campers ask for advice and recommendations, so when we were compiling this book, I decided to create two separate lists of our gear—one with details of what we use and why, and then a checklist for your own use. As you read our detailed list, keep in mind that budget is always the primary consideration with us out of necessity. The detailed list is below, the checklists are provided in the Jot it Down Camping Journal.

The Basics

Tent

We had given away our tents a few years ago, thinking we wouldn't be tent camping any more. But when we decided to embark on this trip, we searched for used tents to better fit our budget. Big mistake that I won't make again. Sure, there are honest people out there, and sure, if you're diligent, you can find bargains. But this experience burned me, and I will buy new from now on.

Tent sizes are deceiving. Manufacturers state a tent is made for two, but don't consider gear or movement inside the tent in that number. Unless you plan to unzip the tent, fall into your sleeping bag, and not move around again until morning, you need a larger tent than the number of occupants. Because I'd experienced this previously, we purchased an eight-person tent, and for the two of us, that's the right size.

Shape of tent is another consideration. The first eight-person tent we bought—the used one—was a 16x8 rectangular tent, with a center height of 74" but the ends were not that tall. With both of us and our gear, it still felt a little snug at times.

After the Texas winds took out that tent, we purchased another eight-person tent, but this one was hexagon-shaped. The center height on this one is 80" and is close to that all the way around it. The room is spacious enough for our beds, our gear, and to move around a bit.

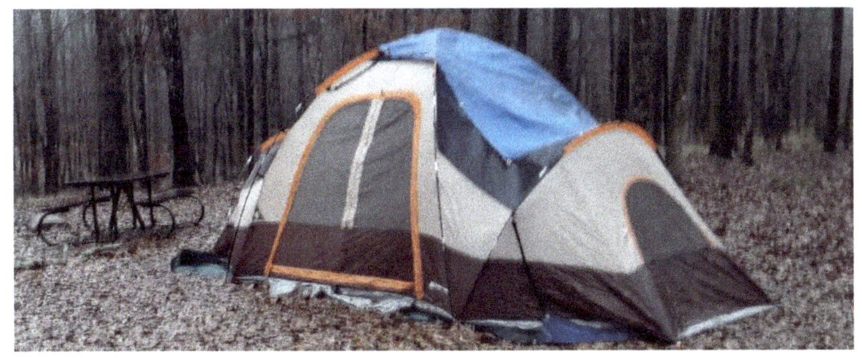

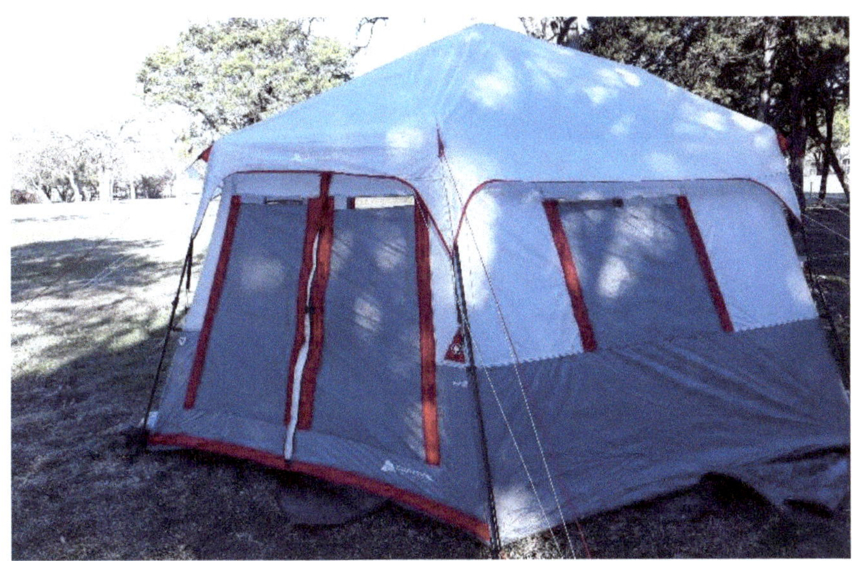

Tent Stakes

A tent camper can never have too many stakes. No joke. We knew that and bought a whole set new when we bought the used tent, then learned when we set up in camp that no stakes were in the bag, even though the seller told us they were. But since the purchase of the first set, we've bought three more sets. We use them to stake our tent, our screen tent, and to add extra guy lines when the winds are strong. They also come in handy when we need to use a tarp for rain. We discard the smallest stakes—they're basically useless—and purchase the thick 10-12" nail type stakes. We also bought a set of twisting plastic stakes for the beach or other really sandy conditions.

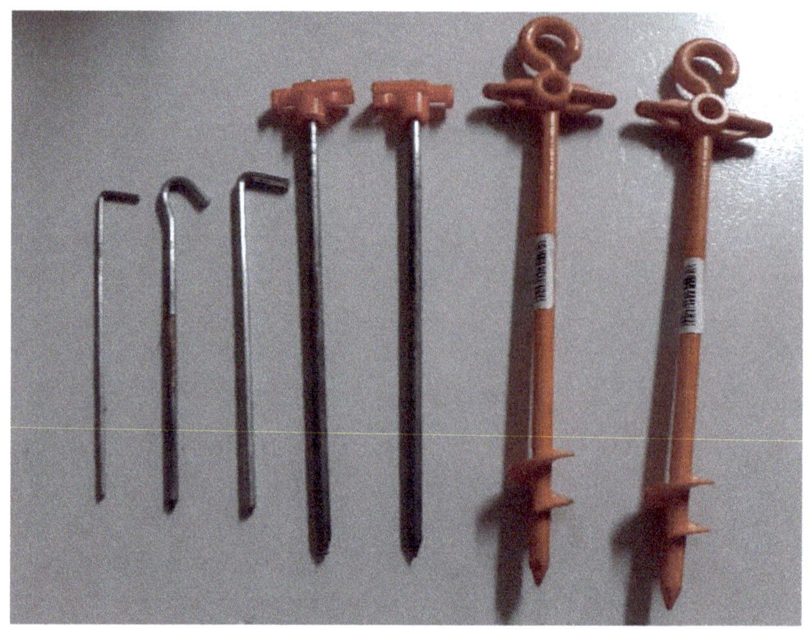

The three stakes on the left are the kind usually provided when you buy tents and screen houses, but not worth much. The plastic stakes on the right are great for sandy soil like the beach. The two orange-topped ones in the middle are the kind we used most because they work well in all kinds of conditions and are strong enough for most normal winds.

Hammers

We use a ball peen hammer for our stakes, but a heavy claw hammer or a small sledgehammer work as well. We also used a flat crow bar or claw hammer to help remove the stakes when the ground doesn't release them so easily.

Rain Fly

Many tents need a rain fly. Some come with them already attached, others come with them as a separate piece. The tent we purchased used was supposed to have one, but when we set up the tent, discovered it did not. If you find yourself in this situation, a tarp will work in a pinch, but we strongly recommend you get and use a rainfly made specifically for your tent. It will save you headaches—and soggy bedding—in the future. Many tent campers also use a tarp on top of their rainfly for extra protection from the elements.

Water proofing

We didn't waterproof our tent when we first started—the new one said it had already been waterproofed. But after a few uses, we discovered the need for it when our tent floor began seeping water, so we bought a couple of cans of 3M Scotchgard.

We sprayed it down, let it dry, and haven't had any seepage since, and we've been in a lot of rain. But we've also learned to better use our tarps, which brings me to the next item on the list.

Tarps

I have a love/hate relationship with tarps, primarily because I'm a short person and can never figure out the best way to utilize the tarps. Like umbrellas, I tend to get wetter using them than not.

But we're learning.

We currently haul around four tarps: one large 20x30, one medium 12x16, and two small ones 6x8. We use the medium one almost exclusively, because it goes under our tent. It's larger than our tent, so we roll the edges under the tent. And yes, in this instance, it matters a great deal which way you roll it. If you roll it inward, where the outer edge rolls on the top inward toward the tent, you'll create a big soggy puddle under your tent. You must roll the outer edges under and down, to serve as a dam, to keep the water at bay.

The extra tarps can be used as canopies for protection from sun, wind, or rain; or for wraps to keep things dry in camp or on the road.

Flooring

Tents have floors, but they need protecting. The tarp protects on the outside—a bit—but I don't like walking around on the tent floor in my bare feet, and an extra layer of protection will provide comfort and protect the floor at the same time. Cheapie that I am, I found upholstery fabric at the thrift store and cut two pieces to fit our bedding at the time. Our beds have since changed, so we've replaced them with cheap moving blankets we learned were sold by Harbor Freight. (Watch for sales to save money.)

Beds

When we first started the journey, I slept on the ground with a sleeping bag while Tim slept in a camping recliner chair. But neither option worked well for us—I'm older and fluffier than I used to be so getting up and down from the ground was a pain, and Tim's recliner chair didn't work like it should, so I ended up having to "tuck him in" every night—and every time he needed to get up all night long. I reached the point of needing sleep, so I got a cot, and then eventually talked Tim into switching over, too. Cots took an adjustment—they make a bit of racket! But the sleep is solid. The cots are each one piece, folding, so setting up and taking down are easy.

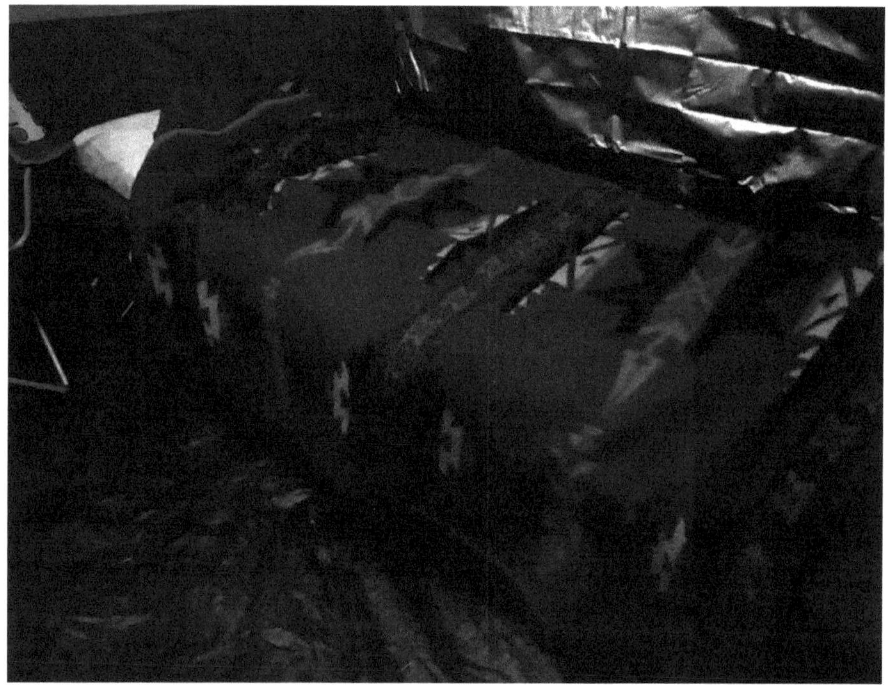

Sleeping Bags

The day we decided to take this journey, I bought myself a new sleeping bag. Tim had an old military mummy bag and planned to use it, but after a couple of nights, realized he couldn't use it with the camper recliner so we swapped bags. That mummy bag was so warm and toasty, I loved it and it worked great for really cold weather. But the bag is too heavy for me, so I switched to other regular blankets and quilts we had with us and stuck with those for all types of weather.

The comfort factor should not be dismissed—traveling for extended periods of time, we needed the comforts of home and having our familiar blankets and pillows have helped immensely.

Heater

Zach recommended getting the Mr. Buddy Heater. I resisted at first, planning to be stay away from cold weather completely. I'm glad he insisted it was needed, because we dealt with crazy weather almost the entire journey. That heater, and the hand warmer packs, helped us survive.

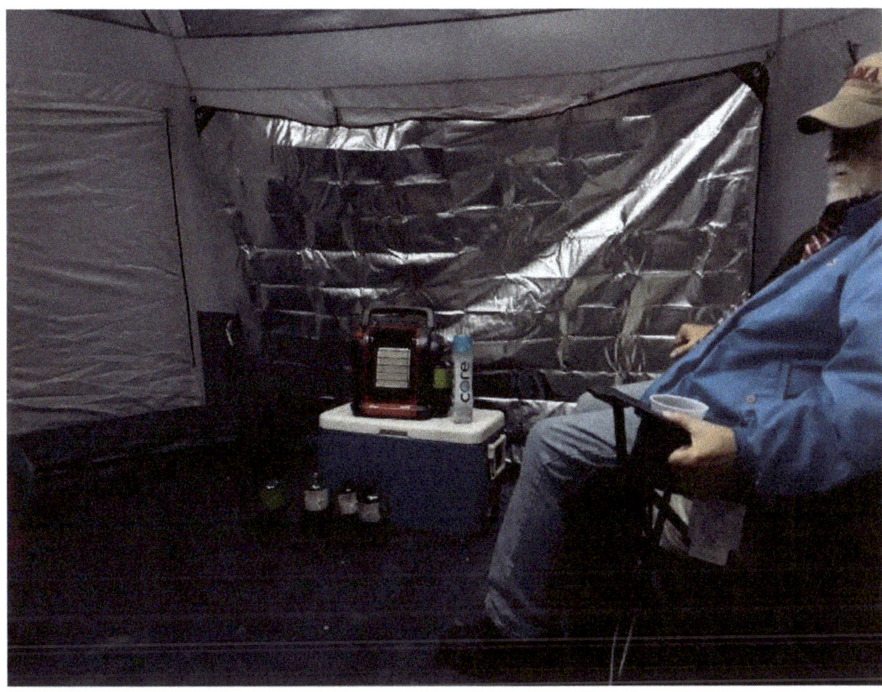

We tried hanging the emergency blankets on the walls, but they were just a bit too heavy to last long.

Propane

The heater and our cookstove run on propane. We didn't want to take up space with the 20 lb tank (15 lb Walmart tanks), but soon learned that the little one-pound cylinders get expensive. Now we carry the larger tank in a laundry basket in the middle of the car and use the single canisters when we stop for a quick meal, coffee, or an overnight stay and don't want to unpack everything.

Tim's had a standard two-burner Coleman camp stove for many years. It's not the prettiest thing, and I try to make him clean it on occasion, but it gets the job done.

We also have a folding grill grate that we use over campfires occasionally, and we make use of grills in campgrounds occasionally, too.

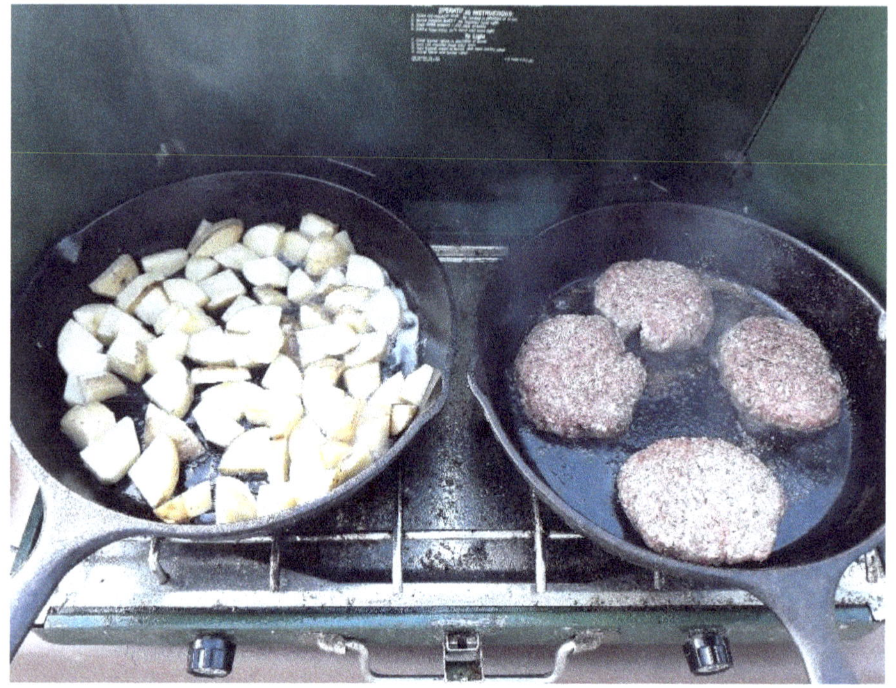

Kitchen

We are foodies and we are cooks. Both of us. Leaving a fully stocked kitchen to go on the road was a challenge. I had to learn how to cook on a cookstove, and Tim is still learning how to cook on any setting below full blaze!

We couldn't take the whole kitchen with us, so we had to whittle it down to bare necessities:

Three iron skillets (Tim's bacon one, which, until I touched it a few weeks ago, had never cooked anything other than bacon. I learned my lesson, and it will never cook anything other than bacon again.) The other two I may use as I wish, and we use those for cooking most everything else.

Two nonstick skillets—I like these for cooking eggs and pancakes mostly.

Three pots of various sizes—we have a 1-, 2-, and 3-quart.

One holey grill basket/bowl thingy—I honestly don't know what they're called, but we brought it. Haven't used it a single time.

One small stock pot. We already had this one from a camp set bought years ago. We use it for boiling water for dishes but may eventually replace it with a slightly larger one so we can use it for other things, but even that is limited, because we don't cook anything that creates leftovers due to lack of refrigeration.

When we were at Fort Anahuac, I found myself washing dishes with nowhere to put them as I washed and rinsed, so we bought a dish drying rack, and that has worked great. We have a divided wash basin made of plastic on our wish list, but never purchased it.

After reading this recommendation in a camping group, I also bought a spray bottle to put bleach and water in, and now all our dishes get a final squirt in the cleaning process.

Utensils—we brought three spatulas (turners), one solid spoon for nonstick and one metal; one slotted spoon for nonstick and one metal, two larger slotted spoons for frying, one ladle, one whisk for nonstick and one metal; and a couple of pairs of tongs; plastic measuring cups and spoons. We also brought our two chef knives, steak knives, and a four-set of our table silverware. I keep most of that in a three-drawer plastic bin; whatever doesn't fit goes in a dedicated stuff sack. [NOTE: the plastic bin works well, but because we went cheap, it wasn't very sturdy and broke as our trip ended. Next time, we'll pay a little more for better quality.]

Coolers

We started out with our regular large cooler, but it was old and we soon discovered it wasn't keeping things cool long, so it took up space without proving useful. We swapped it out for a smaller cooler and also bought a five-gallon round sports jug (one of those orange ones – we chose one with a screw-on lid, rather than one that pops on and off), and those two items take up the same amount of floor space as the big cooler but provides much better functionality. We usually buy fresh food (meats, butter, half & half, eggs) for three to four days, plus a small bag of ice, and that fits perfectly in the cooler. Having the smaller size keeps me from overbuying, too, so there's no waste.

Tools

We started out with what I thought was entirely too many tools, and Tim felt like we had too few. After riding our first leg—from our home to my sister's—he decided to give up some of them, because the only room we had for all he thought we needed was at his feet. A two-hour drive was enough to convince him he needed leg room more than he needed electrical supplies from 50 years ago.

We've since wheedled down the tools to one large tote that also hauls other items. Tools include saws, axes, hammers, screwdrivers, pliers, bungee cords, rope, twine, string, knives and sharpener, duct tape, zip ties, WD-40, automotive tools, small collapsible shovel, machete, small folding rake, and a ton of stuff we'll never use in a million years. But I conceded because I had to bring two small bags of work gear, too.

Bathroom

Skip this section if you think the use of that word is TMI.

When we began camping, we planned to stay primarily in free campsites, and those sites are free because they usually offer little or no amenities like bathrooms or even running water. But our bladders are not spring chicks anymore, so they require frequent emptying. Sure, tinkle behind a tree, is what they told Tim. But what about me? I'm not exposing my fluffy, untanned backside to squat in the woods. Sorry, but it ain't happening.

Then I learned about portable camping toilets and we bought the first one we saw. It was a joke and thankfully we discovered that before we tried using it the first time. The legs wouldn't fold at all once we unfolded them, and while trying to get them to fold, we realized we'd be manhandling the thing a lot after we used it, and that was a no-vote from me. When I returned it, unused, I explored the camping aisle and discovered a snap on toilet seat that fits on a five-gallon bucket (like those Home Depot paint buckets). The store also had bags to fit inside the bucket. These bags come in sets of two—the inner bag is like a black trash bag, has a little bit of "cat litter" in the bottom to help turn liquids to slush, and an outer bag to tuck the inner bag down into and zip closed. Other options include using heavy duty trash bags with diapers. We only use this bucket for nighttime bladders. Any other time, we use vault toilets, campground restrooms, or public restrooms, depending on where we're camping.

Lighting

We already had several of those LED lanterns and flashlights, so we were covered in the lighting department. I'd also recently purchased a couple of boxes of batteries, so that was covered, too. The one lighting purchase we made along the route were headlamps. We bought the cheapo $1 headlamps at Walmart. Until we were in camp using them, we never realized mine didn't work correctly from the beginning, so I've not used it after the first night. Tim uses his regularly. If I find I have a need for one again, I'll probably upgrade to the $3 version next time.

Electronics / Charging

From day one, I knew keeping electronics charged would prove challenging. The two cell phones haven't been too bad, because not only can we charge in the car, we also have one small portable charger that provides one charge at a time, but gives us enough that I can rotate it most of the time between phones and recharge it in the car, even when we're parked remotely for days. Another portable charger would have been a nice bonus, but we never found it necessary enough to buy.

Keeping my laptop charged was another story though—it is next to impossible to keep charged. I'm currently only getting about two hours of use per charge. We have an a/c plug in our car, so I can charge as we travel, but don't always remember to do that, and the computer gets really hot while it charges, so I don't like doing it often, so we end up utilizing fast food joints that offer outlets and public libraries (like I ever need an excuse to visit a library!)

If we continue our travels, I'll invest in a portable solar charger that will hopefully keep me charged enough to get all my work done.

Clothing

I've never been a clothes horse, yet I still had to pare down to hit the road. The clothing situation for both of us has evolved as we traveled. I started out with two pairs of jeans, one pair of cargo pants, and one pair of sweatpants. Now, I have one pair of jeans, one pair of cargo pants, one pair of cargo capris, and one pair of shorts. (Yes, I'm wearing shorts again for the first time in decades.) I'll eventually probably add another pair of cargo pants and/or cargo capris to the mix—I seem to be one pair shy of "enough" for wash rotations. I've learned layering is my friend. I have three summer shirts (short sleeve cotton), three long sleeve shirts, and two long sleeve undershirts, plus one jacket. Eight pairs of panties and six pairs of socks, plus three pairs of fuzzy slipper socks, and one pair of heavy-duty slipper socks. Two pairs of pajamas that I usually layer on top of each other, and a swimsuit. I also packed a tiny overnight bag with one dress and one pair of dress slacks and a top, in case I might need them for something, but so far, have not.

Tim pared down, but still brought three pairs of jeans, four pairs of shorts, six t-shirts, three short sleeve button shirts, three long sleeve button shirts, two pull over casual shirts. One pair of pjs. Two jackets. Four pairs of short socks, three pairs of long socks.

We both added toboggans to our stash, and I discovered how much I liked using mine at night over my eyes – I had much better sleep when my eyes were covered. I've never liked the idea of a mask, but the hat worked great.

We both carry backpacks and one tote bag each. The
backpacks carry toiletries, and stuff we change frequently (socks, underwear, t-shirts). The tote bags carry one change of clothes, our shower shoes, and a towel and washcloth. We take both bags to the showers and rotate dirty for clean when we do laundry. I also kept a separate backpack that held swimsuits, sunscreen, and a beach blanket.

Miscellaneous

Stuff Sacks—buy double what you think you need, maybe triple if your budget can afford them. Stuff sacks of all shapes and sizes have come in handy for us. We started out with a box of three from Walmart—much smaller than I expected, but we've ended up buying two sets, and will likely get a third if we hit the road again. We use the small ones for our toiletries, kitchen utensils, tent stakes, tools, and the pocket rocket. Larger stuff sacks are great for bedding, blankets, sleeping bags, jackets, and towels, also great for hauling laundry to/from laundromats.

Totes. We kept swapping different kinds of totes. What eventually worked best for us were two under-the-bed flat totes for our clothes (one each) that held clothes in rotation. We also bought two totes for the cargo carrier on the back. We went cheap the first time, and they cracked, so we went slightly larger and chose a heavy-duty version the second time around. We made sure I could still lift each one by myself if need be, so we didn't overpack them. And no, that's not a body wrapped in the garbage bag. Those are camp chairs, tarps, and the grill grate.

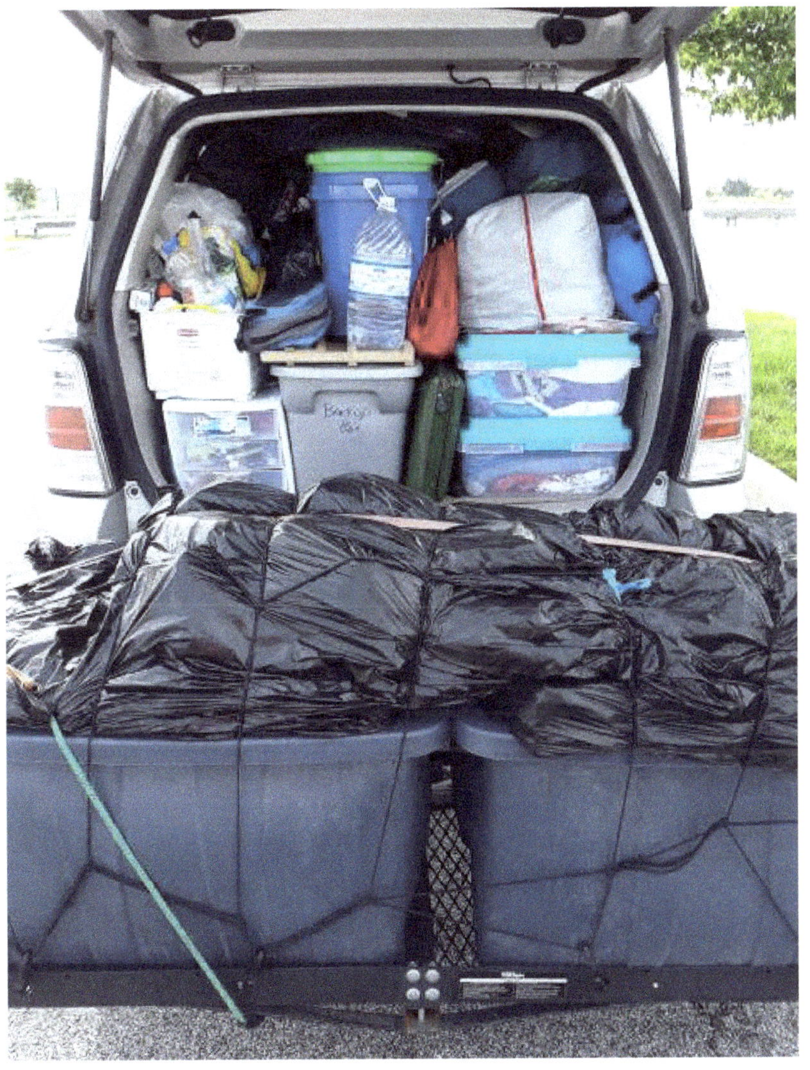

About the Author

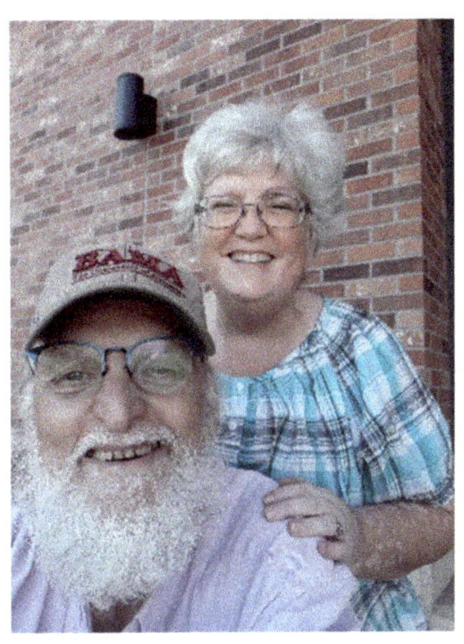

Tracy Ruckman is an upside-down, inside-out kind of creature. She rarely does things the easy way, including raising a family at an early age and going back to college at age 47. She is wife to Tim, and mom to Zach, Jessica, and Jonathan.

The same year she started back to college, Tracy's entrepreneurial spirit led her to open two book publishing companies and has since published more than 200 books for dozens of authors, several of which have earned a variety of awards. In 2014, she added a subsidy press to her offerings, and in 2016, placed the two traditional presses into the capable hands of another publisher. The subsidy press, TMP Books, continues to grow and expand as she helps writers achieve their dreams of publishing books.

After earning her degree, Tracy decided one diploma wasn't enough and is currently one project away from earning her MFA in Screenwriting. She's currently writing a dozen feature-length scripts, most of which are in various stages of the writing and editing process.

Tracy understands spare time as a figment of someone else's imagination, but occasionally she dreams of long, uninterrupted hours to think, write, and create art, unencumbered days spent fishing and photographing, and exploring all those undiscovered roads calling her name.

Visit Tracy on the Web:
www.TracyRuckman.com
www.TMPbooks.com   **www.TMPixArt.com**

Facebook: Tracy Ruckman, Author :
https://www.facebook.com/tracyruckmanauthor/

Facebook TMP Books: https://www.facebook.com/TMPBooks.TR/

Tracy's Amazon Page: www.amzn.to/2ujwEWp

Other Books from the Author

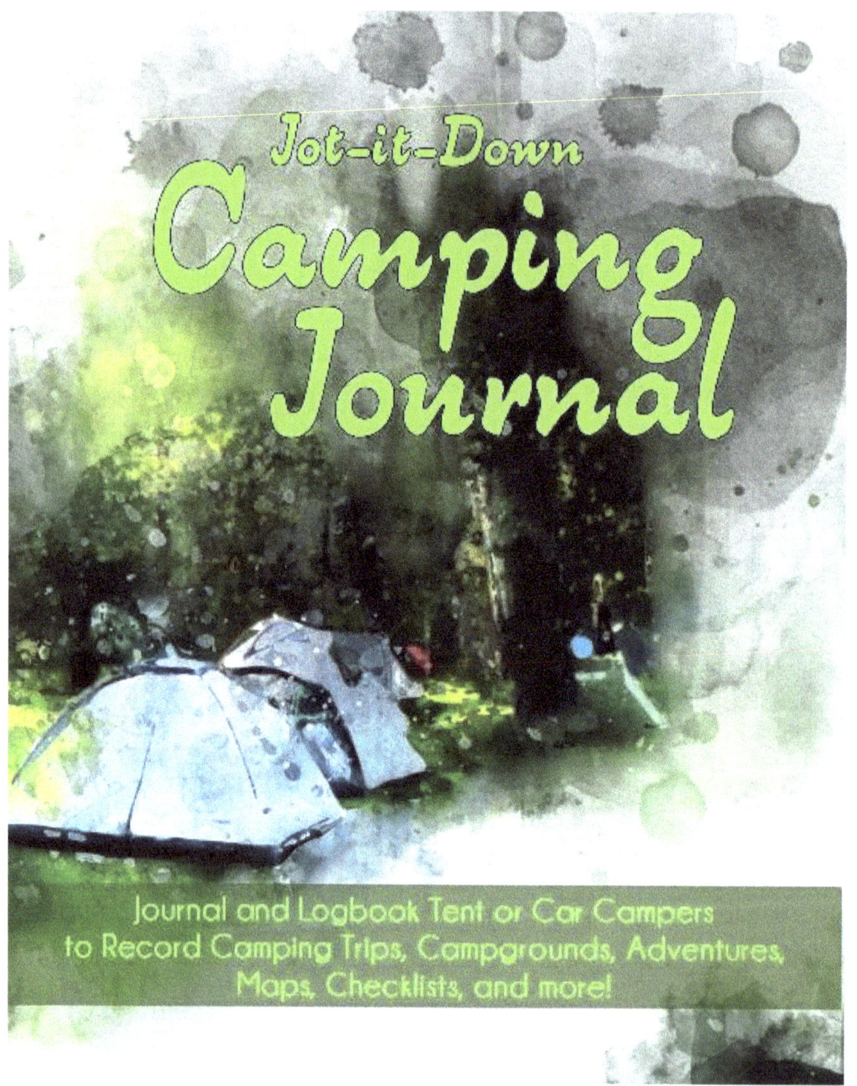

Available on Amazon: https://amzn.to/35pwfP8

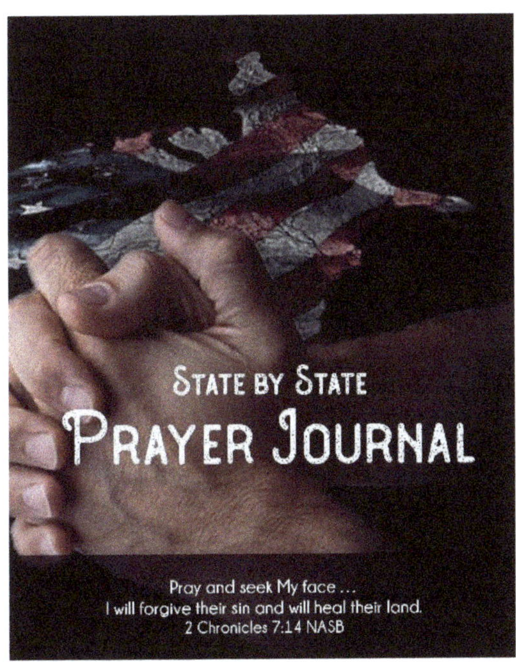

Available on Amazon: https://amzn.to/34bX9tJ

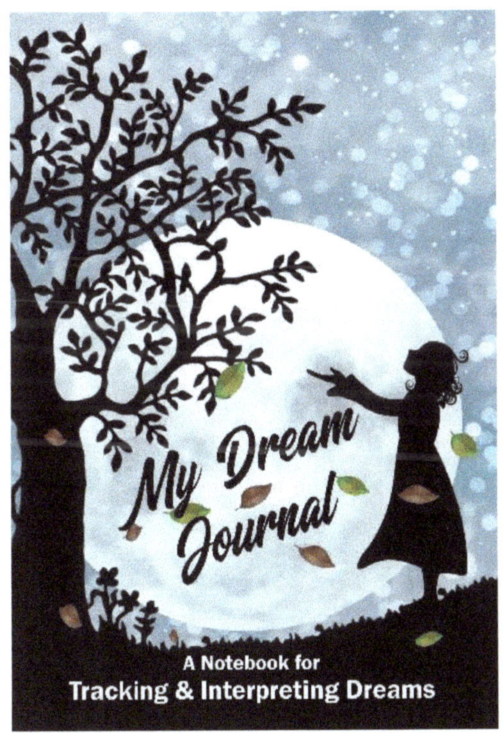

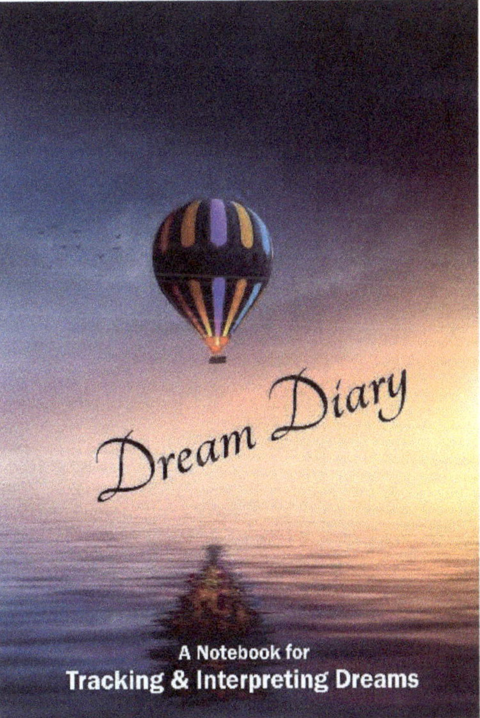

Available on Amazon:

https://amzn.to/35k33sM

Available on Amazon:

https://amzn.to/2pERqxv

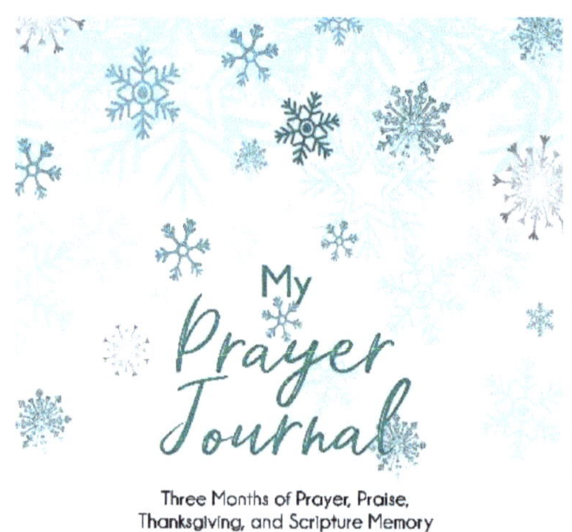

https://amzn.to/34dEuxL

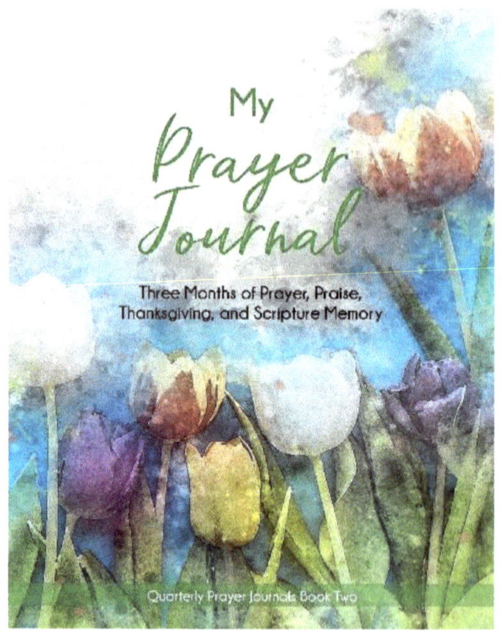

https://amzn.to/2OdaTz2

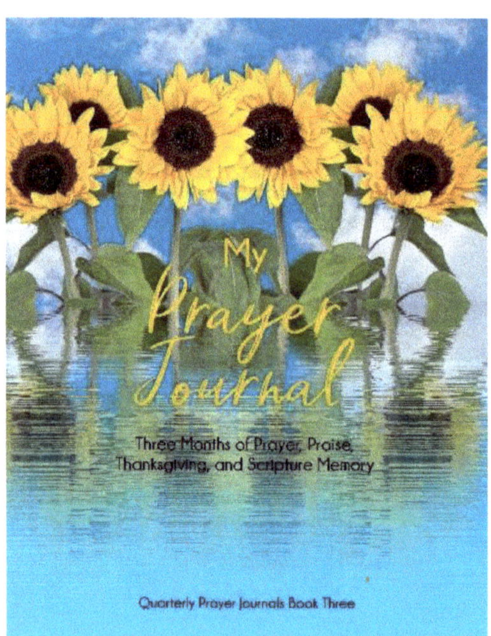

https://amzn.to/2pHP690

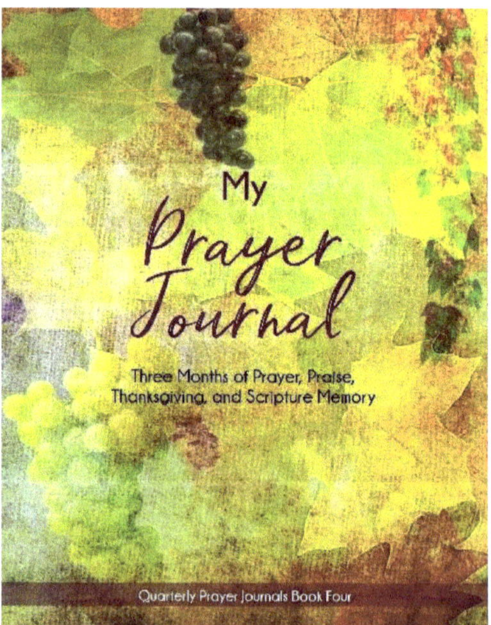

https://amzn.to/2DavtcU

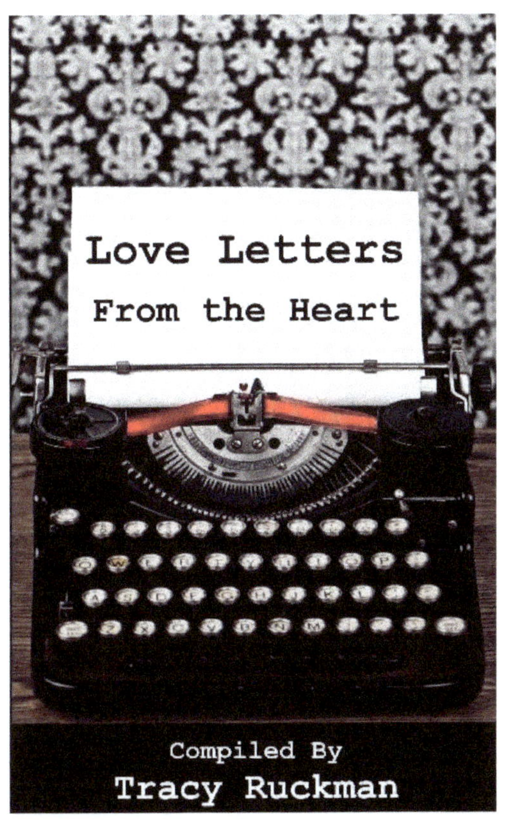

In Paperback and on Kindle: https://amzn.to/2qtHxDt

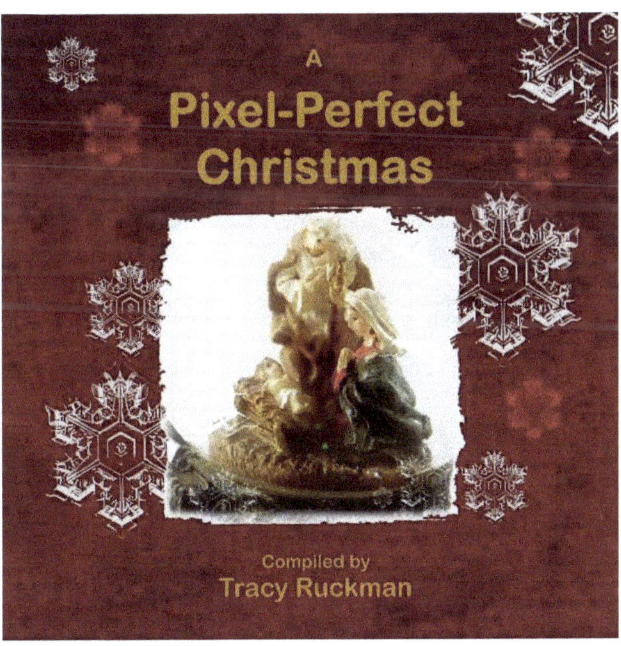

In Paperback and on Kindle: https://amzn.to/2KMnKGi

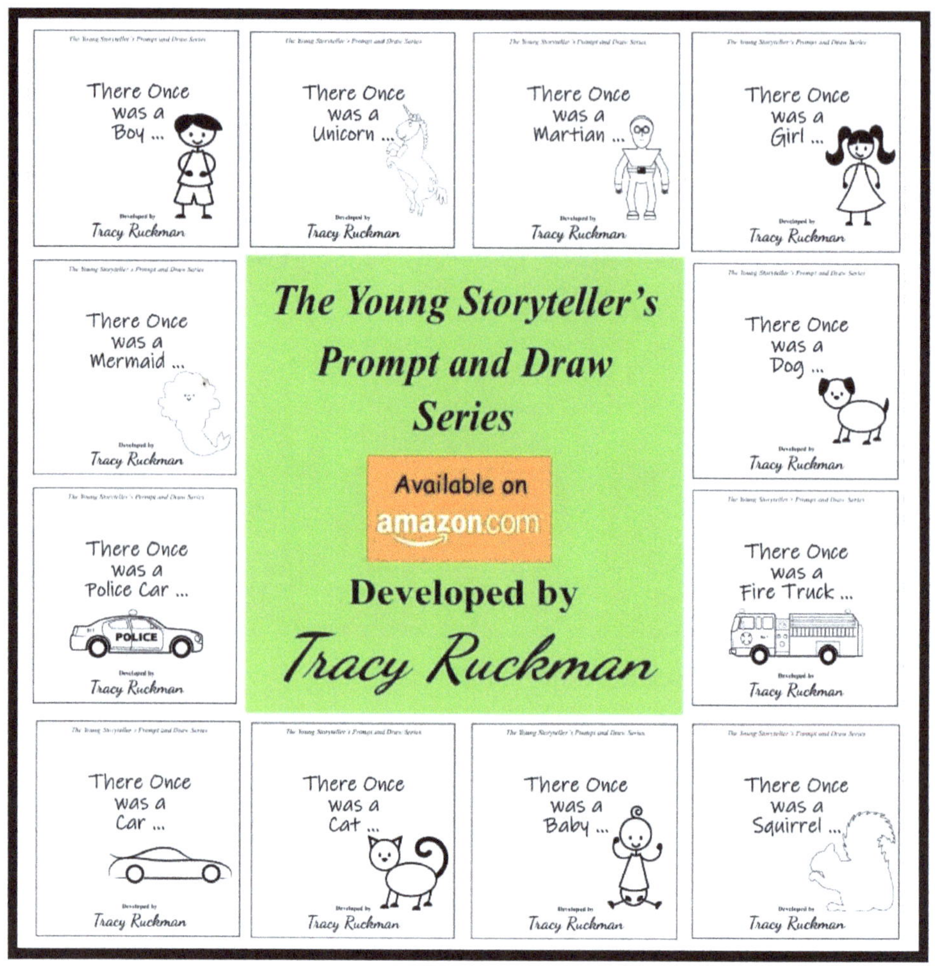

All 12 books available in Paperback:

www.amzn.to/2ObaNb4

Coming Soon!

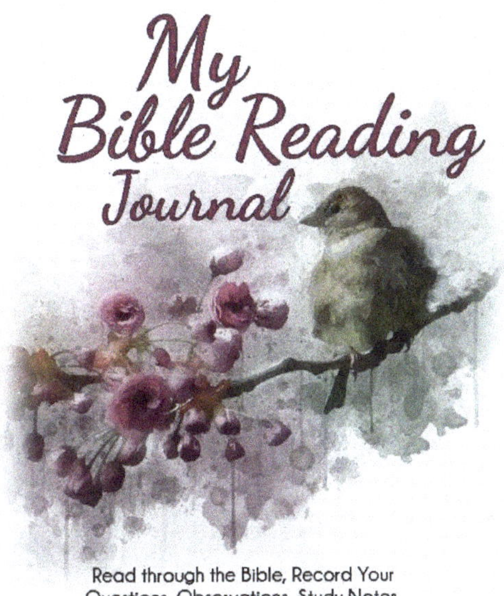

Read through the Bible, Record Your
Questions, Observations, Study Notes,
and Memorize Scripture

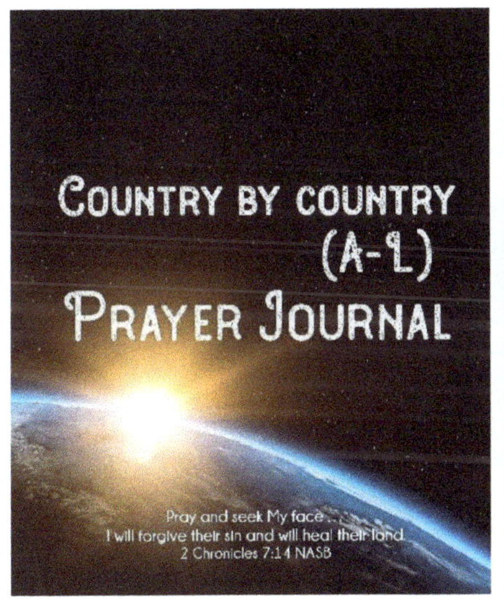

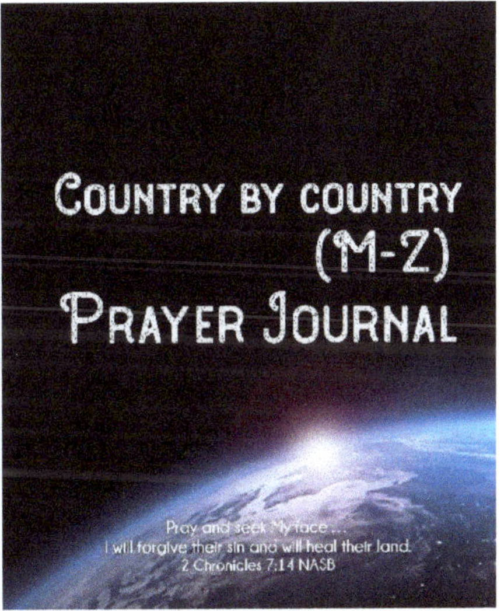

Check Tracy's Author Page for availability

www.amzn.to/2ujwEWp

Thank you for reading our book.

If you enjoyed it, we would appreciate

a brief review.

Reviews help other readers find our books.

Look for other books and merchandise

created by

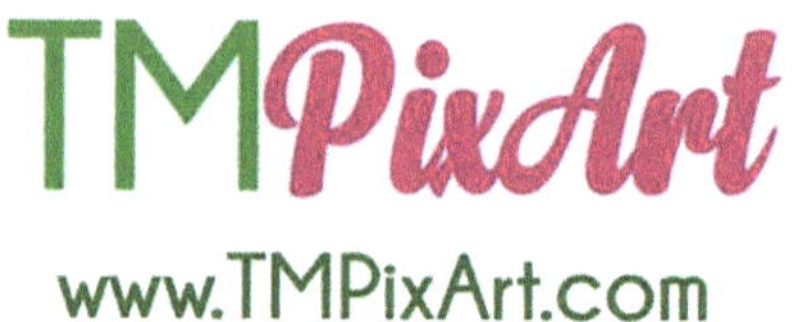

www.TMPixArt.com

www.TMPixArt.com

An Imprint of

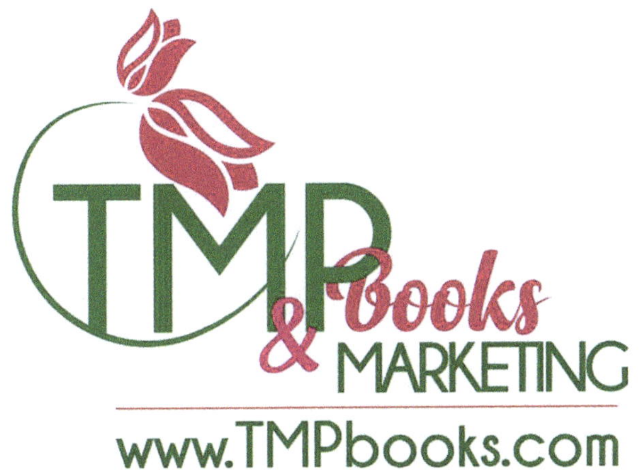

www.TMPbooks.com

Ready to publish a book of your own?
Read client reviews on our website,
then send us an e-mail to discuss your project.

CPSIA information can be obtained
at www.ICGtesting.com
Printed in the USA
BVHW021013220120
570188BV00016B/165